AMERICA AND WORLD WAR I

WARS OF THE UNITED STATES
(Editor: Richard L. Blanco)
Vol. 6

GARLAND REFERENCE LIBRARY OF
SOCIAL SCIENCE
Vol. 259

WARS OF THE UNITED STATES
(Richard L. Blanco, General Editor)

AMERICA AND WORLD WAR I
A Selected Annotated Bibliography
of English-Language Sources

David R. Woodward
Robert Franklin Maddox

GARLAND PUBLISHING, INC. • NEW YORK & LONDON
1985

Library of Congress Cataloging-in-Publication Data

Woodward, David R., 1939–
American and World War I.

(Wars of the United States ; vol. 6) (Garland
reference library of social science ; vol. 259)
Includes indexes.
1. World War, 1914–1918—United States—Bibliography.
2. United States—History—1913–1921—Bibliography.
3. United States—History, Military—20th century—
Bibliography.   I. Maddox, Robert Franklin, 1942–
II. Title.   III. Title: America and World War one.
IV. Title: America and World War 1.   V. Series: Wars of
the United States ; v. 6.   VI. Series: Garland
reference library of social science ; v. 259.
Z6207.E8W67   1985   [D769]   016.9403'73   84-48076
ISBN 0-8240-8939-1 (alk. paper)

Cover design by Alison Lew

Printed on acid-free, 250-year-life paper
Manufactured in the United States of America

To Bonnie and Martha

CONTENTS

C. Specific Aspects

D. Campaigns and Operations

SERIES INTRODUCTION

As Dr. David R. Woodward and Dr. Robert Franklin Maddox of Marshall University note in *America and World War I: A Selected Annotated Bibliography of English-Language Sources*, the Great War was a decisive turning point in global history. This was especially true for the United States. This nation emerged from its traditional diplomatic isolation and plunged into the bloodiest European war yet fought with enthusiasm, patriotism, and humanitarianism in order to make the world "safe for democracy."

Students, scholars, and readers with an interest in the history of their own colorful military heritage will benefit from this thoughtful compilation of published source materials about American participation in World War I. With over 2,000 entries selected from a wide variety of publications and manuscript collections, Professors Woodward and Maddox provide the best annotated selection of printed data in English on the stirring era between 1914 and 1919. The organization of major themes such as reference works, military aspects of the war, and campaigns and operations is astute. Furthermore, the innumerable and conveniently categorized subdivisions of these major topics allow a reader to easily locate the most pertinent literature on subjects such as trench warfare, black troops, the American air role, and so forth. The authors have expanded the scope of typical army-navy-air force history far beyond the battlefield. The coverage of the diplomacy of the war and the peace settlement is quite thorough. Moreover, a large portion of the volume is devoted to the home front which encompasses such fascinating subjects as politics, espionage, mobilization, and, especially, the social and intellectual aspects of the war. Hence, the writers have viewed this great struggle of the United States in its totality—the war itself, and the impact of war on American society.

This volume, the sixth in the series entitled "The Wars of the

United States," should find a receptive audience. Not only have the authors collected the best available materials about World War I, but they have also done so in highly readable prose. To compress into one volume the drama and glory of American fighting men, along with the frustrations and disappointments as well as successes of American politicians and diplomats, is indeed an accomplishment. Professors Woodward and Maddox merit high praise for this distinguished reference work.

Richard L. Blanco
General Editor

PREFACE

On April 6, 1917, the United States took the plunge, becoming directly involved in a great European war that was filled with momentous events and forces: revolutions which saw the triumph of communism in Russia, the destruction or revamping of old empires and with it the European equilibrium, the true industrialization and totality of warfare, a peace settlement of far-reaching consequences, and a profound revolution in Western thought. Affecting the development of the United States more directly was her departure from her diplomatic isolation and her mobilization for total war and all that that implied. The war also forced the United States, as David M. Kennedy has so aptly expressed it, "as almost never before, to measure itself against Europe, even to compete with Europe for a definition of the war's meaning and for the fruits of victory."[1]

Not surprisingly, the sources and literature for the Great War, as it was frequently called before it was surpassed in ferocity and destruction by World War II, are vast. No comparable period in modern history has been so thoroughly written about, from personal accounts to official histories, or documented in sources ranging from the voluminous British Cabinet Papers to the holdings of the National Archives and the Hoover Institution of War, Revolution and Peace Library. Nor have reference works been lacking, as a glance at the first chapter of this volume will attest. The compilers of this bibliography recognize and are greatly indebted to the many existing bibliographies, catalogs, guides, and bibliographical essays on either the war or related aspects of the conflict. This bibliography differs from these reference sources in one or more important ways. The annotations to entries frequently offer a critical evaluation. The bibliography

---

[1] David M. Kennedy, *Over Here: The First World War and American Society* (New York: Oxford University Press, 1980), vii–viii.

reflects the current broader interpretation of military history—
what Edward M. Coffman has called the New American Military
History[2]—because it examines the war's impact on society, institutions, and thought and goes beyond military operations. Its
coverage ranges from war films and literature to civil-military
relations to women and the war. Finally, it treats the European as
well as the American side of the conflict.

In a war that lasted 1,563 days, the United States was at war
for 19 months and was involved in large-scale military operations
for some 110 days. American involvement in the war is the primary focus of this bibliography, but the compilers believe that
the part played by the United States would be presented in a
vacuum if only sources and literature directly pertaining to
America and the war were included. Some of the best accounts
of American neutrality, such as the ones by Arthur S. Link and
Ernest R. May, for example, have been the product of research in
foreign archives; any study of American war objectives is in-
complete if the war aims of the European belligerents are not
fully understood and taken into account; and the military historian who writes a history of the AEF's fight against the German
army will benefit immeasurably from a knowledge of British and
European literature and sources on military operations. The war
was largely a European war, and this bibliography recognizes
that predominance in its selection of subjects and entries.

This bibliography was compiled by two historians: Dr. David
R. Woodward, a Modern European historian with a research
interest in the diplomatic and military history of World War I,
and Dr. Robert Franklin Maddox, a Twentieth-Century American historian who has research interests on the "home front."
Although there was inevitably some overlapping, the rough division of labor was as follows. Dr. Woodward prepared chapters I,
II, III, IV, VII, and VIII. There was equal collaboration on
Chapter VI. Dr. Maddox was responsible for Chapter V. Dr.
Woodward's emphasis was on diplomacy and "over there," including military operations, and Dr. Maddox concentrated on
"over here."

---

[2] Edward M. Coffman, "The New American Military History," *Military Affairs* 48 (January 1984): 1–5.

A majority of the printed works cited by the compilers have been personally sampled by them. When works were unobtainable, abstracts of doctoral dissertations and book reviews and review essays were utilized.

The policy of this series, Wars of the United States, is to use only English-language sources. Given the volume of publication on World War I and the English-language audience to which this bibliography is directed, this restriction seems reasonable. When possible, English editions of foreign works have been included.

The annotated entries include books, published documents, articles, review essays, doctoral dissertations, private papers, libraries and repositories, film, and oral history. With rare exceptions, books published after 1983 are not included. The arrangement is by subject.

The compilers' objective has been to give wide coverage, including both landmark works and a sampling of the literature for a particular subject. Some of the entries will be of more interest to the "history buff" than to the scholar. But this is as we planned it. It would be surprising if every World War I specialist concurs with our choice of subjects or our treatment of them. Either by design or because of the compilers' special interests some subjects have been given more extensive coverage than others. We also recognize that someone's favorite subject or book may not have been included.

Acknowledgment is gratefully made to the Marshall University Foundation which made it possible for Dr. Woodward to have his teaching load reduced from twelve to nine hours during several Spring semesters to work on this bibliography. The authors are also most appreciative of the generous assistance rendered them by librarians, especially the staffs of the Marshall University Library, University of Kentucky Library, and the U.S. Army Military History Institute.

D.R.W.
August 1984

America
and World War I

I. REFERENCE WORKS

A. BIBLIOGRAPHIES, CATALOGS, GUIDES, AND BIBLIOGRAPHICAL ESSAYS

1. General

1. *America: History and Life: A Guide to Periodical Literature.*
   Santa Barbara, Calif.: American Bibliographical Center, Clio
   Press, 1963- .

   This guide offers the researcher a quick reference to articles
   concerning American participation in the Great War. The value of
   the abstracts, however, depends upon the skill of individual ab-
   stracters.

2. Bayliss, Gwyn M. *Bibliographic Guide to the Two World Wars: An
   Annotated Survey of English-Language Reference Materials.* New
   York: R.R. Bowker Co., 1977. 587 pp.

   This is a valuable guide to essential reference works up to
   1976, including general guides, directories, encyclopedias, theses,
   yearbooks, biographies, periodicals, chronologies, and government
   publications. All aspects of the war are covered. There are
   title, author, regional and country, and subject indexes.

3. Enser, A.G.S. *A Subject Bibliography of the First World War:
   Books in English 1914-1978.* London: Andre Deutsch, 1979.
   485 pp.

   Enser, who has also prepared a bibliography on World War II,
   has compiled a massive bibliography of some 5,800 entries under
   340 subject headings. The compilation has a strong British
   flavor and the home front receives far less emphasis than the
   war on land and sea and in the air. In a work of this magnitude,
   it is perhaps not surprising that there are some embarrassing
   mistakes. For example, Alan Clark's blast against the strategy
   and tactics of British generals, *The Donkeys*, is listed under
   the subject heading "Animals."

4. Falls, Cyril, comp. *War Books: A Critical Guide.* London: Peter
   Davies, 1930. 318 pp.

   The compiler has little use for antiwar novels and reminiscences
   and makes no attempt to be comprehensive. Diplomatic works, for
   example, are not included. Still, this is an extremely valuable
   annotated guide because of Falls's vast knowledge of the war.
   Some German and French works are included. There is no index.

5. *Foreign Affairs Bibliography: A Selected and Annotated List of
    Books on International Relations.* Chief compiler and pub-
    lisher vary, 5 vols.

    Prepared under the auspices of the Council on Foreign Rela-
    tions, this important reference work on international affairs
    includes an annotated section on World War I. The first volume
    covers the period 1919-1932, and the fifth and most recent
    volume covers the period 1962-1972.

6. *The Foreign Affairs 50-Year Bibliography: New Evaluations of
    Significant Books on International Relations 1920-1970.*
    New York: R.R. Bowker Co., 1972. 936 pp.

    This volume attempts to single out those works in inter-
    national affairs from 1920 to 1970 that, although not neces-
    sarily the "best" books, were the "landmark" books. There is
    a chapter on World War I.

7. Higham, Robin, ed. *A Guide to the Sources of United States
    Military History.* Hamden, Conn.: Archon Books, 1975. 559 pp.

    Many distinguished historians contributed to this essential
    annotated bibliographical work. The chapter "World War I and
    the Peacetime Army, 1917-1941" was written by Daniel R. Beaver.
    Other contributors deal with topics relevant to World War I
    such as science and technology and military and naval medicine.
    A supplement appeared in 1981.

8. ————, and Mrozek, Donald J., eds. *A Guide to the Sources of
    United States Military History: Supplement I.* Hamden, Conn.:
    Archon Books, 1981. 300 pp.

    This volume does more than bring up to date the sources of
    U.S. military history. New chapters treat such areas as U.S.
    government documents and the U.S. Marine Corps. A quinquennial
    supplement is planned.

9.
    International Commission for the Teaching of History. *The Two
    World Wars: Selective Bibliography.* New York: Pergamon Press,
    1965. 246 pp.

    This is a translation of the 1964 French edition. It is es-
    pecially useful for locating French- and German-language sources
    on World War I.

10.
    Jessup, John E., Jr., and Coakley, Robert W., eds. *A Guide to
    the Study and Use of Military History.* Washington, D.C.:
    Government Printing Office, 1979. 506 pp.

    This is a collection of essays on such topics as "A Perspec-
    tive on Military History," "Military Museums and Collections,"
    "Military History and Army Records," and "The Place of Unit
    History." The student of World War I will find valuable the
    bibliographical essay by Charles B. MacDonald and the chapter
    on the holdings of the US Army Military History Institute by
    Coakley and MacDonald.

11. Leary, William M., Jr., and Link, Arthur S., comps. *The Pro-
     gressive Era and the Great War of 1896-1920*. Arlington Heights,
     Ill.: AHM Publishing Corp., 1978. 106 pp.

     The organization of this important bibliography is topical and
     there are frequent cross-references. This is one of the volumes
     in the *Goldentree Bibliographies in American History*.

12. Millett, Allan R., and Cooling, Benjamin Franklin, III, eds.
     Doctoral Dissertations in Military Affairs: A Bibliography.
     Manhattan: Kansas State University Library, 1972. 153 pp.

     This is a useful bibliography of dissertations in military
     affairs in the English language. It does not cover international
     affairs, and, alas, there is no index.

13. New York Public Library. *Dictionary Catalog of the Research
     Libraries of the New York Public Library, 1911-1971*. Boston:
     G.K. Hall & Co., 1979.

     This is a massive catalog of books, periodicals, and other
     printed materials in the New York Public Library up to 1971.
     Volumes 241-246 cover the World War I period. Over 500 personal
     American narratives are listed. For holdings added since 1972,
     some of them with imprints before 1972, see the *Dictionary Cata-
     log of the Research Libraries*, 1972- .

14. ————. *Subject Catalog of the World War I Collection*. Boston:
     G.K. Hall & Co., 1961. 4 vols.

     The many rare books and the general comprehensiveness of the
     World War I collection in the New York Public Library make it
     a very rich mine indeed for any Great War prospector.

15. Prothero, Sir George W., comp. *A Select Analytical List of Books
     Concerning the Great War*. London: H.M. Stationery Office,
     1923. 431 pp.

     This is an unusually comprehensive pioneer bibliography on the
     Great War, including sections on such topics as "Humour and
     Satire," "Dictionaries and Vocabularies," "Medicine and Surgery,"
     and "Religion."

16. *Readers' Guide to Periodical Literature*. New York: H.W. Wilson,
     1905- .

     Issued twice a month, the *Readers' Guide* serves as the standard
     index to some one hundred important and frequently used periodi-
     cals. There are subject and author indexes.

17. Schaffer, Ronald, comp. *The United States in World War I: A
     Selected Bibliography*. Santa Barbara, Calif.: American Biblio-
     graphical Center. Clio Press, 1978. 224 pp.

     This is an excellent reference work, perhaps the best of its
     kind for the American home front during the Great War. Extremely
     well organized, it is comprehensive in its coverage of subject
     areas.

18. *Writings on American History, 1902-1961*. Chief compiler and pub-
    lisher vary.

    Published by the American Historical Association, this bibliog-
    raphy includes books and articles on American and Canadian his-
    tory, with some brief annotations. This is a particularly good
    source for articles and unit histories immediately after World
    War I. There is an author-title-subject index.

19. *Writings on American History: A Subject Bibliography of Articles,
    1962-* . Millwood, N.Y.: Kraus-Thomson, 1974- .

    James J. Dougherty is the compiler-editor of this recent series
    published under the auspices of the American Historical Associa-
    tion. Its purpose is to provide a current list of article-length
    studies in American history. There is an author index.

2. Specific Subjects

20. Albion, Robert Greenhalgh, comp. *Maritime and Naval History:
    An Annotated Bibliography*. Newton Abbot: David & Charles,
    1973. 370 pp.

    This standard English-language bibliography on maritime and
    naval history includes a section on World War I. There is an
    author-subject index. The first edition was published in 1951.

21. Allard, Dean D.; Crawley, Martha L.; and Edmison, Mary W., comps.
    U.S. Naval History Sources in the United States. Washington,
    D.C.: Naval History Division, Department of the Navy, 1979.
    235 pp.

    This work surveys manuscript, archival, and other special
    collections pertaining to naval history in some 250 U.S. archives
    and libraries. In addition, the volume includes the papers of
    relevant congressmen, records of naval contractors, and official
    U.S. Navy records. This indispensable reference source has an
    unusually comprehensive index.

22. Anderson, Martin, comp. *Conscription: A Select and Annotated
    Bibliography*. Stanford, Calif.: The Hoover Institution Press,
    1976, 453 pp.

    Assisted by Valerie Bloom, Anderson has compiled a thorough
    guide to the literature, including unpublished manuscripts, on
    conscription in the United States and elsewhere. The first volume
    of a projected three-volume series, it includes both author and
    title indexes.

23. Binkley, R.C. "Ten Years of Peace Conference History." *Jour.
    Mod. Hist.* 1 (December 1929): 607-29.

    This bibliographical essay concentrates on the opening stages
    of the peace conference when procedures and organization were the
    central issues.

24. Birdsall, Paul. "The Second Decade of Peace Conference History." *Jour. Mod. Hist.* 11 (September 1939): 362-78.

    This bibliographical essay updates Binkley's earlier survey and focuses on the give and take of the Supreme Council over territorial and economic questions.

25. Bradshaw, Marion J. *The War and Religion: A Preliminary Bibliography of Material in English, Prior to January 1st 1919.* New York: Association Press, 1919. 136 pp.

    The Committee on the War and the Religious Outlook was responsible for this bibliography.

26. Coletta, Paolo E. *A Bibliography of American Naval History.* Annapolis, Md.: United States Naval Institute, 1981. 453 pp.

    Of the twenty-three chapters, Chapter 10, "Naval Power and World War I: Europe, 1914-1917," and Chapter 11, "The U.S. Navy in World War I, 1917-1919," are pertinent. There is an especially useful list of articles.

27. Cresswell, Mary Ann, and Berger, Carl. *United States Air Force History: An Annotated Bibliography.* Washington, D.C.: Office of Air Force History, 1971. 106 pp.

    The compilers include a section on World War I. See also the section "Aircraft." There are both subject and author indexes.

28. Dollen, Charles. *Bibliography of the United States Marine Corps.* New York: Scarecrow Press, 1963. 115 pp.

    Although the focus of this bibliography is on the years 1940-1960, one can find many World War I sources in the some 1,000 entries. There is a subject index.

29. Hager, Philip E., and Taylor, Desmond. *The Novels of World War I: An Annotated Bibliography.* New York: Garland Publishing, 1981. 513 pp.

    Hager and Taylor have compiled an annotated bibliography of American and foreign novels in English. Nine hundred adult and three hundred and seventy juvenile novels are surveyed.

30. Higham, Robin, ed. *Official Histories.* Manhattan: Kansas State University Library Bibliography Series, 1970. 644 pp.

    This work includes a discussion of the official World War I histories of America, Australia, Britain, France, Germany, Italy, and Austria-Hungary. The essays vary in quality; Jay Luvaas' essay evaluating the British official history is outstanding.

31. Hilliard, Jack B., comp. *An Annotated Bibliography of the United States Marine Corps in the First World War.* Washington, D.C.: Historical Division, Headquarters, U.S. Marine Corps, 1967. 16 pp.

    This is a useful bibliography.

32. Johnson, Alexander L.P. "Military Histories of the Great War."
     Jour. Mod. Hist. 3 (June 1931): 266-86.

     This is an excellent review essay on the progress and direction
     of the official military histories of the Great War.

33. Killen, Linda, and Lael, Richard. *Versailles and After: An
     Annotated Bibliography of American Diplomatic Relations,
     1919-1933.* New York: Garland Publishing, 1983. 469 pp.

     This bibliography, which serves as a good reference work for
     the peace settlement, is cross-referenced and has an author-
     subject index. The section on manuscript collections is out-
     standing.

34. Leland, Waldo G., and Mereness, Newton D., comps. *Introduction
     to the American Official Sources for the Economic and Social
     History of the World War.* New Haven: Yale University Press,
     1926. 532 pp.

     This is an excellent summary of the records and official pub-
     lications of the U.S. government in the sphere of social and
     economic history from April 1917 to demobilization in 1920 (al-
     though in some cases the period covered is from 1914 to 1922).

35. Leopold, Richard W. "The Problem of American Intervention,
     1917: An Historical Retrospect." *World Politics* 2 (April
     1950): 405-25.

     In this insightful survey of the literature on American inter-
     vention, Leopold is critical of the "witch-hunting tactics" of
     the early revisionists.

36. Library of Congress. *A List of Atlases and Maps Applicable to
     the World War.* Washington, D.C.: Government Printing Office,
     1918. 202 pp.

     There are author-subject indexes in this work, which includes
     784 atlases and maps arranged by country and by year.

37. Lutz, Ralph H. "Studies of World War Propaganda, 1914-1933."
     Jour. Mod. Hist. 5 (December 1933): 496-516.

     Some one hundred sources on World War I propaganda are sur-
     veyed in this bibliographical article.

38. Nims, Marion R. *Women in the War: A Bibliography.* Washington,
     D.C.: Government Printing Office, 1918. 77 pp.

     The Women's Committee of the American Council of National De-
     fense was responsible for this bibliography.

39. Pappas, George S. *United States Army Unit Histories.* Carlisle
     Barracks, Pa.: US Army Military History Research Collection,
     1971. 405 pp.

     A supplement to this comprehensive bibliography was issued in
     1974.

40. Schmitt, Bernadotte E. "American Neutrality, 1914-1917." *Jour. Mod. Hist.* 8 (June 1936): 200-211.

    This is an enlightening review article, with emphasis on the conclusions of Ray Stannard Baker and Charles Seymour.

41. Slonaker, John. *The US Army and the Negro*. Carlisle Barracks, Pa.: US Army Military History Research Collection, 1971. 116 pp.

    This annotated bibliography includes a section on World War I.

42. Smith, Daniel M. "National Interest and American Intervention, 1917: An Historiographical Appraisal." *JAH* 52 (June 1965): 5-24.

    Smith focuses on some major post-World War II assessments of the American decision for war, with emphasis on the influence of national interest on American statesmen. He concludes that many factors, especially moral and idealistic considerations, were responsible for American intervention and that "the hypothesis that the United States went to war in 1917 to protect its security against an immediate German threat lacks persuasiveness."

43. Smith, Myron J., Jr. *American Naval Bibliography*, vol. 4: *The American Navy, 1865-1918: A Bibliography*. Metuchen, N.J.: Scarecrow Press, 1974. 372 pp.

    Smith includes a section on World War I in his unusually thorough bibliography. There is a subject index.

44. ————. *World War I in the Air: A Bibliography and Chronology*. Metuchen, N.J.: Scarecrow Press, 1977. 271 pp.

    This is an essential reference work of over 2,000 entries. The sources are arranged alphabetically by author and there is a subject index. Some of the sources are annotated and there is an excellent chronology.

45. Smythe, Donald. "Literary Salvos: James G. Harbord and the Pershing-March Controversy." *Mid-Amer.* 57 (July 1975): 173-83.

    This article offers a behind-the-scenes glimpse of the "battle of the books" among three World War I generals. Smythe focuses on Harbord's response to March's account of Pershing's part in the war.

46. U.S. National Archives. *Handbook of Federal War Agencies and Their Records, 1917-1921*. Washington, D.C.: Government Printing Office, 1943. 666 pp.

    The alphabetical list of agencies includes Inter-Allied organizations in which the U.S. participated as well as federal war agencies.

47. Woodward, David R. "The American Expeditionary Force: Published Sources for the Study of Military Operations, 1917-1918." *Der Angriff* (May 1983): 26-27.

    A variety of published sources are critically evaluated.

48. ————. "Official Histories and the War in France and Flanders, 1914-1918: A Review Essay." *Der Angriff* (January 1983): 23.

    The strengths and weaknesses of the official histories of the war on the western front are examined in this review article.

3. Guides to U.S. Collections and Archives

49. Burdick, Charles B. "Foreign Military Records of World War I in the National Archives." *Prologue* 7 (Winter 1975): 213-20.

    Burdick notes that the historical section of the army general staff has acquired a large number of German (96,000), French (66,000), and British (12,000) military documents.

50. Carnegie Institution. *Guides to Manuscript Materials for the History of the United States, 1906-1943.* New York: Kraus Reprint, 1965. 23 vols.

    This fundamental research tool includes European as well as American archives.

51. Hamer, Philip M., ed. *A Guide to Archives and Manuscripts in the United States.* New Haven: Yale University Press, 1961. 775 pp.

    This standard guide, which surveys 1,300 depositories, has a name-subject index.

52. Hayes, John D. "The Papers of Naval Officers: Where Are They." *Mil. Affairs* 20 (Summer 1956): 102-3.

    This article covers the personal papers of naval officers in the Naval Historical Foundation (Library of Congress), the New York Public Library, and other depositories.

53. Library of Congress. *The National Union Catalog of Manuscript Collections.* Publisher and place of publication vary in this series. 1962- .

    This inventory of manuscript collections has indexes by name, subject, and repository and a full annotation of the nature of the collections. Additional volumes have appeared since the first one in 1962.

54. Lutz, Ralph H. "The World War in History." *Amer. Mil. Institute* 1 (Spring 1937): 18-21.

    Lutz surveys source materials housed in the Hoover War Library.

4. Guides to Foreign Collections and Archives

55. *A Catalogue of Files and Microfilms of the German Foreign Ministry Archives, 1867-1920.* Washington, D.C.: American Historical Association, 1959. 1,290 pp.

    This valuable catalog enables the researcher to make his way through the massive German diplomatic records with dispatch and assurance. An AHA committee for the study of war documents compiled this work.

56. Great Britain. Public Record Office. *List of Cabinet Papers 1880-1914*. London: H.M. Stationery Office, 1964. 143 pp.

    Cabinet papers for the first months of the war can be located in this guide.

57. ————. ————. *The Records of the Cabinet Office to 1922*. London: H.M. Stationery Office, 1966. 52 pp.

    This invaluable guide to the important and voluminous Cabinet Papers in the Public Record Office at Kew is useful to the historian of the American as well as the British role in the Great War.

58. ————. ————. *The Records of the Foreign Office 1782-1939*. London: H.M. Stationery Office, 1969. 180 pp.

    One should master the relevant sections in this guide before researching the records of the British Foreign Office for the war years.

59. Grimsted, Patricia Kennedy, comp. *Archives and Manuscript Repositories in the USSR: Moscow and Leningrad*. Princeton: Princeton University Press, 1972. 466 pp.

    This is an essential reference source on the archives and manuscript repositories in the USSR. There is a 1976 Supplement of 218 pages.

60. Herwig, Holger H. "An Introduction to Military Archives in West Germany." *Mil. Affairs* 36 (December 1982): 121-24.

    Although not confined to World War I sources, this article serves as a valuable introduction to war materials in the military archives of West Germany.

61. Kennett, Lee. "Military History in France." *Mil. Affairs* 42 (October 1978): 144-46.

    This University of Georgia professor makes some "practical suggestions" for researching French military history.

62. ————. "World War I Materials in the French Military Archives." *Mil. Affairs* 37 (April 1973): 60-62.

    Kennett provides a valuable survey of French military sources (the N series), many of which are relevant to the military role of the United States.

63. Koenig, Duane. "Archival Research in Italy." *Mil. Affairs* 35 (February 1971): 11-12.

    Koenig includes in this article a few valuable tips for World War I researchers in Italian archives.

64. May, William Edward. "Notes for Historical Research on the
    Royal Navy." *Mil. Affairs* 40 (December 1976): 186-87.

    In this article, May discusses the location of important
    naval archives and official naval records in Great Britain.

65. Mayer, S.L., and Koenig, W.J., comps. *The Two World Wars: A
    Guide to Manuscript Collections in the United Kingdom.* London:
    Bowker Publishing Co., 1976. 317 pp.

    This is an important reference for Anglo-American relations.
    The compilers more often than not surveyed the included collec-
    tions in situ. The libraries and repositories are arranged alpha-
    betically by location. There is a subject index.

66. Scott, Peter T. "Records of the Great War at the PRO. Pt. 1
    and 2." *Stand To!* (Winter 1982-Spring 1983): 16-17, 9.

    This is a valuable discussion of World War I records in the
    Public Record Office at Kew by the editor of *Stand To!* Of par-
    ticular interest to those interested in the AEF is the brief
    discussion of the class WO 106: Directorate of Military Operations
    and Intelligence Papers, which includes much material relating
    to the AEF, including British efforts to brigade American sol-
    diers with the BEF. It should also be noted that a copy of
    Haig's diaries can be found in WO 256, information that could
    make a trip to Edinburgh unnecessary.

67. Skidmore, Thomas E. "Survey of Unpublished Sources on the Central
    Government and Politics of the German Empire, 1871-1918." *AHR*
    65 (July 1960): 848-59.

    Skidmore discusses the availability and location of official
    and unofficial papers concerning the Bismarckian and Wilhelmian
    government and politics. He makes no claim to being exhaustive
    and emphasizes domestic rather than foreign policy.

68. Welsch, Edwin K., ed. *Libraries and Archives in France: A Hand-
    book.* Pittsburgh: Council for European Studies, University of
    Pittsburgh, 1973. 78 pp.

    Researchers are directed to guides to various collections of
    sources in diplomatic, military, and naval history. Welsch also
    provides information on gaining access to these holdings.

                            B. ATLASES

69. Banks, Arthur. *A Military Atlas of the First World War.* New
    York: Taplinger Publishing Co., 1975. 338 pp.

    This is the most useful atlas of World War I yet published.
    The illustrations and charts, which cover topics from the or-
    ganization of armies to weapons, are exceptional in their clarity.
    A commentary by Alan Palmer and a superior index complete the
    volume.

70. Esposito, Vincent J., ed. *The West Point Atlas of American Wars*,
    vol. 2: *1900-1953*. New York: Frederick A. Praeger, 1959.

    This comprehensive collection of maps focuses on land warfare.
    The volume includes a recommended reading list and a narrative
    of military operations for each war. World War I is represented
    by seventy-one maps. There are no page numbers; rather, the
    contents are arranged by section and by map.

71. Gilbert, Martin. *First World War Atlas*. New York: Macmillan Co.,
    1971. 159 pp.

    This handy atlas can be carried without resort to a trolley.
    It is truly an atlas of World War I, for military operations
    from Mesopotamia to the Pacific are given appropriate attention.
    Diagrams of trench warfare are also included in this extremely
    well-planned and reliable atlas.

72. McEntee, Girard L. *Military History of the World War: A Complete
    Account of the Campaigns on All Fronts, Accompanied by 456 Maps
    and Diagrams*. New York: Charles Scribner's Sons, 1937. 583 pp.

    The maps and diagrams make this more an atlas than a narrative
    of the military and naval campaigns. The author was a retired
    colonel in the U.S. Army.

C. BIOGRAPHICAL DICTIONARIES AND ENCYCLOPEDIAS

73. Herwig, Holger H., and Heyman, Neil M., comps. *Biographical
    Dictionary of World War I*. Westport, Conn.: Greenwood Press,
    1982. 480 pp.

    This is an important guide to the major political, military,
    and revolutionary personalities of World War I. The bibliography
    includes works in six languages. The volume also includes maps,
    a brief narrative, and a chronology.

74. *The Marshall Cavendish Illustrated Encyclopedia of World War I*.
    Freeport, N.Y.: Marshall Cavendish Corporation, 1984. 12 vols.

    This comprehensive encyclopedia, which covers the pre-1914
    period to the Treaty of Versailles and the election of Warren G.
    Harding as president, contains over 3,600 pages of text and illus-
    trations. The over 5,000 illustrations include maps, weapons,
    uniforms, cartoons and posters, photographs, and period paintings.
    Published in cooperation with the Imperial War Museum, the en-
    cyclopedia has a foreword by Arthur S. Link and articles by
    authorities written in a popular style. This encyclopedia con-
    tains much material relevant to America and World War I.

75. Paxson, Frederic L.; Corwin, Edward S.; and Harding, Samuel B.
    *War Cyclopedia: A Handbook for Ready Reference on the Great
    War*. Washington, D.C.: Committee on Public Information, 1918.
    321 pp.

    This encyclopedia published by the Creel Committee is an excellent example of how that committee provided propaganda instead of information. For example, "Fright of fullness" is a term used to describe the German method of warfare. On the other hand, the encyclopedia does contain some useful information on, for example, the draft laws. Generally speaking, the information provided has a progressive slant. Since it was edited by scholars, it is a good example of how professors prostituted their craft during the war.

76. *Webster's American Military Biographies.* Springfield, Mass.: G. & C. Merriam Co., 1978. 548 pp.

This excellent biographical source provides a chronology of military engagements that makes it easy to find references to the U.S. officers who fought on land, in the air, and at sea in the Great War.

77. Whitehouse, Arch. *Heroes of the Sunlit Sky.* Garden City, N.Y.: Doubleday & Co., 1967. 384 pp.

This reference work on the aviators of World War I offers biographical vignettes of 134 fliers, with emphasis on those who flew under the American flag. A glossary, bibliography, and numerous photographs are included.

D. STATISTICS

78. Ayres, Colonel Leonard P. *The War with Germany: A Statistical Summary.* Washington, D.C.: Government Printing Office, 1919. 154 pp.

This is the most important statistical study of American involvement in World War I. The student can find here such disparate information as the cost of the war to the United States ($1 million an hour) and American losses to influenza. As with most statistical information, the numbers should be double-checked whenever possible.

79. Creat Britain. War Office. *Statistics of the Military Effort of the British Empire During the Great War, 1914-1920.* London: H.M. Stationery Office, 1922. 880 pp.

This volume constitutes one of the most important statistical sources on military aspects of World War I. It contains material that relates to the American role in the war.

80. U.S. Navy Department. Office of Naval Records and Library, Historical Section. *American Ship Casualties of the World War, Including Naval Vessels, Merchant Ships, Sailing Vessels, and Fishing Craft.* Washington, D.C.: Government Printing Office, 1923. 23 pp.

This is an important statistical source for the American war at sea.

E. BATTLEFIELDS

81. American Battle Monuments Commission. *American Armies and Battlefields in Europe*. Washington, D.C.: Government Printing Office, 1938. 547 pp.

This magnificent work serves as the Baedecker guidebook to European fields drenched in American blood. The superb maps, drawings, photographs, descriptive detail, and directions enable one to retrace the march of American arms.

82. Coombs, Rose E.D. *Before Endeavours Fade: A Guide to the Battlefields of the First World War*. London: Battle of Britain Prints International, 1983. 160 pp.

The title is somewhat misleading because this guide is limited to the battlefields of the western front. Nevertheless, this is an indispensable source for any tour of the battlefields of France and Flanders. The author was until 1982 a special collections officer in the Imperial War Museum; her knowledge of World War I is extensive. The photographs are numerous and generally good, especially those that show the battlefields as they appeared then and appear now. The American war front receives some attention but not in the same depth as can be found in the American Battle Monuments Commission's *American Armies and Battlefields in Europe*.

83. Johnson, Douglas Wilson. *Battlefields of the World War: Western and Southern Fronts, a Study in Military Geography*. New York: Oxford University Press, 1921. 648 pp.

This is a more successful and complete analysis of the geography of the military campaigns in France, Italy, and the Balkans than his earlier *Topography and Strategy in the War*. Many photographs, diagrams, and maps are featured.

84. ————. *Topography and Strategy in the War*. New York: Henry Holt & Co., 1917. 211 pp.

The author discusses the terrain of each theater and attempts to show, through the use of texts, maps, and photographs, how the surface features influenced the strategies and outcomes of various campaigns. Published in September 1917, this work is useful only for the 1914-1916 phase of the war. Johnson was a professor of physiography at Columbia University.

85. Jones, Nigel H. *The War Walk: A Journey Along the Western Front*. London: Robert Hall, 1983. 228 pp.

Jones, whose father was on Haig's staff, has written an account of his 400-mile walk along the western front. Maps, illustrations, and interviews and correspondence with thirty-five veterans add to the worth of this guide to the battlefields of the western front.

86. *Michelin Illustrated Guides to the Battlefields: The Americans in the Great War*. Milltown, N.J.: Michelin & Co., 1920. 3 vols.

The Second Battle of the Marne and the St. Mihiel and Meuse-Argonne offensives are covered in these illustrated volumes. The battlefields, however, are now much changed by man and nature; therefore, more modern guides are recommended.

87. Moss, James A., and Howland, Harry S. *America in Battle: With Guide to the American Battlefields in France and Belgium.* Menasha, Wis.: G. Banta Publishing Co., 1920. 615 pp.

    This is a comprehensive and useful source on the AEF.

II. MANUSCRIPT DEPOSITORIES AND LIBRARIES
(INCLUDING ORAL HISTORY)

88. British Library, Great Russell Street, London WC1B 3DG, England.

    The Department of Manuscripts in the British Library and the
    Public Record Office are the two major British repositories for
    manuscripts. In addition, the book holdings of the British
    Library are vast. Intending researchers should bring with them
    a letter of reference.

89. Hoover Institution of War, Revolution and Peace Library, Stanford
    University, Stanford, Calif. 94305.

    Founded in 1919, this institution began as a repository of
    World War I documents. It has an exceptional collection per-
    taining to social, political, and economic changes during the
    era of World War I. Its holdings range from the records of the
    American Relief Administration to extensive materials on Russo-
    American relations.

90. Imperial War Museum, Lambeth Road, London SE1 6HE, England.

    The private papers, oral history collection, photographs, war
    posters, printed sources, and other records make this one of
    the most important research centers pertaining to the Great War.
    Inquiries concerning any restrictions on the use of the collec-
    tions should be addressed to Keeper of the Department of Docu-
    ments. The important World War I oral history collection is
    organized into five main groups: military and naval aviation,
    1914-1918; western front: life and operations, 1914-1918; Royal
    Navy: lower deck, 1910-1922; the antiwar movement, 1914-1918;
    and war work, 1914-1918. The researcher needs to make arrange-
    ments with the museum's Oral History Programme prior to his or
    her arrival.

91. Library of Congress, Washington, D.C. 20540.

    The Library of Congress and the National Archives are the two
    most important centers for researching American military history.
    The book holdings of the LOC are vast and the Manuscript Division
    (which is the repository for many of the papers of the Naval
    Historical Foundation) has the papers of many American civil and
    military leaders, including General Pershing, Admiral Sims,
    Edward House, and President Wilson. The papers of the American
    peace commission to Versailles are also deposited in the LOC.

92. National Archives, Pennsylvania Avenue and Eighth Street N.W.,
    Washington, D.C. 20408.

    The National Archives documents the history of the United

States. In World War I American military history, all roads
lead to the National Archives. Its records include detailed
information on most of the major World War I agencies and the
records of the American Expeditionary Forces (Record Group 120).
In addition, audio-visual materials, photographs, and other war-
related materials can be found there. The *Guide to the National
Archives of the United States* is the starting point for research
there.

93. Navy Department Library, Building 44, Washington Navy Yard,
     Washington, D.C. 20374.

     The Navy Department Library of some 140,000 volumes has sub-
     stantial holdings relevant to World War I. Along with an ex-
     cellent collection of naval periodicals, the library is very
     rich in graduate theses and dissertations in naval history.
     The library has an open-shelf system.

94. New York Public Library, Fifth Avenue and Forty-Second Street,
     New York, N.Y. 10018.

     The holdings of this great library include many books which
     are classified as rare books and are readily available only in
     this library. The library, for example, has over 500 personal
     American narratives of the war, many of which are not in the
     Library of Congress.

95. Nimitz Library, U.S. Naval Academy, Annapolis, Md. 21402.

     There is a substantial collection of works pertaining to
     World War I naval history in this library of some 500,000 books.
     The library is a depository for transcripts of the interviews
     prepared by the Oral History Office at the U.S. Naval Institute.
     Although this oral history primarily concerns the post-World War I
     period, some material is pertinent to the Great War.

96. Public Record Office, Ruskin Avenue, Kew, Richmond, Surrey
     TW9 4DV, England.

     The World War I records of the Royal Navy, Army, and Air Force,
     the War and Foreign offices, and the Cabinet are deposited in
     the Public Record Office at Kew. U.S. citizens need a letter of
     reference to secure a reader's ticket.

97. U.S. Air Force, Air University Library, Maxwell AFB, Ala. 36112.

     In addition to the Center's extensive book holdings on World
     War I, the special collections of the United States Air Force
     Historical Research Center (formerly the Albert F. Simpson His-
     torical Research Center) contain printed works, manuscript collec-
     tions, and oral history pertaining to the history of the U.S.
     Air Force.

98. US Army Military History Institute, Carlisle Barracks, Pa. 17013.

     The institute's holdings have rapidly expanded since its be-
     ginning in 1967; the institute now has one of the best collections
     of World War I materials in the United States. The holdings best

support research on the Army, but the Navy and Air Force have not been neglected in acquisitions. The archives contain the papers of generals Harry Bandholtz, Tasker Bliss, William Carey Brown, Reynolds Burt, Charles Gerhardt, Johnson Hagood II, Guy V. Henry, Jr., John L. Hines, Lyman Kennon, Michael Lenihan, Robert Mearns, Benjamin Poore, Henry Reilly, Fred Sladen, and Ralph VanDeman. The Oral History Branch of this institute has a fine collection of interviews with a focus on senior officers, a number of which touch upon World War I. Tapes and transcripts do not circulate and must be used in the archives.

99. U.S. Marine Corps Historical Center, Code HDS-5, Building 58, Washington Naval Yard, Washington, D.C. 20374.

This comprehensive repository of Marine materials includes music, art, photographs, operational records, personal papers, and oral history. It is the center for the Marine Corps Oral History Program. This oral history program broadly interprets oral history to mean the spoken history. Thus, for example, its collection contains debriefings and speeches as well as interviews. Many of the interviews concern World War I. World War I materials in special collections include the papers of Smedley D. Butler and a large collection of World War I diaries.

100. U.S. Naval War College. Naval Historical Collection. Newport, R.I. 02840.

World War I materials include attaché reports concerning military capabilities, preparedness, and social and economic conditions of the European powers; compilations on submarine and anti-submarine activities; and war planning for a possible war with Germany. The holdings of the Naval War College Library emphasize theory, tactics, and training.

III. ORIGINS AND OUTBREAK OF WAR

101. Albertini, Luigi. *The Origins of the War of 1914*. New York: Oxford University Press, 1952-1957. 3 vols.

     Originally published in Italian (1942-1943), this study breaks new ground. Exhaustively researched, including many interviews, this work has become a standard analysis of the background of the war. Italian diplomacy is given special emphasis.

102. Barnes, Harry Elmer. *The Genesis of the World War: An Introduction to the Problem of War Guilt*. New York: Alfred A. Knopf, 1929. 754 pp.

     This pioneer revisionist study of the origins of the war, which includes a chapter on American intervention, attempts to debunk the thesis that Germany bore the major responsibility for the war. Barnes points the finger of blame at France and Russia. He also contends that the "turnip winter" of 1916-1917 forced Berlin to resort to unrestricted submarine warfare to save the German people from starvation. Barnes's research is now much dated and his conclusions are in disrepute.

103. Berghahn, V.R. *Germany and the Approach of War in 1914*. New York: St. Martin's Press, 1973. 260 pp.

     This work provides an excellent summary of recent scholarship on German responsibility for the outbreak of war. The author also makes an original contribution in his treatment of German armaments policy and the distorted political perception of German leaders. There are chapter notes, and the bibliography is especially strong in German sources.

104. Bloch, Camille. *The Causes of the World War: An Historical Summary*. London: Allen & Unwin, 1935. 224 pp.

     Bloch, a professor of modern history at the Sorbonne, attempts to reinforce the verdict of the Versailles Treaty with his analysis. This is a good example of the French point of view.

105. Dedijer, Vladimir. *The Road to Sarajevo*. New York: Simon & Schuster, 1966. 550 pp.

     This is a deeply researched and exhaustive evaluation of the events leading to the assassination of Archduke Ferdinand at Sarajevo. It is superior to Remak's 1959 treatment of the same subject.

106. Farrar, L.L., Jr. *The Short-War Illusion: German Policy, Strategy & Domestic Affairs August-December 1914*. Santa

Barbara, Calif.: American Bibliographical Center. Clio Press, 1973. 207 pp.

This monograph, which treats the attitudes of both civil and military authorities, offers an extensive examination of a well-known theme from a German perspective.

107. Fay, Sidney Bradshaw. *The Origins of the World War*. New York: Macmillan Co., 1928. 2 vols.

Based largely on German sources, this classic revisionist study, which stresses collective responsibility, deals with both the underlying and immediate causes of the war. The unavailability of many sources distorts somewhat Fay's portrayal of Serbian and Russian actions. Austria and Russia are assigned more responsibility than Germany for the outbreak of war.

108. Fischer, Fritz. *Germany's Aims in the First World War*. New York: W.W. Norton & Co., 1967. 652 pp.

The author's controversial examination of the origins of the war and German war objectives started afresh the debate over Germany's responsibility for the war. Fischer asserts that Germany practiced brinkmanship in July 1914 to break out of the encirclement created by the Triple Entente. Perhaps his most valuable contribution is his linking of German domestic policy to foreign policy. The expansionist war aims of Germany that emerge from this study are breath-taking in their scope. Many previously unexplored German archival resources are utilized.

109. ————. *War of Illusions: German Policies from 1911 to 1914*. London: Chatto & Windus, 1975. 578 pp.

This single-minded work is a harsh indictment of Germany. The author argues that Germany sought hegemony in Europe and that many of her policymakers considered war as a means of gaining this objective.

110. Fleming, Denna F. *The Origins and Legacies of World War I*. Garden City, N.Y.: Doubleday & Co., 1968. 352 pp.

This study blames the old international system and Germany and Austria-Hungary for World War I. The author concludes that the war resulted in economic chaos, the rise of dictatorships and another world war. This work is not taken seriously by scholars.

111. Geiss, Imanuel. *July 1914. The Outbreak of the First World War: Selected Documents*. London: B.T. Batsford, 1967. 400 pp.

Geiss presents documents and commentary which serve to strengthen the case of Fischer against his critics. The original German edition appeared in two volumes.

112. Gooch, G.P., and Temperley, H. *British Documents on the Origins of the War, 1898-1914*. London: H.M. Stationery Office, 1927-1938. 11 vols. in 13.

Most of these volumes are arranged by subject. The important Vol. 11, which concerns the immediate causes for the outbreak

of war is, however, arranged chronologically. These official
volumes were prepared without any censorship or manipulation
by the British government.

113. Kaiser, David E. "Germany and the Origins of the First World
     War." *Jour. Mod. Hist.* 55 (September 1983): 442-74.

     Kaiser argues that much of the recent literature "has dis-
     torted the domestic aims which foreign policy was designed to
     achieve before 1914, misunderstood the goals of Weltpolitik...
     and obscured the real reasons for the 1914 decisions that
     helped unleash a world war."

114. Keiger, John F.V. *France and the Origins of the First World
     War*. New York: St. Martin's Press, 1983. 201 pp.

     This work debunks the postwar revisionist view that a vengeful
     Poincaré was bent on war with Germany. The French statesman is
     pictured as favoring detente but not rapprochement with Germany.
     This solidly researched volume is an important addition to the
     literature on the origins of the war.

115. Kennedy, Paul. *The Rise of the Anglo-German Antagonism 1860-
     1914*. London: Allen & Unwin, 1980. 604 pp.

     This is a masterful analysis of this important topic. The
     research is thorough and the conclusions balanced. Kennedy
     emphasizes the rapid growth of German power rather than the
     clumsiness of Berlin's diplomacy after Bismarck as the primary
     cause of the deterioration of Anglo-German relations.

116. Koch, H.W., ed. *The Origins of the First World War: Great
     Power Rivalry and German War Aims*. London: Macmillan Press,
     1972. 374 pp.

     This book brings together differing views on Fischer's in-
     terpretation of German policy. The contributors are Epstein,
     Fischer, Geiss, Hatton, Janssen, Joll, Koch, and Zechlin.

117. LaFore, Laurence. *The Long Fuse: An Interpretation of the
     Origins of World War I*. Philadelphia: J.B. Lippincott Co.,
     1971. 284 pp.

     The author emphasizes Slav nationalism and the ramshackle
     nature of the Austro-Hungarian Dual Monarchy as causes for
     World War I. This is an unusually well-written and concise
     study. A useful annotated bibliography is included.

118. Langhorne, Richard. *The Collapse of the Concert of Europe:
     International Politics, 1890-1914*. London: Macmillan Press,
     1981. 137 pp.

     This work provides a fresh approach to the origins of World
     War I. The principal features of international politics from
     1890 to 1914 are discussed thematically. Among other topics,
     the author examines the role of domestic pressures on diplomacy
     and the impact of technological and demographic changes. Chapter
     notes are included, but there is no bibliography.

119. Lee, Dwight E., ed. *The Outbreak of the First World War: Who Was Responsible?* Boston: D.C. Heath & Co., 1963. 81 pp.

     Now outdated by more recent scholarship, this collection of differing views on the causes of the war is of little value. It does not, for example, include a discussion of the debate provoked by Fischer.

120. Montgelas, Count Max. *The Case for the Central Powers.* New York: Alfred A. Knopf, 1925. 255 pp.

     Count Montgelas, a member of the German delegation sent to Versailles to examine the question of responsibility for the war, makes as strong a case as possible for German and Austrian "innocence." This pioneer revisionist study has not stood the test of recent scholarship.

121. Remak, Joachim. "1914--The Third Balkan War: Origins Reconsidered." *Jour. Mod. Hist.* 43 (September 1971): 353-66.

     Remak reconsiders the question of war guilt in this survey of the responsibility of each of the belligerents.

122. ———. *The Origins of World War I.* New York: Holt, Rinehart & Winston, 1967. 162 pp.

     A skillful and thought-provoking synthesis of the causes of World War I, this volume in the Berkshire Studies in European History series contends that the war "was a twentieth century diplomatic crisis gone wrong."

123. ———. *Sarajevo: The Story of a Political Murder.* New York: Criterion Books, 1959. 301 pp.

     This is a popular retelling of Archduke Ferdinand's assassination. Remak's account of the trial of the young assassins breaks new ground, but Dedijer's work in 1966 is based on more recent and more revealing sources.

124. Renouvin, Pierre. *The Immediate Origins of the War: 28th June-4th August, 1914.* New Haven: Yale University Press, 1928. 395 pp.

     This work, which attempts to refute studies that seek to diminish or remove German and Austrian responsibility for the war, is of interest primarily because it was written by France's leading authority for the World War I period. Renouvin was professor of history of World War I at the University of Paris, the editor of the *Revue d'histoire de la guerre mondiale*, and the director of the French War Library. French accounts of the outbreak of the war are not numerous, but the French role can be followed in *Documents diplomatiques français 1871-1914*, one of the best collections of official documents for the prewar period, and in Keiger.

125. Ritter, Gerhard. *The Sword and the Scepter. The Problem of Militarism in Germany*, vol. 2: *The European Powers and the Wilhelminian Empire, 1890-1914.* Coral Gables, Fla.: University of Miami Press, 1970. 328 pp.

This is a readable translation of Ritter's important study of prewar planning and civil-military relations in France, Russia, Britain, and especially Germany. The Schlieffen Plan, Ritter argues, was shaped far too much by military rather than by political considerations. Ritter's interpretation of German motives is often at odds with Fischer.

126. Schmitt, Bernadotte Everly. *The Coming of the War: 1914*. New York: Charles Scribner's Sons, 1930. 2 vols.

This solid study, which concentrates on the July Crisis, is the best anti-revisionist study produced during the interwar period. See Schmitt's later article in the *Journal of Modern History* in which he revises some of his views because of new material.

127. ———. "July 1914: Thirty Years After." *Jour. Mod. Hist.* 16 (September 1944): 169-204.

The author, taking into account new material, revises his interpretation of the July Crisis found in his *The Coming of the War: 1914*.

128. Sontag, Raymond J. "The German Diplomatic Papers: Publication after Two World Wars." *AHR* 68 (October 1962): 57-68.

Sontag discusses Friedrich Thimme's honest and balanced editing of *Die grosse Politik der europäischen Kabinette, 1871-1914*. This fifty-four volume collection of German diplomatic documents remains an essential source for studying the origins of World War I.

129. Steiner, Zara S. *Britain and the Origins of the First World War*. New York: St. Martin's Press, 1977. 305 pp.

This well-researched study examines the role played by external and internal factors in pushing Britain into war. Steiner concludes that the former proved more important. Her work demonstrates that the Fischer model, which stresses domestic tensions as the determining factor in decision making, does not apply in the case of Britain. She argues that "British action was the response to outward events and that these responses were made by a few men who are easily identifiable."

130. ———. *The Foreign Office and Foreign Policy, 1898-1914*. New York: Cambridge University Press, 1969. 262 pp.

This is an important evaluation of the influence of permanent Foreign Office officials such as Hardinge, Tyrrell, Nicolson, and Crowe. Steiner concludes that the anti-German sentiment of Crowe and others has been exaggerated as a factor in Britain's decision to join the anti-German coalition.

131. Taylor, A.J.P. *The Struggle for Mastery in Europe 1848-1918*. Oxford: Clarendon Press, 1960. 638 pp.

Many a graduate student studying European diplomatic history has cut his teeth on this masterful work. Taylor takes exception

with the revisionists who have attempted to shift the blame for
the war away from Germany. There is an excellent annotated bibliography.

132. ————. *War by Time-Table: How the First World War Began*.
      London: Macdonald & Co., 1969. 126 pp.

      This is a stimulating and well-illustrated little book which
      makes a connection between the war plans and the outbreak of
      war in Europe in 1914. Primary attention is given to the
      Schlieffen Plan which served to tie the hands of German states-
      men during the July crisis. As Taylor writes, diplomacy "became
      the servant of strategy."

133. Turner, L.C.F. *Origins of the First World War*. New York: W.W.
      Norton & Co., 1970. 120 pp.

      This survey by a historian from the Royal Military College of
      Australia is valuable because it discusses the diplomatic rami-
      fications of the war plans of the great powers. Turner rejects
      the extreme arguments of the Fischer school and maintains that
      a "tragedy of miscalculation" is the best explanation of the
      outbreak of war.

134. Williamson, Samuel R. *The Politics of Grand Strategy: Britain
      and France Prepare for War, 1904-1914*. Cambridge: Harvard
      University Press, 1969. 409 pp.

      Williamson, utilizing archival sources in Britain, Belgium,
      and France, has thoroughly researched the politics of the
      Entente Cordiale and its strategical consequences. How Britain
      was drawn into participating in a land war in Europe is one
      subject of this balanced study. There is an excellent select
      bibliography.

135. ————, ed. *Origins of a Tragedy: July 1914*. St. Louis: Forum
      Press, 1981. 99 pp.

      The author has collected and evaluated primary source material
      for the student of the causes of the war.

136. Woodward, E.L. *Great Britain and the German Navy*. Hamden,
      Conn.: Archon Books, 1964. 524 pp.

      Recognized as an outstanding work of scholarship, this has
      become a classic account of the Anglo-German naval rivalry in
      the years before 1914. This is a reprint of the 1935 edition.

IV. MILITARY ASPECTS OF THE WAR

A. GENERAL SOURCES OF THE
EUROPEAN WAR, 1914-1918

137. Albrecht-Carrié, René. *The Meaning of the First World War.*
Englewood Cliffs, N.J.: Prentice-Hall, 1965. 181 pp.

The author attempts to assess the significance of the Great
War for the twentieth century. There is a brief bibliography.

138. Aron, Raymond. *The Century of Total War.* Garden City, N.Y.:
Doubleday & Co., 1954. 379 pp.

A central thesis of Aron's thought-provoking study is that
World War I was the catalyst for ruinous forces which have re-
shaped the world, especially in the area of human behavior.

139. Baldwin, Hanson W. *World War I: An Outline History.* New York:
Harper & Row, 1962. 181 pp.

Written in a clear and dramatic style, this short work by the
distinguished military analyst for the *New York Times* ranks with
Barnett's, Taylor's, and Marshall's illustrated histories as a
brief introduction to the war.

140. Barnett, Correlli. *The Great War.* New York: G.P. Putnam's
Sons, 1979. 192 pp.

This illustrated history of World War I by a distinguished
British military historian is one of the best yet produced.
The illustrations and maps, many of them in color, are outstanding. And the commentary is frequently full of insight.
This is more than a survey of military operations because war
aims and the impact of total war, among other topics, are
touched upon.

141. Best, Geoffrey. *Humanity in Warfare.* New York: Columbia University Press, 1980. 400 pp.

The author traces efforts to humanize war as the machine age
and the advent of total war raised the price in blood which
belligerents paid and produced "uncivilized" weapons such as
poison gas and policies such as strategic bombing. The Red
Cross and the Hague Convention are shown to have been two of
the positive results of this movement prior to the Great War.

142. Buchan, John. *A History of the Great War.* Boston: Houghton
Mifflin Co., 1922. 4 vols.

These volumes are chiefly of interest because they constitute
one of the first serious efforts to cover the history of the
war. However, they suffer from the serious defect of having
been written before many essential sources were available to
the author. The style is colorful, but the author's interpretations are frequently neither fair nor balanced.

143. Cameron, James. *1914*. New York: Rinehart & Co., 1959. 278 pp.

The public mood in 1914 was almost carefree when compared to
1939. "Business as usual," for example, continued in Great
Britain. This British journalist succeeds very well in his de-
piction of the reaction of the French, Germans, and especially
the British to the outbreak of general war.

144. Churchill, Winston S. *The World Crisis, 1911-1918*. New York:
      Charles Scribner's Sons, 1927-1930. 4 vols.

Churchill begins his account with the 1911 Agadir Crisis and
concludes with the collapse of Germany in 1918. This is very
personal history because it was written by one of the leading
participants in the war. The literary quality of this wide-
ranging narrative is outstanding.

145. Cruttwell, C.R.M.F. *A History of the Great War 1914-1918*.
      Oxford: Clarendon Press, 1964. 655 pp.

Of considerable literary merit, this history of the war by
an Oxford University historian is a classic. This broad and
comprehensive survey treats diplomatic, political, and military
aspects of the war. Since it was written for an English
audience, the easterner-westerner strategical debate is given
extensive coverage, as is the war in the outer theaters. First
published in 1934, it remains one of the most readable accounts
of the war.

146. Edmonds, Brig.-Gen. Sir James E. *A Short History of World
      War I*. New York: Oxford University Press, 1951. 454 pp.

Written by one of the leading authorities on the war, this
volume concentrates on the western front and is full of the
insight of a man who has seriously studied the war for over
thirty years. Edmonds, however, is often an apologist for the
generals. An extreme westerner, he, like Terraine, argues that
the war in the outer theaters had no military effect on the
outcome of war other than to weaken the British effort in the
"principal theatre" or France.

147. Esposito, Brig.-Gen. Vincent J., ed. *A Concise History of
      World War I*. New York: Frederick A. Praeger, 1964. 414 pp.

Esposito, with the assistance of eight other authorities,
has compiled a valuable collection of essays on various aspects
of the war such as the "Comparative Strength of the Belligerents" and "The War at Sea." There is an annotated bibliography
and the appendices include important statistical material.
Ernest R. May and Cyril Falls are among the distinguished
contributors.

148. Falls, Cyril. *The Great War 1914-1918*. New York: Capricorn Books, 1961. 447 pp.

    Written by a decorated veteran and a member of the team of historians who wrote the British official history of the war, this volume is one of the four or five best general histories of the war. Captain Falls's purpose is to demolish "a myth as preposterous as it is widely believed"; that the generals on both sides were generally incompetent, displaying little tactical or strategical brilliance. This book is exceptionally well written.

149. Ferro, Marc. *The Great War 1914-1918*. London: Routledge & Kegan Paul, 1973. 239 pp.

    This is the English translation of the 1969 French edition. It is a different history of World War I that focuses on economic, political, and social forces. One should look elsewhere for a treatment of military operations. There is a limited bibliography and no footnotes.

150. Fuller, J.F.C. *The Conduct of War, 1789-1961: A Study of the Impact of the French, Industrial, and Russian Revolutions on War and Its Conduct*. New Brunswick, N.J.: Rutgers University Press, 1961. 352 pp.

    This single-minded work by a British military historian and advocate of the tank offers insight into the conduct of total war during 1914-1918.

151. Halsey, Francis Whitling. *The Literary Digest History of the World War*. New York: Funk & Wagnalls Co., 1919-1920. 10 vols.

    These volumes, which are based on American and foreign sources, are valuable for their contemporary treatment of the important events and personalities of the war. Vol. 4 discusses both the American decision for war and preparations for war. There are numerous maps and illustrations. Halsey died as he was finishing the tenth and last volume of this series.

152. Hardach, Gerd. *The First World War, 1914-1918*. Berkeley: University of California Press, 1977. 328 pp.

    This is the English translation of a pioneer economic survey of the war ("the 'crisis' of the capitalist world economy") by a European Marxist. Not surprisingly, Hardach sees the war as an imperialistic conflict. It would seem that in his lights the most important and hopeful event of the war was the Bolshevik Revolution. This study is well documented, has an extensive bibliography, and provides numerous tables.

153. Hayes, Carlton J.H. *Brief History of the Great War*. New York: Macmillan Co., 1920. 461 pp.

    Of the general histories of the war rushed into print during the immediate postwar period, this was the best produced by an American academic. It is, of course, now much dated.

154. King, Jere Clemens, ed. *The First World War*. New York: Walker
      & Co., 1972. 350 pp.

      King has collected documents which deal with military and
      naval operations, diplomacy, and the impact of war on intellec-
      tuals, women, poets, and soldiers. This book is divided into
      three parts: "Martial Glory: The Conduct of Operations," "The
      War's Misery: Attitudes Toward the War," and "The War's Diplo-
      macy." There is a selected bibliography.

155. Liddell Hart, Captain B.H. *The Real War 1914-1918*. Boston:
      Little, Brown & Co., 1930. 508 pp.

      Until his death Liddell Hart was widely recognized as Britain's
      foremost military historian. This work is critical of the
      generals' conduct of the war. Liddell Hart believed that what
      he considered were the tactical and strategical mistakes of the
      war must be underlined to prevent them from being repeated. An
      opponent of the westerners, who wanted to concentrate most
      military resources on the western front, he is sympathetic to
      the easterners, who sought an indirect route to victory over
      the Central Powers. This remains one of the best general his-
      tories of the war in spite of its at times polemical nature.

156. London Times. *The Times History of the War*. 1914-1920. 22
      vols.

      All phases of the Great War are covered in this running ac-
      count of the conflict. The first volume was published in August
      1914. The illustrations are uniformly excellent.

157. New York Times. *Current History of the European War*. 1914-
      1918.

      Published bi-monthly by the *New York Times*, this is a valuable
      serial record of the war. It contains many contemporary docu-
      ments and articles by some of the leading figures of the day.

158. Ropp, Theodore. *War in the Modern World*. Durham, N.C.: Duke
      University Press, 1959. 400 pp.

      This is a concise introduction to warfare from the Renaissance
      through World War II. Political, technological, organizational,
      and institutional or administrative changes in warfare are
      analyzed. Numerous explanatory footnotes enhance the text.

159. Schmitt, Bernadotte E., and Vedeler, Harold C. *The World in the
      Crucible 1914-1919*. New York: Harper & Row, 1984. 553 pp.

      The authors' intent is to write "not a history of the Great
      War but of Europe, and in certain aspects of the world, during
      the period of the war." This is the latest volume in the "Rise
      of Modern Europe" series. Vedeler has incorporated materials
      produced by Schmitt, who died in 1968, in many of the chapters.
      Vedeler's chapters on revolution, however, are his work alone.
      There is a chapter on "Crisis at Sea and American Involvement,"
      and a thorough annotated bibliography.

160. Stallings, Laurence, ed. *The First World War: A Photographic History*. New York: Simon & Schuster, 1933. 298 pp.

Almost three years of research in America and Europe went into the production of this book. The some 500 pictures are generally arranged chronologically and must speak for themselves since there is no commentary.

161. Stokesbury, James L. *A Short History of World War I*. New York: William Morrow & Co., 1981. 348 pp.

This is the first traditional history of World War I which concentrates on military operations that has been written in over two decades. There is a useful annotated bibliography in this volume, which is designed for classroom use.

162. Strachan, Hew. *European Armies and the Conduct of War*. London: Allen & Unwin, 1983. 240 pp.

This is an interpretative work which emphasizes both the conduct of war and the relationship between armies and societies. Clausewitz's influence and the industrialization of war are two of the many issues that are explored.

163. Taylor, A.J.P. *The First World War: An Illustrated History*. New York: Capricorn Books, 1972. 296 pp.

Taylor is as stimulating as he is controversial. The student of the war will almost certainly question some of his interpretations, but will also profit from Taylor's flashes of insight. The some 220 photographs are outstanding. This volume is highly recommended to anyone who desires a quick and thought-provoking introduction to the Great War.

164. Terraine, John. *The Great War, 1914-1918: A Pictorial History*. New York: Macmillan Co., 1965. 400 pp.

Most of the photographs for this volume are from the Imperial War Museum and the Mansell Collection.

165. Tuchmann, Barbara W. *The Guns of August*. New York: Macmillan Co., 1962. 511 pp.

This is a spirited, colorful, and well-written account of the opening battles of the war, based on thorough research in published sources.

166. Vagts, Alfred. *A History of Militarism: Romance and Realities of a Profession*. New York: W.W. Norton & Co., 1937. 510 pp.

This is a standard account of militarism in Europe prior to World War I. The author, a German officer during World War I, focuses on the social and political features of militarism. There are illustrations and chapter notes but no bibliography.

167. Werstein, Irving. *1914-1918: World War I Told with Pictures*. New York: Cooper Square Publishers, 1966. 125 pp.

This pictorial history is intended for a juvenile audience and neither the photographs nor commentary compares favorably

with such popular pictorial works as the ones compiled by Barnett and Taylor.

B. GENERAL SOURCES OF AMERICAN PARTICIPATION,
1917-1919

168. Bassett, John Spencer. *Our War with Germany. A History.* New
      York: Alfred A. Knopf, 1919. 386 pp.

      This matter-of-fact history by a Smith College historian
      avoids controversy. Approximately three-fourths of the volume
      concerns the period of American belligerency and the Paris
      Peace Conference. The research, which depends heavily on news-
      paper accounts, is superficial.

169. Chambrun, Colonel de, and Marenches, Captain de. *The American
      Army in the European Conflict.* New York: Macmillan Co.,
      1919. 436 pp.

      This controversy-free account of the AEF's role in defeating
      the German army was written for the general public. The authors,
      French officers, do not, however, fail to point out the impor-
      tant assistance given the Americans by their French and British
      allies.

170. Coffman, Edward M. *The War to End All Wars: The American Mili-
      tary Experience in World War I.* New York: Oxford University
      Press, 1968. 412 pp.

      Coffman succeeds brilliantly in his objective: to describe
      the war as experienced in the training camps and trenches as
      well as in the War Department and General Pershing's general
      headquarters. This most readable history is a standard account.
      There are no footnotes but there is an outstanding "essay on
      the sources."

171. Dawson, Coningsby W. *Out to Win: The Story of America in France.*
      New York: John Lane Co., 1918. 206 pp.

      This is an account of Dawson's visit to the American army.
      Dawson was working for the British government, and his work
      falls into the category of "morale boosting" books on the war.

172. DeWeerd, Harvey A. *President Wilson Fights His War: World
      War I and the American Intervention.* New York: Macmillan Co.,
      1968. 457 pp.

      This general account of American involvement in the Great War
      is unusual because it does not view the war from a limited
      American perspective. The origins of the war and especially
      the course of the war before U.S. intervention are not slighted.
      The view given is that of the general and statesman and not
      that of the doughboy or tommy. There is little coverage of the
      naval and air war.

173. Dos Passos, John. *Mr. Wilson's War*. Garden City, N.Y.: Double-
     day & Co., 1962. 517 pp.

     Directed toward the layman rather than the scholar, this is
     one of the most readable surveys of the United States and World
     War I. Footnotes are absent, but there are brief "notes on
     sources."

174. Fredericks, Pierce G. *The Great Adventure: America in the
     First World War*. New York: E.P. Dutton & Co., 1960. 253 pp.

     This is an impressionist account written for the general pub-
     lic, treating both the home front and U.S. military and naval
     participation in the war. American intervention in Russia is
     also discussed.

175. Freidel, Frank. *Over There: The Story of America's First Great
     Overseas Crusade*. Boston: Little, Brown & Co., 1964. 385 pp.

     The real value of this work can be found in the excellent
     photographs and the discerning quotations from diaries, letters,
     and memoirs.

176. Hoehling, Adolph A. *The Fierce Lambs*. Boston: Little, Brown
     & Co., 1960. 210 pp.

     This is a descriptive and detailed history of the first
     months of American involvement in the war. The death of the
     first four U.S. soldiers is given special attention. This is
     a book for the layman, not the scholar.

177. Johnson, Thomas M. *Without Censor: New Light on Our Greatest
     World War Battles*. Indianapolis: Bobbs-Merrill Co., 1928.
     411 pp.

     The author, a war correspondent who covered the AEF for the
     New York Sun, tends toward sensationalism. Still there is merit
     in this provocative and at times perceptive study.

178. Johnston, R.M. *First Reflections on the Campaign of 1918*. New
     York: Henry Holt & Co., 1920. 79 pp.

     Johnston was attached to Pershing's staff for twelve months.
     He combines the experience of a soldier with his professional
     skill as a former Harvard historian to evaluate critically the
     American military effort. Many of his proposals for reform,
     however, were not practicable.

179. Kennett, Lee. "The A.E.F. Through French Eyes." *Mil. Rev.* 52
     (November 1972): 3-11.

     The author uses secret French reports on the AEF to show that
     the French were as impressed by the courage and determination
     of the doughboy as they were horrified by Pershing's wasteful
     tactics.

180. Leckie, Robert. *The Wars of America*. New York: Harper & Row,
     1968. 1,052 pp.

     This is a lively survey of America's wars from the colonization

of America to 1967. There are numerous errors of fact in this
broad survey based primarily on secondary sources.

181. McMaster, John Bach. *The United States in the World War.* New
     York: D. Appleton & Co., 1918-1920. 2 vols.

     This detailed narrative by a University of Pennsylvania his-
     torian shows signs of having been rushed into print. There is
     a heavy reliance on newspaper accounts and only a single chap-
     ter, "Fighting in France," is devoted to American military
     operations.

182. Marshall, Brig.-Gen. S.L.A. *The American Heritage History of
     World War I.* New York: American Heritage Publishing Co.,
     1964. 384 pp.

     Beautifully illustrated and written by a distinguished mili-
     tary historian, this book is an excellent introduction to the
     war for the layman. Over half of this work concerns the
     struggle prior to American intervention. The many maps are ex-
     ceptional and enhance the reader's comprehension of campaigns.

183. Moore, William E., and Russell, James C. *U.S. Official Pictures
     of the World War: Showing America's Participation.* Washing-
     ton, D.C.: Pictorial Bureau, 1920. 576 pp.

     The pictures in the War Department were utilized in this com-
     prehensive pictorial record along with some unofficial photo-
     graphs by the compilers. With this volume is bound the authors'
     The United States Navy in the World War (Washington, D.C.: Pic-
     torial Bureau, 1921), a collection of photographs on the U.S.
     Navy and Marine Corps taken for the most part from official
     sources: the files of the Navy and War departments and the U.S.
     Marine Corps.

184. Page, Arthur W. *Our 110 Days' Fighting.* Garden City, N.Y.:
     Doubleday, Page & Co., 1920. 283 pp.

     This is a succinct and generally balanced account of the part
     played by U.S. arms on the western front. There are numerous
     maps and diagrams. The appendix contains many interesting facts
     and figures.

185. Palmer, Frederick. *America in France: The Story of the Making
     of an Army.* New York: Dodd, Mead and Co., 1918. 479 pp.

     Palmer was a war correspondent with unique access to the
     nerve center of the U.S. Army because he was a member of
     Pershing's staff. This book was written when Palmer still
     wore the uniform of an American officer and perhaps did not
     enjoy all of the freedom to relate events and judge military
     leaders that he would have had as a civilian. Nonetheless,
     this work remains a basic source for the creation of an indepen-
     dent American army in France and the role of each American
     division in the line.

186. ———. *Our Gallant Madness.* Garden City, N.Y.: Doubleday,
     Doran & Co., 1937. 320 pp.

Palmer, in reaction to those who would "belittle" the U.S. war effort, attempts to set the record straight. He offers no documentation.

187. Paxson, Frederic L. *American Democracy and the World War*, vol. 2: *America at War, 1917-1918*. Boston: Houghton Mifflin Co., 1939. 465 pp.

Until the more recent works by Coffman and DeWeerd, this was the standard account of America's participation in World War I. Military operations, American relations with the allies, and the development of the AEF are examined. This is a very scholarly work despite the omission of documentation and a bibliography. Several useful tables and maps are provided.

188. Powell, E. Alexander. *The Army Behind the Army*. New York: Charles Scribner's Sons, 1919. 470 pp.

The role of the signal corps, engineers, Chemical Warfare Service, quartermaster corps, army ordnance, air service, military intelligence, tank corps, transportation corps, and the medical department is highlighted to give them the credit they deserve.

189. Stallings, Laurence. *The Doughboys: The Story of the A.E.F., 1917-1918*. New York: Harper & Row, 1963. 404 pp.

The author, a marine in the 2nd Division who was wounded at Belleau Wood, gives a superb portrait of war up close rather than at the high command level. His intention is to chronicle the wartime experiences of the doughboy: "what he was, how he looked, and with what arms and over what fields he fought." He notes that he spares the reader the "ordeal of footnotes" but he provides an excellent annotated bibliography with a strong emphasis on personal accounts and unit histories.

190. Thomas, Captain Shipley. *The History of the A.E.F.* New York: George H. Doran Co., 1920. 540 pp.

In this solid pioneer work, the author, who served in the 1st Division as an intelligence officer of the 26th Infantry Regiment, provides a broad survey of the training and war record of the AEF.

191. U.S. Army. *Order of Battle of United States Land Forces in the World War*, vol. 2: *American Expeditionary Forces. Divisions.* Washington, D.C.: Government Printing Office, 1931. 451 pp.

Prepared by the historical section of the Army War College and based on original sources, this indispensable source pinpoints the command, composition, and operations of American units at the front at any particular time.

192. ———. *Order of Battle of United States Land Forces in the World War*, vol. 1: *American Expeditionary Forces, General Headquarters, Army Corps, Services of Supply, and Separate Forces.* Washington, D.C.: Government Printing Office, 1937. 412 pp.

This volume deals with the participation of U.S. military
organizations larger than a division. When published this volume
was designated as the first volume and the 1931 volume pertaining to divisions was designated as the second volume.

193.   ————. *Order of Battle of United States Land Forces in the
       World War*, vol. 3: *Zone of Interior*. Washington, D.C.:
       Government Printing Office, 1949. 992 pp.

This is an important documentary source for the organization
and activities of the War Department, territorial departments,
and the posts, camps, and stations of the army. Twelve maps
are included.

194.   U.S. Department of the Army. Office of Military History. *The
       United States in the World War 1917-1919*. Washington, D.C.:
       Government Printing Office, 1948. 17 vols.

Approximately three decades in the making, these volumes constitute a representative selection of the records, both American
and foreign, of the AEF overseas. Originally the historical
branch of the general staff planned to describe the United
States at war, including both civilian as well as military activities. Seven of the projected seventeen volumes were to be
devoted to diplomatic relations and economic mobilization.
The scope, however, was narrowed first to just the American
army, and then to the American army "overseas." Despite their
limited horizon and uncritical nature, these volumes are a
basic documentary source on such topics as the amalgamation
controversy. Vol. 1 is a summary narrative of events with
tables of organization; vol. 2 concerns the interior administration of the AEF and its relations with the Allies; vol. 3 is
devoted to training with British and French forces; vols. 4
through 9 concern combat operations; vol. 10 concerns the Armistice; vol. 11 concerns the occupation of Germany; vols. 12
through 15 are devoted to documents, including the preliminary
and final reports of Pershing; and vols. 16 and 17 are devoted
to general orders and bulletins issued by general headquarters,
AEF.

195.   Van Every, Dale. *The A.E.F. in Battle*. New York: D. Appleton
       & Co., 1928. 385 pp.

This detailed record of American fighting forces does not
always live up to Major General Hanson Ely's introduction which
promised that its principal theme was the "experiences of the
soldiers." Giving a complete combat record of the AEF and
describing the day-to-day life of the doughboy were at times
conflicting aims.

196.   Viereck, George S., and Maerker-Branden, A. Paul. *As They Saw
       Us: Foch, Ludendorff and Other Leaders Write Our War History*.
       Garden City, N.Y.: Doubleday, Doran & Co., 1929. 379 pp.

This volume does not always reveal the true feelings of some
European leaders toward the American military effort. In sum,
there is more diplomacy than candid comment in this work.

197. Walton, Robert C. *Over There: European Reaction to Americans
      in World War I.* Itasca, Ill.: F.E. Peacock, 1971. 210 pp.

      This volume in the series "Primary Sources in American His-
      tory" offers many valuable and unbowdlerized views of British,
      Austrian, and German opinions of and assumptions about the
      Americans. The French view has been largely omitted. This is
      an important source for such topics as the German decision to
      resume unrestricted U-boat warfare and the attempt to attach
      American units to British and French divisions.

198. Weigley, Russell F. *History of the United States Army.* New
      York: Macmillan Co., 1967. 688 pp.

      This is not a drum and bugle history of battles but a scholarly
      examination of the institutional development of the American
      army. It is an indispensable source for any examination of
      the development of the American army from its beginnings to
      the wars of the twentieth century.

199. Williams, T. Harry. *The History of American Wars: From Colonial
      Times to World War I.* New York: Alfred A. Knopf, 1981. 435 pp.

      This is a lively and enlightening survey by a Pulitzer Prize-
      winning historian. Both the origins and the course of World
      War I are examined. Williams limited his research to printed
      sources, but his vast knowledge of American wars makes this an
      important and readable work.

                        C. SPECIFIC ASPECTS

                   1. Military and Naval Leadership
                   (Including Manuscript Collections)

a. General Sources

200. Abrahamson, James L. *America Arms for a New Century: The Making
      of a Great Military Power.* New York: Macmillan Publishing
      Co., 1981. 253 pp.

      This volume traces the evolution of the military thought of
      such officers as Hunter Liggett, William S. Sims, Peyton March,
      and John Pershing from 1880 to 1920. These naval and military
      leaders came to the conclusion that U.S. arms needed to be more
      like European arms.

201. Barnett, Correlli. *The Swordbearers: Studies in Supreme Command
      in the First World War.* London: Eyre & Spottiswoode, 1963.
      387 pp.

      Barnett is one of the most perceptive historians of the two
      world wars. In this volume, he focuses on the "decisive effect
      of individual human character on history" by examining four
      World War I commanders-in-chief: Moltke, Jellicoe, Pétain, and

Ludendorff. His treatment of Ludendorff includes a brilliant
analysis of the failure of the German gamble for victory in
1918. Numerous photographs and over forty maps enhance the
value of this work. Documentation is provided, along with a
selected bibliography of German, English, and French sources.

202. Bond, Brian. *The Victorian Army and the Staff College, 1854-
     1914*. London: Eyre Methuen, 1972. 350 pp.

     One of Britain's leading military historians examines the
     selection and training of British officers in the staff college.
     When put to the test in the stalemated warfare of the Great War,
     however, their education was found wanting. But then none of
     Europe's general staffs had prepared officers for trench war-
     fare.

203. Bullard, Robert L. *Fighting Generals*. Ann Arbor, Mich.: J.W.
     Edwards, 1944. 329 pp.

     Bullard provides illustrated biographical sketches of the
     following generals who were his comrades in arms in World War
     I: Joseph T. Dickman, Hanson E. Ely, Henry Allen, Ulysses G.
     McAlexander, Preston Brown, William G. Haan, and John F. O'Ryan.

204. Carver, Field Marshal Sir Michael, ed. *The War Lords: Military
     Commanders of the Twentieth Century*. London: Weidenfeld &
     Nicolson, 1976. 624 pp.

     Fourteen World War I military figures are featured in this
     volume, including Pershing, Hindenburg, Haig, Foch, and Luden-
     dorff. The contributors are authorities on their subjects.
     Donald Smythe's biographical sketch of Pershing is outstanding.
     There are no footnotes or bibliography.

205. Goerlitz, Walter. *History of the German General Staff, 1657-
     1945*. New York: Frederick A. Praeger, 1953. 508 pp.

     Excellent biographical profiles of Schlieffen, the younger
     Moltke, Falkenhayn, Hindenburg, and Ludendorff are drawn in
     this first-rate study of the German General Staff, the "brains"
     of the German army. Neither notes nor a bibliography accompanies
     the text.

206. Hewes, James. "The United States Army General Staff, 1900-1917."
     Mil. Affairs 38 (April 1974): 67-72.

     This is a brief administrative history of the formative years
     of the army general staff by a military historian in the center
     of military history. Edward M. Coffman provides a brief but
     insightful commentary.

207. Hunter, Francis T. *Beatty, Jellicoe, Sims, and Rodman: Yankee
     Gobs and British Tars, as Seen by an Anglomaniac*. Garden
     City, N.Y.: Doubleday, Page & Co., 1919. 204 pp.

     Lieutenant Hunter served under Rear-Admiral Rodman, and his
     personal views of four leading naval commanders are of some
     interest.

208. Liddell Hart, B.H. *Reputations.* London: Murray, 1928. 327 pp.

    This is a tactful but critical evaluation of generalship during the war. Pershing and Liggett are the two Americans discussed by this gadfly to the military establishment.

209. Travers, Tim. "Learning and Decision-Making on the Western Front, 1915-1916." *Can. Jour. of Hist.* 18 (April 1983): 87-97.

    This article constitutes an innovative approach to World War I generalship and has some important things to say about the inability of many British generals to adapt within a reasonable period to trench warfare.

b. United States

Alexander

210. Alexander, Robert. *Memories of the World War, 1917-1918.* New York: Macmillan Co., 1931.

    Unlike Pershing's account of the Meuse-Argonne offensive, this detailed tactical account by General Alexander, who commanded the 77th Division during this battle, gives a very frank appraisal of the failures as well as successes of American generalship. Alexander was a Fort Leavenworth man.

Allen

211. Allen, Maj.-Gen. Henry. Collection in the Division of Manuscripts, Library of Congress.

    Allen's papers consist of some 15,000 items in seventy-eight boxes.

212. ———. *My Rhineland Journal.* London: Hutchinson & Co., 1924. 611 pp.

    Allen's remarks about American relations with the British and French are especially interesting.

213. ———. *The Rhineland Occupation.* Indianapolis: Bobbs-Merrill Co., 1927. 347 pp.

    Allen commanded the American forces on the Rhine.

214. Twichell, Heath, Jr. *Allen: The Biography of an American Officer 1859-1930.* New Brunswick: Rutgers University Press, 1974. 359 pp.

    This volume constitutes a scholarly and balanced treatment of this important U.S. general.

Benson

215. Benson, Admiral William S. Collection in the Division of Manuscripts, Library of Congress.

    Benson was chief of naval operations and played a key role in establishing the inter-allied naval council. After the Armistice

he served as a naval expert for the American peace commission.
There are over 14,000 items in this collection.

Bingham

216. Bingham, Hiram. *An Explorer in the Air Service, U.S.A.* New
     Haven: Yale University Press, 1920. 260 pp.

     Bingham, a Yale history professor, served as chief of "air
     personnel" in Washington before becoming commandant of the
     most important American aviation instruction base overseas at
     Issoudun. He has written a valuable personal account of his
     service, emphasizing the selection and training of American
     pilots. Lieutenant-Colonel Bingham is often critical of the
     direction and policy of the American Air Service.

Bliss

217. Bliss, Tasker H. Collection in the Division of Manuscripts,
     Library of Congress.

     Bliss's papers are especially valuable for any examination of
     America's relations with her allies. Bliss was the U.S. repre-
     sentative on the Allied general staff of the Supreme War Council.
     Much of the Supreme War Council's time was taken up with ques-
     tions of strategy and armed intervention in Russia.

218. ———. "The Evolution of the Unified Command." *For. Affairs* 1
     (December 1922): 1-30.

     Bliss, a strong defender of the Allied experiment in a unified
     command and the American military representative on the Supreme
     War Council, describes the birth and growing pains of this
     organization. The opponents of this scheme gave way, as he
     correctly notes, "only when it was manifest that every other
     course had been tried--and had failed."

219. ———. "Report of General T.H. Bliss on the Supreme War Coun-
     cil." 1920. 121 pp.

     This is an unpublished copy of Bliss's report to the Secretary
     of War on the Supreme War Council. It can be found in the US
     Military History Institute at Carlisle Barracks.

220. Palmer, Frederick. *Bliss, Peacemaker: The Life and Letters of
     General Tasker Howard Bliss.* New York: Dodd, Mead & Co.,
     1934. 477 pp.

     This work includes excerpts from many of Bliss's letters and
     reports. The theme of this volume is that Bliss, although a
     distinguished soldier, was essentially a man of peace.

221. Trask, David F. *General Tasker Howard Bliss and the "Sessions
     of the World," 1919.* Philadelphia: American Philosophical
     Society, 1966. 80 pp.

     This short monograph describes the activities of General
     Bliss.

Bristol

222. Bristol, Rear-Admiral Mark L. Collection in the Division of
     Manuscripts, Library of Congress.

     The papers of this naval officer and diplomat include corres-
     pondence with Admiral Sims and Josephus Daniels.

Bullard

223. Bullard, General Robert Lee. Collection in the Division of
     Manuscripts, Library of Congress.

     In this collection of some 3,250 items, Bullard's diaries,
     which cover his career from the Philippine campaigns through
     the World War I period, are of special importance.

*   ————. *Fighting Generals.* Cited above as item 203.

224. ————. *Personalities and Reminiscences of the War.* Garden
     City, N.Y.: Doubleday & Co., 1925. 347 pp.

     These memories and impressions serve as the memoirs of the
     popular commander of the first U.S. division to go into the
     line. The memoir is written with honesty and without rancor,
     for Bullard, unlike many World War I generals, apparently had
     no axes to grind.

225. ————, and Reeves, Earl. *American Soldiers Also Fought.* New
     York: Longman, Green & Co., 1936. 118 pp.

     Assisted by Reeves, Bullard attempts to highlight the part
     played by the United States in the defeat of Germany to counter
     the view that the United States played only a minor role in the
     war.

226. Millett, Allan R. *The General: Robert L. Bullard and Officer-
     ship in the United States Army, 1881-1925.* Westport, Conn.:
     Greenwood Press, 1975. 499 pp.

     The military career of the Alabamian Bullard, who rose from
     the command of the 1st Division to the head of the III Corps
     during the war, is examined in this well-researched account.
     Millett also provides an astute treatment of American military
     leadership in war and peace.

Butler

227. Butler, General Smedley D. Collection in Marine Corps Personal
     Papers Collection, U.S. Marine Corps Historical Center.

     There are some 3,000 items in this large collection of holo-
     graph and typescript material pertaining to Butler's long service
     in the marines.

228. Carr, Stephen M. "Smedley Butler: Hero or Demagogue." *Amer.
     Hist. Ill.* 15 (April 1980): 31-38.

     This is a sympathetic review of Butler's remarkable career,
     with Carr concluding that this controversial marine was a first-
     rate, albeit maverick, officer.

229. Thomas, Lowell. *Old Gimlet Eye: The Adventures of Smedley D.*
      Butler. New York: Farrar & Rinehart, 1933. 310 pp.

      The exploits of this colorful and outspoken marine, twice the
      recipient of the Medal of Honor, are told in the first person.
      To Butler's great disappointment he saw no combat in France
      during the Great War. Instead he commanded a base at Brest,
      America's chief port of entry. The Haiti phase of Butler's
      World War I tour of duty is also examined. There are illustra-
      tions, but no bibliography, notes, or index.

      Crowder

230. Crowder, General Enoch H. Collection in Western Historical
      Collection, University of Missouri, Columbia.

      The twelve boxes of material include papers relating to
      Crowder's service as Judge Advocate General.

231. Lockmiller, David A. *Enoch H. Crowder: Soldier, Lawyer, and*
      Statesman. Columbia: University of Missouri Press, 1955.
      286 pp.

      This is a thoroughly researched biography of General Crowder,
      who was Judge Advocate General when America became a belligerent.
      Crowder was primarily responsible for administering the draft.
      A graduate of West Point, Crowder was an exceptional army ad-
      ministrator, holding many important positions.

      Dickman

232. Dickman, Maj.-Gen. Joseph T. *The Great Crusade: A Narrative of*
      the World War. New York: D. Appleton & Co., 1927. 313 pp.

      This matter-of-fact account is an important source for the AEF
      because Dickman, a former cavalryman, served as a division and
      corps commander and was in the thick of the fighting from
      Château-Thierry to the Argonne Forest.

      Fiske

233. Fiske, Rear-Admiral Bradley A. *From Midshipman to Rear-Admiral.*
      New York: Century Co., 1919. 694 pp.

      Fiske, a naval officer and inventor whose career spanned
      forty-nine years, has written an interesting and revealing
      account of the obstacles placed by hidebound administrators,
      including Daniels, the Secretary of the Navy, in the way of
      those who wished to make necessary changes in naval administra-
      tion and weaponry.

234. Coletta, Paolo E. *Admiral Bradley A. Fiske and the American*
      Navy. Lawrence: Regents Press of Kansas, 1979. 306 pp.

      Coletta argues that Fiske could have done a better job in
      preparing the navy for World War I if he had not had to deal
      with civilian superiors. This work concludes that the navy was
      ill prepared for World War I.

Gleaves

235. Gleaves, Albert. Collection in Naval Historical Foundation,
      Division of Manuscripts, Library of Congress.

      The some 6,000 items in this collection light on Gleaves's
      career as a naval officer and historian.

236. ————. *A History of the Transport Service: Adventures and
      Experiences of United States Transports and Cruisers in the
      World War.* New York: George H. Doran Co., 1921. 284 pp.

      Gleaves, the commander of convoy operations in the Atlantic,
      was the first American since John Paul Jones to receive the
      French Legion of Honor. His popular history tells the story
      of the struggle with German submarines and the transporting
      of a vast army to Europe to seal the fate of the Central Powers.

Graves

237. Graves, William Sidney. Collection in the Archives, Hoover
      Institution of War, Revolution and Peace.

      This collection of three boxes includes correspondence, re-
      ports, monographs, and other materials pertaining to Allied
      intervention in Russia and Graves's role as commander of the
      AEF in Siberia, 1918-1919.

238. ————. *America's Siberian Adventure.* New York: Peter Smith,
      1941. 363 pp.

      This is an account by the commander of the AEF in Siberia.
      Graves opposed intervention initially and never saw any reason
      to change his mind. This volume describes very well the dif-
      fering motives and tensions between the intervening nations.

Harbord

239. Harbord, James G. Collection in the Division of Manuscripts,
      Library of Congress.

      This collection includes personal diaries, records of conver-
      sations, printed matter, confidential cables, and other materials
      relating to Harbord's service. These papers are especially
      helpful for Harbord's activities as head of the services of
      supply, 1918-1919.

240. ————. *America in the World War.* Boston: Houghton Mifflin
      Co., 1933. 111 pp.

      Harbord's lecture on the achievements of American arms and the
      lessons learned which he delivered at Merton Academy in 1932
      is printed in this volume.

241. ————. *The American Army in France, 1917-1919.* Boston:
      Little, Brown & Co., 1936. 632 pp.

      Harbord was chief of staff of the AEF, 1917-1918, and commander
      of the services of supply, 1918. This work contains information
      on the activities of the services of supply, the amalgamation

controversy, and the combat role of the AEF. Harbord sided
with Pershing in the latter's tug of war with March. This
book, in fact, was largely prompted by March's memoirs, which
presented his side of this controversy. Secretary of War
Newton D. Baker reviewed the typescript and contributed an
anonymous footnote (pp. 110-11) that is critical of March.

242. ———. *The American Expeditionary Forces: Its Organization
      and Accomplishments*. Evanston, Ill.: Evanston Publishing Co.,
      1929. 95 pp.

      This work includes a short biography of Harbord and a dis-
      cussion of his work as chief of staff and commander of the
      services of supply.

243. ———. *Leaves from a War Diary*. New York: Dodd, Mead & Co.,
      1925. 407 pp.

      This work is of special interest because Harbord was both
      Pershing's chief of staff and his friend. It gives a revealing
      record of the thinking of Pershing and his staff about many
      important subjects.

      Johnson

244. Ohl, John K. "Hugh S. Johnson and the Draft, 1917-1918."
      Prologue 8 (Summer 1976): 85-96.

      Johnson is shown as an able and hard-driving organizer, yet
      with certain personality flaws that limited his usefulness.

245. ———. "'Old Iron Pants': The Wartime Career of General Hugh S.
      Johnson 1917-1918." Doctoral dissertation, University of Cin-
      cinnati, 1971. 214 pp.

      Johnson was a member of the general staff and the Office of
      the Provost Marshal General. This dissertation focuses on his
      role in mobilizing American manpower and materiel for war and
      how this experience later shaped his views during the New Deal.

      Lejeune

246. Lejeune, Maj.-Gen. John A. Collection in the Division of Manu-
      scripts, Library of Congress.

      This collection includes some information on Lejeune's com-
      mand of the 2nd Division, AEF, 1918-1919, and his correspondence
      with Josephus Daniels.

247. ———. *The Reminiscences of a Marine*. Philadelphia: Dorrance
      & Co., 1930. 488 pp.

      Lejeune's account is probably the best personal source for
      the adventures of the marines in World War I. Following World
      War I, Lejeune was appointed full Marine Corps Commandant. He
      performed a great service for Marine Corps historiography by
      creating a historical section at Headquarters Marine Corps.

Liggett

248. Liggett, Hunter. *A.E.F. Ten Years Ago in France*. New York: Dodd, Mead & Co., 1928. 335 pp.

   The writing is superior to Liggett's earlier effort. This revision of seven articles which appeared in the *Saturday Evening Post* in 1927 offers considerable insight into the activities and personalities of some of the leading military figures of the day.

249. ————. *Commanding an American Army: Recollections of the World War*. Boston: Houghton Mifflin Co., 1925. 208 pp.

   Liggett, the commander of the 1st Corps, was one of the most respected American generals. His rather pedestrian memoirs describe the American offensives at St. Mihiel and Meuse-Argonne. An interesting section concerns his study in 1917 of French and British tactics. He also discusses the American Army of Occupation, which he briefly commanded.

McCully

250. McCully, Newton Alexander. Collection in Naval Historical Foundation, Division of Manuscripts, Library of Congress.

   This collection contains two personal diaries.

251. Weeks, Charles J., Jr. "The Life and Career of Admiral Newton A. McCully, 1867-1951." Doctoral dissertation, Georgia State University, 1975. 325 pp.

   Vice Admiral Newton A. McCully, who served as the U.S. naval attaché in Petrograd, 1914-1917, commander of the U.S. naval forces in northern Russian waters, 1920, and special agent for the State Department in South Russia, 1920, was in a good position to observe events in Russia during the Great War and the Russian Civil War. Weeks points out, however, that his usually sound advice was often ignored by the State Department.

March

252. March, General Peyton C. Collection in the Division of Manuscripts, Library of Congress.

   Coffman made good use of these papers in his biography of March. The bulk of March's correspondence is for the 1930s.

253. ————. *The Nation at War*. Garden City, N.Y.: Doubleday, Doran & Co., 1932. 407 pp.

   March's memoirs tell us almost as much about his strong disagreements with Pershing as they do about the activities of the War Department where he was chief of staff. This is also an excellent source for the creation of a great American fighting force and its dispatch overseas.

254. Coffman, Edward M. *The Hilt of the Sword: The Career of Peyton C. March*. Madison: University of Wisconsin Press, 1966. 346 pp.

This detailed, thoroughly researched biography of the chief
of staff emphasizes the evolution of the modern military manager.
Written from March's perspective, the study, which contains an
extensive bibliography, treats the general's debates with
Pershing and his insistence upon the power of the chief of
staff.

Marshall

255. Marshall, George C. *Memoirs of My Service in the World War,*
      1917-1918. Boston: Houghton Mifflin Co., 1976. 268 pp.

      This is a valuable narrative of, first, Marshall's overseas
      service in the 1st Division and, second, his position as opera-
      tions officer in the First Army. Written soon after World War I,
      Marshall's memoirs provide an illuminating examination of the
      American military effort in the European war.

256. Pogue, Forrest C. *George C. Marshall: Education of a General,*
      1880-1939. New York: Viking Press, 1963. 421 pp.

      This meticulously researched and well-written volume is a
      first-rate study of American military history for the first
      fifty years of the twentieth century. Marshall's staff work
      during the Great War receives attention.

Mitchell

257. Mitchell, William. Collection in the Division of Manuscripts,
      Library of Congress.

      There is a subject file pertaining to operations by the Air
      Service, AEF. Many of Mitchell's unpublished writings can be
      found in this large collection of some 19,000 items.

258. ————. *Memoirs of World War I: "From Start to Finish of Our*
      Greatest War." New York: Random House, 1960. 312 pp.

      "Billy" Mitchell's World War I diary, which has either been
      lost or destroyed, is the basis of this often one-sided work,
      which provides a personal glimpse of the birth of American air
      power and a portrait of one of America's most famous aviators.
      The original manuscript, which includes technical information
      and official documents omitted in the published volume, is in
      the Library of Congress.

259. ————. *Our Air Force: The Keystone of National Defense.* New
      York: E.P. Dutton and Co., 1921. 223 pp.

      This book is helpful in understanding the pronounced views
      of Mitchell on the future of air power, but adds little to our
      understanding of the role of U.S. air power in World War I.

260. Hurley, Alfred F. *Billy Mitchell: Crusader for Air Power.* New
      York: Franklin Watts, 1964. 180 pp.

      This is a balanced study of Mitchell by a historian who is
      also an officer in the Air Force. The research is thorough and
      the author makes use of oral history.

261. Levine, Isaac Don. *Mitchell: Pioneer of Air Power*. New York: Duell, Sloan & Pearce, 1943. 420 pp.

    Two chapters in this uncritical biography are devoted to Mitchell's service in Europe. A valuable five-page list of Mitchell's published and unpublished writings can be found at the end of this volume.

    Mott

262. Mott, Colonel T. Bentley. *Twenty Years as Military Attaché*. New York: Oxford University Press, 1937. 342 pp.

    Mott was an American officer with an extensive knowledge of the French, having been sent to Paris in 1900 as the American military attaché. During the war he served as a liaison officer between Foch and Pershing, later translating Foch's war memoirs into English. His work includes some general information on Pershing's fight for an independent American army and his relations with Clemenceau and Foch.

    Patrick

263. Patrick, Maj.-Gen. Mason M. *Final Report of the Air Service, A.E.F.* Washington, D.C.: Government Printing Office, 1921. 85 pp.

    Patrick's final report, which includes charts, serves as the official history of the U.S. Air Service during the Great War.

264. ————. *The United States in the Air*. Garden City, N.Y.: Doubleday, Doran & Co., 1928. 191 pp.

    Patrick, an engineer with no flying experience, was plucked from his position as chief engineer, lines of communication, by Pershing in May 1918 to head the Air Service, AEF. Following the war Patrick served as Chief of the Air Service, U.S. Army, publishing this volume the year after he retired. Although most of this work concerns the postwar period, it is revealing on the organization of the American Air Service, its birth pains, and its war with the German air force.

    Patton

265. *The Patton Papers*, vol. 1: *1885-1940*. Edited by Martin Blumenson. Boston: Houghton Mifflin Co., 1972. 966 pp.

    Patton's service in the AEF is revealed through his diary, family letters, memoranda, and official and unofficial army correspondence. Blumenson provides an excellent commentary to assist the reader.

    Pershing

266. Pershing, General John J. Collection in the Division of Manuscripts, Library of Congress.

    This large (over one hundred file boxes) and important collection has recently received new Pershing materials which shed light on his personal life. His diary, 1917-1925, ranks with

Haig's diary as one of the best personal sources produced by an officer during the war. The entire collection is beautifully organized for the researcher.

267. ————. *My Experiences in the World War*. New York: Frederick A. Stokes Co., 1931. 2 vols.

This is a basic source for any study of the AEF. A central theme is Pershing's resistance to amalgamation and his success-ful effort to create an independent American army. This account also reveals that the iron-willed Pershing often differed with the War Department as well as his allies on many fundamental issues. Pershing's diary serves as the framework for the de-tailed narrative.

268. U.S. Army. A.E.F., 1917-1920. *Final Report of Gen. John J. Pershing, Commander-in-Chief American Expeditionary Forces*. Washington, D.C.: Government Printing Office, 1920. 96 pp.

This is an important source for the activities and military operations of the AEF.

269. Andrews, Avery Delano. *My Friend and Classmate John J. Pershing: With Notes from My War Diary*. Harrisburg, Pa.: Military Service Publishing Co., 1939. 291 pp.

Andrews's long friendship with Pershing began in 1882 at a boys preparatory school. During the war, Andrews served as Pershing's assistant chief of staff. Unfortunately there are few nuggets in the commonplace wartime diary kept by Andrews. This work contains some information on the organizational and administrative problems of the AEF.

*   Carver, Field Marshal Sir Michael, ed. *The War Lords: Military Commanders of the Twentieth Century*. Cited above as item 204.

270. Goldhurst, Richard. *Pipe Clay and Drill: John J. Pershing. The Classic American Soldier*. New York: Reader's Digest Press, distributed by Thomas Y. Crowell Co., 1977. 343 pp.

Pershing's command of the AEF receives superficial treatment in this popular work which has no footnotes, other than explana-tory notes, and a very, very selective bibliography. Gold-hurst's study has been dismissed by Allan R. Millett with the following statement: "this is a superfluous book of no value with the possible exception that its errors are good for some hearty laughs."

*   Liddell Hart, B.H. *Reputations*. Cited above as item 208.

271. Palmer, Frederick. *John J. Pershing, General of the Armies: A Biography*. Harrisburg, Pa.: Military Service Publishing Co., 1948. 380 pp.

The author, a war correspondent close to Pershing, finished this biography in 1940 but withheld publication until the com-mander of the AEF was dead. This volume is valuable because of its revealing human interest detail about Pershing.

272. Smythe, Donald. *Guerilla Warrior: The Early Life of John J. Pershing.* New York: Charles Scribner's Sons, 1973. 370 pp.

This is the first attempt at a scholarly biography of Pershing. It treats his career to 1917. The question of the role of political influence in his appointment as head of the AEF receives attention. Very candid and objective, this volume narrowly focuses on Pershing.

273. ─────. "Over There: The Pershing Story." *Army* 30 (December 1980): 34-38.

Smythe explains why a film of Pershing's command of the AEF never became a reality.

274. ─────. "The Pershing-March Conflict in World War I." *Parameters* 11 (December 1981): 53-62.

The numerous disagreements between Pershing and March are critically examined in this well-documented article.

275. ─────. "You Dear Old Jack Pershing." *Amer. Hist. Ill.* 7 (October 1972): 18-24.

A new dimension is added to Pershing's personality by this examination of his courtship.

276. ─────. "'Your Authority in France Will Be Supreme!': The Baker-Pershing Relationship in World War I." *Parameters* 9 (September 1979): 38-45.

Pershing's independence from Washington as commander of the AEF is described. Pershing was forced to back down only on his position concerning the Armistice.

277. Tomlinson, E.T. *The Story of General Pershing.* New York: D. Appleton & Co., 1919. 260 pp.

This popular work focuses on the personality of the commander of the AEF and provides many details on his early years. Those interested in a scholarly and comprehensive biography, however, should look to Smythe and Vandiver.

278. Vandiver, Frank E. *Black Jack: The Life and Times of John J. Pershing.* College Station: Texas A&M University Press, 1977. 2 vols.

A product of multi-national archival research, this detailed biography gives a comprehensive account of the life of General Pershing. Among other topics, his role in the creation of an independent American army in Europe is thoroughly examined. There is also valuable commentary on the course of the war in 1917-1918. Vol. 2 covers the Punitive Expedition and World War I. There are five chapters on Pershing's command of the AEF.

Pratt

279. Pratt, Admiral William V. Collection in Naval Historical Foundation, Division of Manuscripts, Library of Congress.

Pratt, as assistant chief of naval operations, worked closely
with Admiral Sims in London. In 1919 he attended the Paris
Peace Conference as President Wilson's naval adviser.

280. Wheeler, G.E. *Admiral William Veazie Pratt, U.S. Navy: A
      Sailor's Life*. Washington, D.C.: Government Printing Office,
      1974. 456 pp.

      This biography has an extensive bibliography.

Rickenbacker

281. Rickenbacker, Edward V. *Fighting the Flying Circus*. New York:
      Frederick A. Stokes Co., 1919. 371 pp.

      This is an action-filled personal account of the heroics of
      America's leading World War I ace and the 94th (Hat-in-the-Ring)
      pursuit squadron he commanded. There is a useful glossary of
      airmen's terms.

282. Maurer, Maurer. "Another Victory for Rickenbacker." *Air Power
      Hist.* 7 (April 1960): 117-24.

      This article validates another victory for Rickenbacker, the
      famous commander of the 94th Aero Squadron, bringing his total
      to twenty-six (twenty-two airplanes and four balloons).

Rodman

283. Rodman, Hugh. *Yarns of a Kentucky Admiral*. Indianapolis:
      Bobbs-Merrill Co., 1928. 320 pp.

      Rodman commanded all U.S. battleships in the Atlantic. His
      battle squadron served as a unit of the British Grand Fleet.
      He deserves much of the credit for the harmonious relationship
      between British and U.S. naval officers. This is an interesting
      and informal biography which is spiced with many amusing anec-
      dotes.

Scott

284. Scott, Maj.-Gen. Hugh L. Collection in the Division of Manu-
      scripts, Library of Congress.

      Scott, a cavalryman, was chief of staff in the War Department
      and a strong supporter of General Pershing. There are some
      30,000 items in this collection.

Sims

285. Sims, Admiral William S. Collection in Naval Historical Founda-
      tion, Division of Manuscripts, Library of Congress.

      This collection of some 40,000 items contains correspondence,
      memoranda, reports, notes, and other materials. There is much
      information on Sims's interest in naval reforms.

286. ————, and Hendrick, Burton J. *Victory at Sea*. Garden City,
      N.Y.: Doubleday, Page & Co., 1920. 410 pp.

      The "victory" to which Sims refers in his title was the Allied
      triumph over the German submarine. This is a valuable and in-

formative work by one of America's most distinguished naval officers, whose fame in World War I rests on his success as a naval administrator in London rather than as a battle commander on the high seas.

287. Allard, Dean C. "Admiral William S. Sims and United States Naval Policy in World War I." *American Neptune* 35 (April 1975): 97-110.

This is a well-documented article on the part played by Sims in the Great War. His criticisms of U.S. naval policy receive particular attention.

288. Baldridge, Harry A. "Sims the Iconoclast." *U.S. Naval Inst., Proc.* 63 (February 1937): 183-90.

Sims's prewar career is also examined in this general essay by someone who knew him.

*   Hunter, Francis T. *Beatty, Jellicoe, Sims, and Rodman: Yankee Gobs and British Tars, as Seen by an Anglomaniac.* Cited above as item 207.

289. Kittredge, Tracy B. *Naval Lessons of the Great War: A Review of the Senate Naval Investigation of the Criticisms of Admiral Sims of the Policies and Methods of Josephus Daniels.* Garden City, N.Y.: Doubleday, Page & Co., 1921. 472 pp.

In 1920, the naval affairs committee of the U.S. Congress investigated the lack of preparedness of the U.S. Navy on the eve of World War I. Kittredge has given Sims's side of his argument with Josephus Daniels. This is an important, though partisan, source.

290. Leighton, John Langdon. *Simsadus: London.* New York: Henry Holt & Co., 1920. 169 pp.

The author served on the intelligence staff of Admiral Sims. "Simsadus" was the admiral's cable address in London. This firsthand account provides some interesting general information on Sims's role in coordinating American and Allied naval operations.

291. Morison, Elting E. *Admiral Sims and the Modern American Navy.* Boston: Houghton Mifflin Co., 1942. 547 pp.

This is an outstanding biography of one of America's most able and strong-willed naval leaders. Sims's papers were consulted by the author. Although he sheds light on both the career of Sims and the navy of his time, the author did not have access to many government records when he wrote his biography.

Summerall

292. Summerall, General Charles Pelot. Collection in the Division of Manuscripts, Library of Congress.

This collection of some 10,000 items, which include corres-

pondence, diaries, orders, and memoranda, is especially strong
for the period of World War I.

293. Pratt, Fletcher. *Eleven Generals: Studies in American Command*.
      New York: William Sloane Associates, 1949. 355 pp.

      Among the generals Pratt discusses is Summerall, who was a
      great believer in artillery and one of the better officers in
      the AEF.

      ### Wood

294. Wood, General Leonard. Collection in the Division of Manu-
      scripts, Library of Congress.

      This collection includes correspondence, diaries, speeches,
      military papers, and scrapbooks. Wood's friendship with Theodore
      Roosevelt, which went back to their Rough Rider days, helped
      eliminate him from consideration for the command of the AEF.

295. Hagedorn, Hermann. *Leonard Wood: A Biography*. New York: Harper
      & Brothers, 1931. 2 vols.

      This illustrated biography of Wood sheds light on his dif-
      ferences with President Wilson and General Pershing. Wood's
      voluminous papers have been mined in this superior portrait of
      one of America's leading military figures at the beginning of
      the twentieth century.

296. Lane, Jack C. *Armed Progressive: General Leonard Wood*. San
      Rafael, Calif.: Presidio Press, 1978. 329 pp.

      This is a solid study which well describes Wood's rise to the
      position of chief of staff and the important role he played in
      the preparedness movement.

c. Foreign

      #### Allenby

297. Wavell, General Sir Archibald. *Allenby: A Study in Greatness:
      The Biography of Field-Marshal Viscount Allenby of Megiddo
      and Felixstowe, G.C.B., G.C.M.G.* New York: Oxford University
      Press, 1941. 311 pp.

      This biography rightly gives "Bull" Allenby high marks for
      his brilliantly successful campaign against Turkey in 1918, but
      not everyone will agree with the author's contention that
      Allenby was "the best British general of the Great War."
      Wavell does not give J.C. Smuts the credit due him for the
      planning of Allenby's 1918 campaign.

      #### Beatty

298. Roskill, Stephen. *Admiral of the Fleet Earl Beatty: The Last
      Naval Hero*. New York: Atheneum Publishers, 1981. 430 pp.

      Britain's official naval historian has written a masterful
      biography of Vice-Admiral Sir David Beatty, who commanded the
      battle cruisers during the greatest naval battle of the war,

Jutland. As always, Roskill's research is thorough and his style clear. Roskill was given access to the Beatty papers and to Beatty's personal correspondence with Mrs. George Godfrey-Faussett.

Brusilov

299. Brusilov, General A.A. *A Soldier's Note Book, 1914-1918*. London: Macmillan & Co., 1930. 340 pp.

This memoir of the architect of the Brusilov offensive, the only successful offensive of the war to be named after a general, sheds light on Russian military operations. General Brusilov was often frustrated by the stupidity of his fellow officers and with the Tsarist government, which may explain his later decision to join the Red Army.

Chair

300. Chair, Admiral Sir Dudley de. Collection in the Department of Documents, Imperial War Museum, London.

De Chair was the naval adviser for Balfour's 1917 mission to the United States and naval adviser to the Foreign Office on blockade affairs, 1916-1917. His collection includes his war diary and papers on the blockade.

Duff

301. Duff, Admiral Sir Alexander Ludovic. Collection in the Manuscript Division, National Maritime Museum, London.

Admiral Duff was director of the anti-submarine division, 1917, and assistant chief of naval staff, 1918-1919. His papers include a diary of his service on the American mission, September-October 1918.

Falkenhayn

302. Falkenhayn, General E. von. *General Headquarters, 1914-1916, and Its Critical Decisions*. London: Hutchinson & Co., 1919. 299 pp.

Following the failure of the Schlieffen Plan, Falkenhayn directed the German war effort until his fall from grace because of his costly offensive against Verdun in 1916. Although at times self-serving, this is an extremely valuable source. The American title is *German General Staff and Its Decisions*.

Fisher

303. Hough, Richard. *Admiral of the Fleet: The Life of John Fisher*. New York: Macmillan Co., 1970. 392 pp.

This is the first major biography, since Admiral Bacon's study, of John Arbuthnot Fisher, who devised the dreadnought, a new type of battleship, and was first sea lord, 1904-1910, 1914-1915. This is a sympathetic study of one of Britain's greatest naval figures.

Foch

304. *The Memoirs of Marshal Foch.*   Garden City, N.Y.: Doubleday,
     Doran & Co., 1931.   517 pp.

     This is the American edition of Foch's two volumes of war
     memoirs. The excellent translation is by Colonel Mott, who
     served as liaison officer between Foch and Pershing. This im-
     portant source concentrates on the battles of 1914 and 1918
     with little material on the intervening years. It is especially
     valuable for its firsthand treatment of the period when Foch was
     generalissimo.

305. Aston, Maj.-Gen. Sir George.   *The Biography of the Late Marshal
     Foch.* New York: Macmillan Co., 1929.   483 pp.

     When published, this biography was superior to other Foch
     biographies which had been rushed into print in 1918-1919.
     The author, however, did not have access to Foch's papers. A
     more perceptive, and certainly more critical, study is the one
     by Liddell Hart.

306. Hunter, T.M. *Marshal Foch: A Study in Leadership.*   Ottawa:
     Queen's Printer, 1961.   250 pp.

     Hunter, a Canadian army officer, praises Foch's dynamism and
     drive but faults his inability to comprehend fully the military
     significance of airpower, tanks, sea power, and logistics.

307. Liddell Hart, B.H. *Foch: The Man of Orléans.*   Boston: Little,
     Brown & Co., 1932.   480 pp.

     This is a perceptive study of Foch's conduct of military
     operations during World War I. Liddell Hart, one of the war's
     most knowledgeable interpreters, is often critical of Foch's
     generalship. He writes that "Foch's handicap was that he had
     to forget so much before he could learn. And the end of his
     opportunity came before the lesson was complete." On the other
     hand, Liddell Hart gives Foch high marks for his magnetism and
     optimism as generalissimo.

308. Marshall-Cornwall, General Sir James. *Foch as Military Com-
     mander.* New York: Crane, Russak & Co., 1972.   268 pp.

     The author points out that Foch, a serious student of war,
     began the war "with a totally erroneous conception of the con
     duct of war under modern conditions." But Foch grew as both a
     strategist and tactician. By 1918, firmly committed to the
     principle of a unified command, he was the ideal choice as
     generalissimo. Footnotes and a bibliography are included, but
     very little new light is shed on Foch's career.

Gourko

309. Gourko, General Basil. *War and Revolution in Russia, 1914-
     1917.* New York: Macmillan Co., 1919.   420 pp.

     General Gourko was Chief of the Russian Imperial General
     Staff, November 1916-March 1917, and commander-in-chief of the

western armies, March–June 1917. His account is colorful but
not always reliable.

Haig

310. Haig, Field-Marshal Sir Douglas (later first earl). Collection
in the Department of Manuscripts, National Library of Scotland, Edinburgh.

This is an essential collection for any serious student of
World War I. Haig was a meticulous collector and recorder, and
his papers include letters, diaries, military notebooks and
textbooks, maps, and orders. Blake's editing of Haig's papers
is exemplary, but many gems in his papers remained unpublished.
A copy of Haig's diary is in the Public Record Office at Kew.

311. *Sir Douglas Haig's Despatches, December 1915–April 1919.* Edited
by Lieut.-Col. J.H. Boraston. London: J.M. Dent & Sons, 1919.
379 pp.

This serves as Haig's own account of the war. Edited by his
private secretary, it is an important source. The many maps
and sketch plans which accompany this volume are also valuable.

312. *The Private Papers of Douglas Haig 1914–1919.* Edited by Robert
Blake. London: Eyre & Spottiswoode, 1952. 383 pp.

The publication of excerpts from Haig's diary and his correspondence created a sensation. The private Haig as revealed in
his papers shocked many: he appeared petty and small-minded.
The real value of this work, however, is the record it provides
of Haig's command. Blake's introduction remains one of the
best descriptions of civil-military relations during the war.

313. Charteris, Brig.-Gen. John. *Field-Marshal Earl Haig.* New York:
Charles Scribner's Sons, 1929. 407 pp.

The author knew Haig intimately, having served with him in
India and at Aldershot. During the Great War, he was controversial chief of intelligence. Not surprisingly, this is an
uncritical biography. Nonetheless it offers insight into the
personality and actions of the commander-in-chief of the British
forces on the western front.

314. Cooper, Duff. *Haig.* London: Faber & Faber, 1935–1936. 2 vols.

Cooper was given access to Haig's diary, from which he quotes
extensively. This is a well-written defense of Haig's conduct
of military operations. Before Terraine's biography, it was
considered the best study of Haig's generalship.

315. Davidson, Maj.-Gen. John. *Haig: Master of the Field.* London:
P. Nevill, 1953. 158 pp.

This is a sympathetic treatment of Haig which perpetuates the
myth that he continued his 1917 Flanders offensive until
November because the French were insistent that he occupy the
German army to give the war-weary French forces time to recover.

316. Sixssmith, E.K.G. *Douglas Haig*. London: Weidenfeld & Nicolson,
     1976. 212 pp.

     This biography, the most recent of Haig, makes use of some
     unpublished materials, such as the Robertson papers, which
     were unavailable to previous biographers. It is sympathetic
     in tone, but the author asserts that Haig was not "a master of
     the weapons and tactics of his day."

317. Terraine, John. *Ordeal of Victory*. Philadelphia: J.B. Lippin-
     cott Co., 1963. 508 pp.

     Published in Britain under the descriptive title *Douglas Haig:
     The Educated Soldier*, this biography established Terraine as
     one of Britain's foremost authorities on the Great War. This
     is a forceful, although at times dogmatic, defense of Haig's
     strategy and tactics. Extremely well written, it remains the
     best study of Haig's generalship. It succeeds very well in
     demonstrating that he was neither a dunce nor a callous butcher.

     Hindenburg

318. Hindenburg, Marshal von. *Out of My Life*. London: Cassell & Co.,
     1920. 458 pp.

     Hindenburg describes his entire military career, including
     his part in the Seven Weeks and Franco-Prussian wars. Of primary
     interest is his discussion of World War I, during which he be-
     came the commander of the German army. His treatment of his
     command is often more notable for what it omits than for what
     it reveals.

319. Wheeler-Bennett, J.W. *Wooden Titan: Hindenburg in Twenty Years
     of German History, 1914-1934*. Hamden, Conn.: Archon Books,
     1963. 491 pp.

     This remains the best biography of Hindenburg in English. As
     the title indicates, the author is critical in his approach to
     the commander of the German forces, 1916-1918. This is a re-
     print of the 1936 edition.

     Hoffman

320. Hoffman, Max. *War Diaries and Other Papers*. London: Martin
     Secker, 1929. 2 vols.

     The first volume is Hoffman's diary; the second volume is
     divided into two parts: "The War of Lost Opportunities" and
     "The Truth About Tannenberg." Critical of Ludendorff, this is
     an important source for the war on the eastern front. The trans-
     lation is by Eric Sutton.

321. ————. *War of Lost Opportunities*. New York: International
     Publishers, 1925. 246 pp.

     The author, the able chief of the German general staff on
     the eastern front, gives his views on the mistakes of both the
     Germans and Russians in this theater. This account is especially
     useful for the first two years of the war.

Jellicoe

322. Jellicoe, Viscount John Rushworth. *The Grand Fleet, 1914-1916:
      Its Creation, Development and Work.* London: Cassell & Co.,
      1919. 499 pp.

      This volume covers the period when Jellicoe was commander-in-
      chief of the Grand Fleet.

323. ————. *The Submarine Peril: The Admiralty Policy in 1917.*
      London: Cassell & Co., 1934. 240 pp.

      As First Sea Lord in 1917, Jellicoe was an alarmist concerning
      the submarine menace.

324. *The Jellicoe Papers: Selections from the Private and Official
      Correspondence of Admiral of the Fleet Earl Jellicoe.* Edited
      by A. Temple Patterson. London: Publications of the Navy
      Records Society, 1966-1968. 2 vols.

      Most of this collection of papers concerns the war years.

325. Bacon, Admiral Sir Reginald H. *The Life of John Rushworth,
      Earl Jellicoe.* London: Cassell & Co., 1936. 565 pp.

      This is a most sympathetic biography by a friend. The Battle
      of Jutland is given extensive treatment and Bacon takes great
      pains to defend Jellicoe against his critics. There are many
      maps and diagrams.

Joffre

326. *The Personal Memoirs of Joffre, Field Marshal of the French
      Army.* New York: Harper & Brothers, 1932. 2 vols.

      These two volumes cover French prewar planning and the cam-
      paigns in the west from 1914 to 1916. The author's account is
      generally fair and balanced. Many unpublished documents are
      included. The translation by Colonel T. Bentley Mott is ex-
      cellent.

Kitchener

327. Cassar, George H. *Kitchener: Architect of Victory.* London:
      W. Kimber, 1977. 573 pp.

      This biography attempts to rehabilitate Kitchener's reputation
      as a war leader during the first half of World War I. The re-
      search is impressive and the conclusions deserve consideration.

Ludendorff

328. Ludendorff, General Erich. *My War Memoirs, 1914-1918.* London:
      Hutchinson & Co., 1919. 2 vols.

      Since the brilliant and often unstable Ludendorff was the
      architect of the German offensive of 1918, this detailed work
      is of great value. It is not, however, always reliable and
      contains more than its fair share of self-justification. In
      the United States it was published under the title *Ludendorff's
      Own Story.*

329. Goodspeed, Donald J. *Ludendorff: Genius of World War I.* Boston: Houghton Mifflin Co., 1966. 335 pp.

The author, a Canadian officer and military historian, emphasizes that Ludendorff was as inept in politics as he was brilliant in conducting a campaign. There are numerous insights into German strategy in 1918.

330. Parkinson, Roger. *Tormented Warrior: Ludendorff and the Supreme Command.* New York: Stein & Day, 1979. 256 pp.

This is a readable retelling of Ludendorff's part in the German war effort by a former war correspondent specializing in military history. This study, which is based primarily on published sources, does not break new ground. A definitive biography of this brilliant and unstable general remains to be written.

331. Tschuppik, Karl. *Ludendorff: The Tragedy of a Military Mind.* Boston: Houghton Mifflin Co., 1932. 282 pp.

The "tragedy" referred to by this writer of popular biographies is that Ludendorff became the virtual dictator of Germany without possessing the necessary political skills. Tschuppik's account of the campaign of 1918 has its moments, but the subject has been examined with more expertise by Barnett.

Pétain

332. Pétain, Henri Philippe. *Verdun.* New York: Dial Press, 1930. 235 pp.

This is an objective account of one of the most important battles of the Great War. The translation from the French is by Margaret MacVeagh.

333. Ryan, Stephen. *Pétain the Soldier.* South Brunswick, N.J.: A.S. Barnes & Co., 1969. 315 pp.

This is a defense of Marshal Pétain. The first half of this volume examines his early military career and his role during the Great War. Pétain is defended against the charge of "defeatism" in 1917–1918 and is characterized as one of the leading strategists of his day. There is no bibliography and scant documentation.

Robertson

334. Robertson, Field-Marshal Sir William. Collection in Liddell Hart Centre for Military Archives, King's College, London.

Robertson's and Haig's papers constitute the most important private collections of papers for the study of British military operations. As Chief of the Imperial General Staff, Robertson dominated British strategy from 1915 until his forced resignation in early 1918.

335. ———. *From Private to Field-Marshal.* Boston: Houghton Mifflin Co., 1921. 396 pp.

Robertson, whose remarkable rise from private to field-marshal
was without parallel in the British Army, discusses his early
military career as well as his tenure as Chief of the Imperial
General Staff. His *Soldiers and Statesmen 1914-1918* is more
valuable for historians of the Great War.

336. ————. *Soldiers and Statesmen 1914-1918*. New York: Charles
Scribner's Sons, 1926. 2 vols.

Robertson more often than not was in conflict with Lloyd
George over the higher strategy of the war. He has written a
staunch defense of the western strategic school of thought.
These volumes are valuable to anyone studying civil-military
relations in Great Britain. Robertson also touches on topics
pertaining to American participation in the war such as amalgamation.

337. Bonham-Carter, Victor. *The Strategy of Victory, 1914-1918: The
Life and Times of the Master Strategist of World War I: Field-
Marshal Sir William Robertson*. New York: Holt, Rinehart &
Winston, 1964. 417 pp.

Using Robertson's papers, the author attempts to rehabilitate
the military reputation of Robertson. He does not always suc-
ceed, but his points deserve careful consideration. Many documents are published here for the first time and the author's
style is clear and interesting.

Sarrail

338. Tannenbaum, Jan Karl. *General Maurice Sarrail, 1856-1929*.
Chapel Hill: The University of North Carolina Press, 1974.
300 pp.

This examination of the career of the political French general
who commanded the Allied forces in the Balkans sheds light on
military operations in the Balkans and the influence of French
domestic politics on military policy. The author researched
both French and British archives.

Scheer

339. Scheer, Admiral. *Germany's High Sea Fleet in the World War*.
London: Cassell & Co., 1920. 375 pp.

German naval operations are analyzed for the entire war in
this work by the German admiral who commanded at the Battle of
Jutland.

Tirpitz

340. Tirpitz, A.P.F. *My Memoirs*. London: Hurst & Blackett, 1919.
2 vols.

Tirpitz was the motive force in the construction of Germany's
battle fleet and a strong advocate of unrestricted submarine
warfare. He has much of interest to say on both of these topics
in his memoirs.

Wilson

341. Wilson, Field-Marshal Sir Henry. Collection in the Department
      of Documents, Imperial War Museum, London.

      This important collection consists of Wilson's diaries and
      his correspondence. There is much of interest pertaining to
      the question of unity of command and civil-military relations.

342. Callwell, Maj.-Gen. C.E. *Field-Marshal Sir Henry Wilson: His
      Life and Diaries*. London: Cassell & Co., 1927. 2 vols.

      This publication of Wilson's diaries tarnished his reputation.
      Wilson, who replaced Robertson as Chief of the Imperial General
      Staff in 1918, included many self-serving and critical comments
      about the leading figures of his day, including President Woodrow
      Wilson, or "my cousin," as Sir Henry facetiously called him.
      This is a bowdlerized version of Wilson's diary because Callwell
      does not always quote faithfully from the original.

                       2. Civil-Military Relations

343. Beaverbrook, Lord. *Men and Power, 1917-1918*. London: Hutchin-
      son & Co., 1956. 447 pp.

      Beaverbrook served in Lloyd George's ministry as Chancellor of
      the Duchy of Lancaster and minister of information. This is a
      vivid account of the politics of the period and the difficulties
      that Lloyd George had with his generals over strategy.

344. ————. *Politicians & the War 1914-1916*. London: Collins,
      1960. 556 pp.

      This is a fascinating chronicle of ambition and intrigue in
      British wartime politics by someone who knew many of the leading
      figures of the day. There is much material on civil-military
      relations. It must be noted that Beaverbrook was not always a
      dispassionate chronicler, and more recent works have questioned
      some of his conclusions. This work was originally published
      in two volumes (1928-1932). See also Taylor's *Beaverbrook*
      (1972), which brings out differences in Beaverbrook's various
      drafts on the political crisis in late 1916 which destroyed
      Asquith's ministry.

345. Greene, Fred. "The Military View of American National Policy,
      1904-1940." *AHR* 66 (January 1961): 354-77.

      Cooperation, or the lack thereof, between U.S. military and
      civilian policymakers is examined in this article which em-
      phasizes the period between the wars.

346. Guinn, Paul. *British Strategy and Politics 1914-1918*. Oxford:
      Clarendon Press, 1965. 359 pp.

      This scholarly examination of British military operations,
      politics, and war direction is still valuable, although it has
      been dated in some respects by the opening of new archival

materials. Extremely well written, this book is often harsh in
its characterization of British military and political leaders.
This work was awarded the George Louis Beer Prize by the American
Historical Association.

347. Hammond, Paul Y. *Organizing for Defense: The American Military
     Establishment in the Twentieth Century*. Princeton: Princeton
     University Press, 1961. 403 pp.

     The first part of this work discusses military preparation
     and organization prior to World War I. There was progress, but
     not enough to prepare America for participation in a modern war.
     Coordination between civil and military authorities and depart-
     ments was especially lacking. Hammond, a political scientist,
     writes from an administrative or organizational point of view.

348. King, Jere Clemens. *Generals and Politicians: Conflict Between
     France's High Command, Parliament and Government 1914-1918*.
     Berkeley: University of California Press, 1951. 294 pp.

     Civil-military relations in wartime France are carefully
     examined in this important monograph, a revised 1946 University
     of California, Berkeley, doctoral dissertation. The relationship
     between the French civil and military authorities was frequently
     acrimonious, but unlike the German experience, the civilians
     under the fierce-tempered Clemenceau emerged triumphant. Newly
     opened private and official papers have, however, somewhat dated
     this study. See, for example, the biography of Clemenceau by
     Watson.

349. Maurice, Nancy, ed. *The Maurice Case: From the Papers of Major-
     General Sir Frederick Maurice, C.C.M.G., C.B.* Hamden, Conn.:
     Archon Books, 1972. 245 pp.

     The Maurice case concerns the famous letter which the just-
     removed director of military operations wrote to the London
     press in May 1918 accusing the government of deceiving the
     public about its lack of support for Haig's forces. This let-
     ter brought to a head in Parliament the conflict between the
     civil and military authorities. Maurice attempts to defend her
     father's role in this affair by publishing his diary and other
     relevant material. The strident nature of this study detracts
     from its worth.

350. May, Ernest R. "The Development of Political-Military Consulta-
     tion in the United States." *Pol. Sci. Quar.* 70 (June 1955):
     161-80.

     May discusses the haphazard and not particularly successful
     efforts before, during, and after World War I to coordinate the
     efforts of the State, War, and Navy departments.

351. ———, ed. *The Ultimate Decision: The President as Commander
     in Chief*. New York: George Braziller, 1960. 290 pp.

     May discusses Wilson's noninterventionist approach to military
     questions in one of the essays in this collection, arguing that
     Wilson chose to stand aside from military disputes because he

feared that he would be drawn into French and British political decisions.

352. Pohl, James W. "The General Staff and American Defense Policy: The Formative Period, 1898-1917." Doctoral dissertation, University of Texas, 1967. 427 pp.

This is a civil-military study, based for the most part on unpublished sources, of the development of the American general staff. Attention is given to the often critical posture of Congress to the expanding role of the general staff.

353. Repington, Lieut.-Col. C. à Court. *The First World War, 1914-1918*. London: Constable & Co., 1920. 2 vols.

Repington was the brilliant and controversial military analyst for the London *Times* before transferring his pen to the *Morning Post* in 1918. His diary entries and commentary constitute a valuable record of the war both in the trenches and on the home front. During the last stages of the war, Repington conducted a vendetta against the civil authorities, alleging that they had failed to support the military authorities.

354. Ritter, Gerhard. *The Sword and the Scepter: The Problem of Militarism in Germany*. Coral Gables, Fla.: University of Miami Press, 1969-1973. 4 vols.

This monumental work provides a thorough view of civil-military relations in Germany from 1890 to 1918.

355. Woodward, David R. "Britain in a Continental War: The Civil-Military Debate over the Strategical Direction of the Great War of 1914-1918." *Albion* 12 (Spring 1980): 37-65.

This article centers on the at times furious debate over the extent of the British commitment to the western front.

356. ————. "Britain's 'Brass Hats' and the Question of a Compromise Peace, 1916-1918." *Mil. Affairs* 35 (April 1971): 63-67.

This article analyzes the position of Sir William Robertson and other leading British military figures on a negotiated peace.

357. ————. *Lloyd George and the Generals*. Newark: University of Delaware Press, 1983. 367 pp.

Archival sources shed light on the conflict between the military and civil authorities in Great Britain during the war. Woodward examines military, political, and diplomatic questions to demonstrate the often differing perspectives of the politicians and generals.

3. Strategy, Doctrine, and Tactics

358. Allard, Dean C. "Anglo-American Naval Differences During World War I." *Mil. Affairs* 45 (April 1980): 75-81.

This article centers on Anglo-American strategic and operational differences rather than on maritime and mercantile rivalry.

359. Arnold, Joseph C. "French Tactical Doctrine 1870-1914." *Mil. Affairs* 42 (April 1978): 61-67.

Arnold examines the development of the French *offensive à outrance*.

360. Clendenen, Clarence C. *Blood on the Border: The United States Army and the Mexican Irregulars*. New York: Macmillan Co., 1969. 390 pp.

This excellent volume treats Pershing's Mexican intervention. It focuses attention on Pershing's rigorous efforts to train the U.S. Army in the use of airplanes, trucks, and railroads.

361. Coffman, Edward M. "Conflicts in American Planning: An Aspect of World War I Strategy." *Mil. Rev.* 43 (June 1963): 78-90.

Coffman examines the obstacles (for example, the conflict between Pershing and March) to efficient and orderly war planning.

362. Collier, Basil. *The Lion and the Eagle: British and Anglo-American Strategy, 1900-1950*. New York: G.P. Putnam's Sons, 1972. 499 pp.

Using largely printed, many of them secondary sources, the author gives a general account of the strategic background of Anglo-American relations during the first half of the twentieth century. America, however, often receives only peripheral attention in the eight chapters which concern World War I, Allied intervention in Russia, and the peace settlement.

363. Cook, George L. "Sir Robert Borden, Lloyd George and British Military Policy, 1917-1918." *Hist. Jour.* 14 (March 1971): 371-95.

This thoroughly documented article well describes the grand strategic discussions of the leaders of the British Empire, with special emphasis given to the relationship between the British and Canadian prime ministers.

364. Cooper, Malcolm. "The Development of Air Policy and Doctrine on the Western Front, 1914-1918." *Aerospace Hist.* 28 (March 1981): 38-50.

Unlike many studies that concentrate on the heroism of aviators or the development of strategic bombing, this scholarly piece examines the cooperation between air and land forces in World War I.

365. Cruttwell, C.R.M.F. *The Role of British Strategy in the Great War*. London: Cambridge University Press, 1936. 99 pp.

This slim volume discusses the growing British commitment to the western front. The easterners, or exponents of an indirect strategy, are treated sympathetically. The volume is also

valuable for its treatment of the often-dominant French influence on British strategic thinking.

366. Finney, Robert T. "Early Air Corps Training and Tactics."
      Mil. Affairs 20 (Fall 1956): 154-61.

      The impact of World War I on the development of the American
      air arm is the subject of this article.

367. Frothingham, Thomas G. "The Strategy of the World War, and the
      Lessons of the Effort of the United States." *U.S. Naval Inst.,
      Proc.* 47 (May 1921): 669-83.

      This is a survey of the strategy of World War I with emphasis
      on the part played by the United States. An assertion that
      probably raised the eyebrows of European war leaders is that
      the United States demonstrated "the quickest turnover of man-
      power in the world, especially adapted to receive training
      through contact with an infusion of skilled officers and men."

368. Gilmore, Russell. "'The New Courage': Rifles and Soldier In-
      dividualism, 1876-1918." *Mil. Affairs* 40 (October 1976):
      97-102.

      Emphasis on marksmanship in the U.S. Army, according to the
      author, was intended to enhance soldiers' individualism.
      Pershing's influence in this respect receives particular atten-
      tion.

369. Gooch, John. *The Plans of War: The General Staff and British
      Military Strategy c. 1900-1916.* London: Routledge & Kegan
      Paul, 1974. 348 pp.

      This is an outstanding work of scholarship which provides
      many penetrating insights. Gooch demonstrates, for example,
      that the Dardanelles venture was launched without the British
      Imperial General Staff playing its proper role in the development
      of strategy. The research is impressive and the analysis balanced.

370. Gordon-Smith, Captain Gordon. "Errors of Allied Strategy and
      Policy in the World War." *Infantry Jour.* 19 (July 1921):
      22-32.

      The author, a zealous easterner, attempts to make a case for
      an all-out military effort in southeastern Europe, which he
      argues would have destroyed the enemy's "Mittel Europa" position.

371. Gorrell, Colonel Edgar S. "An American Proposal for Strategic
      Bombing in World War I." *Air Power Hist.* 5 (April 1958):
      102-17.

      This 1917 proposal by Gorrell for strategic bombing has been
      called the "earliest, clearest and least known statement of the
      American conception of air power."

372. Greenhous, Brereton. "Evolution of a Close Ground-Support Role
      for Aircraft in World War I." *Mil. Affairs* 39 (February
      1975): 22-28.

This article, based primarily on research in the Public
Record Office, points out that British airpower may have played
an important part in slowing the momentum of the German offensive of March 21, 1918.

373. Greer, Thomas H. "Air Army Doctrinal Roots, 1917-1918." *Mil.
      Affairs* 20 (Winter 1956): 202-16.

      This is a sound article on the influence of World War I on
      the development of American air arm doctrine.

374. Holley, I.B., Jr. *Ideas and Weapons: Exploitation of the Aerial
      Weapon by the United States During World War I: A Study of
      the Relationship of Technological Advance, Military Doctrine,
      and the Development of Weapons*. New Haven: Yale University
      Press, 1953. 222 pp.

      American policymakers are found wanting in this administrative
      history. The United States not only failed to produce acceptable
      war plans, it also developed no coherent doctrine of air power.
      Extensive use has been made of material in the National Archives.
      This monograph was an outgrowth of Holley's 1947 Yale University
      doctoral dissertation.

375. House, Jonathan M. "The Decisive Attack: A New Look at French
      Infantry Tactics on the Eve of World War I." *Mil. Affairs* 40
      (December 1976): 164-65.

      This is a revisionist examination of French massed infantry
      tactics prior to the Great War.

376. Howard, Michael. *The Continental Commitment: The Dilemma of
      British Defence Policy in the Era of the Two World Wars*.
      London: Temple Smith, 1972. 176 pp.

      This is a collection of lectures delivered by Howard at
      Oxford University in the spring of 1971. As Howard freely ad-
      mits, his conclusions must be treated as tentative until further
      research is done in private and official papers. Chapters 2
      and 3 offer flashes of insight into British prewar planning and
      grand strategy during the war.

377. Hunt, Barry, and Preston, Adrian, eds. *War Aims and Strategic
      Policy in the Great War 1914-1918*. London: Croom Helm, 1977.
      131 pp.

      Most of the essays in this collection were presented to the
      Third Annual Military Symposium held at the Royal Military
      College of Canada in 1976. The war aims and strategic policy
      of Britain, France, Canada, America, Italy, and Germany are dis-
      cussed respectively by John Gooch, Douglas Johnson, Robert
      Craig Brown, Edward M. Coffman, John Whittam, and Fritz Fischer.
      Chapter notes are included.

378. Kennedy, Paul, ed. *The War Plans of the Great Powers, 1880-
      1914*. London: Allen & Unwin, 1979. 282 pp.

      This is a useful collection of previously published articles
      on prewar planning. These articles, however, do not represent

a comprehensive treatment of the subject. Grenville is the
author of "Diplomacy and War Plans in the USA, 1890-1917," and
Herwig and Trask have contributed a study on "Naval Operations
Plans Between Germany and the USA, 1898-1913: A Study of Strategic Planning in the Age of Imperialism."

379. Liddell Hart, B.H. *Strategy.* New York: Frederick A. Praeger,
      1967. 430 pp.

      This broad survey of strategy over the centuries includes a
      section on World War I in which Liddell Hart critically eval-
      uates the generals' strategy. This volume is in outline form
      and lacks a bibliography and footnotes. The title of the
      1954 edition, *Strategy: The Indirect Approach*, accurately re-
      flects Liddell Hart's bias.

380. Lucas, Pascal Marie Henri. *The Evolution of Tactical Ideas in
      France and Germany During the War of 1914-1918.* Fort Leaven-
      worth, Kans.: General Service Schools, n.d. 332 pp.

      Written by a lieutenant-colonel in the French army and pub-
      lished in Paris in 1925, this study of tactics was translated
      by P.V. Kieffer. A copy can be found at the US Military History
      Institute at Carlisle Barracks, Pa.

381. Lupfer, Timothy T. *The Dynamics of Doctrine: The Changes in
      German Tactical Doctrine During the First World War.* Washing-
      ton, D.C.: Government Printing Office, 1981. 73 pp.

      This enlightening little volume was issued by the Combat
      Studies Institute as one of the *Leavenworth Papers*. It is a
      well-documented study of the profound changes in German defensive
      and offensive tactics. Of special interest is Lupfer's analysis
      of German elastic defense-in-depth in 1917 and offensive tactics
      of 1918. Lupfer emphasizes that the new German tactical con-
      cepts had a corporative origin and that von Lossberg (defensive
      tactics) and von Hutier (offensive tactics) have previously been
      given too much individual credit.

382. McKenna, Charles D. "The Forgotten Reform: Field Maneuvers in
      the Development of the United States Army, 1902-1920." Doctoral
      dissertation, Duke University, 1981. 279 pp.

      McKenna argues that the system of army field maneuvers was a
      central feature in Root's reforms and played a key role in the
      development of the army from 1902 to 1920.

383. Nenninger, Timothy K. *The Leavenworth Schools and the Old Army:
      Education, Professionalism, and the Officers Corps of the
      United States Army, 1881-1918.* Westport, Conn.: Greenwood
      Press, 1978. 173 pp.

      The Leavenworth influence on the creation of the AEF and its
      operational planning and tactics is examined in this work which
      relies heavily on the papers and memoirs of officers trained at
      Fort Leavenworth and on official army records. This is a re-
      vision of the author's 1974 Wisconsin doctoral dissertation.

384. Rainey, James W. "Ambivalent Warfare: The Tactical Doctrine of the AEF in World War I." *Parameters* 13 (September 1983): 34-36.

The gulf between the way Pershing wanted to train his soldiers (open warfare) and "the way their instincts told them to fight" is highlighted in this study.

385. Ritter, Gerhard, ed. *The Schlieffen Plan: Critique of a Myth*. London: Oswald Wolff, 1958. 195 pp.

The texts of this famous war plan, its variants, addenda, and maps are published for the first time in this volume, which is accompanied by Ritter's astute commentary which stresses that political considerations were either ignored or subordinated to military expediency.

386. Sargent, Herbert Howland. *The Strategy on the Western Front (1914-1918)*. Chicago: A.C. McClurg & Co., 1920. 263 pp.

Colonel Sargent was a member of the War Department general staff, 1917-1918. In that position he prepared memoranda for the chief of staff on the higher strategy of the war. His strongly held view that the German defenses on the western front could not be broken would have pleased many British civilian leaders. Sargent wanted the AEF to fight in the Balkans. This work is an unbalanced defense of his wartime strategic views and an attack on Allied and German generals for their alleged strategic blunders.

387. Schilling, Warner Roller. "Admirals and Foreign Policy 1913-1919." Doctoral dissertation, Yale University, 1953. 375 pp.

Schilling argues that American naval officers linked commercial supremacy to naval dominance in formulating a world policy, overlooking in the process noncommercial factors and the political and strategic significance of land powers.

388. Setzen, Joel A. "Background to the French Failures of August 1914: Civilian and Military Dimensions." *Mil. Affairs* 42 (April 1978): 87-90.

The mistakes of the civilians as well as the generals in the formulation of Plan XVII are highlighted in this article.

389. Sims, Edward H. *Fighter Tactics and Strategy, 1914-1970*. New York: Harper & Row, 1972. 266 pp.

The bulk of this volume concerns the period after World War I. Sims, a fighter pilot during World War II, does not, however, neglect the formative years of air warfare.

390. Spector, Ronald. "'You're Not Going to Send Soldiers Over There Are You!': The American Search for an Alternative to the Western Front 1916-1917." *Mil. Affairs* 36 (February 1972): 1-4.

This is an important and fascinating examination of American strategic thinking, or the lack thereof. There was such a strong

reluctance on the part of many Americans to avoid the human
holocaust on the western front that the United States entered
the war without any coherent general strategy.

*   Travers, Tim. "Learning and Decision-Making on the Western
      Front, 1915-1916." Cited above as item 209.

391. Vigman, Fred K. "The Theoretical Evaluation of Artillery After
      World War I." *Mil. Affairs* 16 (Fall 1952): 115-18.

      This article asserts that writers such as J.F.C. Fuller un-
fairly derogated the utilization of artillery in World War I
to support their particular viewpoints on how future wars should
be fought.

392. Woodward, David R. "The Imperial Strategist: Jan Christiaan
      Smuts and British Military Policy, 1917-1918." *Mil. Hist.
      Jour.* 5 (December 1981): 131-45, 148, 153.

      This article touches upon Smuts's fears that America's ex-
panding diplomatic and military power was detrimental to the
future interests of the British Empire.

393. Wynne, Captain G.C. *If Germany Attacks: The Battle in Depth in
      the West.* London: Faber & Faber Ltd., 1940. 343 pp.

      Written by a British officer involved in the production of
the British official history of the war, this study provides a
comprehensive and intelligent review of German tactics, especially changes in German defensive tactics on the western
front. It is often critical of the failure of British generals
to understand German tactics, either in mastering or imitating
them. Greenwood Press reprinted this work in 1976. See also
the more recent study by Lupfer.

4. Life and Experiences of Ordinary Men in Uniform
(*See also* VI:K, Literature and the War;
IV:C:5, Trench Warfare)

394. Abbey, Edwin A. *An American Soldier: Letters of Edwin Austin
      Abbey.* Boston: Houghton Mifflin Co., 1918. 173 pp.

      This is a collection of letters from an American who fought
with the 4th Canadian Mounted Rifles until he was killed at
Vimy Ridge.

395. *An American for Lafayette: The Diaries of E.C.C. Genet, Lafay-
      ette Escadrille.* Edited by Walt Brown, Jr. Charlottesville:
      University Press of Virginia, 1981. 288 pp.

      Genet has the dubious distinction of being the first American
killed in combat after the United States came into the war.
His diaries, letters, and flight log constitute one of the best
day-to-day records of the Lafayette Escadrille.

396. Baldwin, Fred D. "The American Enlisted Men in World War I."
      Doctoral dissertation, Princeton University, 1964. 261 pp.

This superior dissertation takes a sociological approach in its examination of the noncombat aspects of being an enlisted man in the U.S. Army. Soldiers' letters, government reports, camp newspapers, and records in the National Archives are utilized. Generally of below-average economic and social status, the soldier was trained in camps which emphasized middle-class values. The study concludes that ultimately the soldiers retained their own social and moral values.

397. Berry, Henry. *Make the Kaiser Dance*. New York: Doubleday & Co., 1978. 455 pp.

Berry has compiled a most valuable collection of twenty-four personal reminiscences from some one hundred interviews of World War I veterans from all walks of life and from all branches of service. The photographs are quite good.

398. Biddle, Charles J. *The Way of the Eagle*. New York: Charles Scribner's Sons, 1919. 297 pp.

Biddle, who flew with the Lafayette Escadrille, was credited with seven kills. This volume contains a number of his wartime letters and is a classic work in aerial operations.

399. Blackford, Charles Minor. *Torpedoboat Sailor*. Annapolis, Md.: United States Naval Institute, 1968. 156 pp.

This is a firsthand account of a World War 1 seaman serving aboard a destroyer. It is revealing on the life of the Navy's enlisted men.

400. Brown, J. Douglas. "In Action with the Rainbow Division, 1918-19." *Mil. Rev.* 58 (January 1978): 35-46.

This is an extract from the memoirs of a Princeton premed student who served with the 42nd Infantry Division.

401. Codman, Charles R. *Contact*. Boston: Little, Brown & Co., 1937. 248 pp.

This is an entertaining account by a U.S. pilot who was shot down behind enemy lines during the St. Mihiel offensive. Codman was sent to the German prison camp at Landshut.

402. Depew, Albert N. *Gunner Depew*. Chicago: Reilly & Britton Co., 1918. 312 pp.

This colorful narrative was written by a U.S. citizen who served in the French Foreign Legion on the western front and on an Allied dreadnought. He was taken prisoner by the Germans but U.S. Ambassador Gerard gained his release.

403. Empey, Arthur Guy. *First Call: Guide Posts to Berlin*. New York: Putnam & Sons, 1918. 369 pp.

Empey, an American volunteer in the BEF, followed his smash success, *"Over the Top,"* with this attempt to inform the novice American soldier about the conditions he would encounter on European battlefields. This volume includes much information

concerning the adjustment from civilian to military life, including a definition of army terms.

404.   ———. *"Over the Top" by an American Soldier Who Went.* New
York: Putnam & Sons, 1917. 315 pp.

This is an interesting autobiographical account by a New
Jersey boy who fought with the BEF as a machine gunner. Some
350,000 copies were sold the first year and the book was made
into a popular movie. There are sixteen illustrations and
diagrams.

405.   Flammer, Philip M. "Tragedy and Triumph: The Story of Edmond
C.C. Genet." *Air Power Hist.* 11 (April 1964): 39–44.

The war letters of Genet constitute the chief source of this
account of Genet's career.

406.   Flight (pseud.). *Flying Yankee.* New York: Dodd, Mead & Co.,
1918. 248 pp.

This narrative tells of the experiences of an American volunteer who joined the Royal Flying Corps after his parents went
down on the *Lusitania*.

407.   Ford, Torrey. *Cheer-Up Letters: From a Private with Pershing.*
New York: E.J. Clode, 1918. 192 pp.

This volume of correspondence is filled with positive and
unrealistic news from the front by someone who drove an army
ambulance. Ford does, however, note that censorship prevented
him from being more candid.

408.   Genet, Edmond C. *War Letters of Edmond Genet.* Edited by Grace
E. Channing. New York: Charles Scribner's Sons, 1918. 330 pp.

Genet, a descendant of the controversial Citizen Genet who was
the French minister to the United States, 1793–1794, was killed
in action.

409.   Genthe, Charles V. *American War Narratives, 1917–1918: A Study
and Bibliography.* New York: David Lewis, 1969. 194 pp.

This study serves as a corrective to the notion that all
soldiers were disillusioned by their experiences in the trenches.
This may have been true of many European soldiers, but Genthe's
survey of American war narratives reveals gung-ho patriotism
and muscular idealism. There is a sixty-five-page annotated
bibliography.

410.   Gibson, Preston. *Battering the Boche.* New York: Century Co.,
1918. 120 pp.

This narrative is by a U.S. graduate of Yale who served initially with the French and then later with an American ambulance corps. He comments on the future course of the war as
well as his personal experiences.

411. Gordon, Dennis, ed. *Quartered in Hell: The Story of American North Russian Expeditionary Force, 1918-1919*. Missoula, Mont.: The Doughboy Historical Society and G.O.S., 1982. 320 pp.

Gordon, with the research assistance of Hayes Otoupalik, has compiled an important collection of primary documents dealing with the involvement of U.S. soldiers in the international expeditionary force in North Russia, 1918-1919. Many excellent photographs are included in this valuable record of the reaction of doughboys to a campaign which they did not like or understand.

412. [Grider, John McGavock.] *War Birds: Diary of an Unknown Aviator*. New York: Grosset & Dunlop, c1926. 227 pp.

According to Elliott Springs, the playboy from Princeton who was a World War I aviator, the anonymous author of this illustrated diary was Grider of Pine Bluff, Arkansas. This volume, first published in magazine form, helped create great public interest in the air war in the late 1920s.

413. Hall, Bert. *"En l'air!" (In the Air): Three Years On and Above Three Fronts*. New York: New Library, 1918. 153 pp.

This work tells of the experiences of an American in the Lafayette Escadrille. Hall also flew on the eastern front in Russia and Romania. After the Russian Revolution he returned to America by way of Siberia and Japan.

414. Harrod, Frederick S. "Enlisted Men in the United States Navy, 1899-1939." Doctoral dissertation, Northwestern University, 1973. 511 pp.

This superior dissertation sheds light on Navy personnel and policies during World War I.

415. Hartney, Harold E. *Up and At 'Em*. Harrisburg, Pa.: Stackpole Sons, 1940. 333 pp.

This is one of the best personal accounts by a World War I pilot. Hartley commanded the famous First Pursuit Group, U.S. Air Service, which brought down 285 German planes and balloons unofficially and 201 officially.

416. Hermanns, William. *The Holocaust: From a Survivor of Verdun*. New York: Harper & Row, 1972. 141 pp.

A German veteran provides a graphic account of the longest battle of World War I from the perspective of a foot soldier.

417. Hocking, W.E. "Personal Problems of the Soldier." *Yale Rev.* 7 (July 1918): 712-26.

This article calls for accurate information and broad psychological understanding of personal problems of the soldier. It argues that most U.S. soldiers will maintain their basic morality.

418. Hudson, James J. "Reed G. Landis: America's SE-5 Ace." *Aerospace Hist*. 18 (December 1971): 195-99.

This article describes the distinguished service of the son
of Kenesaw Mountain Landis, who was attached to an RAF unit.

419. Keegan, John. *The Face of Battle: A Study of Agincourt, Water-
      loo and the Somme.* New York: Vintage Books, 1977. 354 pp.

      The author's treatment of the first day of the Somme is the
      best and most original account of perhaps the darkest day in
      British military history. Keegan, a senior lecturer in war
      studies at the Royal Military Academy at Sandhurst, focuses on
      the impact of war on the individual soldier.

420. Kelly, Russell Anthony. *Kelly of the Foreign Legion.* New York:
      M. Kennerley, 1917. 145 pp.

      This volume of letters by a U.S. volunteer in the French
      Foreign Legion deals with the glory and gore of war. In 1916
      Kelly was recorded as "missing."

421. Lane, Allen. *Death's Men: Soldiers of the Great War.* London:
      Allen Lane, 1978. 283 pp.

      Based largely on published and unpublished British memoirs
      and diaries, this illustrated work describes what life was
      really like for the soldiers, especially the tommy, on the
      western front. Unlike many popular works on trench warfare,
      the text is far more important than the forty-nine photographs,
      most of them from the Imperial War Museum. This superior study
      is comprehensive, scholarly, and readable, describing well the
      training of British soldiers, life at the front and in reserve,
      and home leave.

422. Leach, George E. *War Diary.* Minneapolis: Pioneer Printers,
      1923. 205 pp.

      This book concerns the war history of the 151st Field Artil-
      lery in the Rainbow Division. Leach commanded the regiment and
      kept two diaries which are combined in this volume.

423. Leed, Eric J. *No Man's Land: Combat and Identity in World
      War I.* New York: Cambridge University Press, 1979. 257 pp.

      The author makes clear his intention not to write a military
      history, analysis of the war literature, or psychohistory.
      Rather he attempts in an original way to "provide a cultural
      history of the First World War *through* men who participated in
      it." He focuses on the war on the western front. French,
      British, American, and especially German sources are utilized.
      Chapter headings such as "The Defensive Personality," "The Tac-
      tical Realities of Chaos," and "Industrialized War and Neurosis"
      reflect the author's unusual, essentially psychological, approach
      to men at war.

424. McConnell, James Rogers. *Flying for France: With the American
      Escadrille at Verdun.* Garden City, N.Y.: Doubleday, Page &
      Co., 1917. 157 pp.

      This is the personal account of an American who switched from
      driving an ambulance to serving in the Lafayette Escadrille.

425. Macklin, Elton. "'...Suddenly We Didn't Want to Die': A Marine
      Remembers the Battle of Belleau Wood." *Amer. Heritage* 31
      (February/March 1980): 49-64.

      After the war, Macklin, a private in the 67th Company of the
      5th Marine Regiment, recorded these impressions of the fighting
      in Belleau Wood.

426. MacQuarrie, Hector. *How to Live at the Front: Tips for American
      Soldiers*. Philadelphia: J.B. Lippincott, 1917. 269 pp.

      This volume by a British officer of the Royal Field Artillery
      tells of his experiences for the benefit of U.S. soldiers.
      Among other dangers overseas facing the doughboy, MacQuarrie
      warns of the temptations of prostitutes.

427. Merrill, Wainright. *A College Man in Khaki: Letters of an
      American in the British Artillery*. Edited by Charles M.
      Stearns. New York: George H. Doran Co., 1918. 234 pp.

      Merrill describes the training that he received in England
      and the campaign in the mud and blood of Flanders in 1917 which
      claimed his life.

428. Minder, Charles Frank. *This Man's War: The Day-by-Day Record
      of an American Private on the Western Front*. New York:
      Pevensey Press, 1931. 368 pp.

      This contemporary record of an American private on the western
      front captures his pacifistic views and his horror of war.
      Minder wrote his mother almost every day. Gaps in these letters
      caused by censorship have been filled in by the diary he kept.
      The period covered is from Minder's arrival in France in April
      1918 to his gassing in October.

429. Moore, J.R., and others, eds. *History of the American Expedition
      Fighting the Bolsheviki: Campaigning in North Russia, 1918-
      1919*. Hillsdale, Mich.: Polar Bear Publishing, 1920. 303 pp.

      This is the story of intervention in the subzero climate of
      North Russia seen through the eyes of the participants.

430. Rizzi, Joseph N. *Joe's War: Memoirs of a Doughboy*. Edited by
      Richard A. Baumgartner. Huntington, W.Va.: Der Angriff Pub-
      lications, 1983. 160 pp.

      Rizzi served in France with Company A, 110th Engineers, 35th
      Division. During the Meuse-Argonne offensive, he and his com-
      rades found themselves in the thick of things. This book is
      nicely edited and the photographs are excellent.

431. Roberts, Lieutenant E.M. *A Flying Fighter: An American Above
      the Lines in France*. New York: Harper & Brothers, 1918.
      338 pp.

      This narrative by an adventurer who fought in the British
      army and flying service contains some exciting descriptions
      of battle.

432. Rose, Harold W. *Brittany Patrol: The Story of the Suicide
      Fleet.* New York: W.W. Norton & Co., 1937. 367 pp.

      An American naval officer describes his adventures in the
      so-called Suicide Fleet.

433. Skeyhill, Thomas J. *Sergeant York: Last of the Long Hunters.*
      Philadelphia: John C. Winston, 1930. 240 pp.

      York's return to his Tennessee hills as well as his much-
      publicized war heroics during the Meuse-Argonne offensive are
      recounted.

434. Smith, Vice Admiral Allan E. "The Sixth Battle Squadron, A
      Reminiscence." *American Neptune* 40 (January 1980): 50-62.

      These are the reminiscences of a then junior officer aboard
      the U.S.S. *New York.*

435. Smith, Joseph L. *Over There and Back in Three Uniforms: Being
      the Experiences of an American Boy in the Canadian, British
      and American Armies at the Front and Through No Man's Land.*
      New York: E.P. Dutton and Co., 1918. 122 pp.

      Inspired by atrocity stories, the narrator enthusiastically
      joined up to fight the Hun in 1914. He has written a matter-
      of-fact but readable personal account.

*   Stallings, Laurence. *The Doughboys: The Story of the A.E.F.,
      1917-1918.* Cited above as item 189.

436. *Stars and Stripes.* February 8, 1918-June 13, 1919.

      This famous AEF newspaper is a valuable source for the humor,
      interests, and characteristics of the doughboy. Seventy-one
      issues of eight pages each, 14 1/2 by 18 1/2 inches, were pub-
      lished in regular sequence in Paris on the presses of the Con-
      tinental edition of the London *Daily Mail.* Several prominent
      literary figures such as Alexander Woollcott and Harold Ross
      were on the staff. *Stars and Stripes* is now available on micro-
      film through Kraus International Publications/Kraus Microform.

437. Straub, Elmer Frank. *A Sergeant's Diary in the World War.*
      Indianapolis: Indiana Historical Commission, 1923. 356 pp.

      This is the diary, both excerpts and a summary, of an enlisted
      member of the 150th Field Artillery in the 42nd or Rainbow
      Division.

438. Thomason, John W., Jr. *Fix Bayonets!* New York: Charles
      Scribner's Sons, 1926. 245 pp.

      Thomason, a lieutenant in the 1st Battalion, 5th Regiment,
      U.S. Marine Corps, who fought at Belleau Wood, has written a
      colorful and action-filled account of considerable literary
      merit. His drawings are also of a very high quality. Although
      this work is a mixture of fact and fiction, Cyril Falls, the
      distinguished British military historian, considered it "the
      best American book on the War" produced during the first decade
      of the postwar period.

439. Trounce, Harry Davis. *Fighting the Boche Underground.* New York:
     Charles Scribner's Sons, 1918. 236 pp.

     Trounce served with the Royal British Engineers before be-
     coming an officer and sapper in the AEF. His narrative is a
     solid description of the dangerous underground mining operations.

440. Walcott, Stuart. *Above the French Lines: Letters of Stuart
     Walcott, American Aviator, July 4, 1917, to December 8, 1917.*
     Princeton: Princeton University Press, 1918. 93 pp.

     Walcott was killed in action as 1917 came to an end. His
     father, Dr. Charles D. Walcott, the secretary of the Smithsonian
     Institution, contributes a short biography of his son.

441. Westall, Virginia Cooper. "AEF Siberia--The Forgotten Army."
     Mil. Rev. 48 (March 1968): 11-18.

     This article is taken from the unpublished recollections of
     General Robert L. Eichelberger, who served with the AEF in
     Asiatic Russia.

442. Wheeler, Curtis. *Letters from an American Soldier to His
     Father.* Indianapolis: Bobbs-Merrill Co., 1918. 113 pp.

     A young American officer writes his father, the editor of
     Current Opinion, fourteen letters about his experiences in
     France.

443. Winslow, Carroll Dana. *With the French Flying Corps.* New
     York: Charles Scribner's Sons, 1916. 226 pp.

     This American volunteer flying for France describes his view
     of flying. This account succeeds in relating the training an
     aviator received in the French flying corps.

444. Winter, Denis. *The First of the Few: Fighter Pilots of the
     First World War.* Athens: University of Georgia Press, 1983.
     223 pp.

     This important work by a British author takes a different
     approach to the war in the air. Instead of concentrating on
     World War I aces or giving a superficial survey of the air war,
     Winter describes what the war was really like for the pilot from
     his enlistment to demobilization.

445. World War I Survey, US Military History Institute, Carlisle
     Barracks, Pa.

     In the mid-1970s, the Military History Institute began to
     collect the personal papers and military experiences of World
     War I veterans. Appeals were made for personal World War I
     materials and a lengthy questionnaire was sent through the mails.
     By August 1983, some 6,500 responses had been received and cata-
     logued by armies and army corps, divisions, branches of service,
     and camps. In addition, diaries, letters, photographs, and
     items of this nature had been comparably collected and cata-
     logued, including a manuscript history of the 80th Division,
     over 1,000 pages long, prepared by the divisional veterans

association but never published. This remarkable collection,
the largest of its kind in the United States, also includes
some material from Navy, Coast Guard, and Marine veterans.

446. Wright, Jack M. *A Poet of the Air: Letters of Jack Morris
     Wright...April-January 1918.* Boston: Houghton Mifflin Co.,
     1918. 246 pp.

     These letters by an American pilot are of an especially high
     literary quality.

447. York, A.C. *Sergeant York: His Own Life Story and War Diary.*
     Edited by Thomas Skeyhill. New York: Doubleday & Co., 1928.
     309 pp.

     The war diary of Alvin York is supplemented with an account
     in mountain dialect of this war hero's life as a farmer and lay
     preacher.

                          5. Trench Warfare

448. Ashworth, Tony. *Trench Warfare, 1914-1918: The Live and Let
     Live System.* New York: Holmes & Meier Publishers, 1980.
     266 pp.

     A new perspective is gained from this sociological examination
     of the society that developed in the trenches. The "live and
     let live" system which appears in the title refers to the un-
     official truces that developed along certain sectors of the
     front. The author, a teacher at University College, Cardiff,
     used diaries, memoirs, autobiographical fiction, and interviews
     and correspondence with veterans. The emphasis is British.
     There is extensive documentation but no bibliography.

449. Ellis, John. *Eye-Deep in Hell: Trench Warfare in World War I.*
     New York: Pantheon Books, 1976. 215 pp.

     This is one of the best of the recent books on trench warfare.
     Written by a former member of the department of military studies
     at the University of Manchester, this volume effectively por-
     trays life on the western front. The photographs are excellent.
     One can gain, however, the false impression from this and other
     popular accounts of trench warfare that World War I soldiers
     went underground only on the western front. The treatment of
     strategy and tactics is superficial.

450. Hoobler, Dorothy and Thomas. *The Trenches: Fighting on the
     Western Front in World War I.* New York: G.P. Putnam's Sons,
     1978. 191 pp.

     The AEF is virtually ignored in this popular account of trench
     warfare. There is an annotated bibliography. A majority of
     the photographs are from the National Archives.

451. Houlihan, Michael. *World War I Trench Warfare.* London: Ward
     Lock, 1974. 144 pp.

Tactics, both infantry and artillery, conditions in the trenches, the defensive systems, and weapons and equipment are some of the topics discussed in this straightforward and well-organized work. This volume serves as an easy-to-grasp introduction to trench warfare for the general reader. The maps and photographs are quite good.

*   Lane, Allen. *Death's Men: Soldiers of the Great War.* Cited above as item 421.

452.   Lloyd, Alan. *The War in the Trenches.* New York: David McKay Co., 1976. 200 pp.

Many excellent photographs and paintings by war artists, most from the Imperial War Museum, are included in this popular account of trench warfare. There is a strong British emphasis.

453.   Messenger, Charles. *Trench Fighting 1914-1918.* New York: Ballantine Books, 1972. 160 pp.

This is a disappointing work which does not focus on life in the trenches as the title would seem to indicate. Instead it recycles some of the standard works, especially those with a western strategical bias, examining military operations from the perspective of the high command. Many photographs from numerous sources and some maps are provided.

454.   Todd, Frederick P. "The Knife and Club in Trench Warfare, 1914-1918." *Amer. Mil. Institute* 2 (Fall 1938): 139-53.

Todd demonstrates in this illustrated article that men in the trenches showed considerable enterprise in developing weapons for hand-to-hand combat in a war dominated by the machine gun and artillery.

6. Weapons Technology
(*See also* IV:D:2, War in the Air;
IV:D:3, Naval Power and World War I)

455.   Addison, James Thayer. *The Story of the First Gas Regiment.* Boston: Houghton Mifflin Co., 1919. 326 pp.

The training, transportation, and combat role of the First Gas Regiment during its eighteen-month existence is related. Appendix D provides a brief description of weapons used for this new form of warfare.

456.   Armstrong, David A. *Bullets and Bureaucrats: The Machine Gun and the United States Army, 1861-1916.* Westport, Conn.: Greenwood Press, 1982. 239 pp.

This scholarly monograph seeks an explanation for the general lack of interest in the machine gun by military authorities from 1861 to 1916. The Ordnance Department is the focal point of this institutional and technological history. There is a lengthy and valuable bibliography. See also the author's 1976 Duke University doctoral dissertation.

457. Bidwell, Shelford, and Graham, Dominick. *Firepower: British Army Weapons and Theories of War 1904-1945.* Winchester, Mass.: Allen & Unwin, 1982. 320 pp.

This examination of technology's impact on the tactics of the British army is as critical of the advocates of the indirect approach of warfare as it is supportive of the views of John Terraine. The utilization of artillery during World War I receives considerable attention.

458. Brodie, Bernard. *Sea Power in the Machine Age.* Princeton: Princeton University Press, 1943. 462 pp.

This illuminating work examines the impact of the new naval technology on naval strategy and the balance of power on the high seas.

459. Brophy, Leo P. "Origins of the Chemical Corps." *Mil. Affairs* 20 (Winter 1956): 217-26.

The War Department is shown to be quite hidebound in its approach to chemical warfare. Only reluctantly did it establish the Chemical Warfare Service (CWS).

460. Brown, Frederic J. *Chemical Warfare: A Study in Restraints.* Princeton: Princeton University Press, 1968. 355 pp.

Drawing largely upon American sources, including the War Department archives, Brown has written an important study on poison gas policy that is well documented and has a thorough bibliography. The first part of this work examines the history of chemical warfare during the Great War.

461. Chinn, George Morgan. *The Machine Gun.* Washington, D.C.: Government Printing Office, 1951. 688 pp.

Prepared for the Bureau of Ordnance, U.S. Navy, this is an authoritative and profusely illustrated work on the development and use of automatic weapons. The author was a lieutenant-colonel in the marines.

462. Cianflone, Frank A. "The Eagle Boats of World War I." *U.S. Naval Inst., Proc.* 99 (June 1973): 76-80.

The development of the antisubmarine Eagle boats, called "pickle boats" or "cheese boxes" by those who served in them, is well described in this article.

463. Dooly, William G., Jr. *Great Weapons of World War I.* New York: Walker & Co., 1969. 340 pp.

This extensively illustrated survey of World War I weapons is divided into three parts: the land war, the war in the air, and the war at sea. It is written for the popular market.

464. Ellis, John. *The Social History of the Machine Gun.* New York: Pantheon Books, 1975. 186 pp.

This entertaining and well-illustrated work attempts to link the manufacture and use of the machine gun to social history.

465. Emme, Eugene M. "Technical Change and Western Military Thought, 1914-1945." *Mil. Affairs* 24 (Spring 1960): 6-19.

   Emme makes some good points about the way in which new weaponry in World War I led to the development of some questionable post-war theories about how technical changes had altered the art of warfare.

466. Farrow, Edward S. *Gas Warfare*. New York: E.P. Dutton & Co., 1920. 253 pp.

   Farrow was an instructor of tactics at West Point and a military historian of some note. This work, which is especially strong on the tactical use of poison gas, was written to instruct U.S. officers on the importance of chemical warfare.

 * Fiske, Rear-Admiral Bradley A. *From Midshipman to Rear-Admiral*. Cited above as item 233.

467. Foley, John. *The Boilerplate War*. New York: Walker & Co., 1963. 195 pp.

   This is a popular illustrated account that focuses on the development of British tanks.

468. Fries, Amos A., and West, Clarence J. *Chemical Warfare*. New York: McGraw-Hill Book Co., 1921. 445 pp.

   Fries was a brigadier-general who served as chief of the U.S. Chemical Warfare Service, and West was a major in the CWS Reserve Corps. The authors' personal experiences and their ready access to the files of the CWS make this an important source. The volume includes many charts, tables, and illustrations.

469. Fuller, J.F.C. *Memoirs of an Unconventional Soldier*. London: Ivor Nicholson & Watson, 1936. 494 pp.

   Fuller's differences with GHQ while he was chief of the general staff of the British Tank Corps are fully aired. Diagrams and several fold-out maps add to the value of this volume.

470. ————. *Tanks in the Great War, 1914-1918*. London: John Murray, 1920. 331 pp.

   There was no stronger advocate of the tank than Fuller and he is critical of hidebound officers who did not agree with him. Terraine's often conflicting views of the importance of the tank in *The Smoke and the Fire* should be read in conjunction with this work.

471. Hessel, F.A.; Martin, W.J.; and Hessel, M.S. *Chemistry in Warfare: Its Strategical Importance*. New York: Hastings House, 1940. 164 pp.

   F.A. Hessel was a chemist and Martin, and ex-Army officer, inspected the German chemical plants after the war. An informative chapter, "Crucibles of Death," concerns the gases used during the Great War.

472. Jones, Daniel Patrick. "The Role of Chemists in Research on
      War Gases in the United States During World War I." Doctoral
      dissertation, University of Wisconsin, 1969. 279 pp.

      The cooperation of scientists with their government is ex-
      amined through a history of the largest war-related science
      project, the research division of the Chemical Warfare Service,
      which had its center at American University.

473. Jones, Ralph E. *The Fighting Tanks Since 1916.* Washington,
      D.C.: National Service Publishing Co., 1933. 325 pp.

      This was one of the best between-the-wars accounts of the
      development of the tank after it made its first appearance on
      the Somme battlefield in 1916. Photographs and specifications
      add to the usefulness of this volume.

474. Kendall, James. *Breathe Freely! The Truth About Poison Gas.*
      New York: D. Appleton-Century Co., 1938. 179 pp.

      Part two of this work is a good survey of the use of gas in
      the Great War. According to the author, chemical warfare was
      responsible for 100,000 deaths and 1,200,000 injuries. Kendall,
      a lieutenant-commander in the U.S. Naval Reserve, acted as
      liaison officer with Allied services on chemical warfare.

475. Langer, William L. *Gas and Flame in World War I.* New York:
      Alfred A. Knopf, 1965. 120 pp.

      Few American units had a chronicler as able as Company "E"
      of the 1st Gas Regiment of the Chemical Warfare Service.
      Sergeant Langer later became a distinguished professor of diplo-
      matic history at Harvard. This work was originally published
      in 1919 under the title *With "E" of the First Gas.*

476. Liddell Hart, B.H. *The Tanks: The History of the Royal Tank
      Regiment...1914-1945.* New York: Frederick A. Praeger,
      1959. 2 vols.

      The first half of Vol. 1 of this instructive study concerns
      World War I. This remains a standard work for the development
      of the tank.

477. Nenninger, Timothy K. "The Development of American Armor, 1917-
      1940: The World War I Experience." *Armor* 78 (January-February
      1969): 46-51.

      Materials in the National Archives are utilized in this ar-
      ticle focusing on 1917-1918.

478. Orgill, Douglas. *Armoured Onslaught: 8th August 1918.* New
      York: Ballantine Books, 1972. 160 pp.

      Although primarily concerned with the use of the tank in
      achieving a victory over the German army on August 8th (Luden-
      dorff's "Black Day" for German forces), this volume also offers
      a solid introduction to its development. It is richly illus-
      trated.

479. Terraine, John. *The Smoke and the Fire: Myth and Anti-Myths of War, 1861-1945*. London: Sidgwick & Jackson, 1980. 240 pp.

     Terraine's focal point as a military historian remains World War I. In this volume he attempts once again to correct what he considers are misconceptions about this war: the machine-gun myth, the indirect approach myth, the tank myth, the unimaginative general myth, and so on. It is the rare reader who will not be forced to rethink some of his views on World War I.

480. ———. *White Heat: The New Warfare 1914-1918*. London: Sidgwick & Jackson, 1982. 352 pp.

     Terraine evaluates the weaponry, strategy, and tactics of the Great War, which he views as the first war in which all of the consequences of the machine age were manifested. Sea and air warfare as well as land warfare are examined. There are maps, illustrations, and annotations.

481. Trumpener, Ulrich. "The Road to Ypres: The Beginnings of Gas Warfare in World War I." *Jour. Mod. Hist.* 47 (September 1975): 460-80.

     This is an important revisionist study of chemical warfare during the Great War. Among the many interesting assertions in this solid piece of research is that "gas warfare did not begin at Ypres." As early as 1914, Trumpener demonstrates, the French used "small gas-diffusing projectiles."

482. U.S. Army Chemical Corps 1st Gas Regiment. "History of the First Gas Regiment." 1919.

     This unpublished typescript can be found in the holdings of the US Army Military History Institute at Carlisle Barracks, Pa.

483. United States. Infantry School, Fort Benning, Ga. *Compilation of Extracts from Personal Experience Reports of Tank Officers in the First World War*. Fort Benning, Ga.: The Infantry School, 1918. 121 pp.

     This collection includes Colonel Patton's report of his experiences in the tank corps.

484. U.S. War Department. *Gas Warfare*. Washington, D.C.: Government Printing Office, 1918. 4 vols.

     This is an important official source on the use of chemical warfare.

485. ———. *The Medical Department of the United States Army in the World War*, vol. 14: *Medical Aspects of Gas Warfare*. Washington, D.C.: Government Printing Office, 1925. 876 pp.

     This is an important official source on chemical warfare.

486. ———. *The Residual Effects of Warfare Gases*. Washington, D.C.: Government Printing Office, 1933. 93 pp.

Two doctors, Harry L. Gilchrist and Philip B. Matz, examine the "last symptomatic effects" of chlorine and mustard gases.

487. Woollcombe, Robert. *The First Tank Battle: Cambrai 1917*. London: Arthur Barker, 1967. 232 pp.

This scholarly monograph has been called by Liddell Hart "the fullest and best account of this epoch-making battle." Woollcombe conducted extensive research in British archives.

7. Medical and Sanitary Aspects

488. Bayne, Joseph Breckinridge. *Bugs and Bullets*. New York: R.R. Smith, 1944. 256 pp.

This is a vivid account of an American doctor's adventures in Romania during the Great War.

489. Clarke, Walter. "The Promotion of Social Hygiene in War Time." *Ann. Am. Ac. of Pol. Sci. and Soc. Sci.* 79 (September 1918): 178-89.

This essay explains the work of the Sanitary Corps in its attempts to control venereal disease.

490. Cushing, Harvey W. *From a Surgeon's Journal, 1915-1918*. Boston: Little, Brown & Co., 1936. 534 pp.

The atmosphere of the operating room with all of its horror and courage emerges from this journal of an American neurosurgeon who served in a number of capacities on the western front, 1915-1918. Maps and illustrations are included.

491. Gorgas, William Crawford. *Inspection of Medical Services with American Expeditionary Forces. Confidential Report to Secretary of War*. Washington, D.C.: Government Printing Office, 1919. 48 pp.

Gorgas was a retired army general who toured the western front in September-October 1918 to report on AEF medical services.

492. Grissinger, Colonel J.W. *Medical Field Service in France*. Washington, D.C.: Association of Military Surgeons, 1928. 149 pp.

This is a detailed personal account by a member of the medical corps of the American army.

493. Hutchinson, Woods. *The Doctor in War*. Boston: Houghton Mifflin Co., 1918. 481 pp.

Hutchinson was given the freedom to roam the Allied side of the western front in 1917 to survey the activities of medical and sanitary forces. His observations are usually astute, and his writing is of a high quality.

494. Moran, Lord Charles M. *The Anatomy of Courage.* London: Constable, 1945. 216 pp.

This is recognized as a classic account of the infantry of World War I as seen through the medical experiences of a doctor. Lord Moran served with the BEF.

495. Perry, J.C. "Military Health Dependent on Civil Health." *Ann. Am. Ac. of Pol. Sci. and Soc. Sci.* 78 (July 1918): 34-40.

Written by an assistant surgeon-general of the U.S. Public Health Service, this article discusses the problem of civilian health outbreaks and the potential for spreading to soldiers in camps. Perry treats measures taken to ensure public health, treatment of disease, health of workers in war industries, and the health of school children.

496. Pottle, Frederick A. *Stretchers: The Story of a Hospital Unit on the Western Front.* New Haven: Yale University Press, 1929. 366 pp.

This is an account of the hospital unit "Evacuation Eight," which gives an excellent picture of front-line surgery.

497. Seymour, Gertrude. "The Health of Soldier and Citizen." *Survey,* 1 December 1917, pp. 227-32.

The author treats the basic Europe health situation from 1915 until 1917, with emphasis on diseases such as typhus, smallpox, dysentery, trench foot, cerebrospinal fever, trench fever, "soldier's heart," and meningitis. The Germans did a good job in terms of sanitation. The nature of trench warfare, however, contributed greatly to the health problems.

498. ———. "Health of Soldier and Civilian. II. Venereal Disease Abroad." *Survey,* 29 December 1917, pp. 363-67.

This article surveys health problems during the war involving venereal disease. Its control was as much a moral question as it was a physical problem. The author examines the problem in England, Germany, and Italy. Alcohol received much of the blame for the spread of the disease.

499. Shockley, M.A.W. *An Outline of the Medical Service of the Theater of Operations.* Philadelphia: P. Blakiston's Sons & Co., 1922. 230 pp.

This work is based on the postwar conferences and lectures of a lieutenant-colonel in the medical corps of the American Army.

500. Strott, George G. *The Medical Department of the United States Navy with the Army and Marine Corps in France in World War I.* Washington, D.C.: Navy Department, 1947. 322 pp.

This is an official account of the important work of doctors, hospital corpsmen, and dentists of the Navy medical units who treated soldiers and marines in France during World War I.

501. U.S. Bureau of Medicine and Surgery. *Report on the Medico-*

Military Aspects of the European War from Observations Taken Behind the Allied Armies in France. Washington, D.C.: Government Printing Office, 1915. 146 pp.

This 1914 survey was prepared by surgeon A.M. Fauntleroy, instructor in surgery, U.S. Naval Medical School, under the direction of the Bureau of Medicine and Surgery. There are many illustrations of wounds, some of them quite horrific.

502. U.S. Surgeon-General's Office. *The Medical Department of the United States Army in the World War.* Washington, D.C.: Government Printing Office, 1921-1929. 15 vols. in 17.

Begun in 1917 in the Surgeon-General's Office, this monumental official history approaches its subject from both scientific and administrative viewpoints. A wide range of topics is covered, including the medical aspects of gas warfare, sanitation, the nurse corps, field operations, physical reconstruction, and vocational education. Statistics, maps, charts, and illustrations abound. The chief compiler was Major-General M.W. Ireland.

503. ————. *Principles of War Surgery Based on the Conclusions Adopted at the Various Interallied Surgical Conferences.* Washington, D.C.: Government Printing Office, 1918. 80 pp.

This official source may be useful to the specialist.

* U.S. War Department. *The Residual Effects of Warfare Gases.* Cited above as item 486.

504. Walker, George. *Venereal Disease in the American Expeditionary Forces.* Baltimore, Md.: Medical Standard Book Co., 1922. 237 pp.

This is a detailed and important study of venereal disease in the AEF. This volume deals with the attempt by military authorities to control venereal disease and evaluates successful methods of prevention. The author argues that the use of prophylactics increased immorality. The AEF's practice of hospitalizing infected soldiers proved superior to all other methods used to combat and treat venereal disease.

505. Walsh, Joseph. "Tuberculosis and the War." *Ann. Am. Ac. of Pol. Sci. and Soc. Sci.* 80 (November 1918): 23-28.

This essay examines the steps taken by the medical corps to combat tuberculosis.

506. Young, Hugh H. *Hugh Young: A Surgeon's Autobiography.* New York: Harcourt, Brace & Co., 1940. 554 pp.

This is a well-illustrated autobiography by the famous American urologist who played a major role in introducing the doughboy to prophylactics.

8. Intelligence Operations

507. Beesly, Patrick. *Room 40: British Naval Intelligence*. San
     Diego: Harcourt Brace Jovanovich, 1982. 338 pp.

     Among other claims, Beesly argues that the intelligence
     gathered by Hall and his British intelligence group in Room 40
     in the Old Admiralty Building helped bring about U.S. belli-
     gerency.

508. Blankenhorn, Heber. *Adventures in Propaganda: Letters from an
     Intelligence Officer in France*. Boston: Houghton Mifflin
     Co., 1919. 166 pp.

     This volume of letters from Blankenhorn to his wife captures
     the contemporary atmosphere of the AEF in France. It is well
     written but reveals no secrets of American intelligence. The
     illustrations give examples of both Allied and enemy propaganda.

509. Coulter, Captain C.S. "Intelligence Service in the World War."
     Infantry Jour. 20 (April 1922): 376-83.

     This is a worthwhile article on the development and hardships
     of the intelligence section of the 18th Infantry, 1st Division.

510. Dorwart, Jeffrey M. *The Office of Naval Intelligence: The Birth
     of America's First Intelligence Agency, 1865-1918*. Annapolis,
     Md.: Naval Institute Press, 1979. 173 pp.

     This volume traces the development of the Office of Naval
     Intelligence from its beginnings through World War I. At first
     collecting technical data on other navies, the organization by
     1900 had enlarged its covert activities. Approximately one-
     third of this monograph concerns World War I when the ONI ex-
     perienced considerable expansion, even engaging in domestic
     surveillance.

511. Grant, Robert M. *U-Boat Intelligence, 1914-1918*. Hamden,
     Conn.: Archon Books, 1969. 192 pp.

     This is an important work on the Allied intelligence campaign
     against German submarines, notwithstanding the scant documenta-
     tion and absence of an index. Charts and photographs are in-
     cluded.

512. Johnson, Thomas M. *Our Secret War: True American Spy Stories
     1917-1919*. Indianapolis: Bobbs-Merrill Co., 1929. 340 pp.

     The author concentrates on the activities of the American
     secret service (G-2) in Europe during the war. Johnson promises
     many "nuggets of virgin gold" but he has neither notes nor a
     bibliography and admits that there are "international inaccuracies"
     to "protect American secret agents."

513. Kahn, David. "Codebreaking in World Wars I and II: The Major
     Successes and Failures, Their Causes and Their Effects."
     Hist. Jour. 23 (September 1980): 617-39.

     Although most of this article concerns World War II, there is mention of the famous Room 40 in the British Admiralty which intercepted the Zimmermann Note in early 1917.

514. Russell, J.C.E. *True Adventures of the Secret Service.* New
      York: Doubleday, Page & Co., 1923. 316 pp.

      This work is dedicated to the officers and men of the military
      police force and the criminal intelligence service of the AEF.
      It is a potboiler of little or no value and has neither notes
      nor a bibliography.

515. Sweeney, Walter C. *Military Intelligence: A New Weapon in War.*
      New York: Frederick A. Stokes Co., 1924. 259 pp.

      Sweeney, a veteran of military intelligence, does not attempt
      a comprehensive history. Rather, drawing upon his personal
      experiences and study, he discusses the organization and role
      of military intelligence.

516. U.S. Army. A.E.F., 1917-1920. *G.H.Q., General Staff, Second
      Section.* Chaumont? 1918? 2 vols.

      This is a collection of intelligence summaries from January
      to June 1918 which may be researched by date of publication.

517. U.S. War Department. General Staff. *United States Military
      Intelligence, 1917-1927.* New York: Garland Publishing, 1978.
      30 vols.

      There are twenty-six volumes of weekly intelligence summaries
      and four of daily summaries. These summaries are broad in
      their scope, covering political, economic, and social develop-
      ments as well as military events. The four volumes of daily
      summaries provide extensive information on the American military
      role on the western front. Richard D. Challener has written the
      introduction to this collection.

518. Wood, Eric Fisher. *The Note-Book of an Intelligence Officer.*
      New York: Century Co., 1917. 346 pp.

      Major Wood reports on conditions in England in 1917 and the
      Battle of Arras. Wood, who went to Britain to strengthen ties
      between the United States and her European allies, was given a
      staff appointment which enabled him to have something of an
      insider's view.

519. Yardley, Herbert O. *American Black Chamber.* Indianapolis:
      Bobbs-Merrill Co., 1931. 370 pp.

      This solid illustrated work reveals the activities of the
      "Black Chamber," or U.S. cryptographic bureau, which was official-
      ly known as section 8 of the military intelligence division.

                              9. Black Troops, AEF

520. "The American Negro in World Wars I and II." *Jour. Negro Educ.*
      12 (Summer 1943): 263-584.

Thirty essays by such prominent black writers as Emmett J. Scott and W.E.B. Du Bois are included in this yearbook issue devoted to "a comparative analysis of the status and participation of the American Negro in World War I and World War II." The yearbook is divided into three parts. Part one has two sections: the black in American wars prior to World War I and the black's status in the armed services in the two world wars. Part two is also divided into two sections: "The Negro in War Industries and Government War Agencies in World Wars I and II" and "The Role of Morale Agencies Among Negroes in World Wars I and II." Part three is devoted to "The Negro in Post-War Reconstruction in World Wars I and II." A valuable bibliography includes selected references on the part played by blacks in the two world wars.

521. Barbeau, Arthur E., and Henri, Florette. *The Unknown Soldiers: Black Troops in World War I*. Philadelphia: Temple University Press, 1974. 279 pp.

This is a passionate indictment of the Army's treatment of black soldiers, supported by thorough research in the official military records and the personal papers of the soldiers. The authors convincingly demonstrate that blacks made surprisingly good soldiers given their sordid treatment and the smear campaign directed against them. The racist "Disposal of the Colored Drafted Men" of the operations branch of the U.S. Army General Staff is reprinted in an appendix. There is an excellent selection of photographs. See also Barbeau's lengthy 1970 University of Pittsburgh doctoral dissertation.

522. Fletcher, Marvin. *The Black Soldier and Officer in the United States Army 1891-1917*. Columbia: University of Missouri Press, 1974. 205 pp.

This monograph, which emphasizes the racial views of the Army leadership, delineates the role of the black in the Army in both peace and war from 1891 to 1917.

523. Giffin, William W. "Mobilization of Black Militiamen in World War I: Ohio's Ninth Battalion." *Historian* 40 (August 1978): 686-703.

Giffin examines the prevailing views about black soldiers through this study of the mobilization of Ohio's Ninth Battalion. The policy of Newton D. Baker, who had been mayor of Cleveland before becoming secretary of state for war in 1916, receives special attention.

524. Henri, Florette. *Bitter Victory: A History of Black Soldiers in World War I*. Garden City, N.Y.: Doubleday & Co.--Zenith Books, 1970. 120 pp.

Written with high school students in mind, this slim monograph offers a summary of the role of black soldiers in World War I. The photographs are excellent.

525. Heywood, Chester D. *Negro Combat Troops in the World War: The*

Story of the 371st Infantry. New York: Negro Universities
Press (a division of Greenwood Press), 1969. 310 pp.

Heywood, a captain in the 371st Infantry, hoped to counter
the prevalent though distorted picture of the black soldier
"always hot footin' it to the rear" with his account of the
role of his unit in the war. This is a reprint of the 1928
edition. This volume is well illustrated with many original
documents.

526. Little, Arthur W. *From Harlem to the Rhine: The Story of New
York's Colored Volunteers*. New York: Covici Friede, 1936.
382 pp.

The author was a white officer with the Fifteenth New York
Colored Regiment which went into action as part of a French
division.

527. Patton, Gerald W. *War and Race: The Black Officer in the
American Military, 1915-1941*. Westport, Conn.: Greenwood
Press, 1981. 214 pp.

This monograph, which focuses on the years 1917-1920, provides
insight into the trials and tribulations of being a black officer in the American Army. The bibliography reflects extensive
research, and tables and appendices are included.

528. Scott, Emmett J. *Scott's Official History of the American
Negro in the World War*. Chicago: Homewood, 1919. 512 pp.

Scott, who received the assistance of many other blacks in
producing this work, was the special assistant to the secretary
of war. A wide variety of sources was utilized, but there are
no footnotes or bibliography. In addition to the text, there
are ninety-six pages of illustrations, including many official
photographs.

529. Sweeney, W. Allison. *History of the American Negro in the
Great World War: His Splendid Record in the Battle Zones of
Europe*. New York: Negro Universities Press (a division of
Greenwood Press), 1969. 307 pp.

This is a reprint of the 1919 edition. There are no footnotes or bibliography but the author succeeds in showing the
perseverance of black soldiers in the face of the rampant
racism of the period. Numerous photographs enhance this volume.
Barbeau and Henri have produced a much more scholarly treatment
of the same subject.

530. U.S. Army War College. Historical Section. *The Ninety-Second
Division 1917-1918*. N.p., 1923.

The "Buffalo" Division was comprised of black recruits from
across the United States. It sailed for France in June 1918.
Spending two days in active sectors, it captured 38 prisoners
and suffered 176 battle deaths and 1,466 wounded. This confidential report critically evaluates its training and combat
performance. The pages are not numbered consecutively. The
US Military History Institute at Carlisle Barracks, Pa., has a
copy.

531. Williams, Charles H. *Sidelights on Negro Soldiers*. Boston:
      B.J. Brimmer Co., 1923. 248 pp.

      This is one of the better contemporary accounts of the part
      played by the black soldier in the war.

10. Engineers, AEF

532. Collins, Francis A. *The Fighting Engineers: The Minute Men of
      Our Industrial Army*. New York: Century Co., 1918. 200 pp.

      This is a popular, even breathless, account of the achieve-
      ments of American engineers, especially the "Famous 11th En-
      gineers," who fought at Cambrai in late 1917. There are thirty-
      two illustrations but no bibliography, notes, or index.

533. Parsons, W.B. *The American Engineers in France*. New York:
      D. Appleton & Co., 1920. 429 pp.

      This is a detailed examination of the vital work of some
      174,000 American engineers who served overseas. Parsons was a
      colonel who served in the 11th U.S. Engineers, which was with
      the first American forces to participate in active fighting in
      France.

534. Trounce, Harry Davis. *Notes on Military Mining*. Washington
      Barracks, D.C.: Press of the Engineer School, 1918. 88 pp.

      This study is by a Captain in the U.S. Engineers who knew his
      subject. See also his personal account (item 439).

535. U.S. Army. A.E.F. Chief Engineer. *Historical Report of the
      Chief Engineer...American Expeditionary Forces 1917-1919*.
      Washington, D.C.: Government Printing Office, 1919. 437 pp.

      This detailed official history includes appendices and a
      great many illustrations.

536. U.S. Army. A.E.F. Engineer Department. *Report of the Chief
      Engineer, First Army American Expeditionary Forces on the
      Engineer Operations in the St. Mihiel and Meuse-Argonne Of-
      fensives, 1918*. Washington, D.C.: Government Printing Office,
      1929. 151 pp.

      This illustrated volume was the collective effort of numerous
      engineering officers.

11. Artillery, AEF

*   Bidwell, Shelford, and Graham, Dominick. *Firepower: British
      Army Weapons and Theories of War 1904-1945*. Cited above as
      item 457.

537. De Varila, Osborne. *The First Shot for Liberty: The Story of an
      American Who Went Over with the First Expeditionary Force*.
      Philadelphia: John C. Winston Co., 1918. 223 pp.

De Varila served with the 6th U.S. Field Artillery and is
given credit for firing the first shot of the American army.
His work is one of the more interesting accounts of Americans
in the trenches of the western front.

538. DeWeerd, H.A. "American Adoption of French Artillery 1917-
     1919." *Amer. Mil. Institute* 3 (Summer 1939): 104-16.

     DeWeerd discusses the lessons learned from and the long-lasting
     influences of U.S. dependence on French artillery during the
     Great War.

539. Farrow, Edward S. *American Guns in the War with Germany.* New
     York: E.P. Dutton & Co., 1920. 223 pp.

     This work by an instructor of tactics at West Point concerns
     U.S. production of munitions rather than the role of artillery
     on the western front. There is no documentation or discussion
     of sources.

540. Hogg, Ian V. *Barrage: The Guns in Action.* New York: Ballan-
     tine Books, 1970. 160 pp.

     A master gunner in the Royal Artillery examines artillery
     tactics in the two world wars.

541. Olson, Ronald E. "The American 'Schneider.'" *Field Artillery
     Jour.* 48 (November-December 1980): 48-49.

     A U.S. gun, a 155-mm "Schneider," called "Calamity Jane," is
     said to have fired the last artillery shell of World War I.

542. ————. "The 123rd Field Artillery 1917-1919." *Field Artillery
     Jour.* 50 (November-December 1982): 33-35.

     This illustrated article describes the varied adventures of
     this national guard regiment.

543. Ottosen, Major P.H., chief comp. *Trench Artillery, A.E.F.: The
     Personal Experiences of Lieutenants and Captains of Artillery
     Who Served with Trench Mortars.* Boston: Lothrop, Lee & Shep-
     ard Co., 1931. 367 pp.

     This represents a very personal history of those artillerymen
     who shared the fate of the doughboy. This volume was completed
     by Ottosen, who served in the trench artillery or "suicide club"
     as it was sometimes called.

544. U.S. Navy Department. Office of Naval Records and Library,
     Historical Section. *The United States Naval Railway Batteries
     in France.* Washington, D.C.: Government Printing Office,
     1922. 97 pp.

     This is an important source for the often overlooked part
     played by the U.S. Naval railway batteries in the European
     theater.

12. Supplies and Transportation, AEF

545. Crowell, Benedict, and Wilson, Robert Forrest. *How America
      Went to War*. New Haven: Yale University Press, 1921. 6 vols.

      Crowell, who was assistant secretary of war and director of
      munitions, 1917-1920, provides an insider's view of American
      mobilization for war with emphasis on war industry, manpower
      policy, and the transport and supply of the AEF. The last volume
      concerns military and industrial demobilization, 1918-1920. The
      authors conducted interviews with leading administrators. Al-
      though an important source, these volumes are marred by errors
      of fact and an uncritical approach. Wilson, the co-author, was
      an American officer.

546. Cuff, Robert D. "Newton D. Baker, Frank A. Scott, and 'The
      American Reinforcement in the World War.'" *Mil. Affairs* 34
      (February 1970): 11-13.

      This is a survey of the literature on American industrial
      mobilization which highlights the differing interpretations of
      the military and civilian authorities. The civilian or business
      point of view is represented by Crowell and Clarkson and the
      War Department's perspective is put forward by Baker and Scott.

547. Dawes, Charles G. *A Journal of the Great War*. Boston: Houghton
      Mifflin Co., 1921. 2 vols.

      These volumes focus on General Dawes's activities as the
      purchasing agent in Europe for the AEF. The first volume con-
      tains Dawes's wartime diary.

548. Frothingham, Thomas G. *The American Reinforcement in the World
      War*. New York: Doubleday, Page & Co., 1927. 388 pp.

      This is a broad account of American mobilization for war, the
      transport of the AEF, naval operations, and the American military
      effort overseas.

*   Gleaves, Vice-Admiral Albert. *A History of the Transport Ser-
        vice: Adventures and Experiences of United States Transports
        and Cruisers in the World War*. Cited above as item 236.

549. Hagood, Johnson. *The Services of Supply: A Memoir of the Great
      War*. Boston: Houghton Mifflin Co., 1927. 403 pp.

      The memoirs of the chief of staff, services of supply, AEF,
      constitute an important source for any examination of the logis-
      tical efforts of the AEF in France and the creation of an in-
      dependent American army. The author makes extensive use of
      his wartime journal and copies of letters and memoranda he
      saved. This volume is illustrated.

*   Harbord, James G. *The American Army in France, 1917-1919*.
        Cited above as item 241.

*   ————. *The American Expeditionary Forces: Its Organization
        and Accomplishments*. Cited above as item 242.

550. Henniker, Colonel A.M., comp. *Transportation on the Western Front, 1914-1918*. London: H.M. Stationery Office, 1937. 531 pp.

      This volume contains some information, not always accurate, on American lines of communication and transportation on the western front. The index in this British official history is inadequate but there are many helpful maps.

551. Hurley, Edward N. *The Bridge to France*. Philadelphia: J.B. Lippincott Co., 1927. 338 pp.

      A machine tool and appliance manufacturer, Hurley became the chairman of the United States Shipping Board. He recounts, with emphasis on his own views, the massive American effort to build troop and supply ships to support the AEF. He notes that Pershing's goal of eighty divisions in 1919, if met, could not have been transported and supplied by American shipping that would then have been available.

552. Huston, James A. *The Sinews of War: Army Logistics, 1775-1953*. Washington, D.C.: U.S. Army, Office of the Chief of Military History, 1966. 789 pp.

      This is a work of scholarship by a professor of history at Purdue University. Five chapters, "World War I: Industrialization and Procurement," "Interallied Co-ordination," "The Road to France," "Services of Supply in France," and "Demobilization" concern American participation in the war. The shortcomings of the logistical efforts of the AEF are not whitewashed.

553. McClean, Ross H. "Troop Movements on the American Railroads During the Great War." *AHR* 26 (April 1921): 464-88.

      The solid achievements of those who organized and directed American railroads in transporting soldiers to training camps and embarkation ports is told in this article.

554. Mattox, W.C. *Building the Emergency Fleet*. Cleveland: Pepton Publishing Co., 1920. 279 pp.

      The author, who was head of the publication section of the Emergency Fleet Corporation, describes the American crash program to build ships to transport and supply the AEF.

555. Risch, Erna. *Quartermaster Support of the Army: A History of the Corps, 1775-1939*. Washington, D.C.: Office of the Quartermaster General, Quartermaster Historian's Office, 1962. 796 pp.

      Approximately one-sixth of this scholarly history concerns the conversion of the quartermaster's department into the quartermaster corps and its role in the Great War. The corps is shown to be as unprepared for war in 1917 as it had been for the Spanish-American War. Both supply in the zone of interior, 1917-1918, and U.S. operations overseas, 1917-1918, are examined.

556. Shanks, Maj.-Gen. David C. *As They Passed Through the Port*.
      Washington, D.C.: Cary Publishing Co., 1927. 351 pp.

      Shanks was the commander of the port of embarkation, Hoboken,
      New Jersey, which saw almost 1.8 million U.S. soldiers pass
      through on their way to the European war.

557. Sharpe, Henry G. *The Quartermaster Corps in the Year 1917 in
      the World War*. New York: Century Co., 1921. 424 pp.

      The author was quartermaster general of the United States
      Army.

558. U.S. General Staff. War Plans Division. Historical Branch.
      *Organization of the Services of Supply: American Expeditionary
      Forces*. Washington, D.C.: Government Printing Office, 1921.
      130 pp.

      Charts, maps, and appendices are included in this official
      history.

559. Wilgus, William J. *Transporting the A.E.F. in Western Europe,
      1917-1919*. New York: Columbia University Press, 1931. 612 pp.

      The problems and inadequacies of the transportation corps,
      AEF, along with the almost superhuman efforts to overcome them,
      are well described in this work by the director of military
      railways and deputy director general of transportation, AEF.

                     13. Division Histories, AEF

            The following division histories are grouped together
      by division number in ascending order with the ex-
      ception of the first entry, a collection of twenty-
      eight division histories.

560. American Battle Monuments Commission. *Summary of Operations
      in the World War*. Washington, D.C.: Government Printing
      Office, 1944. 28 vols.

      This is an invaluable source for the study of tactical opera-
      tions of the AEF, providing detailed treatment of the operations
      of the twenty-eight divisions which served in the front lines.
      Bound in fabrikoid with detailed fold-out maps in a pocket,
      these slim booklets contain a bibliography, index, table of
      organization, and list of casualties.

561. *History of the First Division During the World War: 1917-1919*.
      Philadelphia: John C. Winston Co., 1922. 450 pp.

      This admirable detailed history, prepared by the Society of
      the First Division, is particularly valuable for studying the
      attack on the small village of Cantigny in late May, the Marne,
      and the St. Mihiel and Meuse-Argonne offensives. First in com-
      bat, the 1st Division was the last complete division to return
      home.

562. Miller, H.R. *First Division*. Pittsburgh, Pa.: Crescent, 1920.
      49 pp.

      This slim volume on the "Big Red One," as it was unofficially
      known, does not compare to the more detailed work by the Society
      of the First Division.

563. Spaulding, Oliver L., and Wright, John W. *The Second Division,
      American Expeditionary Force in France: 1917-1918*. New York:
      Hillman Press, 1937. 412 pp.

      This is a solid piece of historical work. Spaulding served
      for five years as the chief of the historical section of the
      Army War College. Along with McClellan's official history,
      this is a basic source for the marines in France. The so-called
      Indianhead Division was organized in France, spent sixty-six
      days in active sectors, and won more Distinguished Service
      Crosses than any other division.

564. Hemenway, Frederic V. *History of the Third Division, United
      States Army in the World War for the Period December 1, 1917
      to January 1, 1919*. Andernach-on-the-Rhine, 1919. 397 pp.

      Called the "Marne" Division after it helped stop the last
      major German offensive of the war, this division also partici-
      pated in the St. Mihiel and Meuse-Argonne offensives. It was
      commanded by former cavalryman Major General Joseph T. Dickman.

565. Bach, Christian A., and Hall, Henry Noble. *The Fourth Division,
      Its Services and Achievements in the World War*. Issued by the
      Division, 1920. 368 pp.

      This is a superior history of a regular Army division, the
      4th Division or "Ivy" Division. It initially fought in bat-
      talions under French command, but went into action as a complete
      unit during the St. Mihiel and Meuse-Argonne offensives.
      Bach, who was chief of staff of the 4th Division, and Hall,
      who was a London *Times* correspondent attached to the AEF, have
      succeeded well in describing at the division level the role
      played by America in the war.

566. *Official History of the Fifth Division*. *U.S.A.* Washington, D.C.:
      Society of the Fifth Division, 1919. 423 pp.

      The chief compiler of this well-written division history was
      Kenyon Stevenson. The 5th Division, organized at Camp Logan,
      Texas, was called the "Red Diamond" Division. It participated
      in the St. Mihiel and Meuse-Argonne offensives.

567. Fell, Captain Edgar Tremlett. *History of the Seventh Division,
      United States Army 1917-1919*. Philadelphia: Seventh Division
      Officers' Association, 1927. 261 pp.

      This volume includes such disparate information as the number
      of court-martials and the win-loss record of the division's
      basketball team. Dispatched to Europe in August 1918, the
      "Hourglass" Division spent only two days in active sectors.

568. [Densen, G.L. Van, and Muller, W.G.] *Official History of the
     Thirteenth Division, 1918-1919.* Tacoma, Wash.: Robert W.
     Hulbert, 1919. 40 pp.

     Since this division was not organized until July 1918 and was
     not an official division, the slimness of this volume is not
     surprising.

569. Benwell, Harry A. *History of the Yankee Division.* Boston:
     Cornhill, 1919. 283 pp.

     The part played by New Englanders in the 26th Division at
     Seicheprey, the first combat which involved Americans in large
     numbers, is well commemorated in this account. See also the
     excellent accounts by Sibley and Taylor.

570. Ford, Bert. *The Fighting Yankees Overseas.* Boston: Norman E.
     McPhail, 1919. 259 pp.

     The author bills himself as "New England's 'own' war corres-
     pondent."

571. George, A.E., and Cooper, E.H. *Pictorial History of the Twenty-
     Sixth Division, United States Army.* Boston: Ball, 1920.
     320 pp.

     This is a good pictorial history of the first national guard
     division to go into the line.

572. Sibley, Frank P. *With the Yankee Division in France.* Boston:
     Little, Brown & Co., 1919. 365 pp.

     This history of the 26th Division, which was commanded by
     Major General Clarence R. Edwards from February 6 to October 25,
     1918, was written by an American war correspondent with decided
     views.

573. Taylor, Emerson Gifford. *New England in France, 1917-1919: A
     History of the Twenty-Sixth Division, U.S.A.* Boston: Houghton
     Mifflin Co., 1920. 324 pp.

     This important division history by a national guardsman and
     the acting chief of staff of the 26th Division tells the story
     of the first complete division in France. The "Yankee" Division
     was created from New England contingents in July 1917 and by
     November was organized as a complete division overseas. This
     is probably the best single account of the 26th Division.

574. Clarke, William F. *Over There with O'Ryan's Roughnecks.*
     Seattle, Wash.: Superior Publishing Co., 1968. 176 pp.

     These are the illustrated reminiscences of a private who
     served in the 27th Division.

575. O'Ryan, Maj.-Gen. John F. *History of the 27th Division: New
     York's Own.* New York: Bennett & Churchill, 1919. 80 pp.

     This thumbnail sketch does not compare with the author's more
     thorough two-volume history. Citations and names and addresses
     are included.

576.   ────. *The Story of the 27th Division.* New York: Wynkoop,
        Hallenbeck & Crawford, 1921. 2 vols.

        The commander of the 27th Division has written a thorough and
        exemplary unit history. The 27th was attached to the BEF and
        played a role in the breaching of the Hindenburg line.

577.   Starlight, Alexander, comp. *The Pictorial Record of the 27th
        Division.* New York: Harper & Brothers, 1919.

        This pictorial history starts with the "send off" parade in
        New York and concludes with the "welcome home" parade. There
        is no pagination.

578.   Swetland, Maurice J. and Lilli. *"These Men": "For Conspicuous
        Bravery Above and Beyond the Call of Duty."* Harrisburg, Pa.:
        Military Service Publishing Co., 1940. 312 pp.

        Two-thirds of this volume concerns the 27th Division, in which
        Maurice Swetland served in the Great War.

579.   Gilbert, Eugene. *The 28th Division in France.* Nancy: Berger-
        Levrault, 1919.

        This is a slim volume of drawings. There is no pagination.

580.   Martin, Col. Edward. *The Twenty-Eighth Division: Pennsylvania's
        Guard in the World War.* Pittsburgh, Pa.: 28th Division Pub-
        lishing Co., 1923-1924. 5 vols.

        This division history also gives the "History and Traditions
        of the Pennsylvania National Guard and its predecessor the
        Pennsylvania Militia."

581.   *Pennsylvania in the World War: An Illustrated History of the
        Twenty-Eighth Division.* Pittsburgh, Pa.: States Publications
        Society, 1921. 2 vols.

        The photographs in this pictorial usually do justice to the
        exploits of the "Keystone" Division, which spent forty-nine days
        in active sectors.

582.   Proctor, Henry G. *The Iron Division: National Guard of Penn-
        sylvania in the World War.* Philadelphia: Winston, 1919.
        296 pp.

        This is the story of the 28th Division, which was commanded
        in order by Major General Charles H. Muir, Brigadier General
        Frank H. Albright (temporary), and Major General William H. Hay.

583.   Warner, Frank A. *Journal of Operations. Twenty-Eighth Division,
        A.E.F. August 5, 1917-November 30, 1918.* N.p., 1919. 71 pp.

        This is "a complete chronological record of events pertaining
        to this Division from date of embarkation overseas." The 28th
        Division fought at Château Thierry, the Marne, the Vesle and
        Thiaucourt sectors, and at Meuse-Argonne.

584.   Cutchins, Lieut.-Col. John A. *History of the Twenty-Ninth*

Division: "Blue and Grey," 1917-1919. Philadelphia: MacCalla & Co., 1921. 493 pp.

The 29th Division saw heavy action in Vosges and at Verdun, sustaining over 5,000 casualties. The appendix contains a roster of all officers and enlisted men who served in the 29th.

585. U.S. Army. 29th Infantry Division. *Operations of the 29th Division, East of the Meuse River, October 8th to 30th, 1918.* Fort Monroe, Va.: Coast Artillery School, 1922. 410 pp.

This volume contains operations reports and field orders.

586. Murphy, Elmer A., and Thomas, Robert S. *The Thirtieth Division in the World War.* Lepanto, Ark.: Old Hickory Publishing Co., 1936. 342 pp.

This volume sheds light on the U.S. assault against the Saint-Quentin Tunnel complex. Attached to the British, this unit was called the "Old Hickory" Division.

587. Garlock, G.W. *Tales of the Thirty-Second.* West Salem, Wis.: Badger Publishing Co., 1927. 275 pp.

The author of this illustrated history was a lieutenant colonel in the "Red Arrow" Division.

588. Wisconsin War History Commission. *The 32nd Division in the World War, 1917-1919.* Milwaukee: Wisconsin Printing Co., 1920. 319 pp.

Commanded by Major General William G. Haan, this division was composed of national guardsmen from Michigan and Wisconsin. In the Amiens sector, some of its detachments served with the Australians.

589. Harris, Barnett W. *33rd Division Across No-Men's Land.* Chicago: R.R. Donnelley & Sons Co., 1919. 92 pp.

In addition to the photographs, there are illustrations by Dudley J. Nelson, a private in the 132nd Infantry.

590. Huidekoper, Frederic L. *Illinois in the World War: The History of the 33rd Division, A.E.F.* Springfield: Illinois State Historical Society, 1921. 4 vols.

Vols. 2 through 4 of this division history consist of appendices and maps. The author, the division adjutant of the "Prairie" Division, has done a thorough job of relating the activities of his division.

591. *Illinois in the World War: An Illustrated History of the Thirty-Third Division.* Chicago: States Publications Society, 1921. 2 vols.

This solid unit history was written either by or under the supervision of the officers of the 33rd Division. Donald F. Biggs of the States Publication Society was the general editor.

592. Carter, Robert L. *Pictorial History of the 35th Division*.
      Kansas City, Mo., 1933.

      Most of the photographs are from the U.S. Signal Corps. There
      is no pagination.

593. Hoyt, Charles B. *Heroes of the Argonne: An Authentic History
      of the Thirty-Fifth Division*. Kansas City, Mo.: Franklin
      Hudson Publishing Co., 1919. 259 pp.

      The narrative, written in a popular style, is accompanied by
      photographs and maps.

594. Kenamore, Clair. *From Vauquois Hill to Exermont: A History of
      the Thirty-Fifth Division of the United States Army*. St.
      Louis: Guard Publishing Co., 1919. 435 pp.

      Not always written with balance, this work is nevertheless
      useful for any examination of the Meuse-Argonne offensive.
      The 35th also served in brigades in the Vosges sector and as
      a division in the Gerardmer and Sommedieu sectors.

595. Chastaine, Capt. Ben H. *Story of the 36th: The Experiences of
      the 36th Division in the World War: 1917-1918*. Oklahoma
      City: Harlow Publishing, 1920. 291 pp.

      After its training at Camp Bowie, Texas, this division sailed
      for France in July 1918 and as a division spent twenty-three
      days in active sectors.

596. Cole, Ralph D., and Howells, W.C. *The Thirty-Seventh Division
      in the World War 1917-1918*. Columbus, Ohio: Thirty-Seventh
      Division Veterans Association, 1926-1929. 2 vols.

      Organized from Ohio and West Virginia national guardsmen, the
      "Buckeye" Division had varied experiences on the western front
      in 1918. The authors were division historians.

597. Koons, Jack, and Palmer, Don. *Billets and Bullets of the 37th
      Division: Cartoons and Ragtime*. Cincinnati: Bacharach Press,
      1919. 79 pp.

      This volume offers a representative example of doughboy humor.

598. *The Thirty-Seventh's Bit in the World War of 1914-1918: A Brief
      Story*. N.p., 1918. 16 pp.

      This brief account includes maps.

599. *History of the Fortieth (Sunshine) Division...1917-1919*.
      Los Angeles: C.S. Hutson & Co., 1920. 179 pp.

      The "Sunshine" Division, which sailed for Europe in August,
      never made it into the line. It served as a depot division,
      filling the ranks of depleted units.

600. Reilly, Henry J. *Americans All. The Rainbow at War: Official
      History of the 42nd Rainbow Division in the World War*. Colum-
      bus, Ohio: F.J. Herr, 1936. 888 pp.

The author was an officer in both the infantry and artillery in the "Rainbow" Division, which got its name because it included national guardsmen from twenty-six states and Washington, D.C., covering the country, so it was said, like a rainbow. This division arrived in France in November and spent 39 days in active sectors and 125 days in quiet sectors.

601. Sherwood, Elmer W. *Diary of a Rainbow Veteran.* Terre Haute, Ind.: Moore-Langen Co., 1929. 217 pp.

General Charles P. Summerall contributed the foreword to this volume, which was first published by a newspaper syndicate under the title "Ten Years Ago with the Rainbow Division."

602. Tompkins, Raymond S. *The Story of the Rainbow Division.* New York: Boni & Liveright, 1919. 264 pp.

This history is one of the most readable of the division histories. The author, a correspondent for a Baltimore newspaper, includes many anecdotes.

603. Wolf, Walter B. *A Brief Story of the Rainbow Division.* New York: Rand, McNally & Co., 1919. 61 pp.

This brief history was rushed into print to enable the members of the division to have a copy when they returned to the United States.

604. *History of the Seventy-Seventh Division, August 25, 1917-November 11, 1918.* New York: W.H. Crawford Printers, 1919. 228 pp.

Designed and written in the field, this unit history was the work of several division historians, but the primary compiler was the chief editor, Major Julius Ochs Adler. Sailing for Europe in April 1918, the 77th was the first national army division to arrive in France. Its sixty-six days in active sectors, including the Meuse-Argonne offensive, were surpassed only by the 1st and 3rd Divisions.

605. Milham, Charles G. "'Atta Boy!': The Story of New York's 77th Division." *Brooklyn Daily Eagle*, 26 January 1919.

This extensive newspaper article describes the contributions to victory made by the "Liberty" Division. The 77th Division was one of the few U.S. divisions that both started and finished the Meuse-Argonne offensive.

606. Rainsford, Kerr. *From Upton the Meuse.* New York: D. Appleton & Co., 1920. 298 pp.

Written with a sense of humor, this volume examines the role of the 307th Infantry and 77th Division. The sketches are especially good. The foreword is by General Alexander.

607. Meehan, Thomas F., ed. *History of the Seventy-Eighth Division in the World War, 1917-18-19.* New York: Dodd, Mead & Co., 1921. 243 pp.

Composed of recruits from New York, New Jersey, and Delaware,

the "White Lightning" Division covered itself with glory when
it took Grandpré in house-to-house fighting.

608. *History of the Seventy-Ninth Division, A.E.F., During the World
      War, 1917-1919.* Lancaster, Pa.: Steinman & Steinman, 1922.
      509 pp.

      The history of the 79th Division, which is said to have cap-
      tured the two highest points during the Meuse-Argonne offensive,
      was prepared by the history committee of the 79th Division
      Association. The division is covered from its training at
      Camp Meade, Maryland, to its demobilization. The 79th sailed
      for France in July 1918.

609. Young, Rush Stephenson. *Over the Top with the 80th by a Buck
      Private, 1917-1919.* Washington, D.C., 1933.

      There is no pagination in this brief history of the "Blue
      Ridge" Division, which was made up of draftees from West Vir-
      ginia, Virginia, and western Pennsylvania. This division served
      with the British at Artois and participated in the St. Mihiel
      and Meuse-Argonne offensives. It sailed for France in May 1918.

610. *Official History of 82nd Division American Expeditionary Forces,
      "All American" Division, 1917-1919.* Indianapolis: Bobbs-
      Merrill Co., 1919. 310 pp.

      The history of this division from its training to the St.
      Mihiel and Meuse-Argonne offensives to its role after the armis-
      tice is covered in this superior division history. A thorough
      account of York's heroism is included. Made up of men from Ten-
      nessee, Alabama, and Georgia, this division sailed for France
      in May 1918. The principal author is Lieutenant-Colonel G.
      Edward Buxton, Jr.

611. *The Official History of the Eighty-Sixth Division.* Chicago:
      States Publications Society, 1921. 319 pp.

      Although the 86th Division did not make it into the line,
      many of its officers and men saw action during the Meuse-Argonne
      offensive. The "Black Hawk" Division, comprised of recruits
      from Illinois, sailed for France in September 1918.

612. *The 88th Division in the World War of 1914-1918.* New York:
      Wynkoop Hallenbeck Crawford Company, 1919. 236 pp.

      The history of the 88th Division is divided into four parts:
      training and transportation to France; life in the trenches;
      post-Armistice service abroad and demobilization; and a roster
      of all who served in this division abroad. Sailing for France
      in August, the 88th spent its time in quiet sectors.

613. Larson, E.J.D. *Memoirs of France and the Eighty-Eighth Division.*
      Minneapolis: Webb, 1920. 172 pp.

      This history includes a section of personal narratives and a
      photographic album section of many of the members of the
      division.

614. English, George H., Jr. *History of the 89th Division, U.S.A.* Denver, Colo.: The War Society of the 89th Division, 1920. 511 pp.

    Maps, photographs, official reports, and honor and casualty lists are included in this unit history. The "Middle West" Division sailed for Europe in June 1918 and participated in the St. Mihiel and Meuse-Argonne offensives.

615. Masseck, C.J., comp. *Official Brief History of the 89th Division, U.S.A., 1917-1918-1919.* N.p., 1919. 48 pp.

    Major General Leonard Wood was this division's first commander, but he was removed before it sailed for France.

616. *Report on St. Mihiel Offensive, 89th Division, September 12-13, 1918.* Fort Leavenworth, Kans.: Army Service Schools Press, 1919. 72 pp.

    Some of the problems associated with the 89th Division's role in the St. Mihiel offensive, especially those problems relating to communications and transportation, are discussed in official reports written following this operation.

617. *Operations 90th Division, A.E.F., August 18th 1918-November 11th 1918.* Fort Leavenworth, Kans.: General Services Schools, n.d.

    This volume of documents, compiled and issued by the operations section of the general staff of the 90th Division, constitute an important source for the study of the St. Mihiel and Meuse-Argonne offensives. The pages are not numbered consecutively.

618. Wythe, Maj. George. *A History of the 90th Division.* New York: Ninetieth Division Association, 1920. 259 pp.

    Most of the text concerns the "battle period" of the 90th Division which spent twenty-six days in active sectors. The author was the division historian.

619. Henderson, Alice Palmer. *The Ninety-First. The First at Camp Lewis.* Tacoma, Wash.: John C. Barr, 1918. 510 pp.

    This is a good source for U.S. training camps.

620. *The Story of the 91st Division.* San Francisco: 91st Division Publication Committee, 1919. 177 pp.

    The "Evergreen" Division sailed for Europe in July 1918 and participated in the Meuse-Argonne offensive. This history gives a blow-by-blow account of the combat role of the 91st.

*   U.S. Army War College. Historical Section. *The Ninety-Second Division 1917-1918.* Cited above as item 530.

14. Uniforms

621. Mollo, Andrew. *Army Uniforms of World War I: European and United States Armies and Aviation Services.* New York: Arco Publishing Co., 1978. 219 pp.

The illustrations are in color, the coverage comprehensive, and the commentary erudite. There is also a section on "personal equipment."

622. Schulz, Paul J.; Otoupalik, Hayes; and Gordon, Dennis. *World War One: Collectors Handbook.* Missoula, Mont.: GOS Incorporated, 1977. 50 pp.

This is a useful illustrated reference work on the uniforms, insignia, equipment, and weapons of the AEF.

15. Others

623. Haycock, Ronald G. "The American Legion in the Canadian Expeditionary Force, 1914-1917: A Study in Failure." *Mil. Affairs* 43 (October 1979): 115-19.

Haycock concludes that the American Legion in the CEF was "a military, political, and diplomatic embarrassment to all concerned."

624. *Journal of Forest History* 22 (October 1978): 180-234.

The use of forest resources in World War I is the unifying theme of this issue. Articles of special interest are: "All Wooden on the Western Front" by Frank N. Schubert; "The Biggest Regiment in the Army" and "The Woodsmen of the AEF: A Bibliographical Note" by David A. Clary; "The National Park Service and the First World War" by Marcella M. Sherfy; and "The Deterioration of Forest Grazing Land: A Wider Context for the Effects of World War I" by Daniel E. Mortensen.

625. Lishchiner, Jacob B. "Origin of the Military Police: Provost Marshall General's Department, A.E.F., World War I." *Mil. Affairs* 11 (Summer 1947): 67-79.

This is a solid administrative study.

626. Pease, Theodore Calvin. "Notes and Suggestions: A Caution Regarding Military Documents." *AHR* (January 1921): 282-84.

Pease discusses "certain characteristics of military documents that necessitate the application to them of the most careful critique."

627. Ryan, Garry D. "Disposition of AEF Records of World War I." *Mil. Affairs* 30 (Winter 1966-1967): 212-19.

Ryan faults the War Department for its records management during the Great War.

628. Silverman, Alberl J. "Kidnapping the Kaiser." *Amer. Hist. Ill.*
14 (January 1980): 36-43.

     This is an interesting account of the curious postwar attempt
     by four American soldiers to kidnap the former German emperor
     from his place of refuge in Holland.

629. Van Dam, T., ed. *The Postal History of the AEF, 1917-1923.*
State College, Pa.: American Philatelic Society, 1980. 242 pp.

     This superbly illustrated work is a valuable contribution to
     the historiography of the war. Numerous individuals have con-
     tributed chapters on subjects ranging from the North Russian
     campaign to the postal markings of the AEF.

D. CAMPAIGNS AND OPERATIONS

1. Land War

a. *France and Flanders* (*See also* IV:C:13, Division Histories, AEF)

630. Bean, C.E.W., gen. ed. and principal author. *The Official History of Australia in the War of 1914-1918.* Sydney: Angus &
Robertson, 1921-1942. 12 vols.

     Bean, who was the official war correspondent with the AIF,
     has written an outstanding official history of the Australian
     part in the war in France and Flanders. Given wide latitude
     by his government, Bean writes with balance and intellectual
     honesty. The result is probably the most dispassionate account
     of the war by an official historian. Vols. 3 through 6 cover
     the AIF in France, 1916-1918. Six of the twelve volumes were
     written by Bean. The University of Queensland Press is presently
     in the process of reissuing the entire twelve-volume set.

631. Brook-Shepherd, Gordon. *November 1918.* Boston: Little, Brown
& Co., 1981. 461 pp.

     This narrative by a British journalist takes a different
     approach from most of the recent accounts of Germany's defeat
     in late 1918. Rather than focusing almost exclusively on the
     western front, Brook-Shepherd analyzes the cumulative effect
     of Allied military efforts in all theaters.

632. Coffman, Edward M. "The Second Battle of the Marne." In *Trans-
formation of a Continent: Europe in the Twentieth Century*,
edited by Gerhard L. Weinberg, pp. 11-58. Minneapolis:
Burgess Publishing Co., 1975.

     The part played by American troops in this crucial 1918 battle
     is given special emphasis in this clearly written article which
     includes numerous unpublished documents in a "Sources" section.

633. Cotton, Major R.C. "A Study of the St. Mihiel Offensive." *Infantry Jour.* 17 (July 1920): 43-59.

This is a generally laudatory account of the planning and execution of the St. Mihiel offensive.

634. Edmonds, Brig.-Gen. J.E., gen. ed. and chief compiler. *Official History of First World War: Military Operations, France and Belgium*. London: Macmillan & Co., 1922-1949. 14 vols.

The British official history, prepared under the direction of the historical section of the Committee of Imperial Defence, is a monumental achievement. Years in the making--the last volume was published in 1949--this is an essential source for the study of military operations on the western front. These volumes combine factual material, buttressed by official documents, with many astute observations. Edmonds, however, views events from an extreme westerner point of view; his revision upward of German casualties to defend the attrition strategy of British generals is a case in point. The reader should be aware that Edmonds made corrections concerning earlier volumes, usually of no great significance, in each new volume. The three volumes for 1917 and the five volumes for 1918 are of particular interest to the student of American participation in the war.

635. Essame, H. *The Battle for Europe 1918*. New York: Charles Scribner's Sons, 1972. 216 pp.

Essame served with the British 8th Division in 1918 and this volume reflects his extensive military experience. He does not merely recycle the views of those who preceded him in describing and evaluating the last campaigns of the war. Essame is more complimentary of Pershing and his staff than many British and French observers in 1918 or later. Maps, illustrations, and a short bibliography are provided, but there is no documentation.

636. Evarts, Jeremiah M. *Cantigny: A Corner of the War*. Privately printed, 1938. 96 pp.

Evarts, a captain in the 18th Infantry, 1st Division, has written a lively account of the capture of Cantigny. General Bullard wrote the preface.

637. Farrar-Hockley, Anthony. *Death of an Army*. New York: William Morrow & Co., 1968. 195 pp.

At the end of 1914, few members of the original BEF were still on their feet. The author, a professional soldier, has written a balanced and well-researched account of the BEF's first encounter with trench warfare during the First Battle of Ypres. Sir John French's generalship is criticized, but this is not a polemic against the Army leadership. It is much more an account of ordinary soldiers in war.

638. Gies, Joseph. *Crisis 1918: The Leading Actors, Strategies and Events in the German Gamble for Total Victory on the Western Front*. New York: W.W. Norton & Co., 1974. 288 pp.

This popular, fast-moving treatment of the last year of the war places emphasis on Ludendorff's desperate strategy to win

the war before the United States could play a major role.
Chapter 11, entitled "The Americans," includes no revelations
about the U.S. role in the war. A bibliography is included
but there is no documentation.

639. Gregory, Barry. *Argonne 1918: The AEF in France*. New York:
      Ballantine Books, 1972. 160 pp.

      An introduction to the role of the AEF with emphasis on the
      Argonne offensive can be gained from this slim but well-illustrated
      volume in the Ballantine series, "The Illustrated History of
      the Violent Century." Attention is given to German as well as
      Allied and U.S. strategy. A very brief bibliography is included.

640. Hallas, James. "Doughboys at Cantigny." *Amer. Hist. Ill.* 18
      (November 1983): 36-45.

      This is a popular account of America's first victory in World
      War I. The author is a free-lance writer who specializes in
      military history.

641. Horne, Alistair. *The Price of Glory: Verdun 1916*. New York:
      St. Martin's Press, 1963. 371 pp.

      This is a popular account of the longest battle of World War
      I. Many German, French, and English sources were utilized and
      the author also interviewed survivors of Verdun. This work
      remains the best English-language account of this 1916 German
      offensive against the fortress town of Verdun.

642. Johnson, Thomas M., and Pratt, Fletcher. *The Lost Battalion*.
      Indianapolis: Bobbs-Merrill Co., 1938. 338 pp.

      The stand of the "Lost Battalion" in the Argonne Forest has
      become an American legend. Fact is separated from fiction in
      this solid and interesting joint effort by a "sometime war
      correspondent" and a military historian.

643. Keegan, John. *Opening Moves: August 1914*. New York: Ballan-
      tine Books, 1971. 160 pp.

      Well illustrated with excellent photographs, this slim volume
      describes the first battles on the western front and evaluates
      the French and German war plans. There are no startling reve-
      lations, but the style is clear and readable.

644. Liddell Hart, B.H. "The Basic Truths of Passchendaele." *JRUSI*
      104 (November 1959): 433-39.

      Liddell Hart is critical of the views of Terraine concerning
      the 1917 Flanders offensive. Among other points, Liddell Hart
      contends that the continuation of the British offensive into
      the fall was neither requested by the French high command nor
      necessary to prevent the Germans from launching massive assaults
      against the French. He also accuses Edmonds of "a fantastic
      juggling with figures" to inflate German casualties to make
      Haig's conduct of the battle appear in a more favorable light.

645. McCarthy, Joe. "The Lost Battalion." *Amer. Heritage* 28 (October 1977): 86-91, 93.

     This is a succinct account of the adventures of the "Lost Battalion."

646. Maddox, Robert J. "The Meuse-Argonne Offensive." *Amer. Hist. Ill.* 10 (June 1975): 22-35.

     In this well-illustrated article, Maddox highlights the role played by the AEF in knocking Germany out of the war.

647. ————. "Ordeal of the 'Lost Battalion.'" *Amer. Hist. Ill.* 10 (December 1975): 22-33.

     The so-called Lost Battalion, according to Maddox, was in actual fact a collection of several units and was never truly lost.

648. ————. "The Saint-Mihiel Salient. Pershing's 'Magnificent' Victory." *Amer. Hist. Ill.* 16 (April 1981): 43-50.

     Maddox argues that Pershing's staff developed an "almost flawless plan of operations." The mistakes made were mistakes of execution, especially in the area of communications and transportation.

649. Middlebrook, Martin. *The First Day on the Somme, 1 July 1916.* New York: W.W. Norton, 1972. 346 pp.

     The greatest value of this volume is that it is written from the perspective of the ordinary soldier. Middlebrook's focus is on the first day of this prolonged British offensive, but his final three chapters, "Aftermath," "Cost," and "An Analysis," help to provide a comprehensive analysis.

650. Miles, L. Wardlow. *History of the 308th Infantry 1917-1919.* New York: G.P. Putnam's Sons, 1927. 357 pp.

     This is one of the basic sources for the so-called Lost Battalion.

651. Palmer, Frederick. *Our Greatest Battle: The Meuse-Argonne.* New York: Dodd, Mead & Co., 1919. 629 pp.

     This is an insider's account by a journalist of the Meuse-Argonne offensive in which more than a million Americans participated. Palmer does not ignore the transportation difficulties and the inevitable problems caused by inexperienced staff officers.

652. Pitt, Barrie. *The Last Act.* New York: W.W. Norton & Co., 1963. 318 pp.

     This is an always entertaining account of the last year of the war. Pitt's description of Corporal York's exploits serves as one example of his often anecdotal approach. When asked how many prisoners he had taken, York responded: "Jesus, Lieutenant, I ain't had time to count them yet!"

653. Smythe, Donald. "St. Mihiel: The Birth of an American Army."
     Parameters 13 (June 1983): 47-57.

     This well-documented article addresses the problems associated
     with this American offensive.

654. Spears, Brig.-Gen. E.L. *Prelude to Victory*. London: Jonathan
     Cape, 1939. 640 pp.

     Spears gives a superior account of the planning and launching
     of the Allied spring attacks of 1917; his work is of the highest
     literary quality. Spears, fluent in French, was a British
     liaison officer with an intimate knowledge and understanding
     of both the French and British positions. His work remains
     one of the best English-language sources for the controversial
     Calais conference and the ill-fated Nivelle offensive. It is
     based on research in primary materials and personal experiences
     but there is neither documentation nor a bibliography.

655. Stokesbury, James L. "The Aisne-Marne Offensive." *Amer. Hist.
     Ill.* 15 (July 1980): 8-17.

     Stokesbury asserts that the turning point of the war was July
     18, 1918, when the Aisne-Marne offensive, which was to involve
     some 250,000 U.S. soldiers, began.

656. Sweitzer, Captain J.S., Jr. "The Champagne-Marne Defensive."
     Infantry Jour. 19-20 (December 1921-June 1922): 653-58, 34-40,
     184-91, 263-69, 401-7, 526-31, 653-59.

     This seven-part series by an infantry officer provides detail
     on this significant battle. The part played by U.S. soldiers
     is emphasized.

657. Swindler, Henry O. "The So-Called Lost Battalion." *Amer.
     Mercury* 15 (November 1928): 257-65.

     Swindler, a veteran and historical research officer at the
     Army War College, attempts to separate fact from fiction con-
     cerning this most celebrated incident of American World War I
     military operations.

658. Terraine, John. *To Win a War: 1918, The Year of Victory*. Garden
     City, N.Y.: Doubleday & Co., 1981. 268 pp.

     This pithy account of the last year of the war, although its
     primary focus is on the successful British offensives, is
     superior to more voluminous studies such as the one by John
     Toland. Terraine's central objective is to show the greatness
     of Haig and the magnitude of the achievements of his army, but
     there are flashes of insight on many other subjects, including
     the role of the AEF and the tank in the defeat of the German
     Army.

659. ————. *The Western Front 1914-1918*. Philadelphia: J.B.
     Lippincott Co., 1965. 321 pp.

     This is a collection of essays previously published by Ter-
     raine in such journals as *History Today*. These interpretative

essays on various aspects of the war on the western front are
frequently thought-provoking.

660.   ————, ed. *The Road to Passchendaele*. *The Flanders Offensive
        of 1917: A Study in Inevitability*. London: Leo Cooper, 1977.
        365 pp.

    On the sixtieth anniversary of the controversial Passchen-
    daele offensive, or the Third Battle of Ypres as it was official-
    ly known, Terraine published this volume of largely primary
    documents. Terraine has always defended Haig's Flanders offen-
    sive. His method this time is to let the record speak for it-
    self, although his explanatory footnotes, introduction, and
    short conclusion make his point of view very clear. Terraine
    includes a note on German and British casualty figures, a sub-
    ject on which there remains little agreement.

661.   Toland, John. *No Man's Land: 1918--The Last Year of the Great
        War*. Garden City, N.Y.: Doubleday & Co., 1980. 651 pp.

    Toland, no stranger to military history, does not always
    succeed in this retelling of the last year of the war. The
    reader can lose his way in the mass of detail. His use of
    firsthand accounts of soldiers, however, is to be applauded.

662.   U.S. Army. A.E.F. General Staff, Intelligence Section. *The
        German and American Combined Daily Order of Battle, 25 Septem-
        ber, 1918 to 11 November, 1918, Including the Meuse-Argonne
        Offensive*. Chaumont, 1919. 26 pp.

    The tables and graphs make this a useful source.

663.   Watt, Richard M. *Dare Call It Treason*. New York: Simon &
        Schuster, 1963. 344 pp.

    The French army mutiny after the failure of Nivelle's offen-
    sive certainly deserves attention. Unfortunately this work by
    an amateur historian, although good on military operations and
    the morale of the French soldier, does not deal satisfactorily
    with the often Byzantine character of French politics in 1917.
    But, then, there exists no English-language source that gives
    comprehensive treatment to French politics during the war.

664.   Werstein, Irving. *The Lost Battalion*. New York: W.W. Norton
        & Co., 1966. 191 pp.

    This is a well-illustrated and popularly written account of
    the "Lost Battalion." A soldier in the "Lost Battalion" is
    alleged to have remarked" "Lost! Hell, we weren't lost! The
    Krauts knew just where to find us!"

665.   Williams, M.J. "Thirty Per Cent: A Study in Casualty Statis-
        tics." *JRUSI* 109 (February 1964): 51-55.

    Williams makes a convincing case that the compiler of the
    British official history, J.E. Edmonds, cooked German casualty
    figures to make the tactics and strategy of British generals
    appear in a more favorable light. Edmonds's figures are shown
    to have little if any relationship to his evidence.

666. Wise, Jennings C. *The Turn of the Tide: American Operations at*
      Cantigny, Château Thierry, and the Second Battle of the Marne.
      New York: Henry Holt & Co., 1920. 255 pp.

      This American officer generally lives up to his promise of
      avoiding "the all too common error of overrating our physical
      contribution to the result."

667. Wolff, Leon. *In Flanders Fields: The 1917 Campaign.* New York:
      Viking Press, 1958. 308 pp.

      This is a gripping account of the 1917 British offensive
      which has become known as the Passchendaele offensive. Wolff
      is critical of Haig and his staff. Notes and a bibliography
      are provided. For another perspective see the collection of
      documents compiled by Terraine in *The Road to Passchendaele.*

668. Woodward, David R. "Did Lloyd George Starve the British Army
      of Men Prior to the German Offensive of 21 March 1918?"
      Hist. Jour. 27 (March 1984): 241-52.

      This article serves as a corrective to the standard interpre-
      tation of Lloyd George's use of British reserves on the eve of
      the March 21 German offensive.

b. Russian Front

669. Churchill, Winston S. *The Unknown War: The Eastern Front.*
      New York: Charles Scribner's Sons, 1931. 396 pp.

      The war on the eastern front remained "unknown" for so long
      because the military operations there received little attention
      from English-language writers. Until recently Churchill's
      account was the most comprehensive discussion by a British or
      American writer of Russia's struggle with the Central Powers.
      Churchill's primary focus is on the battles of 1914-1915.
      Stone's *The Eastern Front, 1914-1917*, published in 1975, is
      more comprehensive and up to date.

670. Clark, Alan. *Suicide of the Empires: The Battles on the Eastern*
      Front 1914-1918. New York: American Heritage Press, 1971.
      127 pp.

      This is a popular and richly illustrated account by a British
      author.

671. Golovin, Lieut.-Gen. Nicholas N. *The Russian Army in the World*
      War. New Haven: Yale University Press, 1931. 287 pp.

      Golovin was a professor in the Russian Imperial General Staff
      College and chief of staff of the Russian armies on the Romanian
      front. He takes a sociological approach in analyzing the im-
      pact of the war on the Tsarist army. Along with military opera-
      tions, he describes the organization of the army and the morale
      of the ordinary soldier.

672. Ironside, Sir Edmund. *Tannenberg: The First Thirty Days in*
      East Prussia. Edinburgh: W. Blackwood & Sons, 1925. 306 pp.

The crushing defeat, a modern-day Cannae, suffered by the Tsarist army in East Prussia is described in this work.

673.   Jukes, Geoffrey. *Carpathian Disaster: Death of an Army*. New York: Ballantine Books, 1971. 160 pp.

The Russian army made a surprising recovery in 1916 from its defeats of the previous year. A great offensive led by General Brusilov against Austria-Hungary in the region of the Carpathian Mountains at first showed great promise. In the end, however, massive losses led to widespread defeatism both in the army and on the home front. Written for the layman rather than the scholar, this book discusses both military operations and their impact on Russian morale.

674.   Knox, Maj.-Gen. Sir Alfred. *With the Russian Army, 1914-1917*. London: Hutchinson & Co., 1921. 2 vols.

Knox was the British military attaché in Russia before the war. Fluent in Russian, he spent much of the war at the front; most of these volumes consist of extracts from the diary he kept. His evaluation of Russian arms is one of the best by a foreigner. Following the overthrow of the Tsar, he became one of London's best intelligence sources about events in Russia. Numerous photographs taken by the author are included.

675.   Pares, Sir Bernard. *Day by Day with the Russian Army*. London: Constable & Co., 1915. 287 pp.

During the Great War, Pares, a noted Russianist, served as an officer with the Russian army. He was with the Third Caucasian Corps in Galicia when it was almost annihilated by an Austro-German offensive in the spring of 1915. His comments reflect a rare understanding of Russian conditions by someone from the west.

676.   Rutherford, Ward. *The Russian Army in World War I*. London: Gordon Cremonisi Publishers, 1975. 303 pp.

This volume is a convenient and easy-to-read account of the war on the eastern front by a writer of novels and popular military history. There is documentation, but this work does not reflect much depth of scholarship. Russian prewar planning receives some attention.

677.   Stone, Norman. *The Eastern Front, 1914-1917*. New York: Charles Scribner's Sons, 1975. 348 pp.

This is a revisionist account of the Tsarist army's performance in the Great War. Stone differs from the standard interpretation of Russian manpower and war industry. He argues that the Russian army was actually short of men (the *per capita* strength of the army was below that of her allies), and that Russian industry was capable of supplying the needs of the army. He concludes that the inefficiency and incompetence of the generals and bureaucrats were largely responsible for the decline of the army. This is a well-researched work that includes maps.

678. Wildman, Allan K. *The End of the Russian Imperial Army: The Old Army and the Soldiers' Revolt (March-April 1917)*. Princeton: Princeton University Press, 1980. 402 pp.

This impressively researched work, which makes use of Soviet sources, is the best examination of the impact of revolution on the Tsarist army. It complements Stone's examination of the army from 1914 to 1916. A sequel is planned.

c. Dardanelles, Gallipoli, and Balkans

679. Aspinall-Oglander, Brig.-Gen. C.F. *Official History of First World War, 1914-1918: Gallipoli*. London: William Heinemann, 1929-1932. 2 vols.

Aspinall-Oglander comes closest to Bean as an official historian who speaks his mind. His often critical evaluation of the Gallipoli campaign remains the starting point for all other accounts of that military venture. Still, as Aspinall-Oglander admitted in a private letter, "I was not a free agent, and could not say exactly what I liked. Many happenings had to be omitted altogether, and many (as I thought) fair criticisms were deleted by the official blue pencil."

680. Cassar, George H. *The French and the Dardanelles: A Study of Failure in the Conduct of War*. London: Allen & Unwin, 1971. 276 pp.

There have been many studies of the controversial Dardanelles campaign, but until Cassar's work, none had examined in depth the role of the French. This valuable study is based on thorough research in private and official French documents, some of which the author has omitted citing at the request of literary executors. Cassar's work is illuminating on the growing conflict over strategy among Joffre and the French politicians and the inability of the French and British to develop a truly common plan for the Dardanelles campaign.

681. Falls, Captain Cyril. *Official History of First World War, 1914-1918: Macedonia*. London: H.M. Stationery Office, 1933-1935. 2 vols.

These two volumes examine the Allied campaign in the Balkans, 1915-1918.

682. Higgins, Trumbull. *Winston Churchill and the Dardanelles: A Dialogue in Ends and Means*. New York: Macmillan Co., 1963. 308 pp.

Higgins is strongly critical of Churchill and other ministers who were enthusiastic about the Dardanelles campaign. Some of Higgins's critical comments about the higher direction of the war in Britain are valid, but a fuller, better researched, and more balanced account of Churchill's role in the Dardanelles disaster can be found in Martin Gilbert's *Winston S. Churchill*, vol. 3: *The Challenge of War, 1914-1916* (1971).

683. James, Robert Rhodes. *Gallipoli*. New York: Macmillan Co.,
     1965. 384 pp.

     In his history of the eight-and-a-half month Gallipoli cam-
     paign of 1915, James is critical of Churchill's part in this
     ill-fated venture. If he had had access to unpublished sources
     that were available to Churchill's biographer, Gilbert, he might
     have moderated some of his criticism of the then First Lord of
     the Admiralty.

684. Moorehead, Alan. *Gallipoli*. New York: Harper & Brothers, 1956.
     384 pp.

     The publication of this lucid and entertaining study of the
     Gallipoli campaign revived interest in this controversial mili-
     tary operation. Moorehead, who relied almost exclusively on
     published sources, has been superseded by James and Gilbert.

*   Tannenbaum, Jan Karl. *General Maurice Sarrail, 1856-1929*.
     Cited above as item 338.

d. *Italian Theater*

685. Edmonds, Brig.-Gen. Sir James E., and Davies, H.R. *Official
     History of First World War, 1914-1918: Italy, 1915-1919*.
     London: H.M. Stationery Office, 1949. 450 pp.

     This is the basic English-language source for military opera-
     tions on the Italian front.

686. Falls, Cyril. *Caporetto, 1917*. London: Weidenfeld & Nicolson,
     1966. 200 pp.

     This is a solid and interesting account of the Austro-German
     breakthrough at Caporetto in October 1917.

687. McEntee, G.L. *Italy's Part in Winning the World War*. Princeton:
     Princeton University Press, 1934. 114 pp.

     This is one of the few English-language sources on Italy's
     role in the war. The author was an American army officer.

688. McLaughlin, Patrick D. "Doughboy Diplomats: The U.S. Army in
     Italy, 1917-19." *Army* 21 (January 1971): 30-37.

     The Americans are shown to have raised Italian morale with
     their limited participation on the Italian front. The role of
     Fiorello La Guardia is given special attention.

689. Rothenberg, Gunther E. *The Army of Francis Joseph*. West Lafay-
     ette, Ind.: Purdue University Press, 1976. 298 pp.

     Political, diplomatic, economic, and social forces are con-
     sidered in this scholarly examination of the Austro-Hungarian
     army. Approximately one-fourth of the text concerns World War I.
     Contrary to some other accounts, Rothenberg contends that the
     morale of the multinational army was reasonably good until the
     last year of the war. The war on the Austro-Hungarian side of
     the Italian front can be followed in this volume.

690. Villari, Luigi. *The War on the Italian Front*. London: Cobden-Sanderson, 1932. 308 pp.

The chief value of this work is that it is one of the very few English-language surveys of the war on the Italian front. The author, a bilingual Italian, gives particular emphasis to the Italian contributions to victory. Advocates of increased emphasis on the Italian front as an alternative to the western front will find support for their views in this volume. There is documentation but no bibliography.

e. *Other Theaters*

691. Aldington, Richard. *Lawrence of Arabia: A Biographical Enquiry*. Chicago: Henry Regnery Co., 1955. 448 pp.

This is a single-minded and not really successful attempt to prove that Lawrence was a fraud.

692. Barker, A.J. *The Bastard War: The Mesopotamian Campaign of 1914-1918*. New York: Dial Press, 1967. 449 pp.

Cyril Falls views this work as the best treatment of the Mesopotamian conflict since Moberly's official history. This study provides numerous examples of British military blunders as Britain fought with the Turks for control of the Persian Gulf and the oil fields of Mesopotamia.

693. Burdick, Charles B. *Japanese Siege of Tsingtau: World War I in Asia*. Hamden, Conn.: Archon Books, 1976. 274 pp.

This work of considerable scholarship examines the Japanese conquest of Tsingtau in 1914 which, according to the author, "destroyed Germany's colonial aspirations and empire." There is extensive documentation.

694. Falls, Cyril. *Armageddon: 1918*. Philadelphia: J.B. Lippincott Co., 1964. 200 pp.

This is a superior account of Allenby's brilliant campaign against the Turks in 1918. The Battle of Megiddo (which is Armageddon in the Hebrew) and the exploits of the British cavalry are highlighted.

695. Hordern, Lt.-Col. Charles. *Official History of First World War: Military Operations in East Africa, August 1914-September 1916*. London: H.M. Stationery Office, 1941. 603 pp.

This official history was based on a draft by Major H. Fitz Stacke. A second volume was planned but never published.

696. Knightley, Philip, and Simpson, Colin. *The Secret Lives of Lawrence of Arabia*. New York: McGraw-Hill, 1970. 333 pp.

This popular account is neither a work of hagiography nor a polemical treatment designed to demolish the "myth" of Lawrence. Some new material from the Foreign Office archives is utilized.

697. Lawrence, T.E. *Revolt in the Desert*. New York: George H. Doran
     Co., 1927. 335 pp.

     Lawrence's first account of his part in the Arab revolt was
     stolen in the Reading train station and never recovered. He
     then rewrote from memory another account and privately published
     eight copies. This is an abridgement of that personal account.

698. ————. *Seven Pillars of Wisdom: A Triumph*. Garden City, N.Y.:
     Doubleday, Doran & Co., 1936. 672 pp.

     This literary *tour de force* served to reinforce the Lawrence
     legend.

699. Lettow-Vorbeck, Paul Emil von. *East African Campaigns*. New
     York: Speller, 1957. 303 pp.

     John Gunther is the author of the Foreword.

700. ————. *My Reminiscences of East Africa*. London: Hurst &
     Blackett, 1920. 335 pp.

     Lettow-Vorbeck conducted a classic campaign of guerilla war-
     fare against superior Allied forces in East Africa. Against
     all odds, he held out until November 25, 1918, some two weeks
     after the Armistice. His accounts represent the best German
     source of the war in German East Africa. Twenty-two maps and
     sketch maps and thirteen drawings by Lettow-Vorbeck's adjutant
     are included.

701. Liddell Hart, B.H. *"T.E. Lawrence": In Arabia and After*. Lon-
     don: J. Cape, 1934. 454 pp.

     This is an important source on both Lawrence and the tactics
     of the Arabs. Nine maps are included.

702. Liman von Sanders, Otto Viktor Earl. *Five Years in Turkey*.
     Annapolis, Md.: United States Naval Institute, 1927. 326 pp.

     This is an excellent source for both German assistance to
     Turkey and the state of that country's armed forces during the
     Great War. Liman von Sanders, a German cavalryman who had
     fought in the Gallipoli Peninsula, succeeded Falkenhayn as
     commander of a large Turkish force in Palestine in 1918. He
     was accorded the Turkish rank of marshal.

703. Mack, John E. *A Prince of Our Disorder: The Life of T.E. Law-
     rence*. New York: Little, Brown, 1976. 561 pp.

     Well written, this is a solid historical and psychological
     examination of Lawrence's controversial life. An extensive
     bibliography is included.

704. MacMunn, Lieut.-Gen. Sir George, and Falls, Captain Cyril. *Of-
     ficial History of First World War, 1914-1918: Egypt and Pal-
     estine*. London: H.M. Stationery Office, 1928-1930. 2 vols.

     Vol. 1 covers the history of the Egyptian Expeditionary Force
     from August 1914 to June 1917. Vol. 2 examines the capture of

Jerusalem and "Bull" Allenby's spectacular victory over the Turks in September-October 1918.

705. Miller, Charles. *Battle for Bundu: The First World War in East Africa.* New York: Macmillan Publishing Co., 1974. 353 pp.

This is a fast-moving account of Major-General Paul von Lettow-Vorbeck's brilliant campaign against the Allies in East Africa. This book was written for a popular audience and the research is based on printed sources.

706. Moberly, Brig.-Gen. F.J. *Official History of First World War 1914-1918: Mesopotamia.* London: H.M. Stationery Office, 1923-1927. 4 vols.

This is the most comprehensive account of the British effort in the Mesopotamian theater, a campaign which ultimately involved over 500,000 men, most of whom were Indian soldiers.

707. ────. *Official History of First World War: Togoland and the Cameroons, 1914-1916.* London: H.M. Stationery Office, 1931. 469 pp.

This official history provides a solid treatment of one of the war's "sideshows." It was compiled by arrangement with the British Colonial Office.

708. Townshend, Sir C.V.F. *My Campaign in Mesopotamia.* London: T. Butterworth, 1920. 400 pp.

This is the personal account of the controversial British general who was forced to surrender his army at Kut-el-Amara to the Turks in 1916.

709. Wavell, General Sir Archibald. *Allenby; A Study in Greatness: The Biography of Field-Marshal Viscount Allenby of Megiddo and Felixstowe, G.C.B., G.C.M.G.* Cited above as item 297.

2. War in the Air

a. General Sources

710. Bright, Charles D. "Air Power in World War I: Sideshow or Decisive Factor." *Aerospace Hist.* 18 (June 1971): 58-62.

The author argues that airpower at the very least "was a decisive factor in creating and maintaining the stalemate which was characteristic of the Great War." See also the more thorough study by Cooper (item 364 above).

711. Brown, Charles R. "The Development of Fleet Aviation During the World War." *U.S. Naval Inst., Proc.* 64 (September 1938): 1297-303.

This article emphasizes the British experience in fleet aviation.

712. Clark, Alan. *Aces High: The War in the Air over the Western Front 1914-1918.* New York: Ballantine Books, 1974. 216 pp.

     This is a useful and competent survey of the men and their machines who fought in the skies over the western front. Richthofen, Guynemer, Mannock, and Rickenbacker are some of the aces featured. There is a chapter on the Lafayette Escadrille. Over one hundred illustrations and some useful appendices are included.

713. Cooke, David C. *Sky Battle, 1914-1918: The Story of Aviation in World War I.* New York: W.W. Norton & Co., 1970. 304 pp.

     This richly illustrated work is an example of good popular history.

714. Cuneo, John R. *Winged Mars,* vol. 2: *The Air Weapon, 1914-1916.* Harrisburg, Pa.: Military Service Publishing Co., 1947. 503 pp.

     This is a competent and thorough treatment of the role and significance of air power during the first half of the war. The many maps and charts are excellent and there is an extensive bibliography.

715. Norman, Aaron. *The Great War: The Men, the Planes, the Saga of Military Aviation, 1914-1918.* New York: Macmillan Co., 1968. 558 pp.

     This is a comprehensive history which destroys some of the myths of World War I aviation. The U.S. air role is not slighted in this well-illustrated work, which has documentation and a bibliography.

716. Reynolds, Quentin. *They Fought for the Sky: The Dramatic Story of the First War in the Air.* New York: Rinehart & Co., 1957. 304 pp.

     This is a dramatic account of the war in the air written for the general public. There is a bibliography but no documentation.

717. Toliver, Raymond F., and Constable, Trevor J. *Fighter Aces.* New York: Macmillan Co., 1965. 354 pp.

     This work includes a brief and not very satisfactory chapter on American aces of World War I. A list of all the American aces can be found at the end of this volume.

718. Whitehouse, Arch. *Heroes and Legends of World War I.* Garden City, N.Y.: Doubleday & Co., 1964. 368 pp.

     This is a popular and richly illustrated history which focuses on the great events and legends of the Great War. It is written for the layman rather than the scholar.

719. ————. *The Years of the Sky Kings.* Garden City, N.Y.: Doubleday & Co., 1959. 336 pp.

This is a gripping account of the air war by a pilot who
dueled with German aviators in 1917-1918. It includes an interesting glossary of the popular terms used by World War I
pilots. Chapter 6 concerns the U.S. part in the air war.

720. ————. "The Years of the Yammering Guns." *Aerospace Hist.* 15
      (Spring 1968): 12-15.

      Whitehouse examines the reasons for the sudden interest by
      the American public in the late 1920s in World War I aviators.

b. American Air Role

721. Bolling, Maj. R.C. "A Lesson in Timing." *Air Power Hist.* 7
      (October 1960): 222-32.

      The 1917 report of the aeronautical commission is published
      in full. This report by Bolling is interesting for its contem-
      porary view of the problems that must be dealt with in the
      development of an American air arm.

722. Craven, Wesley Frank, and Cate, James Lea. *The Army Air Forces
      in World War II.* Chicago: The University of Chicago Press,
      1948. Vol. 1. 788 pp.

      There is a brief but superior survey of the American Air
      Service in the Great War in this authoritative official history.

723. Edwards, W. Atlee. "The U.S. Naval Air Force in Action, 1917-
      1918." *U.S. Naval Inst., Proc.* 48 (November 1922): 1863-82.

      This is a valuable account by a naval officer of the combat
      role of the U.S. Naval Air Force.

724. Felice, Maj. Carmen P. "The Men and the Machines. Part V,
      Air Operations in World War I." *Air Power Hist.* 5 (January
      1958): 37-52.

      A short biography of Gorrell can be found in this survey which
      concentrates on U.S. air operations.

725. Frank, Sam H. "American Air Service Observation in World War I."
      Doctoral dissertation, University of Florida, 1961. 496 pp.

      Frank focuses on observation aviation of the American Air
      Service, emphasizing its role in the development of American
      air power.

726. Frey, Royal D. "Setting the Record Straight: The First of Many
      American Air-to-Air Victories." *Aerospace Hist.* 21 (Fall
      1974): 156-59.

      Lieutenant Stephen Thompson is given credit for being the
      first American to destroy an enemy plane while wearing the
      uniform of his country.

727. Gorrell, Edgar S., comp. "History of the U.S. Army Air Services."
      Unpublished manuscript in National Archives. 286 vols. (58
      microfilm rolls).

Often referred to as the "Gorrell Histories," this unpublished
typescript provides an exhaustive history of the American Air
Service in World War I. It includes unit histories, statistics,
combat reports, pictures, and other materials. Gorrell was a
colonel in the air service. There was little or no organization
until the National Archives prepared a thorough guide to this
important collection in 1975. See also the first volume of
Maurer's *The U.S. Air Service in World War I.*

*   Hartney, Harold E. *Up and At 'Em.* Cited above as item 415.

728.   Herbert, Craig. "Gasbags Preferred: The American Balloon Ser-
        vice in World War I." *Aerospace Hist.* 15 (Summer 1968):
        26, 39-51.

        The tables and photographs add considerably to the worth of
        this article.

729.   Hooper, Bruce C. "American Day Bombardment in World War I."
        Air Power Hist. 4 (April 1957): 87-97.

        The 94th Aero Squadron is followed from its formation at
        Kelly Field in 1917 to its participation in the St. Mihiel and
        Meuse-Argonne offensives.

730.   Hudson, James J. *Hostile Skies: A Combat History of the
        American Air Service in World War I.* Syracuse: Syracuse
        University Press, 1968. 338 pp.

        This scholarly work remains the single best treatment of the
        American Air Service in World War I. In addition to footnotes
        and a bibliography, there are illustrations, maps, and tables.
        Although the author examines the American squadrons that fought
        on the British front and the American aviators who served with
        the French and Italians, he omits the achievements of U.S. naval
        pilots.

731.   Johnson, Lieut.-Col. Edward C., and Cosmas, Graham A. *Marine
        Corps Aviation: The Early Years, 1912-1940.* Washington, D.C.:
        History and Museums Division, Headquarters, U.S. Marine Corps,
        1977. 106 pp.

        This official history includes bibliographical notes.

732.   La Guardia, Fiorello H. *The Making of an Insurgent: An Auto-
        biography, 1882-1919.* Philadelphia: J.B. Lippincott Co.,
        1948. 222 pp.

        La Guardia's colorful career included a period when he was a
        Congressman-officer in the American Air Service in Italy. In
        fact, he was largely responsible for American aviators serving
        with the Italians. His biography was dictated just before he
        died.

733.   Mason, Herbert Molloy, Jr. *The United States Air Force: A
        Turbulent History, 1907-1975.* New York: Mason/Carter, 1976.
        287 pp.

The first five chapters are pertinent to the air role of the United States in the Great War. Mitchell receives particular attention. The author was a marine in World War II, serving on both battleships and aircraft carriers.

734. Maurer, Maurer. "The 1st Aero Squadron--1913-1917." *Air Power Hist.* 4 (October 1957): 207-12.

This concise article describes the early years of America's first air tactical unit.

735. ———. "Flying with Fiorello: The U.S. Air Service in Italy, 1917-1918." *Air Power Hist.* 11 (October 1964): 113-18.

This well-documented study examines the wartime activities of the "Little Flower."

736. ———, ed. *The U.S. Air Service in World War I.* Washington, D.C.: Government Printing Office, 1978-1979. 4 vols.

This is an indispensable collection of documents with commentary on the part played by the United States in the air war. The result of extensive research, these volumes contain much hitherto unpublished material. Vol. 1, which includes "Gorrell's History," concerns the final report of the chief of Air Service, AEF, and a tactical history; Vol. 2 focuses on early concepts of military aviation; Vol. 3 contains documents relating to the St. Mihiel offensive; and Vol. 4 provides a postwar review, with emphasis on "lessons learned" and intelligence reports on the effects of bombing.

737. Sweetser, Arthur. *The American Air Service: A Record of Its Problems, Its Difficulties, Its Failures, and Its Achievements.* New York: D. Appleton & Co., 1919. 384 pp.

Although dated, Captain Sweetser's account is still an important source on the American Air Service. He labors in most respects to defend the record of the American Air Service against its critics in this well-illustrated volume. Although this study is often technical in nature, it was intended for the general reader.

738. Toulmin, H.A., Jr. *Air Service, American Expeditionary Force, 1918.* New York: D. Van Nostrand Co., 1926. 388 pp.

Toulmin, a lieutenant-colonel who served in the American Air Service as chief of the coordination staff, has written a worthwhile study of the growth and organization of the American Air Service. Many charts and tables are provided.

739. Turnbull, Archibald D., and Lord, Clifford L. *History of United States Naval Aviation.* London: Oxford University Press, 1949. 345 pp.

Although not an official history, this is an authoritative account by Turnbull, the deputy director of naval records and history, and Lord, the former head of the naval aviation history unit. The authors were given free access with no limitations to the Navy Department records.

740. Van Wyen, Adrian O. *Naval Aviation in World War I.* Washington, D.C.: Government Printing Office, 1969. 90 pp.

     This is a collection of articles published previously in *Naval Aviation News.*

741. Williams, Edwin L., Jr. "Legislative History of the Air Arm." *Mil. Affairs* 20 (Summer 1956): 81-93.

     The legislative enactments that made possible the development of an American air force are chronicled. Approximately half of this article concerns World War I.

c. Foreign Air Services (Including Lafayette Escadrille)

*   *An American for Lafayette: The Diaries of E.C.C. Genet, Lafayette Escadrille.* Cited above as item 395.

*   Biddle, Charles J. *The Way of the Eagle.* Cited above as item 398.

742. Flammer, Philip M. "Lufbery: Ace of the Lafayette Escadrille." *Air Power Hist.* 8 (January 1961): 13-22.

     The colorful, mysterious, and varied life of Gervais Raoul Lufbery is detailed in this documented article.

743. ———. "The Myth of the Lafayette Escadrille." *Aerospace Hist.* 22 (March 1975): 23-28.

     The author examines some of the reasons for the many distortions about the famed Lafayette Escadrille.

744. ———. *The Vivid Air: The Lafayette Escadrille.* Athens: University of Georgia Press, 1981. 249 pp.

     This work by a historian and former Air Force officer is the best study of the American volunteer unit that fought with the French. Many interviews were utilized and there is an excellent annotated bibliography. See also Flammer's 1963 Yale dissertation, "Primus Inter Pares: A History of Lafayette Escadrille."

745. Hall, Captain James N., and Nordhoff, Lieutenant Charles B. *The Lafayette Flying Corps.* Boston: Houghton Mifflin Co., 1920. 2 vols.

     This is the authorized history of the Lafayette Escadrille.

746. Hennessy, Juliette A. "The Lafayette Escadrille: Past and Present." *Air Power Hist.* 4 (July 1957): 150-61.

     This article carries the history of the 94th Squadron up to 1955.

747. Longacre, Edward G. "The Lafayette Escadrille." *Amer. Hist. Ill.* 17 (September 1982): 16-27.

     This is an entertaining retelling of the exploits of the Lafayette Escadrille, which Longacre views as a "living symbol of American idealism."

748. Mason, Herbert Molloy, Jr. *The Lafayette Escadrille*. New York: Random House, 1964. 340 pp.

The author's extensive research includes a tour in the air and on the land of the western front. The result is a popular history that reads quite well. There is a brief essay on the sources used.

749. Morrow, John H., Jr. *German Air Power in World War I*. Lincoln: University of Nebraska Press, 1982. 267 pp.

This is not a history of the German war in the air. Rather this scholarly monograph focuses on German aircraft production.

750. Neumann, Georg Paul. *The German Air Force in the Great War*. London: Hodder & Stoughton, 1921. 297 pp.

This is a translation of the German history of the German air force by a German officer. It was published in German in 1920.

751. Raleigh, Walter, and Jones, H.A. *Official History of First World War, 1914-1918: The War in the Air*. Oxford: Clarendon Press, 1922-1937. 6 vols.

This history is full of important information, but it is really not independent history. Its principal author, Jones, is an unbalanced advocate for an independent air force. Raleigh, a university professor, was the author of the first volume. Following his death, his pen passed to another professor, D.G. Hogarth, but he, too, died. The last five volumes are the work of Jones. Vol. 1, which contains a summary of the history of aviation, was reissued in 1939.

752. Robinson, Douglas H. *The Zeppelin in Combat: A History of the German Naval Airship Division, 1912-1918*. London: G.T. Foulis & Co., 1962. 417 pp.

This superior treatment of the development and use of the German rigid airship utilizes German and British primary sources.

753. Whitehouse, Arch. *Legion of the Lafayette*. Garden City, N.Y.: Doubleday & Co., 1962. 338 pp.

This is a most readable and very personal examination of the American volunteers who served with the Lafayette Escadrille. A short bibliography is included.

754. Woodward, David R. "Zeppelins over London." *Brit. Hist. Ill.* 2 (June 1975): 40-51.

This illustrated article provides a general treatment of the German bombing of London with Zeppelins.

3. Naval Power and World War I

a. Background

755. Braisted, William Reynolds. *The United States Navy in the
      Pacific, 1909-1922.* Austin: University of Texas Press, 1971.
      741 pp.

      This massive work is a study of naval policy rather than naval
      operations in the Pacific. Braisted demonstrates that nonmili-
      tary factors often determined naval policy. American, Japanese,
      and some British sources were consulted. There is a twenty-two-
      page bibliography.

756. Challener, Richard D. *Admirals, Generals and American Foreign
      Policy, 1898-1914.* Princeton: Princeton University Press,
      1973. 433 pp.

      The influence of the military, especially the navy, on American
      policy in Asia and Latin America is explored in this monograph,
      which is solidly based on archival research.

757. Clinard, Outten J. *Japan's Influence on American Naval Power,
      1897-1917.* Berkeley: University of California Press, 1947.
      235 pp.

      This is a pioneering study of American naval policy in the
      Pacific. The basic naval archival sources, however, were not
      consulted.

758. Davis, George T. *A Navy Second to None: The Development of
      Modern American Naval Policy.* New York: Harcourt, Brace &
      Howe, 1940. 508 pp.

      This work examines the fluctuations of American public opinion
      toward the navy, especially in regard to naval appropriations.

759. Dingman, Roger. *Power in the Pacific: The Origins of Naval Arms
      Limitation, 1914-1922.* Chicago: University of Chicago Press,
      1976. 318 pp.

      Dingman presents a fresh interpretation of American, British,
      and Japanese naval politics based on multi-archival research.
      He focuses on the reasons why naval limitations replaced the
      tremendous naval expansion of the prewar era. A strength of
      this volume is that it shows the connection between domestic
      politics and foreign policy.

760. Halpern, Paul G. *The Mediterranean Naval Situation, 1908-1914.*
      Cambridge: Harvard University Press, 1971. 415 pp.

      The naval situation in the Mediterranean just prior to World
      War I is given comprehensive treatment in this monograph which
      is based on multi-archival research. Each great naval power
      receives its own chapter. The last chapter carries the story
      into the first weeks of the war in the Mediterranean.

761. Healy, David. *Gunboat Diplomacy in the Wilson Era: The U.S.*

Navy in Haiti, 1915-1916. Madison: University of Wisconsin Press, 1976. 268 pp.

The author of this well-researched monograph contends that American policy in the Caribbean was shaped by the army and navy. The focus is on naval officers in Haiti rather than on policymakers in Washington. But, then, Healy's point is that American policy largely originated in Haiti rather than in the White House or State Department.

762. Herwig, Holger H. *"Luxury Fleet": The Imperial German Navy 1888-1918*. London: Allen & Unwin, 1980. 314 pp.

This is an important revisionist examination of the German navy, including an excellent treatment of its personnel. Naval operations during the war are not treated in depth. There are many excellent photographs.

763. Livermore, S.W. "The American Navy as a Factor in World Politics, 1903-1913." *AHR* 63 (July 1958): 863-79.

The U.S. Navy with its tilt toward the Entente powers is shown to have moved the United States away from isolation and into international politics.

764. Lumby, E.W.R., ed. *Policy and Operations in the Mediterranean, 1912-1914*. London: Publications of the Navy Records Society, 1970. 481 pp.

This documentary work focuses on the British response to the naval situation in the Mediterranean during a three-year period. The papers of the Cabinet, Foreign Office, and Admiralty make up the bulk of the collection.

765. Mitchell, Donald W. *History of the Modern American Navy, from 1883 Through Pearl Harbor*. New York: Alfred A. Knopf, 1946. 334 pp.

This expanded doctoral dissertation is a comprehensive and detailed history of the U.S. Navy from 1883 to 1941. It ranges from ship construction to policy to diplomacy.

766. Rappaport, Armin. *The Navy League of the United States*. Detroit: Wayne State University Press, 1962. 271 pp.

This well-researched study of the Navy League traces the history of that pro-navy lobbying group to 1952. Prior to World War I, the Navy League worked hard to promote a strong navy. With the advent of war, it pushed even harder and did contribute to the passage of the Naval Act of 1916. The author disagrees with the assertion that the Navy League was the mouthpiece for the munitions makers.

767. Sprout, Harold and Margaret. *The Rise of American Naval Power, 1776-1918*. Princeton: Princeton University Press, 1939. 398 pp.

This volume remains the best introduction to the role of the American navy in World War I. The authors correctly point out

that the naval bill of 1916 did not meet the needs of the
American navy. Little attention was paid to antisubmarine
warfare. Although naval authorities recognized that a German
invasion of the United States was out of the question, the
construction of capital ships was emphasized.

768.   ———. *Toward a New Order of Sea Power: American Naval Policy
        and the World Scene, 1918-1922.* Princeton: Princeton Univer-
        sity Press, 1946. 336 pp.

        The "changing role of sea power, especially American sea
        power," is the primary subject of this first-rate interpretative
        study. The 1946 edition differs in some significant ways from
        the original 1940 edition.

769.   Still, William N., Jr. *American Sea Power in the Old World:
        The United States Navy in European and Near Eastern Waters,
        1865-1917.* Westport, Conn.: Greenwood Press, 1980. 291 pp.

        This detailed treatment of the activities of the U.S. Navy in
        European and Near Eastern waters from the end of the Civil War
        until U.S. intervention in World War I illustrates how the navy
        was used as an adjunct of foreign policy.

b. *The War on the Sea*

770.   Bennett, Geoffrey. *Naval Battles of the First World War.* New
        York: Charles Scribner's Sons, 1969. 319 pp.

        This is a popular account of the Anglo-German confrontation
        on the high seas during the Great War. It does not compare in
        scope or scholarship with Marder's account.

771.   Breckel, H.F. "The Suicide Flotilla." *U.S. Naval Inst., Proc.*
        53 (June 1927): 661-70.

        The "Suicide Flotilla" was a fleet of sea-going yachts sent
        to patrol French waters. The author served on the yacht U.S.S.
        Corsair, which was owned by J.P. Morgan.

772.   Corbett, Sir Julian S., and Newbolt, Sir Henry. *Official His-
        tory of First World War, 1914-1918: Naval Operations.* London:
        Longmans, Green & Co., 1920-1931. 5 vols.

        Like many official histories, this naval history could not
        escape certain restraints placed upon it by the service depart-
        ment concerned. The first three volumes were written by Cor-
        bett, a successful barrister, who, despite having had no active
        naval experience, was a naval authority. When Corbett died in
        1922, Newbolt, a poet and well-known writer, completed the work.
        The revised edition of Vol. 3, published in 1940, should be
        used instead of the original 1923 edition for it contains new
        Jutland material on that controversial naval battle.

773.   Fitzsimons, Bernard, ed. *Warships and Sea Battles of World
        War I.* London: BPC Publishing, 1973. 160 pp.

        Richly illustrated and with a historical narrative written by
        numerous authorities, this is an excellent introduction to the

war at sea, 1914-1918. Not surprisingly, primary attention is given to submarine warfare and the Battle of Jutland. There is no index or bibliography, but most chapters have a section on suggestions for further reading.

774. Frothingham, Thomas G. *The Naval History of the World War.* Cambridge: Harvard University Press, 1924-1926. 3 vols.

Captain Frothingham's account of Jutland, among other topics, is controversial, and new information has dated some of his interpretations. The historical section of the U.S. Navy, it has been suggested, provided the author with some of his material and also perhaps influenced his interpretations. Still, Vol. 3, which examines America's role in the war, remains a standard work.

775. Gill, C.C. *Naval Power in the War (1914-1918).* New York: George H. Doran Co., 1919. 302 pp.

Gill, a U.S. naval officer, provides a clear and nontechnical account of some of the major naval battles of the war. Eleven of the twelve chapters were published in *Current History.* The appendices contain a section on America's part in the development of naval weapons and tactics.

776. Hoehling, Adolph A. *The Great War at Sea: A History of Naval Action, 1914-1918.* New York: Thomas Y. Crowell, 1965. 336 pp.

Although the author uses numerous primary sources, he wrote for the general public rather than for the naval authority. The maps contribute to the reader's understanding of the war at sea.

777. Hough, Richard. *The Great War at Sea.* New York: Oxford University Press, 1983. 353 pp.

This study focuses on the naval conflict between Germany and Great Britain. Hough argues that Britain's naval power ultimately decided the fate of the Central Powers. Eleven maps are provided.

778. Marder, Arthur J. *From the Dreadnought to Scapa Flow: The Royal Navy in the Fisher Era, 1914-1919.* New York: Oxford University Press, 1961-1970. 5 vols.

A model of balanced scholarship, this is an indispensable study, perhaps the best of its kind, of the Royal Navy during the World War I period. Fleet operations, leadership in the Admiralty, and the convoy system are some of the subjects given detailed treatment. This American naval historian's mastery of the sources is unrivalled.

779. Newbolt, Henry. *A Naval History of the War, 1914-1918.* London: Hodder & Stoughton, 1920. 350 pp.

This popular survey was written before Newbolt became the official naval historian. It of course cannot compare with his later naval history based on official records.

780. Perry, Lawrence. *Our Navy in the War.* New York: Charles
     Scribner's Sons, 1918. 279 pp.

     This is a general description of the naval role of the United
     States in the Great War.

781. Potter, Elmer B., ed. *Sea Power: A Naval History.* Englewood
     Cliffs, N.J.: Prentice-Hall, 1960. 932 pp.

     This broad survey places the U.S. Navy in the context of
     world naval history. An earlier edition (1955) was published
     under the title *The United States and World Sea Power.*

*   Sims, William Snowden, and Hendrick, Burton J. *Victory at Sea.*
     Cited above as item 286.

782. Taussig, Joseph K. "Destroyer Experiences During the Great
     War." *U.S. Naval Inst., Proc.* 48 (December 1922): 2015-40;
     49 (January-March 1923): 39-69, 221-48, 393-408.

     The activities of the destroyer division sent abroad to
     operate from Brest against enemy submarines receive a detailed
     examination by a U.S. Navy officer.

783. U.S. Congress. Senate. Committee on Naval Affairs. *Naval In-*
     vestigation: Hearings Before the Subcommittee on Naval Affairs.
     66th Cong., 2nd Sess. Washington, D.C.: Government Printing
     Office, 1920. 2 vols.

     These hearings into the lack of preparedness of the U.S. Navy
     prior to participation in World War I constitute an important
     source for the American navy during the Great War. Many docu-
     ments are included.

784. Wilson, Henry B. *An Account of Operations of the American Navy*
     in France During the War with Germany. N.p., 1919. 176 pp.

     Vice-Admiral Wilson commanded American naval forces in France
     from Brest, overseeing operations and the convoy system.

c. The War Beneath the Sea

785. Alden, Carroll S. "American Submarine Operations in the War."
     U.S. Naval Inst., Proc. 46 (June-July 1920): 811-50, 1013-48.

     A thorough accounting of U.S. submarine activity is given by
     a professor of English at the U.S. Naval Academy.

786. Cope, Harley F. "U.S. Submarines in the War Zone." *U.S. Naval*
     Inst., Proc. 56 (August 1930): 711-16.

     That the U.S. was not prepared for submarine warfare against
     Germany is abundantly demonstrated in this essay.

787. Fayle, Charles Ernest. *Official History of First World War,*
     1914-1918: Seaborne Trade. London: John Murray, 1920-1924.
     3 vols.

     These important volumes serve as a supplement to the volumes
     on naval operations by Corbett and Newbolt. Vol. 1 covers the

enemy's surface attacks during the first eight months of the
war. Vol. 2 covers the period from the opening of the submarine
campaign to the appointment of a shipping controller in December
1916. Vol. 3 covers the period of unrestricted submarine warfare.

788. Frost, Wesley. *German Submarine Warfare: A Study of Its
       Methods and Spirit, Including the Crime of the Lusitania.*
       New York: D. Appleton and Co., 1918. 243 pp.

       Frost, the U.S. consul at Queenstown, has recorded detailed
       testimony of survivors of over fifty torpedoed ships. This
       work indicates how German submarines shelled defenseless ships,
       including passenger liners, along the southern Irish coast.
       This work captures the contemporary view of the submarine.

789. Gibson, Richard H., and Prendergast, Maurice. *The German Sub-
       marine War, 1914-1918.* London: Constable & Co., 1931. 438
       pp.

       This is probably the most complete and authoritative British
       study of the U-boat menace in the Great War.

790. Grant, Robert M. "Aircraft Against U-Boats." *U.S. Naval Inst.,
       Proc.* 65 (June 1939): 824-28.

       The author examines attempts to utilize aircraft against
       U-boats, a tactic which was not tried until the later stages of
       the war. This article makes especially interesting reading
       in view of the extensive use of air planes against submarines
       during World War II.

791. ————. *U-Boats Destroyed: The Effect of Anti-Submarine Warfare
       1914-1918.* London: Putnam & Co., 1964. 172 pp.

       The convoy system and the employment of new and old weapons
       in greater quantity and often in new ways are given credit for
       the Allied success against undersea assault.

792. Gray, Edwyn A. *The Killing Time: The U-Boat War 1914-1918.*
       New York: Charles Scribner's Sons, 1972. 280 pp.

       This is a fast-moving narrative by a British author that
       makes extensive use of interviews with former U-boat captains.
       Several useful appendices are provided.

793. Herwig, Holger H., and Trask, David F. "The Failure of Germany's
       Undersea Offensive Against World Shipping, February 1917–
       October 1918." *Historian* 33 (August 1971): 611-36.

       Using material recently made available, the authors try to
       answer questions concerning unrestricted German U-boat warfare
       during the last stages of World War I.

794. Hurd, Archibald. *Official History of First World War, 1914-
       1918: Merchant Navy.* London: J. Murray, 1921-1929. 3 vols.

       This is the official history of the merchant navy. It pro-
       vides extensive treatment of the German campaign of underseas

assault. The sinking of the *Lusitania* is covered in the first
volume.

795. James, Henry J. *German Submarines in Yankee Waters: First
      World War*. New York: Gotham House, 1940. 208 pp.

      This is an account of the U.S. Navy's war against German
      submarines in American waters. There is no bibliography or
      footnotes, but it is apparent that considerable research went
      into the production of this volume.

796. Ludeberg, Philip K. "The German Naval Critique of the U-Boat
      Campaign, 1915-1918." *Mil. Affairs* 27 (Fall 1963): 105-18.

      This is a valuable survey of how German naval writers viewed
      their country's U-boat strategy during the Great War.

797. Merrill, James M. "Submarine Scare, 1918." *Mil. Affairs* 17
      (Winter 1953): 181-90.

      The U-boat campaign in American waters which began in the
      spring of 1918 demonstrated that the United States was now sub-
      ject to attack by a power thousands of miles away. Although
      this brought into serious question any future American isola-
      tionist policy, this lesson was not always remembered in the
      postwar period.

798. Millholland, Ray. *The Splinter Fleet at the Otranto Barrage*.
      Indianapolis: Bobbs-Merrill Co., 1936. 307 pp.

      This interesting book concerns the activities of an American
      subchaser, including the attack against Durazzo.

799. Nutting, William W. *The Cinderellas of the Fleet*. Jersey City,
      N.J.: Standard Motor Construction Company, 1920. 178 pp.

      This volume concerns American subchasers.

800. U.S. Navy Department. Office of Naval Records and Library,
      Historical Section. *German Submarine Activities on the At-
      lantic Coast of the United States and Canada*. Washington,
      D.C.: Government Printing Office, 1920. 163 pp.

      This is an important source for any study of the German cam-
      paign of undersea assault against Allied and American shipping.

801. Whitaker, Herman. *Hunting the German Shark: The American Navy
      in the Underseas War*. New York: Century Co., 1918. 310 pp.

      The writer, the author of several novels, spent nearly a
      year with the British Grand Fleet and a week aboard a U.S. sub-
      marine. His anecdotal narrative describes the experiences of
      chasing U-boats.

d. Blockade of the Central Powers

802. Arnold-Forster, Lieutenant Commander W.E. *The Economic Block-
      ade, 1914-1919, Before the Armistice--and After*. London:
      Oxford University Press, 1939. 40 pp.

Among the topics covered are visit and search of ships and controls over various commodities. In 1920, the author, the Admiralty's representative on various committees concerned with economic warfare, prepared a naval staff monograph, *The Economic Blockade, 1914-1919*, which was not declassified until 1942.

803. Belknap, Reginald R. *The Yankee Mining Squadron: or, Laying the North Sea Mine Barrage*. Annapolis, Md.: U.S. Naval Institute, 1920. 110 pp.

Captain Belknap commanded the Americans who were involved in the dangerous work of laying mines in the North Sea. The author has avoided technical language to inform the nonexpert of what has been called the "biggest 'mine planting stunt' in the world's history."

804. Bell, A.C. *A History of the Blockade of Germany and of the Countries Associated with Her in the Great War: Austria-Hungary, Bulgaria and Turkey, 1914-1918*. London: H.M. Stationery Office, 1937. 845 pp.

This official history, written by Bell, a member of the historical section of the Committee of Imperial Defence, was kept secret until 1961 when it was released for public sale. This volume is based on extensive research in official papers. Unfortunately there is little documentation to guide to researcher to the original source. There are, however, many long citations from unpublished materials.

805. Clapp, Edwin J. *Economic Aspects of the War: Neutrals Rights, Belligerent Claims, and American Commerce in the Years 1914-1915*. New Haven: Yale University Press, 1915. 340 pp.

This contemporary book focuses on the British attempt to limit with their orders in council trade between Germany and neutral states.

806. Consett, Rear-Admiral M.W.W.P. *The Triumph of Unarmed Forces (1914-1918): An Account of the Transactions by Which Germany During the Great War Was Able to Obtain Supplies Prior to Her Collapse Under the Pressure of Economic Forces*. London: Williams & Norgate, 1923. 344 pp.

Consett, the British naval attaché in Scandinavia during the war, gives an interesting account of how Britain bungled her economic warfare against Germany in Scandinavia. The author received the assistance of Captain O.H. Daniel.

807. Davis, H.W. Carless. *History of the Blockade, Emergency Departments*. 217 pp.

The preface is dated June 1, 1920, but this official history, a copy of which is deposited in the British Library, was not made available until the late 1950s. The author was a historian who served as the vice-chairman of the war trade intelligence department. The theme of this study is the organization of the blockade.

808. Farrar, Marjorie Milbank. "French Blockade Policy, 1917-1918:
      A Study in Economic Warfare." Doctoral dissertation, Stan-
      ford University, 1968. 445 pp.

      This dissertation, based primarily on unpublished private
      and official papers, focuses on the French role in attempting
      to isolate the enemy economically through diplomacy rather than
      through a maritime blockade.

809. Guichard, Lieutenant Louis. *The Naval Blockade, 1914-1918*.
      London: Philip Allan, 1930. 324 pp.

      This is the English translation of an important French study
      written by a member of the historical section of the French
      ministry of marine.

810. Riste, Olav. *The Neutral Ally: Norway's Relations with Belli-
      gerent Powers in the First World War*. Oslo: Universitets-
      forlaget, 1965. 295 pp.

      Riste traces Norway's ultimately unsuccessful attempt to be
      genuinely neutral in a war between Germany and Britain. The
      British blockade undermined the Norwegian economy and forced
      Norway to become Britain's "neutral ally" during the last
      years of the war. Extensive use has been made of unpublished
      German and Norwegian sources.

811. Savage, Carlton. *Policy of the United States Toward Maritime
      Commerce in War*. Washington, D.C.: Government Printing
      Office, 1934-1936. 2 vols.

      The second volume covers the 1914-1918 period.

812. Siney, Marion Celestria. *The Allied Blockade of Germany, 1914-
      1916*. Ann Arbor: University of Michigan Press, 1957. 339 pp.

      The legal, political, and diplomatic aspects of the blockade
      (or more accurately economic warfare) against Germany are
      carefully examined in this excellent monograph. This volume
      is solidly based on archival research in the United States,
      Great Britain, the Netherlands, and the Scandinavian countries.
      New light is shed on the negotiations with the border neutrals.

813. ————. "British Negotiations with American Meat Packers, 1915-
      1916: A Study of Belligerent Trade Controls." *Jour. Mod.
      Hist*. 23 (December 1951): 343-53.

      This article is based on the files of Henry Veeder, who was
      the counsel for Swift and Company.

814. ————. "British Official Histories of the Blockade of the
      Central Powers During the First World War." *AHR* 68 (January
      1963): 392-401.

      This article discusses the official histories by Bell, Davis,
      and Arnold-Forster which were classified between the wars.

815. U.S. Navy Department. Office of Naval Records and Library,
      Historical Section. *The Northern Barrage and Other Mining*

Activities. Washington, D.C.: Government Printing Office, 1920. 146 pp.

The role of the American mining force in mining the strait between Scotland and Norway receives particular attention in this official history.

816. Vandenbosch, Amry. *The Neutrality of the Netherlands During the World War*. Grand Rapids, Mich.: William B. Eerdmans, 1927. 349 pp.

This scholarly work by a political scientist delineates the efforts of the Dutch government to protect its neutral rights. Many official Dutch documents are utilized.

e. Other Specific Subjects

817. Andrade, Ernest. "The Battle Cruiser in the United States Navy." *Mil. Affairs* 45 (February 1980): 18-22.

This article examines the debate during the Great War over the construction of U.S. battle cruisers.

818. Beers, Henry P. "The Development of the Office of the Chief of Naval Operations, Part II and III." *Mil. Affairs* 10 (Fall 1946): 10-38; 11 (Summer 1947): 88-99.

Parts II and III of Beers's study cover the period of World War I.

819. DeNovo, John A. "Petroleum and the United States Navy before World War I." *MVHR* 41 (March 1955): 641-56.

The decision to convert the U.S. Navy from coal fuel to oil is elucidated in this article.

820. Dyer, George P. "A Navy Supply Department in War Time." *U.S. Naval Inst., Proc.* 46 (March 1920): 379-92.

The author was the commander of the supply corps, U.S. Navy.

821. Horn, Daniel. *The German Naval Mutinies of World War I*. New Brunswick, N.J.: Rutgers University Press, 1969. 346 pp.

The origins of the mutiny in the German navy which served as a spark for the German Revolution, 1918-1919, have been the subject of considerable controversy. Horn's thorough research reveals that the mutinous sailors were not motivated by any desire to create a communist state in Germany. Long-standing grievances of the sailors against their officers and opposition to a suicide mission by the German navy against the British were the factors largely responsible for the revolt.

822. Melhorn, Charles M. *Two-Block Fox: The Rise of the Aircraft Carrier, 1911-1929*. Annapolis, Md.: Naval Institute Press, 1974. 181 pp.

This volume examines the origins of aircraft carriers during the World War I era. The debate within the general board and in congressional hearings is carefully followed.

823. Saul, Norman E. *Sailors in Revolt: The Russian Baltic Fleet in 1917.* Lawrence: The Regents Press of Kansas, 1978. 312 pp.

This volume centers on the growth of revolutionary sentiment among sailors of the Baltic Fleet and their role in the Russian Revolution. Like Horn's work on the German naval mutinies, this book is an excellent study of the relationship between war and revolution.

824. Sumrall, Robert F. "Ship Camouflage (WW I): Deceptive Art." *U.S. Naval Inst., Proc.* 97 (July 1971): 57-77.

Commentary accompanies this profusely illustrated pictorial. The compiler makes the point that fewer than one percent of the camouflaged ships were sunk by U-boats.

825. U.S. Navy Department Bureau of Engineering. *History of the Bureau of Engineering Navy Department During the World War.* Washington, D.C.: Government Printing Office, 1922. 176 pp.

This official source has an index and includes numerous photographs and tables.

4. U.S. Marines

826. Asprey, Robert B. *At Belleau Wood.* New York: Putnam, 1965. 375 pp.

Numerous interviews with participants are utilized in this detailed and solid history of the offensive of the 2nd Division at Belleau Wood. Excellent maps enable the reader to follow the action.

827. Edwards, Lieut.-Col. H.W. "Harbord and Lejeune: A Command Precedent." *Marine Corps Gazette* 37 (July 1953): 12-15.

The relationship of Harbord, who commanded the 4th Brigade (Marines), and Lejeune, who commanded the 2nd Division (Army), is discussed.

828. Gatlin, Albertus W., and Dyer, Walter A. *"With the Help of God and a Few Marines."* Garden City, N.Y.: Doubleday & Co., 1919. 425 pp.

Gatlin commanded the Sixth Regiment of marines and was wounded at Belleau Wood. This volume focuses on that battle and Château Thierry.

829. Hewitt, Captain Linda L. *Women Marines in World War I.* Washington, D.C.: History and Museums Division, Headquarters, U.S. Marine Corps, 1974. 80 pp.

This is the official history of the often overlooked part played by women marines in the Great War.

*   Lejeune, John A. *The Reminiscences of a Marine.* Cited above as item 247.

830. McClellan, Edwin N. "The Aisne-Marne Offensive." *Marine Corps
      Gazette* 6 (March-June 1921): 66-84, 188-232.

      In this two-part account, McClellan makes a good case for
      treating as a single battle the part played by the marines and
      other troops of the 2nd Division in the Aisne defensive and
      the Second Battle of the Marne. This study is illustrated and
      features fold-out maps.

831. ————. "American Marines in Siberia During the World War."
      Marine Corps Gazette 5 (June 1920): 173-81.

      This article describes the part played by U.S. Marines from
      the *Brooklyn* in Allied intervention.

832. ————. "The Fourth Brigade of Marines in the Training Areas
      and the Operations in the Verdun Sector." *Marine Corps
      Gazette* 5 (March 1920): 81-110.

      McClellan offers a detailed account of the activities of the
      Fourth Brigade from its days at the Gondrecourt training area
      to its dispatch to the Château-Thierry sector.

833. ————. "Operations of the Fourth Brigade of Marines in the
      Aisne Defensive." *Marine Corps Gazette* 5 (June 1920): 182-
      214.

      A blow-by-blow account of marine operations during the so-
      called Aisne defensive is given in this article.

834. ————. "The St. Mihiel Offensive." *Marine Corps Gazette* 6
      (December 1921): 375-77.

      This is a detailed account of the part played by the marines
      in the St. Mihiel offensive. A fold-out map and tables of
      marine casualties are included.

835. ————. *The United States Marine Corps in the World War*. Wash-
      ington, D.C.: Government Printing Office, 1920. 108 pp.

      This slim official history offers a good introduction to the
      rapid wartime expansion of the U.S. Marine Corps and its part
      in the war in Europe. Numerous statistical tables are included.

836. Millett, Allan R. *Semper Fidelis: The History of the United
      States Marine Corps*. New York: Macmillan Publishing Co.,
      1980. 782 pp.

      This solid work is one of the volumes in the "Macmillan Wars
      of the United States" series. Chapters 10 and 11 are pertinent
      to World War I. There is an excellent annotated bibliography.

837. Moskin, J. Robert. *The U.S. Marine Corps Story*. New York:
      McGraw-Hill Co., 1977. 807 pp.

      Based on considerable research, this fast-moving history pro-
      vides an excellent introduction for the general public to the
      U.S. Marine Corps. There is a good annotated bibliography.
      This volume, however, is not as comprehensive as the recent
      study by Millett.

838. Shulimson, Jack. "The First to Fight: Marine Corps Expansion,
      1914-1918." *Prologue* 8 (Spring 1976): 5-16.

      The wartime expansion of the marines and its efforts to play
      a role on the European battlefields are described in this
      article.

*   Spaulding, Oliver L., and Wright, John W. *The Second Division,
      American Expeditionary Force in France: 1917-1918.* Cited
      above as item 563.

839. Suskind, Richard. *Do You Want to Live Forever?* New York:
      Bantam Books, 1964. 147 pp.

      This narrative succeeds in giving a succinct history of the
      exploits of the marines at Belleau Wood. An abridged edition
      with numerous illustrations was published by Macmillan in 1969
      under the title *The Battle of Belleau Wood: The Marines Stand
      Fast.*

*   Thomason, John W., Jr. *Fix Bayonets!* Cited above as item 438.

840. ————. "The Marine Brigade." *U.S. Naval Inst., Proc.* 54
      (November 1928): 963-68.

      Captain Thomason illustrates this account of the part played
      by the 4th Marine Brigade at Belleau Wood with his own drawings.

841. Wise, Frederic M., and Frost, Meigs O. *A Marine Tells It to
      You.* New York: J.H. Sears & Co., 1929. 366 pp.

      Colonel Wise related the adventures and heroism of the marines
      on the battlefields of Europe and elsewhere to Frost who then
      put Wise's words into writing.

V. HOME FRONT

A. GENERAL AND COMPARATIVE SOURCES

842. Chambers, Frank P. *The War Behind the War 1914-1918: A History of the Political and Civilian Fronts.* New York: Arno Press, 1972. 620 pp.

    Where can the World War I historian turn to find the ministers and their respective responsibilities in the numerous French wartime governments or a concise summary of Belgium under German occupation? The answer to this and many other questions concerning the war on the home front can be found in this comprehensive account, which succeeds admirably in the ambitious task of surveying the political, social, and economic conditions in the major belligerents. This is a reprint of the 1939 edition.

843. Churchill, Allen. *Over Here!: An Informal Re-Creation of the Home Front in World War I.* New York: Dodd, Mead & Co., 1968. 240 pp.

    This is a general, popular work on the American home front during the Great War. This volume is well written, but it is obviously based on secondary sources and adds nothing new to the historiography of the home front. The author does not include documentation.

844. Hale, Oron J. *The Great Illusion, 1900-1914.* New York: Harper & Row, 1971. 361 pp.

    This is a masterful synthesis of European politics, culture, and economics on the eve of war. Hale argues that war was not inevitable or predestined by conditions in Europe and that the period from 1900 to 1914 belongs more to the twentieth than to the nineteenth century.

845. Hawley, Ellis W. *The Great War and the Search for a Modern Order: A History of the American People and Their Institutions, 1917-1933.* New York: St. Martin's Press, 1979. 264 pp.

    This survey of the years 1917-1933 concludes that the theme of that period was the evolution of new managerial and bureaucratic institutions concerned with solving peacetime problems. The wartime experience proved to be the guide for the development of that evolution.

846. Jantzen, Steven. *Hooray for Peace. Hurrah for War. The United States During World War I.* New York: Alfred A. Knopf, 1971. 327 pp.

This is an entertaining history of the impact of World War I
on America. It contains extensive quotations, including many
of the songs of the day, and is illustrated. There is an annotated bibliography.

847. Kennedy, David M. *Over Here: The First World War and American
      Society*. New York: Oxford University Press, 1980. 404 pp.

      This is a wide-ranging, interpretative, committed, and well-
      written volume that treats American participation in World War I
      as a turning point in American history. The emphasis is on the
      home front, but Chapter 4 centers on the AEF's fight with the
      German army. Kennedy's research in both primary and secondary
      sources is impressive. This is an indispensable source for
      understanding the American wartime experience.

848. Lauzanne, Stéphane. *Great Men and Great Days*. New York: D.
      Appleton & Co., 1921. 262 pp.

      Lauzanne, the editor of *Le Matin* and a member of a French
      mission to the United States, has written sketches of some of
      the leading figures of the war, including House, Wilson, and
      Roosevelt. He also comments on the mood of America in 1918.

*   McMaster, John Bach. *The United States in the World War*.
      Cited above as item 181.

849. Paxson, Frederic L. *American Democracy and the World War*.
      Boston: Houghton-Mifflin Co., 1936-1939. 2 vols.

      This well-written narrative of the World War I period
      focuses attention on Wilson's policies at home and abroad.
      Paxson treats the major questions of intervention with a favor-
      able view of the Wilson administration. Although this work
      does not contain footnotes or a bibliography, it remains a
      classic.

850. Roth, Jack J., ed. *World War I: A Turning Point in Modern His-
      tory: Essays on the Significance of the War*. New York: Al-
      fred A. Knopf, 1967. 137 pp.

      This is a valuable collection of lectures by Craig, Friedrich,
      Kohn, and Hirschfield which were delivered at Roosevelt Univer-
      sity. Craig examines how total war influenced diplomacy and
      the conduct of war; Friedrich discusses the connection, or lack
      thereof, between war and totalitarianism; Kohn looks at the
      cultural environment; and Hirschfield analyzes the impact of
      the war on the American home front.

851. Slosson, Preston William. *The Great Crusade and After 1914-
      1928*. New York: Macmillan Co., 1931. 486 pp.

      In a well-written volume, Slosson examines the impact of
      World War I, including the great moral decline which resulted
      from the war. Moreover, he emphasizes how temporary the eco-
      nomic prosperity was. Slosson concludes that the United States
      learned much about organization from the experiences of war.

852. Soule, George. *Prosperity Decade: From War to Depression, 1917-1929*. New York: Rinehart & Co., 1947. 365 pp.

   This is a readable survey.

853. Trask, David F., ed. *World War I at Home: Readings on American Life, 1914-1920*. New York: John Wiley & Sons, 1970. 212 pp.

   This useful collection of forty-four articles from magazines such as the *Independent* and the *New Republic* treats certain aspects of the home front. The articles are organized into three sections: neutrality, 1914-1917; belligerency, 1917-1918; and peacemaking, 1919-1920.

854. Williams, John. *The Other Battleground. The Home Fronts: Britain, France, and Germany, 1914-1918*. London: Constable & Co., 1972. 326 pp.

   This is a well-written, interesting, but at times impressionistic attempt at comparative history of the home fronts of three belligerents. It does not, however, supplant the standard work by Chambers on the war behind the front lines.

B. CIVILIAN LEADERSHIP
(INCLUDING MANUSCRIPT COLLECTIONS)

1. U.S.

Baker, Newton

855. Baker, Newton D. Collection in the Division of Manuscripts, Library of Congress.

   This collection includes Baker's correspondence when he was secretary of war. Palmer made extensive use of these papers when he prepared his biography of Baker. Some of the papers of Ralph Hayes, Baker's secretary, are included in this collection.

856. ———. "Invisible Armor." *Survey*, 17 November 1917, pp. 159-60.

   In this speech before a national conference on war-camp community recreation, the secretary of war argues that soldiers going to war must have an "invisible armor" of positive and clean social habits.

857. Beaver, Daniel R. *Newton D. Baker and the American War Effort, 1917-1919*. Lincoln: University of Nebraska Press, 1966. 273 pp.

   This is a well-researched, stimulating study of Woodrow Wilson's World War I secretary of war. Written from Baker's perspective, this volume examines the major controversies of the War Department as well as Baker's contributions to the war

effort. A good essay on sources and an outstanding bibliography add to the value of this study. See also Beaver's 1962
Northwestern University doctoral dissertation.

858. Cramer, C.H. *Newton D. Baker: A Biography.* Cleveland, Ohio:
World Publishing Co., 1961. 310 pp.

This is a fascinating but somewhat impressionistic biography
of Baker.

859. Hayes, Ralph A. *Secretary Baker at the Front.* New York:
Century, 1918. 185 pp.

This volume, written by the war secretary's secretary, tells
of Baker's experiences during a visit to the front.

860. Palmer, Frederick. *Newton D. Baker: America at War.* New York:
Dodd, Mead & Co., 1931. 2 vols.

This is a running narrative of Baker's role as secretary of
war. Based on Baker's papers, this work shows how a pacifist
developed into a capable war leader who helped the mobilization
process and stood solidly behind General Pershing.

Baker, Ray Stannard

861. Baker, Ray Stannard. Collection in the Division of Manuscripts,
Library of Congress.

This collection includes the valuable interviews which Baker
conducted with intimates of the president when he prepared his
biography of Wilson.

Baruch

862. Baruch, Bernard Mannes. Collection in Princeton University
Library.

This rich collection contains Baruch's papers from 1905 to
1965. Valuable information may be gleaned from his work on
the War Industries Board, his position as adviser at Versailles,
his role on the Council of National Defense, and his role in
the National Industrial Conference.

863. ———. *American Industry in the War: A Report of the War Industries Board.* New York: Prentice-Hall, 1941. 498 pp.

This report on the activities of the War Industries Board was
ghostwritten for Baruch, and it focuses attention on the accom-
plishments of the board rather than on the personalities involved. The report represents an important synthesis of how
the board worked during World War I. Of course it makes the
person who chaired the board look good.

864. Coit, Margaret L. *Mr. Baruch.* Boston: Houghton Mifflin, 1957.
784 pp.

Based upon solid documentary evidence, including the Baruch
Papers, this sympathetic biography of Baruch carries him into
the period after World War II. It focuses much attention on

Baruch's activities during World War I. Coit sees Baruch as
the man who had the best understanding of the economy and who
as head of the War Industries Board mobilized the American
economy during World War I.

865. Schwarz, Jordan A. *The Speculator: Bernard M. Baruch in Washington, 1917-1965.* Chapel Hill: The University of North
Carolina Press, 1981. 679 pp.

This is the standard biography of Bernard M. Baruch. This
well-researched, analytical work focuses attention on Baruch's
relationship with Woodrow Wilson and his successful role as
head of the War Industries Board during World War I. Baruch
was converted to Wilson's practical idealism and remained a
Wilson spokesman for the rest of his career.

Beck

866. Keller, Morton. *In Defense of Yesterday: James M. Beck and
the Politics of Conservatism, 1861-1936.* New York: Coward,
McCann, 1958. 320 pp.

This well-written work deals with a conservative corporate
lawyer who held a number of important high-level government
positions. It presents a good example of right-wing thought
in the period from 1900 to 1936.

Beveridge

867. Beveridge, Albert J. *What Is Back of the War.* Indianapolis:
Bobbs-Merrill Co., 1915. 430 pp.

Senator Albert Beveridge's opposition to U.S. intervention
was strengthened by his visit to the western front.

Borah

868. Borah, William Edgar. Collection in the Division of Manuscripts, Library of Congress.

Borah's papers from 1907 to 1940 represent an extensive collection on his senatorial career. A few other papers can be
found at the Idaho State Historical Society.

Brandeis

869. Mason, Alpheus Thomas. *Brandeis: Lawyer and Judge in the
Modern State.* Princeton: Princeton University Press, 1933.
203 pp.

Well written and well researched, this study examines the
public welfare activities, ideology, and constitutional principles of Brandeis.

870. Urofsky, Melvin I. *Louis D. Brandeis and the Progressive
Tradition.* Boston: Little, Brown & Co., 1981. 183 pp.

This well-written general biography of Brandeis traces the
career of one of the foremost legal minds of the twentieth
century. Urofsky treats the Wilson-Brandeis relationship and
Brandeis's role in the "New Freedom" philosophy, his appointment

to the Supreme Court and his role in World War I. Wilson frequently turned to Brandeis for advice during the war, and
Urofsky concludes that Brandeis played a major role in the
appointments of Hoover and Baruch.

Creel

871. Creel, George. Collection in the Division of Manuscripts,
     Library of Congress.

     This collection contains some correspondence, scrapbooks, and
     bound volumes of writings.

872. ————. *How We Advertised America.* New York: Harper & Brothers,
     1920. 467 pp.

     This book details the activities of the Committee on Public
     Information during World War I. Written by the committee's
     chairman, this work shows how the committee attempted to
     mobilize world opinion in terms of U.S. participation in the
     war. The author treats: censorship, relations with Congress,
     news division, four-minute men, films, war expositions, speaking,
     advertising, women's war work, world news service, enemy censor-
     ship, work in various countries, and demobilization. This book
     is essential to an understanding of the war's propaganda effort.

873. ————. "Public Opinion in War Time." *Ann. Am. Ac. of Pol. Sci.
     and Soc. Sci.* 78 (July 1918): 185-91.

     The chairman of the Committee on Public Information points
     out that the mobilization of public opinion is part of any mili-
     tary program. He explains in general how the committee is
     functioning; he emphasizes that his job is to sell America.

874. ————. *The War, the World and Wilson.* New York: Harper &
     Brothers, 1920. 366 pp.

     Creel presents a one-sided lawyer's brief in support of the
     ratification of the Treaty of Versailles.

Crowell

875. Crowell, Benedict. Collection in Western Reserve University
     Library.

     This collection includes correspondence, papers, and printed
     matter relating to Crowell's activities as assistant secretary
     of war and director of munitions. These papers shed light on
     war mobilization.

*   ————, and Wilson, Robert Forrest. *How America Went to War.*
     Cited above as item 545.

Daniels

876. Daniels, Josephus. Collection in the Division of Manuscripts,
     Library of Congress.

     The researcher has a monumental task in separating the wheat
     from the chaff in the papers of the frequently controversial

secretary of the navy. His voluminous correspondence and his diary, which has been superbly edited by E. David Cronon, constitute the most important part of the partially indexed collection.

877. ————. *The Wilson Era*. Chapel Hill: The University of North Carolina Press, 1944-1946. 2 vols.

The important memoirs of Daniels cover the Wilson period. Daniels compares Bryan favorably to Lansing as secretary of state. Other personal evaluations of the leading figures of the day are interesting and valuable.

878. Cronon, E. David, ed. *The Cabinet Diaries of Josephus Daniels, 1913-1921*. Lincoln: University of Nebraska Press, 1963. 648 pp.

This is an important and useful account of the Wilson years through the eyes of the secretary of the navy. The diary sheds light on Wilson's cabinet meetings as well as the relationship between Daniels and his abrasive assistant secretary, Franklin D. Roosevelt.

Frankfurter

879. Frankfurter, Felix. Collection in Harvard University Law School Library.

Frankfurter's personal papers, memoranda, speeches, and other items can be found in this important collection.

Gompers

880. Gompers, Samuel. Collection in New York Public Library.

This collection contains much documentation on Gompers's career during World War I.

881. ————. *Seventy Years of Life and Labor*. New York: Augustus M. Kelley, 1967. 2 vols.

This memoir of the founder of the American Federation of Labor includes several chapters dealing with his role during World War I.

882. Grubbs, Frank L., Jr. *The Struggle for Labor Loyalty: Gompers, the A.F. of L. and the Pacifists, 1917-1920*. Durham, N.C.: Duke University Press, 1968. 172 pp.

This narrowly focused, well-researched book argues that Gompers and the American Federation of Labor worked to suppress radical opposition to the war. Gompers's American Alliance for Labor and Democracy, financed by the Creel Committee, was used to counter the more radical People's Council. The reader should take into account some basic errors when examining the book.

883. Mandel, Bernard. *Samuel Gompers: A Biography*. Yellow Springs, Ohio: Antioch Press, 1963. 566 pp.

This general biography of Gompers documents his role during World War I as he supported the restraint of civil liberties.

Hay

884. Herring, George C., Jr. "James Hay and the Preparedness Con-
      troversy, 1915-1916." *JSH* 30 (November 1964): 383-404.

      This article examines James Hay's attempt to get a prepared-
      ness measure through Congress at a time when public opinion
      opposed any preparedness. Hay claimed partial credit when a
      proposal to nationalize and upgrade the National Guard was
      passed.

Hoover

885. Hoover, Herbert Clark. Collection at Hoover Institution of
      War, Revolution and Peace, Stanford University.

      Hoover's papers on his World War I career are located here.

886. ————. *America's First Crusade*. New York: Charles Scribner's
      Sons, 1942. 81 pp.

      Hoover wrote his memoirs of the Great War in 1934-1935, in-
      tending that they be published following his death. Another
      world war and promptings from the *Saturday Evening Post* led
      him to publish his views on peacemaking in 1919, first in the
      Saturday Evening Post, and then later, in a more complete
      fashion, in this slim volume.

887. ————. *The Memoirs of Herbert Hoover: Years of Adventure,
      1874-1920*. New York: Macmillan Co., 1953. 496 pp.

      These memoirs are especially rich in revealing Hoover's World
      War I experiences.

888. ————. *The Ordeal of Woodrow Wilson*. New York: McGraw-Hill
      Book Co., 1958. 318 pp.

      This is an extremely important work because of Hoover's posi-
      tion and insight. Much of the study is devoted to Wilson and
      Versailles, including the failure of the treaty to be ratified.
      Hoover, loyal to Wilson, sees the president losing politically
      but winning a moral victory. This book is a must for those
      wanting to gain an understanding of the economic problems of
      the peace.

889. Burner, David. *Herbert Hoover: A Public Life*. New York: Alfred
      A. Knopf, 1979. 433 pp.

      This biography, aimed at the general and scholarly audience,
      deals with a very complex figure. Three chapters are devoted
      to Hoover's World War I activities in Belgium, his work as war
      food administrator, and his hunger-relief activities after the
      war.

890. Gelfand, Lawrence E., ed. *Herbert Hoover: The Great War and Its
      Aftermath, 1914-23*. Iowa City: University of Iowa Press,
      1979. 242 pp.

      This is a collection of papers presented at the Herbert Hoover
      Centennial Seminar in 1974. Papers range from "Herbert Hoover,

Launching the American Food Administration, 1917" to "Herbert Hoover and the Russian Revolution."

891. O'Brien, Francis William. *The Hoover-Wilson Wartime Correspondence, September 24, 1914 to November 11, 1918.* Ames: The Iowa State University Press, 1974. 297 pp.

Gleaned from four depositories, this correspondence reveals a good relationship between Hoover and Wilson. Evidence exists in these letters that Wilson sought Hoover's advice in foreign affairs. This volume is important to understanding the Hoover-Wilson relationship.

892. Vincent, Charles Paul. "The Post-World War I Blockade of Germany: An Aspect in the Tragedy of a Nation." Doctoral dissertation, University of Colorado, 1980. 300 pp.

This dissertation devotes considerable space to the activities of Hoover, the U.S. food administrator.

893. Willis, Edward F. *Herbert Hoover and the Russian Prisoners of World War I: A Study in Diplomacy and Relief, 1918-1919.* Stanford, Calif.: Stanford University Press, 1951. 67 pp.

This slim volume actually focuses on the negotiations concerning Russian prisoners in Germany rather than on Hoover.

894. Wilson, Joan Hoff. *Herbert Hoover: Forgotten Progressive.* Boston: Little, Brown & Co., 1975. 307 pp.

This biography synthesizes the career of Herbert Hoover. The author concludes that in foreign affairs Hoover emerged as a figure who opposed U.S. military interventions as a matter of routine policy.

Houston

895. Houston, David F. *Eight Years with Wilson's Cabinet: 1913 to 1920.* Garden City, N.Y.: Doubleday, Page & Co., 1926. 2 vols.

This memoir is an important and useful account of the Wilson administration through the eyes of the secretary of agriculture. It reveals his views on major events from his perspective.

Hughes

896. Perkins, Dexter. *Charles Evans Hughes and American Democratic Statesmanship.* Boston: Little, Brown & Co., 1956. 200 pp.

Hughes played a number of successful roles as a lawyer, governor, presidential candidate, secretary of state, and chief justice of the Supreme Court. Perkins, in an interpretative biography, sees his subject as a statesman. His chapters on the 1916 election and the fight over the League of Nations are useful to those interested in World War I.

Hurley

897. Hurley, Edward Nash. Collection in University of Notre Dame
      Archives.

      This brief collection concentrates on Hurley's work on the
      U.S. Shipping Board.

*   ————. *The Bridge to France.* Cited above as item 551.

Johnson

898. Johnson, Hiram W. Collection in Bancroft Library, University
      of California, Berkeley.

      The bulk of Johnson's official and personal papers are con-
      tained in this collection. Other papers can be found in other
      collections.

899. DeWitt, Howard A. "Hiram Johnson and World War I: A Progressive
      in Transition." *So. Cal. Quar.* 61 (Fall 1974): 295-305.

      This essay examines the impact of World War I on the foreign
      policy attitudes of Senator Hiram W. Johnson of California.
      Ultimately Johnson emerged as a strong isolationist who opposed
      Wilsonian internationalism.

Kitchen

900. Kitchen, Claude. Collection in Southern Historical Collection,
      University of North Carolina.

      This collection is rich in materials documenting Kitchen's
      role on the House Ways and Means Committee during World War I.

901. Arnett, Alex Mathews. *Claude Kitchen and the Wilson War Policies.*
      Boston: Little, Brown & Co., 1937. 341 pp.

      This volume examines the antiwar efforts of Representative
      Kitchen of North Carolina. Extensive use is made of the Kitchen
      papers.

LaFollette

902. LaFollette, Belle Case and Fola. *Robert M. LaFollette, June 14,
      1855-June 18, 1925.* New York: Macmillan Co., 1953. 2 vols.

      This sympathetic biography, based in large part on manuscript
      sources, is valuable despite the fact that it was coauthored by
      the wife and daughter of the subject. LaFollette opposed U.S.
      intervention in the war and voted against the Wilson declaration
      of war. Because of this stand, he was charged with disloyalty
      and his opponents tried to get him removed from the Senate.
      He also opposed the Treaty of Versailles as being unjust.

Lodge

903. Lodge, Henry Cabot. Collection in Massachusetts Historical
      Society, Boston.

      The bulk of Lodge's official and personal correspondence is

included in this collection. However, other Lodge documents
are scattered in other collections.

904. Fischer, Robert James. "Henry Cabot Lodge's Concept of Foreign
Policy and the League of Nations." Doctoral dissertation,
University of Georgia, 1971. 254 pp.

This is a revisionist treatment of Lodge's opposition to the
League of Nations. Fischer emphasizes Lodge's long and genuine
commitment to the position he took during the debate. If a
Republican had been president, Fischer argues, Lodge's opposition, which was based on principle, would have been just as
strong.

905. Francesconi, Robert A. "A Burkeian Analysis of Selected Speeches
of Woodrow Wilson and Henry Cabot Lodge on the League of
Nations." Doctoral dissertation, Bowling Green State University, 1975. 269 pp.

Kenneth Burke's analytic method is employed in this speech
dissertation to analyze the speeches of Wilson and Lodge.
Wilson, it is asserted, exhibited "characteristics of a mystic"
while Lodge displayed "a pragmatic ideology."

906. Garraty, John A. *Henry Cabot Lodge: A Biography*. New York:
Alfred A. Knopf, 1968. 433 pp.

Garraty's biography of Lodge is one of the best political
biographies in existence. Written from Lodge's point of view,
this book is balanced and well written. It reveals Lodge's
role in the fight over the Versailles Treaty. Lodge's reservations prove that he was a responsible, constructive critic who
wanted workable collective security.

907. Widenor, William C. *Henry Cabot Lodge and the Search for an
American Foreign Policy*. Berkeley: University of California
Press, 1980. 389 pp.

This study of Lodge's impact on U.S. foreign policy argues
that both Lodge and Wilson were internationalists. Wilson
believed that U.S. interests would be best served through an
international system, while Lodge placed more emphasis on
nationalism in an international setting. Ultimately each man
blocked the other's course of action.

McAdoo

908. McAdoo, William Gibbs. Collection in the Division of Manuscripts, Library of Congress.

This rich collection provides much information on McAdoo's
career during the war. Likewise, it helps provide a different
view of Wilson's career.

909. ———. *Crowded Years: The Reminiscences of William G. McAdoo*.
Boston: Houghton Mifflin Co., 1931. 542 pp.

This well-written memoir of Wilson's treasury secretary
during World War I is valuable for providing a view of the

part played by both McAdoo and others in the Wilson cabinet.
Interestingly, he compares Wilson with Robert E. Lee.

Norris

910. Norris, George W. *Fighting Liberal*. New York: Macmillan Co.,
      1945. 419 pp.

      This well-written autobiography surveys the political career
      of one of the most important senators of the twentieth century.
      Norris presents his views on U.S. involvement in World War I
      and outlines his opposition to the Versailles Treaty.

911. Lowitt, Richard. *George W. Norris: The Persistence of a Pro-
      gressive, 1913-1933*. Urbana: University of Illinois Press,
      1971. 590 pp.

      This superior volume concerns Norris's opposition to U.S.
      involvement in World War I. This important progressive opposed:
      the armed-ship bill, the war resolution, war profiteering, and
      the Versailles Treaty.

Palmer

912. Coben, Stanley. *A. Mitchell Palmer: Politician*. New York:
      Columbia University Press, 1963. 351 pp.

      This important biography of Wilson's attorney general reveals
      a progressive reformer who violated civil liberties on an un-
      precedented scale during World War I. Palmer subordinated his
      idealism to his powerful political ambition. His hope for
      national attention motivated his persecution of socialists
      during the "Red Scare."

Rainey

913. Waller, Robert A. *Rainey of Illinois: A Political Biography,
      1903-34*. Urbana: University of Illinois Press, 1977. 260 pp.

      This biography is important to those interested in World
      War I because Rainey, a member of the House Ways and Means
      Committee, played an important role in the passage of Wilson's
      tax measures during the war.

Roosevelt, Franklin D.

914. Freidel, Frank. *Franklin D. Roosevelt: The Apprenticeship*.
      Boston: Little, Brown & Co., 1952. 456 pp.

      The first volume of this outstanding multivolume biography
      treats FDR's role during World War I. In a definitive way,
      Freidel examines Roosevelt's disagreements with Navy Secretary
      Daniels, his militance as World War I broke out, his work in
      the Caribbean, his role as war administrator, and his trip to
      Paris after the war. This work is a must to understanding the
      activities of the Navy Department during the Wilson years.

915. ————. *Franklin D. Roosevelt: The Ordeal*. Boston: Little,
      Brown & Co., 1954. 320 pp.

The second volume of Freidel's biography of Roosevelt contains
a description of FDR's trip to Paris after the war.

Roosevelt, Theodore

916. Roosevelt, Theodore. *Fear God and Take Your Own Part.* New
     York: George H. Doran, 1916. 414 pp.

     This collection of Roosevelt's prewar magazine articles re-
     flects vividly his concern for preparedness. The colorful
     articles are pure Roosevelt.

917. Morison, Elting E., ed. *The Letters of Theodore Roosevelt.*
     Cambridge: Harvard University Press, 1951-1954. 8 vols.

     Vol. 8 of this set concentrates on Roosevelt's World War I
     correspondence. The letters are filled with his strong anti-
     German and anti-Wilson attitudes.

918. *Talks with T.R.: From the Diaries of John J. Leary, Jr.* Boston:
     Houghton Mifflin Co., 1920. 334 pp.

     Leary was a journalist whom Roosevelt took into his con-
     fidence. The extracts published from his diary for the most
     part concern the war and reveal T.R.'s low regard for Wilson.

Scott

919. Scott, Frank. Collection in the Division of Manuscripts,
     Princeton University Library.

     These papers, which include correspondence and minutes of
     meetings, relate to Scott's founding and leadership of the U.S.
     War Industries Board.

Stone

920. Stone, William Joel. Collection in the Manuscript Collections,
     University of Missouri.

     This collection contains information on Stone's World War I
     activities.

921. Towne, Ruth Warner. *Senator William J. Stone and the Politics
     of Compromise.* Port Washington, N.Y.: Kennikat, 1979.
     278 pp.

     In April 1917, Stone, chairman of the Senate Foreign Relations
     Committee, cast the lone dissenting vote against getting the
     war resolution out of committee. He was considered disloyal
     even though he later supported war measures. This biography
     traces his role in national politics.

Tumulty

922. Tumulty, Joseph Patrick. Collection in the Division of Manu-
     scripts, Library of Congress.

     This collection contains important communications with Presi-
     dent Wilson while he was in Europe as well as correspondence
     with Mrs. Wilson.

923. Blum, John M. *Joe Tumulty and the Wilson Era*. Boston: Hough-
      ton Mifflin Co., 1951. 337 pp.

      Based upon rich primary sources, including the Tumulty papers,
      this biography deals with the single politician who stood close
      to Wilson throughout his political career. The primary politi-
      cal relationship is chronicled; during the war Tumulty's role
      increased as a buffer, a political manipulator, and loyal friend.
      Blum gives Tumulty some credit for Wilson's unsuccessful poli-
      tical intervention in the 1918 election.

      Wilson

924. Wilson, Woodrow. Collection in the Division of Manuscripts,
      Library of Congress.

      This important collection of the president's private papers
      is arranged chronologically. The extracts found in Baker's
      Woodrow Wilson: Life and Letters represent only a fraction of
      this voluminous collection.

925. Bell, H.C.F. *Woodrow Wilson and the People*. Garden City, N.Y.:
      Doubleday, Doran & Co., 1945. 392 pp.

      The intention of this popular work is to show how Wilson
      attempted to reach the people and draw strength from them. It
      offers interesting discussions of Wilson's appeals to the people
      by making American intervention a people's war as well as his
      appeal to get the Treaty of Versailles approved.

926. Blum, John Morton. *Woodrow Wilson and the Politics of Morality*.
      Boston: Little, Brown & Co., 1956. 275 pp.

      This work surveys Wilson's career from the perspective of
      the impact of Calvinistic morality on his decision-making
      process. Blum places the blame for Wilson's unwillingness
      at times to compromise on his adherence to moral precepts.
      Convinced that he was morally right, he often was unyielding.
      Well written, this work has been outdated by subsequent re-
      search.

927. Cronon, E. David, ed. *The Political Thought of Woodrow Wilson*.
      New York: Bobbs-Merrill Co., 1965. 559 pp.

      In a series of edited documents, the author attempts to
      reveal Wilson's political thought. About half of the volume
      deals with World War I.

928. Diamond, William. *The Economic Thought of Woodrow Wilson*.
      Baltimore, Md.: Johns Hopkins Press, 1943. 195 pp.

      This systematic approach to Wilson's economic thinking reveals
      a middle-class, progressive approach to industrialization.
      Wilson's thinking at Versailles receives special attention.

929. Dodd, William E. *Woodrow Wilson and His Work*. New York:
      Doubleday, Page & Co., 1920. 369 pp.

      A contemporary defense of Wilson and his policies, this volume
      underlines Wilson's moralistic approach to politics.

930. Dudden, Arthur P., ed. *Woodrow Wilson and the World of Today: Essays by Arthur S. Link, William L. Langer, Eric F. Goldman.* Philadelphia: University of Pennsylvania Press, 1957. 96 pp.

This is a collection of lectures given at Bryn Mawr College. Link discussed Wilson the political leader, Goldman spoke on his management of the war, and Langer evaluated certain aspects of Wilsonian diplomacy.

931. Freud, Sigmund, and Bullitt, William C. *Thomas Woodrow Wilson, Twenty-Eighth President of the United States: A Psychological Study.* Boston: Houghton Mifflin Co., 1967. 307 pp.

This "psychological study" is pure character assassination by an elderly Freud and a disillusioned Bullitt.

932. Grayson, Rear Admiral Cary T. *Woodrow Wilson: An Intimate Memoir.* New York: Holt, Rinehart & Winston, 1960. 143 pp.

Grayson served as Wilson's doctor for almost ten years, and the publication of this manuscript, which was found in his papers, gives an intimate glimpse of Wilson during the period of World War I.

933. Link, Arthur, ed. *The Papers of Woodrow Wilson.* Princeton: Princeton University Press, 1979-1983.

Fourteen volumes of the Wilson papers that deal with the World War I period have been published. Volume 29 deals with the period December 2, 1913-May 5, 1914; Volume 30 deals with the period May 6-September 5, 1914; Volume 31 deals with the period September 6-December 31, 1914; Volume 32 deals with the period January 1-April 16, 1915; Volume 33 deals with the period April 27-July 21, 1915; Volume 34 deals with the period July 21-September 30, 1915; Volume 35 deals with the period October 1, 1915-January 27, 1916; Volume 36 deals with the period January 27-May 8, 1916; Volume 37 deals with the period May 9-August 7, 1916; Volume 38 deals with the period August 7-November 19, 1916; Volume 40 deals with the period November 20, 1916-January 23, 1917; Volume 41 deals with the period January 24-April 6, 1917; Volume 42 deals with the period April 7-June 23, 1917; Volume 43 deals with the period June 24-August 20, 1917.

934. ————. *Wilson: Campaigns for Progressivism and Peace, 1916-1917.* Princeton: Princeton University Press, 1965. 464 pp.

This book treats Wilson and his era from the 1916 election to the passage of the war resolution against Germany. Link's sympathetic portrayal sees Wilson as the leader of a new progressive coalition which carried him to victory in 1916, and as an international leader who saw the role which the United States must play in international affairs. Moreover, Link concludes that Wilson was truly neutral in his policies. In addition, he argues that Wilson went to war to protect American rights on the high seas and to hasten the war's end in Europe.

935. ————. *Wilson: Confusions and Crises, 1915-1916.* Princeton: Princeton University Press, 1964. 386 pp.

This volume of Wilson's biography deals with preparedness,
a second *Lusitania* problem, and the House-Grey Memorandum. Link
sees Wilson as vacillating on many issues in 1915 and 1916.
Moreover, Link blames Colonel House for the problems which resulted from the House-Grey Memorandum. He concludes that Wilson's policies were guided too much by public opinion.

936. ———. *Wilson: The Struggle for Neutrality, 1914-1915.*
Princeton: Princeton University Press, 1960. 736 pp.

This superb volume in Link's multivolume biography of Wilson
concentrates on the first fifteen months of World War I. It
focuses attention on the foundations of U.S. neutrality policy,
and it examines problems in Mexico, the Caribbean, and the Far
East. Throughout, Wilson emerges as an embattled president who
attempted to keep the United States free from involvement in
the European war.

937. ———. *Woodrow Wilson and the Progressive Era, 1910-1917.*
New York: Harper & Brothers, 1954. 331 pp.

This important survey in the "New American Nation Series"
examines progressivism and the question of U.S. entrance into
World War I. Link concludes that Wilson was influenced by the
question of unrestricted submarine warfare and the public's response to it.

938. Reid, Edith Gittings. *Woodrow Wilson: The Caricature, the
Myth, and the Man.* New York: Oxford University Press, 1934.
242 pp.

This is a most sympathetic biography by a friend of Wilson
since their student days.

939. Seymour, Charles. *Woodrow Wilson and the World War.* New Haven:
Yale University Press, 1921. 382 pp.

Seymour critically examines Wilson's provincialism in dealing
with the European war. Yet he points out the importance of
Wilson's idealism. The treatment of the peace conference is
very strong.

940. ———. "Woodrow Wilson in Perspective." *For. Affairs* 34
(January 1956): 175-86.

This highly interpretative article places Woodrow Wilson's
career in perspective. Seymour believes that Wilson deserves
more credit for getting more significant reforms in place than
he has received. He gives Wilson high marks for his determined
steps to maintain U.S. neutrality.

941. Tumulty, Joseph P. *Woodrow Wilson as I Know Him.* New York:
Doubleday, Page & Co., 1921. 553 pp.

This favorable portrait of Wilson by his secretary emerges
as a narrative on events with Wilson as the focus. There is
much of interest in Tumulty's views of events from 1913 to
1921.

942. Walworth, Arthur. *Woodrow Wilson*. New York: Longmans, Green
      & Co., 1958. 2 vols.

      This sympathetic biography of Wilson won the Pulitzer Prize
      for biography in 1958. A high-minded Wilson who sees himself
      as a prophet emerges from the pages of this work. Concerning
      the debate over the Versailles Treaty, Walworth sees Wilson as
      beset on all sides by enemies, and he captures well the failure
      of Wilson to compromise.

943. Watson, Richard L., Jr. "Woodrow Wilson and His Interpreters,
      1947-1957." *MVHR* 44 (September 1957): 207-36.

      This important bibliographical essay treats a decade of
      debate concerning Wilson.

944. Weinstein, Edwin A. "Woodrow Wilson's Neurological Illness."
      JAH 57 (September 1970): 324-51.

      The author, a professor of neurology, claims that President
      Wilson was afflicted as early as 1906 by a brain-damaging
      stroke that was not diagnosed as such. He reveals that after
      1906 Wilson's behavior patterns changed.

945. White, William Allen. *Woodrow Wilson, the Man, His Times, and
      His Task*. Boston: Houghton Mifflin Co., 1924. 527 pp.

      Part III of this well-written biography is devoted to the
      war. White is very favorable to the president.

946. Wilson, Edith Bolling. *My Memoir*. Indianapolis: Bobbs-Merrill
      Co., 1939. 386 pp.

      This memoir reveals little that is new, but it does contain
      some intimate portraits of important people. This work con-
      tains the details of the attempt to prevent the Wilson-Galt
      marriage. Mrs. Wilson is extremely critical of House, Lansing,
      Balfour, and Clemenceau. This volume is strongest in its dis-
      cussion of the ratification crusade and Wilson's subsequent
      collapse.

                              2. Foreign

      Asquith

947. Asquith, Herbert H. (later first earl of Oxford and Asquith).
      Collection in the Department of Western Manuscripts, Bodleian
      Library, Oxford.

      The papers of the British prime minister shed light on cer-
      tain aspects of Anglo-American relations, 1914-1916, and have
      been utilized with profit by such scholars as Link.

948. Jenkins, Roy. *Asquith*. London: Collins, 1964. 572 pp.

      This is an outstanding biography of Asquith, who was replaced
      by Lloyd George as prime minister in December 1916. The por-
      trait which the author, a prominent British politician and

writer, paints is a sympathetic one based on extensive research
and a thorough knowledge of the politics of the period.

Bethmann Hollweg

949. Jarausch, Konrad H. *The Enigmatic Chancellor: Bethmann Hollweg
      and the Hubris of Imperial Germany.* New Haven: Yale Univer-
      sity Press, 1973. 560 pp.

      This important biography of "'the last imperial chancellor
      who actually governed'" is a good source for German-American
      relations during the first years of the Great War.

950. Ritter, Gerhard. *The Sword and the Scepter. The Problem of
      Militarism in Germany,* vol. 3: *The Tragedy of Statesmanship--
      Bethmann Hollweg as War Chancellor (1914-1917).* Coral Gables,
      Fla.: University of Miami Press, 1972. 611 pp.

      Ritter portrays Bethmann Hollweg as a "good" German, a charac-
      terization that not all historians will accept. However, his
      view of Ludendorff as an aggressive expansionist is the standard
      view. This is a very valuable study of wartime German politics.

Churchill

951. Churchill, Randolph Spencer, and Gilbert, Martin. *Winston S.
      Churchill.* Boston: Houghton Mifflin, 1966- .

      Churchill's son Randolph had brought his famous father's
      career up to 1914 when he died. Gilbert was then given the
      task of completing this exhaustive bibliography. Three of
      Gilbert's volumes cover the war years, intervention in Russia,
      and the peace conference. This monumental biography sheds
      considerable light on both Churchill and the politics of the
      World War I period.

Clemenceau

952. Clemenceau, Georges. *Grandeur and Misery of Victory.* New York:
      Harcourt, Brace & Co., 1930. 432 pp.

      Clemenceau's pugnacious personality is well revealed in his
      autobiography. But one should look elsewhere for a balanced
      view. There are numerous errors of fact and many questionable
      interpretations.

953. Bruun, Geoffrey. *Clemenceau.* Hamden, Conn.: Archon Books,
      1962. 219 pp.

      This excellent biography of Clemenceau's long and turbulent
      political career was until recently the standard work on the
      "Tiger" in the English language. It has now, however, been
      superseded in some respects by the more recent biography by
      Watson which utilizes many sources not available to Bruun.
      This is a reprint of the 1943 edition.

954. Watson, David Robin. *Georges Clemenceau: A Political Biography.*
      New York: David McKay Co., 1974. 463 pp.

      This is a first-rate biography of Clemenceau based on original
      documentary research in French and British private and official

papers. Chapters 13 through 18 cover the war years, intervention in Russia, and the peace settlement.

955. Williams, Wythe. *The Tiger of France: Conversations with
Clemenceau*. New York: Duell, Sloan & Pearce, 1949. 315 pp.

The dynamism of Clemenceau is apparent in these interviews
which the French leader had with an American journalist.
Williams's approach is uncritical, but the result is both entertaining and enlightening, especially concerning Clemenceau's
personality.

Hankey

956. Hankey, Maurice (later first baron). Collection in Archives
of Churchill College, Cambridge.

Hankey was at the center of policymaking in Britain during
the war. His papers consist of 135 boxes of official and
personal papers. His diary is an important source, but most
of it has been published in either Hankey's memoirs or Roskill's
biography.

957. ————. *The Supreme Command 1914-1918*. London: Allen & Unwin,
1961. 2 vols.

This remains an indispensable source for the study of the
wartime government of Great Britain. Written by the most important behind-the-scenes figure in the government, this work
contains valuable material on Anglo-American relations. Lord
Hankey, however, does not tell all that he knows and the first
volume of Roskill's biography should be used as a corrective
on many important questions.

958. Roskill, Stephen. *Hankey, Man of Secrets*, vol. 1: *1877-1918*.
London: Collins, 1970. 672 pp.

This excellent biography of the record keeper of the British
government and confidant of prime ministers Asquith and Lloyd
George is an essential source. Roskill was one of Britain's
most outstanding historians and his understanding of Britain's
war policies on the diplomatic and military front is rarely
equalled. This account should be used to supplement Hankey's
memoirs.

Lloyd George

959. Lloyd George, David (later first earl). Collection in House of
Lords Records Office, London.

This voluminous and beautifully catalogued collection is an
extremely important source for Anglo-American relations during
the war and at the peace conference. These papers serve as a
corrective to the Welshman's misleading memoirs.

960. ————. *War Memoirs of David Lloyd George*. London: Odhams
Press, 1938. 2 vols.

Many official documents and his own papers are utilized by
Lloyd George in this spirited defense of his actions and policies

during World War I. The opening of Lloyd George's papers in
the 1960s confirmed what many suspected about these memoirs:
they should be used with care. Lloyd George's account of the
British response to Wilson's attempt at mediation in 1916 is
only one example of his distortion.

961. Jones, Thomas. *Lloyd George*. Cambridge: Harvard University
      Press, 1951. 330 pp.

      Until Rowland's biography, this study of Lloyd George was
      considered the best biography of one of Britain's greatest
      prime ministers. It is remarkable that Jones was able to
      portray Lloyd George so well in only 330 pages. His publisher
      made him scale down his original manuscript, an ordeal known
      to many authors, and thus many important topics could not be
      expanded upon. Jones was the assistant secretary to the
      Cabinet and War Cabinet during the last half of the war.

962. Rowland, Peter. *David Lloyd George: A Biography*. New York:
      Macmillan Publishing Co., 1975. 872 pp.

      This is a well-written and stimulating biography based on
      many sources that were unavailable to earlier biographers of
      Lloyd George. About one-fourth of this work covers the war
      years and the peace settlement.

*   Woodward, David R. *Lloyd George and the Generals*. Cited
      above as item 357.

Poincaré

963. Poincaré, Raymond. *The Memoirs of Raymond Poincaré*. London:
      William Heinemann, 1926-1929. 3 vols.

      It is a shame that the memoirs of this French statesman do
      not cover the entire war. Only Vol. 3 concerns the war, and
      then only 1914. This work is most useful for its insight into
      prewar diplomacy and politics.

William II

964. William II. *My Memoirs*. London: Cassell & Co., 1922. 348 pp.

      This apologia by the Hohenzollern ruler who lost his throne
      because of the Great War is of some interest.

965. Balfour, Michael. *The Kaiser and His Times*. Boston: Houghton
      Mifflin Co., 1964. 524 pp.

      The last chapters of this standard biography shed light on
      American-German relations during the war.

C. CONGRESS AND NATIONAL POLITICS

966. Burner, David. *The Politics of Provincialism: The Democratic Party in Transition, 1918-1932.* New York: Alfred A. Knopf, 1968. 293 pp.

This excellent study of the Democratic party from World War I until the Roosevelt election in 1932 examines the period when the party moved from being a rural party to an urban party. The book contains a good discussion of the Wilson coalition in the party.

967. Decker, Joe Frank. "Progressive Reaction to Selective Service in World War I." Doctoral dissertation, University of Georgia, 1969. 188 pp.

The Selective Service Act of 1917 brought strong disagreement among progressives. The views on the draft reflected their conflicting views on the war. The study concludes that the schism among the progressive idealists proved to be long lasting in the postwar period.

968. Edwards, John Carver. "The Price of Political Innocence: The Role of the National Security League in the 1918 Congressional Election." *Mil. Affairs* 42 (December 1978): 190-95.

Carver analyzes the NSL's attempt to unseat representatives who were unsupportive of preparedness. The role of Charles D. Orth receives special attention.

969. Grantham, Dewey W., Jr. "Southern Congressional Leaders and the New Freedom, 1913-1917." *JSH* 13 (November 1947): 439-59.

This well-researched article shows the role played by southern congressional leaders in getting Wilson's reform bills through Congress. It reveals that there was close cooperation between the president and Congress.

970. Livermore, Seward W. *Politics Is Adjourned: Woodrow Wilson and the War Congress, 1916-1918.* Middletown, Conn.: Wesleyan University Press, 1966. 324 pp.

This well-documented study challenges the idea that there was bipartisan cooperation during World War I. The author argues that partisan Republican politicians worked behind the scenes to undermine Wilson's policies. The Democratic failure to maintain control of Congress in 1918 was caused by Democratic ineptness and Republican astuteness.

971. ————. "The Sectional Issue in the 1918 Elections." *MVHR* 35 (June 1948): 29-60.

This significant article on the surprising defeat of the Democratic party in the 1918 congressional elections concludes that the defeat was caused by Democratic overconfidence on the war issue and the issue of cotton regulation.

972. McDonald, Timothy Gregory. "Southern Democratic Congressmen
      and the First World War, August 1914-April 1917. The Public
      Record of Their Support for or Opposition to Wilson's Poli-
      cies." Doctoral dissertation, University of Washington,
      1962. 272 pp.

      The author examines through the *Congressional Record* the
      division of southern Democratic senators over Wilson's policies.
      McDonald shows that the majority supported Wilson on all issues
      (better than eighty percent) and that after unrestricted sub-
      marine warfare the dissenters dropped off sharply. McDonald
      also made extensive use of the *New York Times*.

973. Morlan, Robert L. *Political Prairie Fire: The Nonpartisan
      League, 1915-1922*. Minneapolis: University of Minnesota
      Press, 1955. 408 pp.

      This work examines the political history of an organization
      which was formed to call upon government intervention in the
      economy on behalf of farmers. Unfortunately, Morlan fails to
      examine in depth some of the League's state enterprises.

974. Ryley, Thomas W. *A Little Group of Willful Men: A Study of
      Congressional-Presidential Authority*. Port Washington, N.Y.:
      Kennikat, 1975.

      This competent narrative examines the armed-ship controversy
      which concerned President Wilson's failure to get Congress to
      approve the arming of American merchant ships. Wilson was
      blocked by a handful of antiwar progressive senators.

975. Thompson, J.A. "American Progressive Publicists and the First
      World War, 1914-1917." *JAH* 58 (September 1971): 363-83.

      This important article examines how various progressives re-
      lated to World War I. Different progressives reacted in dif-
      ferent ways and some even modified their ideas along the way.
      There existed some relationship between a concern for social
      reform and the hope that there would be a lasting peace. Since
      the stakes were high, failure could lead to "disillusionment
      and guilt."

976. Ward, Robert D. "The Origin and Activities of the National
      Security League, 1914-1919." *MVHR* 47 (June 1960): 51-65.

      This article treats the development of an organization that
      was concerned about preparedness.

977. Watson, Richard L., Jr. "A Testing Time for Southern Congres-
      sional Leadership: The War Crisis of 1917-1918." *JSH* 48 (Feb-
      ruary 1978): 3-40.

      This article examines how the southern congressional leader-
      ship responded to the crisis of World War I. Despite political
      differences between northern and southern congressmen, they
      worked together during the period of American participation in
      the war.

D. STATE AND LOCAL STUDIES

978. Alabama. State Council of Defense. *Report of the Alabama Council of Defense Covering Its Activities from May 17, 1917 to December 31, 1918.* Montgomery, Ala.: Brown Printing, 1919. 116 pp.

This report surveys the activities of the Alabama Council of Defense, which, among other things, attempted to coordinate the local defense councils. It also worked to promulgate government policies, to detect deserters, to establish a speaker's bureau, to organize a livestock conservation campaign, to organize an illiteracy campaign, to help in administering the selective service law, to create a State Highway Transport Committee, to establish a committee on negro organization, and to cooperate with many other facets of the war program. The report also deals with the Woman's Committee.

979. Anderson, Claude H. "The Civic Work of State Councils of Defense." *Nat. Mun. Rev.* 7 (September 1918): 472-83.

The State Councils of Defense contributed to national cohesion by emphasizing the ideals of self-government, a free economy, and industrial well being.

980. Arizona State Council of Defense. *A Report of the Activities of the Arizona State Council of Defense from Formation April 8, 1917 to Dissolution June 1919.* Phoenix, Ariz.: Republican Print Shop, 1919. 50 pp.

This slim report outlines the activities of the Arizona State Council of Defense. The report is bare-bones and gives only a superficial account of the work of the council. It is not as thorough as many other reports of state councils.

981. Arkansas. State Council of Defense. *Report of the Arkansas State Council of Defense, May 22, 1917 to July 1, 1919.* Little Rock, Ark., 1919. 88 pp.

This report outlines the activities of the Arkansas State Council of Defense. It treats, among other things: the organization of the council, its meetings, county and community councils, patriotic education, war conferences, conservation activities, state protection, welfare work, shipbuilding, selective service boards, government activities, services for military men, food administration, fuel administration, Liberty Loan campaigns, Arkansas war history, the Red Cross, the Y.M.C.A., U.S. Employment Service, explosives regulation, and historical records work.

982. Baines, May, ed. *Houston's Part in the World War.* Houston, Texas, 1919. 205 pp.

This privately printed volume is a survey of the war activities of Houston. Among the topics discussed are: the War Mothers, Houston's Gold Stars, the Red Cross, librarians, the Salvation Army, the National League of Women's Service, the

Lutheran Brotherhood of America, the preachers, the Y.M.C.A.,
the Y.W.C.A., officers, nurses, War Camp Community Service,
clubs and organizations, the Chamber of Commerce, entertainers,
schools, Boy Scouts, chronology, League of Nations, and the
Houston Ship Channel.

983. Bickelhaupt, W.G. "South Dakota Fuel Administration." *So.
      Dak. Hist. Coll.* 10 (1921): 279-88.

      South Dakota coal and the conservation campaign which re-
      sulted from wartime shortages receive attention in this article.

984. Blackmar, Frank W., ed. *History of the Kansas State Council
      of Defense*. Topeka, Kans.: State Printing Plant, 1921.
      137 pp.

      This history is limited in value because of the paucity of
      records. It lists the activities of the council, and shows
      how various committees which dealt with agricultural problems
      functioned. Brief reports in various councils are also in-
      cluded.

985. Blatt, Heimank K., comp. *Sons of Men: Evansville's War Record*.
      Evansville, Ind.: A.P. Madison, 1920. 316 pp.

      This volume contains sketches of the Evansville soldiers who
      were killed during the war. These sketches of the "Gold Stars"
      are very well done. It also includes an honor roll, a section
      on the war mothers, a chapter on the local war organizations,
      a look at Red Cross activities and at the activities of the
      American Legion.

986. Brown, Earl S. *A History of Switzerland County's Part in the
      World War*. Connersville, Ind.: Express Printing, 1919.
      142 pp.

      This volume focuses attention on the war activities of Swit-
      zerland County, Indiana, at home and overseas. Like most works
      of this type, biographical sketches of native sons who lost
      their lives receive much attention. What is positive about
      this book is that it captures the daily impact of the war on
      this county. Outline treatments of the various war agencies
      are also included. Of major significance, the volume contains
      accounts of a number of firsthand experiences of World War I
      veterans. This is a good work.

987. Connecticut. State Council of Defense. *Report of the Connecti-
      cut State Council of Defense, December 1918*. Hartford, Conn.,
      1919. 236 pp.

      This report outlines the activities of the Connecticut State
      Council of Defense during World War I. It deals with: the
      Connecticut Council of Defense, the Executive Department, pub-
      licity, food supply, transportation, the Americanization Depart-
      ment, child welfare, health and recreation, nonwar construction,
      historical records, industrial surveys, commercial economy and
      relations, employment service, coal committee, fuel conservation,
      education, Military and Naval Committee, sanitation medicine,

manpower and labor, war savings, the Woman's Division, and the committee's financial support.

988. Costrell, Edwin. *How Maine Viewed the War, 1914-1917*. Orono: Published at the University of Maine Press, 1940. 101 pp.

This slender volume, well written and well documented, purports to examine Maine's public opinion on the subject of the war. However, it actually examines the opinion of the newspaper editors who supported the war when it came.

989. Cottman, George S. *Jefferson County in the World War*. Madison, Ind.: Jefferson County Historical Society, 1920. 127 pp.

This volume examines the war-related activities of Jefferson County, Indiana. It outlines the military functions of the county as it treats the organization of the county's companies and the work of the draft board. In addition, civilian activities such as fund raising and Red Cross work, and the impact of war on business, are examined. This volume also includes a section of letters from soldiers.

990. Cram, Ralph W., ed. *History of the War Activities of Scott County, Iowa, 1917-1918*. Davenport, Iowa: State Council of National Defense, 1919. 145 pp.

This volume examines the activities of the Scott County Council of National Defense, the Medical Advisory Board, and the Registration Board; recruitment of soldiers; the Red Cross; Liberty Loans; the various service clubs; the fuel committees; activities of professionals; housing; Rock Island Arsenal; and the honor roll. It gives a good account of the local wartime activities in middle America.

991. Davis, Arthur K., ed. *Virginia War History in Newspaper Clippings*. Richmond: Virginia War History Commission, 1924. 32 pp.

Virginia's war history is given from a selection of some 30,000 newspaper clippings. Some of the topics included are as follows: distilled newspapers, facts intrinsic and composite, newspapers as history, Virginia editorials, political contributions, draft law and Virginia organizations, economic conditions, Virginia communities in wartime, the Chesapeake Bay area, soldiers and sailors overseas, the Red Cross, and war relief.

992. Dennis, Roger L. "War Savings Stamp Campaign in South Dakota for Year 1918." *So. Dak. Hist. Coll.* 10 (1921): 269-78.

This article outlines the 1918 war bond sale in South Dakota.

993. Eilers, Tom D., ed. *Buena Vista's Part in the World War: One Iowa County's Record of Service and Sacrifice*. Storm Lake, Iowa: T.D. Eilers, 1920. 770 pp.

This rather detailed volume treats the war activities of a rural county in northwestern Iowa. Over 200 pages treat those

who died during the war. Photographs of local dignitaries
abound along with battlefield photographs. The strength of
this work is that the editor, in some detail, carefully weaves
the story of the local county's activities into the national
and international story of the war.

994. Fraser, Bruce. "Yankees at War: Social Mobilization on the
      Connecticut Home Front, 1917-1918." Doctoral dissertation,
      Columbia University, 1976. 375 pp.

      Connecticut was selected because it had a major munitions
      industry and was rich in primary materials for the war period.
      Fraser concludes that ideological characteristics resulted from
      the old elites rather than from propaganda, that the old line
      establishment controlled the Council of Defense and its activi-
      ties, and that the dominant influence on Connecticut mobiliza-
      tion was local rather than federal.

995. Gibbs, Christopher Cochran. "Patriots and Slackers: The Impact
      of World War One on Missouri." Doctoral dissertation, Uni-
      versity of Missouri-Columbia, 1980. 357 pp.

      This dissertation examines the impact of the war on local
      communities in Missouri and explores the reasons why a majority
      of Missourians opposed American involvement in the war.

996. Greenough, Walter. *The War Purse of Indiana: The Five Liberty
      Loans and War Savings and Thrift Campaigns in Indiana During
      the World War*. Indianapolis: Indiana Historical Commission,
      1922. 278 pp.

      This work chronicles the process by which Indiana raised
      $5 million in war bonds.

997. Hancock County, Indiana. Council of Defense. *Hancock County,
      Indiana, in the World War*. Greenfield, Ind.: Board of Com-
      missioners of Hancock County, 1921. 368 pp.

      This county historical work is a cut above the average. It
      includes coverage of the local Council of Defense, the county
      food administration, the county fuel administration, public
      improvements, Liberty Bonds, the Red Cross and the Y.M.C.A.,
      the draft board, those from the county who were killed, and an
      interesting sampling of letters from soldiers.

998. Hansen, Marcus L. *Welfare Campaigns in Iowa*. Iowa City: State
      Historical Society in Iowa, 1920. 297 pp.

      This volume chronicles Iowa's war welfare campaigns. Hansen
      utilizes newspapers, bulletins, letters, and interviews.

999. Hart, Hastings H. *Social Problems of Alabama: A Study of the
      Social Institutions and Agencies of the State of Alabama as
      Related to Its War Activities*. New York: Russell Sage Foun-
      dation, 1918. 87 pp.

      This general survey of social problems in Alabama during the
      war is an excellent beginning on the topic and points the way

to further research. It treats: war work and social work, problems in state institutions, the state debt, the convict system, education, State Council of Defense, woman's division of the Council of Defense, state war historian, the deficiency in support of state institutions, hospitals for the insane, reformatories, public health and sanitation, public education, welfare board, child welfare institutions, social work and social work of corporations.

1000. ———. *The War Program of the State of South Carolina.* New York: Russell Sage Foundation, 1918. 61 pp.

This brief report on the social agencies and institutions of South Carolina came about as a result of a two-week study by Hart. It treats the 1917 mobilization, the governor's actions, the State Council of Defense, the future of the war program, the state board of charities and corrections, the work of the Red Cross, care of various groups, and the quality of recruits and education. This pamphlet reveals some interesting facts. The average white teacher, for example, was paid $935 per year while the typical black teacher received $116 per year.

1001. Hayworth, Clarence U. *History of Howard County in the World War.* Indianapolis: W.B. Burford, 1920. 352 pp.

This excellent volume treats the impact of war on Howard County, Indiana. It includes biographical sketches of many of the county's leading participants in the war. It also touches upon the activities of the militia, activities at home, conscription, munitions, the food administration, the Liberty Loan drive, the fuel administration, the work of relief organizations, and the Howard County war organizations.

1002. Henson, Joseph M. *South Dakota in the World War, 1917-1919.* Pierre, S.D.: State Historical Society, 1940. 447 pp.

This is one of the best state histories in print. It includes a well-written account of the training and military activities of South Dakota units. This account is well researched and well organized.

1003. Herreid, Charles N. "The Federal Food Administration in South Dakota During the World War." *So. Dak. Hist. Coll.* 10 (1921): 295-314.

This is an account by the head of federal food administration in South Dakota during the war.

1004. Hilton, Ola A. *The Minnesota Commission of Public Safety in World War I, 1917-1919.* Stillwater: Oklahoma Agricultural and Mechanical College, 1951. 44 pp.

This pamphlet chronicles the activities of the Minnesota Commission of Public Safety during World War I. It discusses the commission's activities in propaganda, promotion of loyalty, and Liberty Bond and war savings campaigns, as well as other war-related drives. It also reveals the antilabor attitude of the commission in its treatment of the I.W.W. It is a good basic study of a midwestern state in the war.

1005. Hodges, Leroy. "Virginia War Economy and Budget System."
       Proc. Acad. Pol. Sci. 8 (1918-1920): 50-53.

       This brief discussion of the Virginia budget shows that it
       was modernized during the war.

1006. Holbrook, Franklin F. "The Collection of State War Service
       Records." *AHR* 25 (October 1919): 72-78.

       Holbrook gives a progress report on the collecting and pre-
       serving of state records relating to American participation
       in the war.

1007. ————, and Appel, Livia. *Minnesota in the War with Germany.*
       St. Paul: Minnesota Historical Society, 1928. 374 pp.

       Well documented, this state study treats some of the problems
       of a state in which the war was controversial due to its ethnic
       composition. Minnesota had a very strong peace movement which
       was overridden by a prowar Commission of Public Safety. The
       chapters dealing with training camps are strong.

1008. Holmes, Frederick L. *Wisconsin's War Record.* Madison, Wis.:
       Capitol Publishing, 1919. 191 pp.

       Among the topics examined in this competent history are:
       the National Guard in service, draft registration, legislative
       support, the State Council of Defense, women's war work, help
       for soldiers' dependents, the Red Cross and Liberty Loans,
       the school system, the role of farmers, the food and fuel
       administrations, health care, and the war history commission.
       Wisconsin was the first state to organize a Council of Defense.

1009. Hornik, Anna. *Danbury and Our Boys in the World War.* Danbury,
       Conn., 1923. 37 pp.

       This privately published booklet briefly examines Danbury's
       contribution to the war effort. It contains lists of those
       who contributed in various ways with a special emphasis on the
       activities of the American Legion. This work is not very
       useful to the serious scholar.

1010. Iowa State Council of Defense. *The Alleged "Reign of Terror,"
       the Non-Partisan League, the Expulsion of Mr. Pierce, Full
       Proceedings of the Council of Defense upon the Foregoing
       Important Subject, "There Is Only One Question Now Before
       the People of Iowa--How Best to Win the War."* Des Moines,
       Iowa, 1918. 8 pp.

       This report attacks the attempt to establish a nonpartisan
       league, arguing that such a movement would be divisive and
       attacking former Congressman Charles A. Lindbergh, a leader
       of the nonpartisan league.

1011. Jenison, Marguerite Edith, ed. *War Documents and Addresses.*
       Springfield: Illinois State Historical Library, 1923. 522 pp.

       This volume in the series "Illinois in the World War" sur-
       veys documents relevant to Illinois and World War I.

1012. Koch, Felix J. *Cincinnati Sees It Thru: The Camera's Story of How the Great World War Came to the Queen of the West.* Cincinnati, Ohio: Meyer Engraving, 1917. 55 pp.

This little volume contains about six or seven small photographs per page. It deals primarily with the activities of the home front.

1013. Lovin, Hugh T. "World War Vigilantes in Idaho, 1917-1918." *Idaho Yesterdays* 18 (Fall 1974): 2-11.

This article surveys the anti-German attitudes of the councils of defense and illustrates the ways in which they harassed some German immigrants.

1014. Ohio State Council of Defense. *A History of the Activities of the Ohio Branch, Council of National Defense, 1917-1919: How Ohio Mobilized Her Resources for the War.* Columbus: F.J. Heer, 1919. 205 pp.

This report treats the activities of the Ohio Council of National Defense. It deals with county and community organizations, the Woman's Committee, industrial relations and employment, postwar activities, food supply and conservation, and other activities. This volume should be the starting point for any research on the home front in Ohio during World War I.

1015. Philadelphia. War History Committee. *Philadelphia in the World War, 1914-1919.* New York: Wynkoup Hallenbeck, 1922. 785 pp.

This detailed volume is one of the most thorough treatments of World War I on the local level. It deals with the Philadelphia war chronology, the various war committees, the 28th Division, draft boards, casualty lists, marines, the navy, wartime industries, the newspapers' role in the war, the Red Cross, relief work, religious works, women's clubs, men's clubs, the return of the troops, and the service flag. This is one of the superior local treatments and it is must reading for scholars interested in Philadelphia and the war.

1016. Smith, George W. "New Mexico's Wartime Food Problems, 1917-1918: A Case Study in Emergency Administration." *New Mexico Hist. Rev.* 18 (October 1943): 349-85; 19 (January 1944): 1-54.

This is an excellent analysis of the problems of the mobilization of agricultural products. It also shows the impact of the policies of the food administration.

1017. Whitney, Nathaniel R. *The Sale of War Bonds in Iowa.* Iowa City: State Historical Society, 1919. 236 pp.

This volume treats: Iowa as a field for sales, the bonds, machinery of sales, the campaigns, resistance to sales, and the success of the drives. Despite the state's large foreign-born population, the Iowa bond sales campaign was successful. A statistical breakdown on a county-by-county basis is included.

1018. Wycoff, Minnie E., ed. *Ripley County's Part in the World War
       1917-1918: Compiled under the Direction and Censorship of
       the Ripley County Historical Society.* Batesville, Ind.,
       1920. 388 pp.

       This volume represents a good case study of the war's im-
       pact on a local area. This volume is divided into two parts.
       Part one deals with the home front and the second deals with
       the boys "over there." Part one concerns the Red Cross, loan
       drives, food conservation, service organizations, and the
       draft board. Part two examines the various divisions which
       included soldiers from Ripley County.

                            E. ENEMY ESPIONAGE

1019. Goltz, Capt. Horst von der. *My Adventures as a German Secret
       Agent.* New York: Robert McBride & Co., 1917. 288 pp.

       These are the adventures of an admitted German agent, who
       describes himself as the "sometime confidential aide to Captain
       von Papen."

1020. Hall, Admiral Sir W. Reginald, and Peaslee, Amos J. *Three
       Wars with Germany.* New York: G.P. Putnam's Sons, 1944.
       309 pp.

       Hall headed British intelligence and Peaslee directed the
       American Courier Service (called the "Silver greyhounds")
       during the Great War. Their correspondence, especially as it
       relates to the Black Tom-Kingsland case, constitutes an im-
       portant source on counter-espionage activities during the war.
       Joseph P. Sims has edited and illustrated this work.

1021. Hough, Emerson. *The Web.* Chicago: Reilly & Lee, 1919. 511
       pp.

       This volume is the authorized history of the American Pro-
       tective League. It surveys the work of the League during the
       war with an emphasis on propaganda, the spy cases, disloyal
       aliens, the I.W.W. trial, slacker raids, and the arts of the
       operatives. It also details the League's activities in dif-
       ferent sections of the country. In a rather melodramatic way,
       the League's activities are described as good versus the evil
       German influence.

1022. Jensen, Joan M. *The Prince of Vigilance.* New York: Rand
       McNally & Co., 1968. 367 pp.

       This study of the American Protective League during World
       War I is based primarily upon private papers, Justice Depart-
       ment files, and military records. This organization kept a
       vigilant eye on the patriotism of thousands of people but
       failed to catch a single spy.

1023. Jones, John Price, and Hollister, Paul Merrick. *The German Secret Service in America*. Boston: Small, Maynard & Co., 1918. 340 pp.

Jones, the author of *America Entangled* (1917), an account of German spying in the United States, and Hollister have written a careful and generally well-researched study of German espionage in the United States. Like other spy books of this genre, it is written in a popular style and is directed toward the general public.

1024. Landau, Captain Henry. *The Enemy Within: The Inside Story of German Sabotage in America*. New York: G.P. Putnam's Sons, 1937. 323 pp.

The author, a former member of the British secret service during the war, focuses on the destruction of munitions by alleged German sabotage in 1916 and 1917 in the United States. The book jacket contends that "no fiction can match this story."

1025. Pintelen, Captain von. *The Dark Invader: Wartime Reminiscences of a German Naval Intelligence Officer*. London: Lovat Dickson, 1933. 288 pp.

This is the story of a German officer who was engaged in espionage in America during the period of American neutrality.

1026. Skaggs, William H. *German Conspiracies in America: From an American Point of View by an American*. London: T. Fisher Unwin, 1915. 332 pp.

This study is interesting only because of its polemical nature and anti-German passion. The author was a native of Alabama.

1027. Strother, French. *Fighting Germany's Spies*. New York: Doubleday, Page & Co., 1918. 275 pp.

Seven articles written by the managing editor of *The World's Work*, which appeared in that magazine in 1918, make up the bulk of this book. The last chapter by Dr. Scheele is new. Strother claims that much of his information was gained from the bureau of investigation of the Justice Department.

1028. Tunney, Thomas J. *Throttled! The Detection of the German and Anarchist Bomb Plotters*. Boston: Small, Maynard & Co., 1919. 277 pp.

Tunney, a New York police department inspector, has written an interesting account of his detective work in thwarting would-be bombers. Paul Merrick Hollister assisted Tunney in putting his story on paper.

F. FOREIGN HOME FRONTS

1. Entente

*   Beaverbrook, Lord. *Men and Power, 1917-1918*. Cited above as
         item 343.

*   ———. *Politicians & the War 1914-1916*. Cited above as item
         344.

1029. Browder, Robert Paul, and Kerensky, Alexander F., eds. *The
         Russian Provisional Government, 1917: Documents*. Stanford,
         Calif.: Stanford University Press, 1961. 3 vols.

         Fourteen hundred primary documents have been selected and
         translated in this important source for the brief life of the
         Russian Provisional Government. The editors provide commentary
         and notes. Kerensky was the premier when the Bolsheviks
         destroyed the Provisional Government.

1030. Carr, E.H. *The Bolshevik Revolution, 1917-1923*. London:
         Macmillan & Co., 1950-1953. 3 vols.

         This monumental work remains the standard analysis of "the
         political, social and economic order" which developed after
         the Bolshevik Revolution. Carr, a British authority on Russian
         affairs, takes a more sympathetic approach to the development
         of the Soviet system than is usually found in western historiog-
         raphy.

1031. Chamberlin, William Henry. *The Russian Revolution, 1917-1921*.
         New York: Grosset & Dunlap, 1965. 2 vols.

         Although there are more recent histories of the Russian
         Revolution by such western scholars as Daniels, Katkov, and
         Rabinowitch, these volumes, originally published in the mid-
         1930s, still give perhaps the best overall view of the tumultu-
         ous and confusing events of this period of history. Written
         by an American journalist who was close to the events that he
         describes, this remains an essential background source for any
         examination of Russo-American relations from 1917 to 1921.

1032. Daniels, Robert V. *Red October: The Bolshevik Revolution of
         1917*. New York: Charles Scribner's Sons, 1967. 269 pp.

         Daniels gives considerable credit to luck and accident for
         the successful Bolshevik coup d'état in 1917 in this well-
         written and scholarly narrative.

1033. Gide, Charles, ed. *The Effects of the War upon French Economic
         Life*. Oxford: Clarendon Press, 1923. 197 pp.

         This volume is a collection of five monographs dealing with
         the war's impact on the French merchant marine, textile indus-
         try, finance, commercial policy, and labor. The war's impact
         was obviously negative in all these areas.

1034. Hazlehurst, Cameron. *Politicians at War, July 1914 to May
       1915: A Prologue to the Triumph of Lloyd George.* New York:
       Alfred A. Knopf, 1971. 346 pp.

       This is an original and comprehensive treatment of British
       politics from the "July Crisis" to the formation of a coalition
       government in May 1915. It presents Lloyd George in a sym-
       pathetic light and takes exception with Koss's conspiracy
       thesis. The Cabinet Papers and many private papers were
       examined. Two documents on military planning prior to the
       war are reprinted in an appendix.

1035. Hirst, Francis W. *The Consequences of the War to Great
       Britain.* New York: Greenwood Press, 1968. 311 pp.

       This is a reprint of Hirst's volume in the British series
       "Economic and Social History of the World War," which was
       first published by Yale University Press in 1934. Although
       some of the chapters, such as the one on conscription and
       pacifism, are dated by more recent research, this work still
       contains much useful information. See, for example, the chap-
       ter "Losses in Killed and Wounded."

1036. Hurwitz, Samuel J. *State Intervention in Great Britain: A
       Study of Economic Control and Social Response, 1914-1919.*
       New York: Columbia University Press, 1949. 321 pp.

       This is a scholarly monograph which traces the British
       government's transition from "business as usual" in 1914 to
       massive state intervention in its relations with labor and in-
       dustry. Section III focuses on labor's reaction to increased
       state intervention.

1037. Johnson, Paul Barton. *Land Fit for Heroes: The Planning of
       British Reconstruction, 1916-1919.* Chicago: University of
       Chicago Press, 1968. 540 pp.

       The effort to build a more just society in Britain following
       the war was a failure for the most part. But Johnson's
       thorough research in the Public Record Office demonstrates
       that this failure was not the fault of the planners, who,
       sincere in their efforts, were unable to overcome Britain's
       extensive postwar economic problems. This is superior and
       fair-minded institutional history.

1038. Katkov, George. *Russia 1917: The February Revolution.* New
       York: Harper & Row, 1967. 489 pp.

       This is a revisionist study of the February Revolution which
       attempts to debunk the view that the revolution was spontaneous
       and leaderless. Katkov argues that German agents and Russian
       Freemasons combined to provoke the February riots which led to
       the abdication of Nicholas II.

1039. ————. *Russia 1917: The Kornilov Affair, Kerensky and the
       Break-Up of the Russian Army.* London: Longman, 1980. 210
       pp.

This is, by and large, a defense of Kornilov's actions and an attack on the head of the Provisional Government, Kerensky, whom Katkov charges with having manufactured the so-called Kornilov affair. Not everyone will be convinced by Katkov's argument, and a better account of the collapse of the Tsarist army is found in Wildman's recent monograph.

1040. Kernez, Peter. *Civil War in South Russia, 1918: The First Year of the Volunteer Army.* Berkeley: University of California Press, 1971. 351 pp.

This masterful monograph, which centers on the Volunteer Army and its Cossack allies, is the best examination of an anti-Bolshevik army, especially its leaders, during the Russian Civil War. The research is impressive and the style clear.

1041. Page, Thomas Nelson. *Italy and the World War.* New York: Charles Scribner's Sons, 1920. 422 pp.

Page was the American ambassador to Italy from 1913 to 1919. He provides some insight into Italian diplomacy and military operations. There is some mention, not always accurate, of American forces operating in Italy.

1042. Pares, Bernard. *The Fall of the Russian Monarchy: A Study of the Evidence.* New York: Alfred A. Knopf, 1939. 510 pp.

This is a narrative of the last years of the Romanov dynasty by a distinguished British historian with an intimate knowledge of the Russian scene. Pares concludes that Nicholas II and his inept officials were largely responsible for the collapse of the Russian monarchy in 1917.

1043. Rabinowitch, Alexander. *The Bolsheviks Come to Power: The Revolutions of 1917 in Petrograd.* New York: W.W. Norton & Co., 1976. 393 pp.

This detailed monograph takes exception to many basic assumptions of Soviet historians about the Bolshevik seizure of power and makes an outstanding contribution to the historiography of the Bolshevik Revolution.

1044. Taylor, A.J.P. *Beaverbrook.* London: Hamish Hamilton, 1972. 712 pp.

This is a splendid biography of the Canadian millionaire journalist, public servant, and power broker. Taylor's chapters on World War I offer insight and serve as a corrective to certain aspects of Beaverbrook's lively but not always accurate chronicle of wartime politics.

1045. ————. *English History 1914-1945.* New York: Oxford University Press, 1965. 708 pp.

There exists no better short account of Britain at war, 1914-1918, than the first three chapters of this volume. The explanatory footnotes are a joy to read and the annotated bibliography is erudite and thorough.

1046. Thayer, John A. *Italy and the Great War: Politics and Culture, 1870-1915*. Madison: University of Wisconsin, 1964. 463 pp.

   This work is especially helpful to an understanding of Italian politics on the eve of Italian belligerency.

1047. Wilson, Trevor, ed. *The Political Diaries of C.P. Scott 1911-1928*. London: Collins, 1970. 509 pp.

   This book, which serves as a model of scholarly editing, offers an enlightening glimpse into the thinking of one of Britain's foremost liberals, the editor of the *Manchester Guardian*. There is useful information also on British war objectives.

1048. Woodward, Sir Llewellyn. *Great Britain and the War of 1914-1918*. London: Methuen & Co., 1967. 610 pp.

   Woodward, a World War I veteran and one of Britain's most distinguished historians, has written a much-needed general history of Britain's involvement in the Great War that goes well beyond the coverage of military operations. It is, however, unfortunate that the writing and production of this book coincided with the opening of many official and private papers and the publication of many scholarly articles. Woodward was unable to utilize these new sources or the most recent scholarship.

2. Central Powers

1049. Bartholdy, Albrecht Mendolssohn. *The War and German Society: The Testament of a Liberal*. New York: Howard Fertig, 1971. 299 pp.

   First published in 1937, this study examines the general impact of the war on Germany. This book was written by a German liberal who saw much development during the war, but also much moral decay.

1050. Craig, Gordon A. *The Politics of the Prussian Army 1640-1945*. New York: Oxford University Press, 1964. 538 pp.

   Craig discusses prewar operational planning, the political effects of the Schlieffen Plan, the supreme command, war objectives, the German army, and the German Revolution, 1918-1919.

1051. Emin, Ahmed. *Turkey in the World War*. New Haven: Yale University Press, 1930. 310 pp.

   This is a standard work on the politics, economy, and diplomacy of Turkey during the era of the Great War. There is a bibliography but no index.

1052. Feldman, Gerald D. *Army, Industry and Labor in Germany, 1914-1918*. Princeton: Princeton University Press, 1966. 572 pp.

Military and socioeconomic history are brought together in
this excellent account of the confrontation of army, labor,
and industry in Germany during the war. Feldman demonstrates
that the German high command, despite its dictatorship during
the last two years of the war, was often unable to master
internal affairs. The research in German sources is impressive
and there is extensive documentation.

1053. Holborn, Hajo. *A History of Modern Germany, 1840-1945*. New
      York: Alfred A. Knopf, 1969. 818 pp.

      This is an outstanding history of Germany in the nineteenth
      and twentieth centuries. The author embraces Fritz Fischer's
      view on German responsibility for the war and the expansionist
      nature of German war objectives. An introduction to the
      German home front can be obtained in this superior work of
      scholarship.

1054. Jászi, Oscar. *The Dissolution of the Habsburg Monarchy*.
      Chicago: University of Chicago Press, 1929. 488 pp.

      This impressive analysis argues that the Habsburg Monarchy
      was doomed because of the shortsightedness of political
      leaders who refused to grant autonomy to the numerous subject
      nationalities. According to Jászi, this, rather than the
      war, was the basic cause for the collapse of the Dual Monarchy.

1055. Kann, Robert A.; Király, Béla K.; and Fichtner, Paula S. *The
      Habsburg Empire in World War I: Essays on the Intellectual,
      Military, Political and Economic Aspects of the Habsburg
      War Effort*. Boulder, Colo.: East European Quarterly, 1977.
      247 pp.

      Most of the papers published in this book were the product
      of conferences sponsored by the East European section of the
      center for European studies at the graduate school and uni-
      versity center, CUNY. Of special interest to those interested
      in the performance of the Austro-Hungarian army during World
      War I are the contributions by Rothenberg and Luvaas.

1056. Lutz, Ralph Haswell, comp. *Fall of the German Empire, 1914-
      1918*. Stanford, Calif.: Stanford University Press, 1932.
      2 vols.

      Some 500 documents concerning every aspect of the German
      war effort are published in these volumes. This work is based
      on the rich collection of German materials in the Hoover War
      Library.

1057. May, Arthur J. *The Passing of the Hapsburg Monarchy, 1914-
      1918*. Philadelphia: University of Pennsylvania Press, 1966.
      2 vols.

      May provides a detailed account based on exhaustive research
      on the last years of the Habsburg Monarchy. This work is also
      useful for understanding the diplomacy and military campaigns
      of Austria-Hungary during the war.

1058. Mitrany, David. *The Effect of the War in Southeastern Europe*.
New Haven: Yale University Press, 1936. 282 pp.

This volume provides a historical background and examines
the impact of war on the governments and economies of southeastern Europe. In his epilogue, the author criticizes some
aspects of the peace settlement.

1059. Müller, Georg Alexander von. *The Kaiser and His Court: The
Diaries, Note Books and Letters of Admiral Georg Alexander
von Müller, Chief of the Naval Cabinet, 1914-1918*. Edited
by Walter Goerlitz. London: Macdonald, 1961. 430 pp.

This is one of the few English-language sources that provides
a revealing behind-the-scenes account of the German government
and of the Kaiser's circle. It is especially useful in examining American-German relations and the U-boat issue.

* Ritter, Gerhard. *The Sword and the Scepter*. *The Problem of
Militarism in Germany*, vol. 3: *The Tragedy of Statesmanship--
Bethmann Hollweg as War Chancellor (1914-1917)*. Cited above
as item 950.

1060. ———. *The Sword and the Scepter: The Problem of Militarism
in Germany*, vol. 4: *The Reign of German Militarism and the
Disaster of 1918*. Coral Gables, Fla.: University of Miami
Press, 1973. 496 pp.

Ritter died as he was finishing the fourth and last volume
of his study of militarism in Germany. This volume covers the
period from Bethmann Hollweg's fall to the defeat of the
German army and the beginning of the German revolution. Ritter
has been criticized for generally attempting to limit German
responsibility for the outbreak of war and grandiose war objectives to the generals.

1061. Rosenberg, Arthur. *Imperial Germany: The Birth of the German
Republic 1871-1918*. Boston: Beacon Press, 1964. 286 pp.

This remains one of the best surveys of internal developments in Germany during the war. The author was a member of
the Reichstag committee of inquiry into the causes of Germany's
defeat. There is no bibliography in this English edition but
there are notes at the end of each chapter. The first English
edition was published in 1931.

1062. Sachar, Howard M. *The Emergence of the Middle East, 1914-1924*.
New York: Alfred A. Knopf, 1969. 518 pp.

This excellent history sheds light on the convulsions of the
Middle East and the emergence of modern Turkey out of the
destruction of the Ottoman Empire.

1063. Seton-Watson, Hugh and Christopher. *The Making of a New Europe:
R.W. Watson and the Last Years of Austria-Hungary*. Seattle:
University of Washington Press, 1981. 470 pp.

This is an important study of the breakup of the Austro-
Hungarian Dual Monarchy. The central figure is the elder

Seton-Watson, who influenced British perceptions of the subject
nationalities during the war as an expert in the British
government on East-Central Europe. Seton-Watson also attended
the Peace Conference in an unofficial capacity as a lobbyist
and consultant to the various peace delegations.

1064.   Zeman, Z.A.B. *The Break-Up of the Habsburg Empire, 1914-1918:
        A Study in National and Social Revolution.* London: Oxford
        University Press, 1961. 274 pp.

        Zeman researched the Vienna archives to analyze the factors
        responsible for the destruction of the Dual Monarchy. One
        controversial question that receives particular attention is:
        was the Habsburg Empire destroyed by internal forces or was
        its demise a result of Entente policy? Military developments
        are dealt with only peripherally.

                            G. MOBILIZATION

                          1. General Sources

1065.   Baker, Charles Whiting. *Government Control and Operation of
        Industry in Great Britain and the United States During the
        World War.* New York: Oxford University Press, 1921. 138 pp.

        This Carnegie Endowment study examines governmental adminis-
        tration of industry in Britain and the United States during
        the war. It treats efficiency in government-operated indus-
        tries, organization, railways in Great Britain and the United
        States, public utilities in the United States, shipping,
        labor, capital, food, popular views, and executive and legis-
        lative conflict.

1066.   Bogart, Ernest L. *Direct and Indirect Costs of the Great
        World War.* Washington, D.C.: Carnegie Endowment for Inter-
        national Peace, 1919. 330 pp.

        Bogart, an economist, puts the direct and indirect cost of
        the war at the mind-boggling figure of $337,946,179,657.
        Given the inexact nature of such a study, however, this dollar
        figure is certainly open to question.

1067.   Carnegie, David. *The History of Munitions Supply in Canada,
        1914-1918.* New York: Longmans, Green & Co., 1925. 336 pp.

        The author was intimately involved during the war in the
        Canadian supply of munitions to Britain. There is some material
        on Canadian cooperation with the United States.

1068.   Clark, J. Maurice; Hamilton, Walton H.; and Moulton, Harold G.,
        eds. *Readings in the Economics of War.* Chicago: University
        of Chicago Press, 1918. 676 pp.

        This is a broad and extensive collection of writings on the
        economics of World War I which focuses most on the economic and
        fiscal mobilization of the United States for the war.

1069. Coffman, Edward M. "The Battle Against Red Tape: Business Methods of the War Department General Staff, 1917-1918." *Mil. Affairs* 26 (Spring 1962): 1-10.

    Peyton C. March's gifts as an administrator receive special emphasis in this well-written article.

1070. Cooling, Benjamin Franklin. *Gray Steel and Blue Water Navy: The Formative Years of America's Military-Industrial Complex, 1881-1917.* Hamden, Conn.: Shoe String Press, 1979. 286 pp.

    This important, well-written, and well-researched book argues that the U.S. military-industrial complex was started with the construction of the modern steel navy in the post-Civil War period. The study explores the relationship between the government and the steel industry as disputes arose over the price of armor plating and gun forgings. Cooling approaches his subject from the government's perspective.

1071. Cuff, Robert D. "The Dollar-a-Year-Men of the Great War." *Princeton Lib. Chron.* 30 (Autumn 1968): 10-24.

    This well-written article samples and surveys the attitudes and work of the World War I dollar-a-year-men. They learned that with a mandate to plan without being hindered by the antitrust laws, industry could achieve great things.

1072. ———. "Organizing for War: Canada and the United States During World War I." In *Historical Papers, 1969*, pp. 141-56. Ottawa: Canadian Historical Association, 1969.

    This paper examines World War I industrial mobilization in Canada and the United States. Generally, Canadian mobilization moved more slowly than U.S. mobilization. In fact, the United States quickly overtook Canada in war production.

1073. ———. "We Band of Brothers—Woodrow Wilson's War Managers." *Can. Rev. Amer. Stud.* 5 (Fall 1974): 135-48.

    This well-thought-out article analyzes Wilson's war managers. Cuff concludes that idealism sets the Wilson war machine off from more recent war management situations.

1074. Fesler, James W. "Areas for Industrial Mobilization, 1917-1938." *Pub. Admin. Rev.* 1 (Winter 1941): 149-66.

    This article traces the evolution of industrial mobilization concepts and organization from World War I until 1938, and discusses the organizational structure and problem areas during that period.

1075. Finnegan, John P. *Against the Specter of a Dragon: The Campaign for American Military Preparedness, 1914-1917.* Westport, Conn.: Greenwood Press, 1975. 252 pp.

    This well-researched and sprightly work is the best study of American military preparedness. The preparedness movement, whose impetus came primarily from isolationism, did not result in a military establishment capable of fighting a war in Europe, but it did, according to the author, create, "almost accidentally,

the necessary preconditions for a full-scale effort." One important point Finnegan emphasizes is the lack of coordination
between military policy and U.S. foreign policy. An excellent
annotated bibliography is included. See also the author's
1969 University of Wisconsin dissertation.

1076. Gray, Howard L. *Wartime Control of Industry*. New York: Mac-
       millan Co., 1919. 307 pp.

       This study examines the British control of industry during
       World War I. Control came in three phases: the first involved
       ten months of tentative action; the second involved a year
       and a half of regulation; and the third dealt with determined
       control. This work details the various stages of government
       control of industry, from railroad control to the fixing of
       consumer prices, and contains a brief comparison with the
       United States.

1077. Hull, William I. *Preparedness: The American Versus the Military
       Programme*. New York: Fleming H. Revell Co., 1916. 271 pp.

       This work, written from a pacifistic point of view, attacks
       the inadequacy of the military preparedness programs, but it
       points out the evils of an adequate military preparedness
       system. This is a clearly stated, critical view of the prewar
       preparedness movement. It questions the argument that the
       United States must be the world's policeman. Moreover, the
       book contains a useful description of the period's military
       hardware.

1078. Kaufman, Burton I. *Efficiency and Expansion: Foreign Trade
       Organization in the Wilson Administration*. Westport, Conn.:
       Greenwood Press, 1974. 300 pp.

       The study is an insightful analysis of Wilson's foreign
       trade policy. Wilson brought government and business together
       in promoting foreign trade--a policy followed by subsequent
       administrations. During World War I, the wartime agencies
       continued to promote overseas trade. The volume is thoroughly
       researched and based on manuscript sources.

1079. Knoeppel, C.E. *Industrial Preparedness*. New York: Engineering
       Magazine Co., 1916. 145 pp.

       This contemporary work examines German military and indus-
       trial preparedness and had the purpose of pointing the way
       toward preparedness in the United States. The book treats
       the condition of industrial preparesness in the United States,
       German military accomplishments, German military principles,
       German industrial efficiency, lessons from German industrial
       preparedness, and how those lessons should be implemented.

1080. Koistinen, Paul A.C. "The 'Industrial-Military Complex' in
       Historical Perspective: World War I." *Bus. Hist. Rev.* 41
       (Winter 1967): 378-403.

       This article examines the origins of "the industrial-military
       complex" in World War I. Ultimately the War Industries Board

brought industry, government, and the military together. Industry generally experienced self-rule because of the emergency
situation and the military's dependence on it. Private businessmen worked hand-in-hand with army personnel to modernize
military supply procedures.

1081. Kreidberg, Marvin A., and Henry, Merton G. *The History of
Mobilization in the U.S. Army, 1775-1945*. Washington, D.C.:
Government Printing Office, 1948. 721 pp.

Many charts and tables appear in this comprehensive examination of the use of American manpower in war from the American
Revolution to World War II.

1082. Magoffin, Ralph Van Deman. "Historical Work by Army General
Staffs." *AHR* 24 (July 1919): 630-36.

Magoffin notes the broadening of general staff histories to
include civilian activities.

1083. Paxson, Frederic L. "The American War Government, 1917-1918."
AHR 26 (October 1920): 54-76.

The author surveys the creation and activities of emergency
boards and administrations to enable America to fight a total
war. By September 1918 the state had achieved an astonishing
degree of intervention in social and economic matters.

1084. Scherer, James A.B. *The Nation at War*. New York: George H.
Doran Co., 1918. 285 pp.

This volume, written in a popular style, is a personal
account by a field agent of the Council of National Defense.
It treats U.S. entrance into the war, the Council of Defense,
experiences in northern and southern states, the experiences
of dealing with western states, the Research Council and
Shipping Board, various personalities encountered, Paul
Petrigard, and America's future. The work captures the contemporary flavor and feeling of the war.

1085. Urofsky, Melvin I. *Big Steel and the Wilson Administration:
A Study in Business-Government Relations*. Columbus: Ohio
State University Press, 1969. 364 pp.

This study, a narrative of the relationship between the
steel industry and the Wilson administration, is important
for those who are interested in understanding how the industrial war machine operates.

1086. Van Dorn, Harold Archer. *Government Owned Corporations*. New
York: Alfred A. Knopf, 1926. 311 pp.

This study traces the evolution of government-owned corporations. It also attempts to predict the future value of such
organizations. Among others, it looks at Federal Land Banks,
the Emergency Fleet Corporation, the War Finance Corporation,
the United States Housing Corporation, the United States Sugar
Equalization Board, the Federal Intermediate Credit Banks, the

Inland Waterways Corporation, and various minor corporations.
Van Dorn concludes that government-owned corporations represented a major advance in governmental administration.

1087. Willoughby, William Franklin. *Government Organization in War
Time and After: A Survey of the Federal Civil Agencies
Created for the Prosecution of the War*. New York: D. Apple-
ton & Co., 1919. 370 pp.

This contemporary work examines in a general way the federal
civil agencies utilized during World War I. It treats the
mobilization of science, public opinion, finance, industry,
foreign trade, shipping, inland transportation and communica-
tion, labor, food, fuel, aircraft construction, and war-risk
insurance. The author points out that in finance the existing
machinery worked well. In addition, other successful areas
included direct authority, negotiation, licensing, subsidiary
corporations, and public relations.

1088. Wright, Chester W. "American Economic Preparation for War,
1914-1917 and 1939-1941." *Can. Jour. Econ. Pol. Sci.* 8
(May 1942): 157-75.

This article illustrates how the United States had learned
from the World War I experience as it prepared for World
War II. Much emphasis is placed on the organizational structure before the world wars.

2. Agencies

a. Aircraft

1089. "The Aircraft Production Board." *Proc. Acad. Pol. Sci.* 7 (February 1918): 104-14.

This board was brought into existence to act in an advisory
way to help create an industry where none existed. The main
focus of the board was to provide support for training in the
United States and support for combat activities in France.

1090. Knappen, Theodore M. *Wings of War: An Account of the Important
Contribution of the United States to Aircraft Invention,
Engineering, Development and Production During the World
War*. New York: G.P. Putnam's Sons, 1920. 289 pp.

The author attempts to refute the view that U.S. aircraft
production was "the outstanding industrial fiasco of America's
part in the World War." This work includes forty-three illustrations.

b. Council of National Defense

1091. Martin, Franklin H. *Digest of the Proceedings of the Council
of National Defense during the World War: Prepared in Narrative Form*. Washington, D.C.: Government Printing Office,
1934. 700 pp.

Based upon the experiences of Franklin Martin as a member of the Council of National Defense, this work summarizes the work of that important body. It should be treated as a primary document with good insights on the medical side of World War I.

c. *Food*

1092. "The Battle of the Plow." *Outlook* 116 (2 May 1917): 11-12.

This essay is an excellent example of an attempt to influence American public opinion to mobilize its food resources.

1093. Bernhardt, Joshua. "Government Control of Sugar During the War." *Quar. Jour. Econ.* 33 (August 1919): 672-713.

This article examines the four periods of government control, sugar crop problems in 1918-1919, price problems, supply and distribution problems, the United States Sugar Equalization Board, sugar agreements, and solutions. The author concludes that the sugar program was a success.

1094. Brand, Charles J. "Truth About the Food Situation." *Forum* 59 (January 1918): 43-50.

In this article the chief of the United States Bureau of Markets asserts that there will be no food shortages in the United States. Nevertheless, he warns the people to conserve food.

1095. Cooke, Jay. "The Work of the Federal Food Administration." *Ann. Am. Ac. of Pol. Sci. and Soc. Sci.* 78 (July 1918): 175-84.

This article outlines the work of the Federal Food Administration in terms of basic commodities. It also treats market and distribution problems.

1096. Coville, Frederick V. "War, Patriotism, and the Food Supply." *National Geographic* 31 (March 1917): 254-56.

The author equates patriotism with food conservation and increased production.

1097. Cuff, Robert D. "Herbert Hoover, the Ideology of Voluntarism and War Organization During the Great War." *JAH* 64 (September 1977): 358-72.

This important article examines the concept of voluntarism during World War I with a particular focus on Herbert Hoover. Basically, the author sees voluntarism as conservative, and that Hoover did not want to change the governmental structure as it responded to the stress of war. The voluntarist viewed the war as temporary, and argued that the response during the emergency must lead only to temporary measures.

1098. Dewey, John. *Enlistment for the Farm*. New York: Columbia University Division of Intelligence and Publicity, 1917. 10 pp.

This very brief essay is primarily a statement to school

boards, principals, and teachers to show how school children
can help the war program.

1099. Dickson, Maxcy R. *The Food Front in World War I*. Washington,
       D.C.: American on Public Affairs, 1944. 194 pp.

       This book synthesizes the national activities of the World
       War I food program. It deals with propaganda aimed at the
       conservation of food. It contains little information on the
       activities of the agencies, but it does shed light on the
       problems and policies of the period.

1100. Edgar, William C. "Bureaucracy and Food Control." *American
       Review of Reviews* (June 1917): 626-28.

       The editor of the *Northwestern Miller* warns against govern-
       ment functionaries who were scaring the populace with tales of
       grain scarcity.

1101. Eldred, Wilfred. "The Wheat and Flour Trade Under Food Ad-
       ministration Control: 1917-1918." *Quar. Jour. Econ.* 33
       (November 1918): 1-70.

       This article examines the commercial situation and prices
       for 1916-1917. It treats the necessity for government control,
       the wheat price committee, the resentment of the wheat millers,
       the stabilization of the market, the decline in milling ac-
       tivity, evasions, and conclusions. The author concludes that
       the program worked well.

1102. Gilman, Charlotte P. "The Housekeeper and the Food Problem."
       Ann. Am. Ac. of Pol. Sci. and Soc. Sci. 74 (November 1917):
       123-31.

       This practical look at the food problem sees it as being
       threefold: first, the problem of production at a minimum cost;
       second, the problem of distribution in a fast and efficient
       manner; and third, the problem of economy of preparation.
       The article argues for practical solutions for the management
       and preparation of food in the home.

1103. Houston, David F. "The Department of Agriculture and the Food
       Situation." *Science* 46 (23 November 1917): 528-29.

       The Secretary of Agriculture indicates how the various
       agencies concerning agriculture can cooperate for the common
       good in increasing food production.

1104. ———. "Soldiers of the Soil." *National Geographic* 31
       (March 1917): 273-79.

       In this essay the Secretary of Agriculture calls for an
       increase of food production in all areas.

1105. Merrill, Sara. "What Retail Merchants Are Doing for Food
       Conservation." *Jour. Home Econ.* 10 (June 1918): 264-65.

       This article explains how local retailers, especially through
       advertising, were encouraging people to conserve food.

1106. Mullendore, William C. *History of the United States Food Administration, 1917-1919.* Stanford, Calif.: Stanford University Press, 1941. 399 pp.

This official history of the U.S. Food Administration focuses much attention on the role of Herbert C. Hoover. Basically, it views the agency's response to great problems as a record of much accomplishment.

1107. Pack, Charles Lathrop. *The War Garden Victorious.* Philadelphia: J.B. Lippincott Co., 1919. 174 pp.

This contemporary volume treats the story of the war garden in World War I. It examines: the establishment of the National War Garden Commission, how the garden helped, the types of war gardens, the first war garden, the role of big business, the role of the railroads, school gardens, community gardens, cooperative gardening, war gardens as city assets, the role of daylight saving time, the future of war gardens, conserving the surplus, community conservation, the future of dehydration, and the support of the press. The appendix contains manuals on the home storage of vegetables and canning and drying of vegetables and fruits.

1108. Pollock, Ivan L. *The Food Administration in Iowa.* Iowa City: State Historical Society, 1923. 2 vols.

These volumes chronicle the work of the people of Iowa as they contributed to the war effort by conserving food. By war's end the organization to conserve food functioned smoothly.

1109. Powell, G. Harold. "Regulation of the Perishable Food Industries After the War." *Ann. Am. Ac. of Pol. Sci. and Soc. Sci.* 82 (March 1919): 183-88.

This article calls for the extension of the concept of regulation of the perishable food industry into the postwar period. The author offers suggestions as to how that could be accomplished.

1110. Stoddard, Ralph G. "Mobilizing Unused Land and Forces to Meet an Unprecedented Crisis." *American City* 16 (May 1917): 471-81.

The author outlines methods which could be employed in growing food on vacant lots and on people's lawns in order to combat the food shortage created by the war.

1111. Surface, Franklin, and Bland, Raymond L. *American Food in the World War and Reconstruction Period: Operations of the Organizations Under the Direction of Herbert Hoover, 1914-1924.* Stanford, Calif.: Stanford University Press, 1931. 1,033 pp.

This volume treats the Commission for Relief in Belgium, the United States Food Administration, the Armistice period, and the Reconstruction period. Basically statistical, the

study shows the organizational genius of Herbert Hoover as
the relief program spent over $5 billion.

d. *Fuel*

1112.   Garfield, Harry A.   "The Task of the Fuel Administration."
        Proc. Acad. Pol. Sci. 7 (February 1918): 50–54.

        Written by the head of the fuel administration, this article
        emphasizes the importance of bringing order out of the chaos
        in Washington through cooperation among the various agencies.

1113.   Johnson, James P.   *The Politics of Soft Coal: The Bituminous
        Industry from World War I Through the New Deal.*   Champaign:
        University of Illinois Press, 1979.   258 pp.

        A well-researched study of the relations between management,
        labor, and government, this book shows that the failure of the
        mine operators to stabilize the soft coal industry forced
        the government to create the U.S. Fuel Administration during
        World War I.   Thus, the government intervened in labor dis-
        putes and fixed prices.   However, this wartime cooperation
        failed to carry over into the postwar period.

e. *Housing*

1114.   Childs, Richard S.   "The Government's Model Villages."   *Survey*,
        1 February 1919, pp. 584–92.

        The author, the secretary of the committee on new industrial
        towns, explains the development of model villages during World
        War I.   Photographs and general plans complement the article,
        which touches on such towns as Buckmer Village, Yorkship
        Village, Gloucester, Union Park Gardens, Sun Village, and
        other planned communities.   Basically, the communities were
        well planned and attractive.

1115.   Hitchcock, Curtice N.   "The War Housing Program and Its
        Future."   *Jour. Pol. Econ.* 27 (April 1919): 241–79.

        This article examines the problems in the housing program
        which developed during the war.   The basic problem was that
        there existed no single agency which had responsibility for
        housing.   Ultimately, the Housing Corporation took over the
        construction and management of many housing projects.   ·It
        dealt with nonshipping industrial projects, while a division
        of the emergency fleet corporation dealt with housing in the
        shipping industry.   The war ended before the housing projects
        were completed.

1116.   National Housing Association.   *A Symposium on War Housing.*
        New York: National Housing Association, 1918.   141 pp.

        This interesting document contains the proceedings of a
        meeting on war housing.   Among other items examined were:
        the question of housing war workers, the ownership of this
        housing, housing for women war workers, and discussions of the

housing situation in a number of northeastern cities. This is a good starting point for researchers who are interested in examining the housing question during World War I.

1117. Veiller, Lawrence. "The Housing of the Mobilized Population." *Ann. Am. Ac. of Pol. Sci. and Soc. Sci.* 78 (July 1918): 19-24.

The director of the national housing association treats the housing problems brought on by World War I mobilization. For soldiers, the solution was small barracks to house around 66 men. The housing of the industrial army presented greater problems and would be solved by building small houses and even small communities to handle the war workers.

f. Labor

1118. Bing, A.M. *War-Time Strikes and Their Adjustment.* New York: E.P. Dutton & Co., 1921. 329 pp.

The organization and role of government agencies responsible for mediating industrial disputes are examined in this work.

1119. Conner, Valerie Jean. *The National War Labor Board: Stability, Social Justice, and the Voluntary State in World War I.* Chapel Hill: University of North Carolina Press, 1983. 234 pp.

This well-written volume focuses attention on the National War Labor Board as a good example of cooperation between management and labor. The board set important precedents by supporting the minimum wage concept and the eight-hour day. The author feels that the board turned voluntarism toward a social orientation. However, the book breaks little new ground.

1120. Frankfurter, Felix. "The Conservation of the New Federal Standards." *Survey,* 7 December 1918, pp. 291-93.

The author, the chairman of the United States Labor Policies Board, discusses the labor standards which emerged from World War I. The standards included hours, wages, safeguards against industrial accidents, employment of women and children, arbitration of disputes, labor organizations, and community standards. He argues that in the period after the war the government should act only as a moderator in labor relations.

1121. Lindsay, Samuel M. "Purpose and Scope of War Risk Insurance." *Ann. Am. Ac. of Pol. Sci. and Soc. Sci.* 79 (September 1918): 52-68.

This essay treats the War Risk Insurance Act and its ramifications. Basically, the U.S. government was in the business of underwriting the insurance for the merchant marine.

1122. Love, Thomas B. "The Social Significance of War Risk Insurance." *Ann. Am. Ac. of Pol. and Soc. Sci.* 79 (September 1918): 46-51.

This article examines the social impact of war risk insurance. It shows the concept of insurance was an important part of the

relationship between the United States government and all of
its workers.

1123. Macy, V. Everit. "Labor Policies That Will Win the War."
      Ann. Am. Ac. of Pol. Sci. and Soc. Sci. 78 (July 1918):
      74-80.

      The article argues against national conscription of war
      workers as a means of mobilizing labor. The author calls for
      cooperation, a national wage, working standards, and the co-
      operation of labor boards.

*   Mandel, Bernard. *Samuel Gompers: A Biography.* Cited above
        as item 883.

1124. Marshall, L.C. "The War Labor Program and Its Administration."
      Jour. Pol. Econ. 26 (May 1918): 425-60.

      This important contemporary article deals with some of the
      problems coming out of the war labor program and its adminis-
      tration. It treats the establishment of the War Labor Board
      and outlines its structure. This is a good starting point
      for an examination of the war labor program.

1125. Nash, Gerald D. "Franklin D. Roosevelt and Labor: The World
      War I Origins of the Early New Deal Policy." *Labor Hist.* 1
      (Winter 1960): 39-52.

      This important article shows how Assistant Secretary of the
      Navy Franklin D. Roosevelt through the Committee of Labor and
      the National War Labor Board helped keep production moving
      forward in the shipyards. This experience influenced him as
      president in his handling of labor problems.

1126. Rayback, Joseph G. *A History of American Labor.* New York:
      The Free Press, 1966. 491 pp.

      This survey of the American labor movement as an integral
      part of American history deals with World War I's impact on
      labor in both a positive and negative way.

1127. Sullivan, J.W. "The Maintenance of Labor Standards." *Ann.
      Am. Ac. of Pol. Sci. and Soc. Sci.* 78 (July 1918): 90-96.

      This article discusses some of the work of the Council of
      National Defense and the question of labor standards. Written
      from the perspective of labor, it points out ways in which
      labor is still being treated unfairly.

1128. Wehle, Louis B. "The Adjustment of Labor Disputes Incident
      to Production for War in the United States." *Quar. Jour.
      Econ.* 32 (November 1917): 122-41.

      This article examines labor problems in contracts for can-
      tonments, adjustments, emergency shipbuilding in private yards,
      adjustment with longshoremen, and conclusions. It also con-
      tains some basic documents dealing with labor adjustments.

1129. Wolfe, S.H. "Eight Months of War Risk Insurance Work." *Ann. Am. Ac. of Pol. Sci. and Soc. Sci.* 79 (September 1918): 68-79.

In this essay an official of the Quartermaster Corps analyzes the war risk insurance plan after its first eight months of operation. The bureau which administers the act broke new ground since it had no precedents to follow.

g. Railroads

1130. Crennan, C.H., and Warrington, W.E., comps. "Documents and Statistics Pertinent to Current Railroad Problems." *Ann. Am. Ac. of Pol. Sci. and Soc. Sci.* 76 (March 1918): 272-304.

This section consists of legislation and proclamations dealing with the railroads during World War I. In addition, it contains basic statistics about railroads in the United States and other countries as well. Of more importance to the researcher, it includes a statistical bibliography.

1131. Cunningham, William J. *American Railroads: Government Controls and Reconstruction Policies*. Chicago: A.W. Shaw, 1922. 409 pp.

This work focuses attention on the period from January 1, 1918, to March 1, 1920. The author served on the staff of the director general of the railroads. After a brief survey of railroad history to 1916, the author examines a number of topics, including: the railroad's war board, unification under federal control, contracts between the government and the railroads, unification policies, standardization, accounting and statistical innovations, passenger and freight service in 1918, operating results in 1918, relations with state commissions, upkeep of physical property, financial results, political influence, and the Transportation Act of 1920.

1132. Dixon, Frank H. "Federal Operation of Railroads During the War." *Quar. Jour. Econ.* 33 (August 1919): 577-631.

This article treats the reasons why roads were taken over by the government, the contract, federal operation, labor, rate increases, financing, relations with other agencies, and speculation on the future. This essay indicates that the system worked for the public good and that a call for total nationalization might be in the future.

1133. ————. *Railroads and Government: Their Relations in the United States, 1910-1921*. New York: Charles Scribner's Sons, 1922. 384 pp.

This work deals with the federal regulation of railroads from 1910 to 1921. This competent volume treats: rate regulation, the long and short haul, commerce court, administration, railroad water lines, labor problems, war board, federal control, federal operation, state regulation, government and labor financial results, reconstruction, postwar rate problems,

jurisdictional conflicts, railroad consolidation, capitaliza-
tion, regulation of wages and working conditions, water
traffic, and future specialization.

1134.   ————, and Parmelee, Julius H. *War Administration of the*
Railways in the United States and Great Britain. New York:
Oxford University Press, 1918. 155 pp.

This monograph examines the historical background of the
railroads and their wartime usage. It focuses attention on
the period when the U.S. entered the war and railroads had to
move from a period of competition to a period of voluntary
cooperation. It examines the war organization of railroads,
the attempts to achieve operating efficiency, growing cooperation of government and railways, and the end of voluntary
cooperation. The work also surveys the British railway system
during the war.

1135.   Dunn, Samuel O. "The Railways in Peace and War." *Yale Rev.* 7
(January 1918): 362-81.

This essay treats questions of ownership of the railroads.
It argues for government regulation and against government
ownership.

1136.   Godfrey, Aaron A. *Government Operation of the Railroads: Its*
Necessity, Success, and Consequences, 1918-1920. Austin,
Texas: Jenkins Publishing, 1974. 190 pp.

This well-researched study examines how the government took
over the railroads during the war and ran them in a monopolis-
tic way. The war measures upset shippers and management.
However, labor made significant financial gains and thus was
the only group to complement the system in the period after
the war.

1137.   Kerr, K. Austin. *American Railroad Politics, 1914-1920: Rates,*
Wages, and Efficiency. Pittsburgh: University of Pittsburgh
Press, 1968. 250 pp.

This book examines the way in which various special-interest
groups attempted to influence federal railroad policy during
World War I. The author points out that the shippers lost
their prewar influence during the war. Yet in the postwar
period, the shippers regained their influence.

1138.   ————. "Decision for Federal Control: Wilson, McAdoo, and
the Railroads, 1917." *JAH* 54 (December 1967): 550-60.

This competently researched essay deals with the takeover
of the railroad system by the government during World War I.
Political, rate, and labor problems forced Wilson to national-
ize the railroads under the pressure of a war. Much pressure
came from McAdoo and the railroads themselves. Kerr concludes
that the nationalization sharpened the political conflict but
that it was the best solution available at the time.

1139.   Parmalee, Julius H. "Physical Needs of the Railways Under

Government Control." *Ann. Am. Ac. of Pol. Sci. and Soc. Sci.* 76 (March 1918): 42-58.

This essay concerns congestion caused by an inadequate supply of equipment as well as improper utilization of equipment. It surveys railroad traffic and projects the traffic problems and physical needs of the railroads. The author predicts that over $500 million of capital improvements would be needed on an annual basis.

1140. Smith, Alexander W. "A Suggested Plan for Permanent Governmental Supervision of Railroad Operation After the War." *Ann. Am. Ac. of Pol. Sci. and Soc. Sci.* 76 (March 1918): 142-56.

This article offers a proposal for the government supervision of railroads on a permanent basis. The plan involves the establishment of a government department for the operation of railroads. Thus, political meddling should be kept to a minimum.

1141. Thelen, Max. "Federal Control of Railroads in War Time." *Ann. Am. Ac. of Pol. Sci. and Soc. Sci.* 76 (March 1918): 14-24.

This article surveys all facets of government control of the railroads during the war. The article concludes that William Gibbs McAdoo would successfully handle the operations of the railroads as a single system.

1142. Thorne, Clifford. "Government Operation of American Railroads." *Ann. Am. Ac. of Pol. Sci. and Soc. Sci.* 76 (March 1918): 84-110.

Thorne treats the operation of the railroads by the government in light of legal and public policy questions. The article concludes that railroads would retain ownership and that railroad stockholders would be protected from loss of investment while other industries were in danger of getting into financial difficulty.

h. *Shipping*

1143. Adams, John W. "The Influences Affecting Naval Shipbuilding Legislation, 1910-1916." *Nav. War Col. Rev.* 22 (December 1969): 41-70.

Adams surveys the naval building programs from 1910 to 1916. Likewise, he examines the influence of the politicians and government agencies. Ultimately, the government apparatus reflected the will of the people.

1144. Smith, J. Russell. *Influence of the Great War upon Shipping.* New York: Oxford University Press, 1919. 357 pp.

This report, published under the auspices of the Carnegie Endowment for International Peace, examines the impact of the war on commercial shipping. The author treats the organization

of world shipping before and during the war with a look at
topics from freight rates to shipbuilding in the United States
and Great Britain.

1145. Stevens, Raymond B. "Problems Before the Shipping Board."
      Proc. Acad. Pol. Sci. 7 (February 1918): 93-99.

      This article argues that the shipping board faced two major
      problems. One concerned creating the shipping necessary to
      get supplies to the Allies and to transport the American Ex-
      peditionary Force to Europe. The other involved the proper
      utilization of the shipping which was already in existence.

1146. Still, William N., Jr. "Shipbuilding in North Carolina: The
      World War I Experience." *American Neptune* 41 (July 1981):
      188-207.

      This is a well-documented case study of the rapid expansion
      of shipbuilding after the United States entered the war.

1147. Webb, William J. "The United States Wooden Steamship Program
      During World War I." *American Neptune* 35 (October 1975):
      275-88.

      As a result of the war, the Fleet Corporation decided that
      wooden vessels could be used in coastwise shipping. Ultimate-
      ly, over sixty wooden or composition ships were put into ser-
      vice during the war.

i. War Finance Corporation

1148. Goldman, Michael Abbot. "The War Finance Corporation in the
      Politics of War and Reconstruction 1917-23." Doctoral dis-
      sertation, Rutgers University, 1971. 416 pp.

      This well-researched volume examines the War Finance Corpora-
      tion as a case study of the relations between the government
      and private economic groups from World War I through the early
      1920s. Corporate banking reformers led the fight in war
      finances, foreign trade financing, and rural credits to
      rationalize the American economy in a progressive way. This
      agency served as a precedent for the Reconstruction Finance
      Corporation.

j. War Industries Board

1149. Beaver, Daniel R. "Newton D. Baker and the Genesis of the
      War Industries Board, 1917-1918." *JAH* 52 (June 1965):
      43-48.

      From late March to mid-June of 1917, Newton D. Baker helped
      to make three decisions that shaped American industry's part
      in World War I. These dealt with raising, training, and dis-
      patching American troops to France. Baker believed that the
      military should have the final authority in industrial mobili-
      zation. Treasury secretary William G. McAdoo believed that
      the power should be in the hands of a civilian. This conflict

led to the appointment of Bernard Baruch as head of the War
Industries Board with strong central powers. Baker stayed on
with the War Department after threatening to resign.

*   Coit, Margaret L. *Mr. Baruch.* Cited above as item 864.

1150.   Crissey, Forrest. *Alexander Legge, 1866-1933.* Chicago:
        Alexander Legge Memorial Committee, 1936. 232 pp.

        This "memorial" biography of Alexander Legge treats the
        career of an important agriculturalist and industrialist
        with McCormick Company. During World War I, he served as
        vice chairman of the War Industries Board under Bernard
        Baruch. He served well as a practical economist, and he was
        taken to the Paris Peace Conference as an economic expert.
        The biography is not footnoted and is based to some degree on
        oral history. This work is important in that it reveals some
        insights into a key, but little-known, World War I figure on
        the economic scene.

1151.   Cuff, Robert D. "Bernard Baruch: Symbol and Myth in Indus-
        trial Mobilization." *Bus. Hist. Rev.* 43 (Summer 1969):
        115-33.

        This essay examines Bernard Baruch's role in industrial
        mobilization during World War I. Cuff attacks the importance
        given to Baruch in Grosvenor B. Clarkson's work *Industrial
        America in the World War.* Giving credit to Newton D. Baker
        for helping to shape the War Industries Board, Cuff sees
        Baruch as a symbol of stability for the nation during a period
        of relentless uncertainty. Baruch made the change from the
        private to the public sector, but he failed to achieve all of
        his goals.

1152.   ———. "A 'Dollar-a-Year-Man' in Government: George N. Peek
        and the War Industries Board." *Bus. Hist. Rev.* 41 (Winter
        1967): 404-20.

        This well-researched essay examines George N. Peek's role
        with the WIB during World War I. Peek, unable to free himself
        from his business ties to the private sector, based many de-
        cisions on his connection with the farm implements industry.
        However, some decisions he made were based on the good of the
        country as a whole. Cuff concludes that Peek aided the war
        effort by protecting and stabilizing industry.

1153.   ———. *The War Industries Board: Business-Government Rela-
        tions During World War I.* Baltimore, Md.: Johns Hopkins
        University Press, 1973. 304 pp.

        In a major study, Robert Cuff examines the role of the WIB
        during the war and analyzes the impact of the businessmen who
        worked on it during the war. Cuff concludes that the business-
        men failed in their goal to protect business interests in the
        period after the war.

1154.   DeWeerd, Harvey A. "American Industrial Mobilization for

War, 1917-1918." *Ohio Archaeol. and Hist. Quar.* 49 (July-
September 1940): 249-61.

This article surveys the background to U.S. mobilization.
It highlights some of the major organizational and technical
developments. A major development was the adoption of the
Springfield rifle and its interchangeable parts. It was eleven
months before the War Industries Board had sufficient power to
mobilize truly. The author argues that a history of British
mobilization would have been useful to the United States.

1155. Himmelberg, Robert F. "The War Industries Board and the Anti-
       Trust Question in November 1918." *JAH* 52 (June 1965): 59-
       74.

This well-researched article deals with the War Industries
Board's perceived power to set policies for demobilization
and reconstruction. During the war the WIB had abandoned the
antitrust policy and engaged in price-fixing, a practice industry wanted continued into the postwar period to prevent
deflation. The simplest way to continue the policy would be
the continuation of the WIB. However, President Wilson opposed
this plan and the WIB accepted it, thus preserving its image
as an impartial and honorable agency serving the national interest during the war.

1156. Ohl, John K. "The Navy, the War Industries Board, and the In-
       dustrial Mobilization for War, 1917-1918." *Mil. Affairs* 40
       (February 1976): 17-22.

This article analyzes the expansion of the so-called military-industrial complex during the time of America's involvement
in World War I.

*   Schwarz, Jordan A. *The Speculator: Bernard M. Baruch in Wash-
       ington, 1917-1965.* Cited above as item 865.

                    3. Manpower and Training Camps

1157. Camfield, Thomas M. "'Will to Win'--The U.S. Army Troop Morale
       Program of World War I." *Mil. Affairs* 41 (October 1977):
       125-28.

Based almost exclusively on archival research, this article
examines the "first systematic troop morale program" in the
U.S. Army.

1158. Clifford, John Garry. *The Citizen Soldiers: The Plattsburg
       Training Camp Movement, 1913-1920.* Lexington: The University
       Press of Kentucky, 1972. 386 pp.

This well-researched study of the Plattsburg Training Camp
movement focuses attention on Grenville Clark as the man behind
the training camp movement. Moreover, Clifford analyzes Leonard
Wood's role in getting the movement started and pushing diligent-
ly for it to come to fruition.

1159. Dickinson, John Moore. *Building of an Army: A Detailed Account*
      of Legislation, Administration and Opinion in the United
      States, 1915-1920. New York: Century Co., 1922. 398 pp.

      This is a useful reference source because of its mass of facts
      and figures.

1160. Durham, Weldon. "'Big Brother' and the 'Seven Sisters': Camp
      Life Reforms in World War I." *Mil. Affairs* 42 (April 1978):
      57-60.

      The author describes the activities of the Commission on
      Training Camp Activities (CTCA).

1161. Durr, Ernest. "The Training of Recruits." *U.S. Naval Inst.*
      Proc. 43 (January 1917): 99-123.

      Some suggestions for the improvement of the training of
      naval recruits can be found in this article.

1162. Fosdick, Raymond B. "The Commission of Training Camp Activi-
      ties." *Proc. Acad. Pol. Sci.* 7 (February 1918), 163-70.

      This article explains why the CTCA was formed and how the
      War Department used it to improve the environment in camps and
      training centers. Basically, the commission attempted to es-
      tablish recreational facilities, and to utilize organizations
      such as the Young Men's Christian Association.

1163. ———. "The War and Navy Departments, Commissions on Train-
      ing Camp Activities." *Ann. Am. Ac. of Pol. Sci. and Soc.*
      Sci. 79 (September 1918): 130-42.

      This essay details the activities of service organizations
      such as the Y.M.C.A. in helping to improve the life of the
      soldier in the training camps.

1164. Mooney, Chase C., and Layman, Martha E. "Some Phase of the
      Compulsory Military Training Movements, 1914-1920." *MVHR* 38
      (March 1952): 633-57.

      This examination of the compulsory military training movement
      from the perspective of Congress reveals the tendency of con-
      gressmen to avoid politically explosive issues such as the com-
      pulsory training movement. Thus, the process of adding amend-
      ments and engaging in filibusters reflects an attempt to avoid
      controversy.

1165. Ruml, Beardsley. "The Extension of Selective Tests to Indus-
      try." *Ann. Am. Ac. of Pol. Sci. and Soc. Sci.* 81 (January
      1919): 38-46.

      This article examines the way in which the army used testing
      to place men in the proper jobs. It concludes that testing
      should be utilized by private industry in the placement of men
      in industry.

1166. United States War Department. *Home Reading Course for Citizen*
      Soldiers. Washington, D.C.: Government Printing Office, 1917.
      62 pp.

This pamphlet contains thirty daily lessons for U.S. soldiers. They include lessons on making a good soldier, preparing for camp, camp cleanliness, good health, marching, equipment, recreation, teamwork, branches of the service, training systems, and the soldier in battle.

1167. Walter, Henrietta R. "Output and Hours: A Summary of the English Experience." *Survey*, 21 April 1917, pp. 51-53.

This brief article discusses the work of the English committee on the health of munition workers. The committee concluded after a year's survey that the labor supply could be exhausted by overwork. Thus, it recommended the establishment of canteens, a welfare department in industry, improvements in housing, and the end of the seven-day work week and the eight-hour day for women.

4. Finance

1168. Adams, George P., Jr. *Wartime Price Control*. Washington, D.C.: American Council on Public Affairs, 1942. 153 pp.

This volume examines the price control effort of World War I and concludes that it is surprising it "succeeded as well as it did."

1169. Clark, John Maurice. *The Costs of the World War to the American People*. New Haven: Yale University Press, 1931. 316 pp.

The gigantic cost of the war is subjected to a statistical and social analysis by an economist. This is one of the volumes in the massive "Economic and Social History of the World War" series.

1170. Davies, Joseph E. "Price Control." *Ann. Am. Ac. of Pol. Sci. and Soc. Sci.* 74 (November 1917): 288-93.

This article surveys the wartime price rise and explains the legislation which had recently been passed to deal with the problem. The author argues that the fixed price should be based on a production cost that would not starve production.

1171. Fisher, Irving. "How the Public Should Pay for the War." *Ann. Am. Ac. of Pol. Sci. and Soc. Sci.* 78 (July 1918): 112-17.

This article argues that war bonds should be held to the end of the war and that savings and thrift must be encouraged.

1172. Gilbert, Charles. *American Financing of World War I*. Westport, Conn.: Greenwood Publishing Co., 1970. 256 pp.

This study deals with federal financial policies during the war. The work focuses attention on taxation as well as economic and political factors in the determination of economic policies. Based on printed sources, this book concludes that the Treasury Department did as well as it could have under the circumstances.

1173. Hillje, John W. "New York Progressives and War Revenue Act of 1917." *New York History* 53 (October 1972): 437-59.

Amos Pinchot and other New York progressives provided leadership to the American Committee on War Finance, which lobbied successfully that the war revenue acts should tax the wealthy. Thus, the progressive impulse did not die with the war.

1174. Seligman, Edwin R.A. "Loans Versus Taxes in War Finance." *Ann. Am. Ac. of Pol. Sci. and Soc. Sci.* 75 (January 1918): 52-82.

This well-written article analyzes the pros and cons of loans and taxes in war finance. The author concludes that government loans are necessary for sound finance.

1175. Taussig, Frank W. "Price Fixing as Seen by a Price-Fixer." *Quar. Jour. Econ.* 33 (February 1919): 205-41.

This article examines the three agencies which fixed prices, their different methods, the price-fixing committee, commodities regulated by the committee, cost of production as the basis, proposals for an average or pooled price, and objections to these methods.

1176. Vanderlip, Frank A. "Financing with War Savings Certificates." *Ann. Am. Ac. of Pol. Sci. and Soc. Sci.* 75 (January 1918): 31-37.

This essay by the president of the National City Bank of New York City explains the process and mechanism of how war savings certificates can be utilized in financing the war. It captures the contemporary view of how these certificates can be used.

1177. Van Hise, Charles R. "The Necessity for Government Regulation of Prices in War Time." *Ann. Am. Ac. of Pol. Sci. and Soc. Sci.* 74 (November 1917): 224-35.

Written by the president of the University of Wisconsin, this article presents an argument favoring price regulation. It surveys major industries and the upward spiral of prices fueled by the war. It concludes that businesses took advantage of the war to increase prices, and therefore price regulation was imperative.

1178. Whitney, Nathaniel R. *The Sale of War Bonds in Iowa.* Iowa City: State Historical Society of Iowa, 1923. 236 pp.

This well-written and well-organized work details the methods by which a rural state was sold on the idea of war bonds.

1179. Zoller, J.F. "A Criticism of the War Revenue Act of 1917." *Ann. Am. Ac. of Pol. Sci. and Soc. Sci.* 75 (January 1918): 182-90.

Written by a tax attorney for General Electric, this essay attacks the War Revenue Act of 1917 as being discriminatory against corporations. Zoller expresses concern that this tax could upset the financial and business structure of the country.

5. Science and Medicine
(*See also* IV:C:7, Medical and Sanitary Aspects)

1180.   Andrews, John B.   "National Effectiveness and Health Insurance."
        Ann. Am. Ac. of Pol. Sci. and Soc. Sci. 78 (July 1918): 50-
        57.

        This article examines the question of a national health in-
        surance program.   The author argues that the returning soldiers
        will demand some sort of health program.

1181.   Brackett, Elliot G.   "Rehabilitation of Diseased and Injured
        Soldiers Due to the War."   *Amer. Jour. of Pub. Health* 8
        (January 1918): 11-13.

        This address before a meeting of the American Public Health
        Association examines the question of the treatment of casualties
        in World War I.   It calls for giving these men a chance after
        the war.

1182.   Burnham, John C.   *Psychoanalysis and American Medicine, 1894-
        1918.*   New York: International Universities Press, Inc.,
        1967.   249 pp.

        This well-researched monograph analyzes the impact of psycho-
        analysis upon the medical profession.   The author concludes
        that by the time of World War I there existed a body of full-
        time analysts in the United States.   There is a brief dis-
        cussion of the impact of World War I in enhancing the stature
        of psychoanalysis and in the concept of "shell shock."

1183.   Camfield, Thomas Marley.   "Psychologists at War: The History
        of American Psychology and the First World War."   Doctoral
        dissertation, The University of Texas at Austin, 1969.   334
        pp.

        This study traces the development of psychology in the
        United States from the 1870s to 1918.   It focuses attention
        on the concentrated effort of the discipline to aid the war
        effort with the army and navy.   Ultimately, psychology emerged
        from the war with an enhanced position and broad acceptance.

1184.   Coffin, Howard E.   "The Automobile Engineer and Preparedness."
        S.A.E. Bull. 10 (July 1916): 461-74.

        Coffin, in this essay, preferred the term "prearrangement"
        to preparedness.   He called for industrial preparedness, stan-
        dardization of munitions, and for engineers to solve the prob-
        lems of preparedness.

1185.   Costello, Charles A.   "The Principal Defects Found in Persons
        Examined for Service in the United States Navy."   *Amer. Jour.
        of Pub. Health* 7 (May 1917): 489-92.

        The major defect in persons examined for the navy was problems
        with vision.

1186.   Crosby, Alfred W., Jr.   *Epidemic and Peace, 1918.*   Westport,
        Conn.: Greenwood Press, 1976.   337 pp.

This interesting study surveys the influenza epidemic of
1918-1919. Over 675,000 people died in the United States and
43,000 died in the military. Despite this, the epidemic took
second place to the war in the public mind.

1187. Devine, Edward T., and Brandt, Lilian. *Disabled Soldiers and
Sailors Pensions and Training*. New York: Oxford University
Press, 1919. 471 pp.

This preliminary study of how the disabled soldiers should
be dealt with was completed in October of 1918, before the
war was over. This important work surveys the disabilities
caused by.the war, how disabled veterans have coped in the
past, and developments in Great Britain, Canada, France,
Germany and Austria, and the United States. It also examines
in some detail the proposed new program in the United States.
Artillery fire caused more casualties than anything else.

1188. Fleming, Winston. "Testing the Brains of Our Naval Fighters."
Illus. World 29 (August 1918): 897-900.

This brief article treats psychological tests for naval personnel.

1189. Galishoff, Stuart. "Newark and the Great Influenza Epidemic
of 1918." *Bull. Hist. of Med.* 43 (May-June 1969): 246-58.

This study outlines the impact of the influenza epidemic on
Newark, which stimulated the public health movement.

1190. Haynes, William. *American Chemical Industry*, vol. 5: *Decade
of New Products*. Princeton: D. Van Nostrand Co., 1954.
622 pp.

Written by a top historian of chemistry, this volume examines
in a chronological fashion the major developments, men, and
processes in the chemical industry. The chemical role during
World War I is discussed as is the chemical industry's development as a depression-proof industry by 1940.

1191. Jones, Daniel Patrick. "The Role of Chemists in Research on
War Cases in the United States During World War I." Doctoral dissertation, University of Wisconsin, 1967. 279 pp.

This important study examines the cooperation between scientists and the government during World War I. Well-researched,
the work deals primarily with the activities of the research
division of the Chemical Warfare Service at American University
in Washington, D.C. to show that scientists from many different
disciplines could work together and that peacetime chemical
warfare research was relevant to the war effort.

1192. Kevles, Daniel H. "Testing the Army's Intelligence: Psychologists and the Military in World War I." *JAH* 55 (December
1968): 565-82.

This article examines the impact of the intelligence test on
the army in 1917. Robert M. Yerkes, president of the American
Psychological Association in 1917, pushed a testing program on

the military which was modified in line with a proposal being developed by Walter D. Scott and Walter V. Bingham. By 1918 the program had been approved and was in operation. The author concludes that the program made testing more acceptable and that it was ended after the war due to military objections. The author is too dependent on Yerkes for his sources.

1193. Layton, Edwin Ti, Jr. *The Revolt of the Engineers: Social Responsibility and the American Engineering Profession.* Cleveland: The Press of Case Western Reserve University, 1971. 285 pp.

This competent study of engineering progressivism from 1900 to 1940 shows that the engineering profession led by Herbert Hoover tried to apply engineering expertise to the great problems of the day. It peaked during and immediately after World War I. The emphasis on planning during World War I stimulated the reform thrust of engineering into the postwar period.

1194. Macmahon, Arthur W. "Health Activities of State Councils of Defense." *Ann. Am. Ac. of Pol. Sci. and Soc. Sci.* 79 (September 1918): 239-45.

This article explains the activities of the State Councils of Defense in an attempt to improve the health status of civilians.

1195. Scott, Lloyd N. *Naval Consulting Board of the United States.* Washington, D.C.: Government Printing Office, 1920. 288 pp.

This report details the civilian contribution of the naval consulting board headed by Thomas A. Edison. Basically made up of engineers, the board came into being in 1915 to study naval problems. The board put its scientific and engineering talents to work to tackle naval problems during the war. The special problems committee dealt with submarine detection, while the ship protection committee devised ways to make it more difficult to sink a ship. The work outlines the numerous naval inventions developed by this board and underlines the war work of Thomas A. Edison.

1196. Shryock, Richard H. *American Medical Research Past and Present.* New York: The Commonwealth Fund, 1947. 350 pp.

This pioneering study surveys American medical roots with emphasis on British, French, and German development. Moreover, it examines the influence of the Johns Hopkins Medical School and William Welch in influencing medical research and teaching traditions. In the broad context of the work, the author emphasizes that World War I showed the superiority of German science.

1197. ————. *The Development of Modern Medicine: An Interpretation of the Social and Scientific Factors Involved.* Madison: The University of Wisconsin Press, 1979. 473 pp.

First published in 1936, this work portrays medical development in its intellectual and social aspects. The work discusses in a broad sense the impact of World War I on the American experience.

1198. Silk, Leonard S. *The Research Revolution*. New York: McGraw-Hill Book Co., 1960. 244 pp.

Silk's well-written study examines the impact of technological innovation on the American economy. Devoid of footnotes and bibliography, the book concentrates on the economy in the twentieth century.

1199. Talbot, Henry P. "Chemistry at the Front." *Atlantic Monthly* 122 (August 1918): 265-74.

This article surveys the use of chemistry on the battlefield.

1200. ————. "Chemistry Behind the Front." *Atlantic Monthly* 122 (November 1918): 651-63.

This article discusses some of the research procedures developed during the war in the field of chemistry.

1201. Tobey, James A. *The National Government and Public Health*. Baltimore, Md.: The Johns Hopkins Press, 1926. 423 pp.

This book examines the history of the American public health movement through World War I. It is especially good at outlining public health activities in the various government agencies. Tobey's discussion of the war and navy departments and public health organizations is relevant to World War I.

1202. Yerkes, Robert M., ed. *The New World of Science: Its Development During the War*. New York: Century, 1920. 443 pp.

This important volume, edited by the chairman of the research information service of the National Research Council, deals with science mobilization during the war. It contains important articles dealing with "Science and War," "War Services of the National Research Council," "Contributions of Physical Science," "Some Scientific Aspects of the Meteorological Work of the United States Army," "Sound Ranging in the American Expeditionary Forces," "War-Time Photography," "Optical Glass for War Needs," "The Supply of Nitrogen Products for the Manufacture of Explosives," "The Chemical Warfare Service," "Contributions of Geography," "Contributions of Geology," and articles on the role of engineering, biology and medicine, psychology, and the relations of war to scientific progress.

1203. ————. *Psychological Examining in the United States Army*. Washington, D.C.: Government Printing Office, 1921. 890 pp.

This detailed volume explains in an excellent fashion the role, process, and methodology of psychological testing during World War I. It deals with the history and organization of psychological examining, testing materials, and preliminary results, and presents a detailed breakdown of the intelligence results during the war. There is an abundance of statistical data concerning a comparison of kinds of materials gathered.

This report represents a milestone in the history of psychological testing.

1204. Yoakum, Clarence S., and Yerkes, Robert M. *Army Mental Tests*. New York: Henry Holt & Co., 1920. 303 pp.

This handbook helps toward understanding and utilizing the War Department's mental tests. The basic purposes for the testing were to identify the mentally incompetent, to aid in the classification of the men, and to identify competent men for responsible positions. The work treats the way the tests were made, the results and methods, the examiner's guide, students' tests, practical application, and blanks and forms. This work spells out the state-of-the-art on psychological testing during World War I.

6. Other Sources

1205. DeNovo, John A. "The Movement for an Aggressive American Oil Policy Abroad, 1918-1920." *AHR* 61 (July 1956): 854-76.

The shift in American policy toward foreign oil sources from apathy to intense interest and anxiety is examined in this article. By 1920, DeNovo concludes, it was "established dogma" in the oil industry and Washington that the national interest was involved in the aggressive exploitation of foreign oil fields.

1206. Ise, John. *The United States Oil Policy*. New York: Arno Press, 1972. 547 pp.

This reprint of a 1926 study discusses the history of oil from its early years of development to the early 1920s.

1207. Keller, Charles. "Electric Power During the World War." *Mil. Engin.* 17 (November-December 1925): 462-68.

This article surveys the electric power situation in western Pennsylvania during the war. It shows how the demands of the war created power shortages.

1208. ————. *The Power Situation During the War*. Washington, D.C.: Government Printing Office, 1921. 300 pp.

This Corps of Engineers report surveys the electric power situation during World War I. Complete with maps and graphs, this volume treats public power development nationally and shows where shortages existed during the war. It is important to the understanding of the state of electric power during the war.

1209. Kelsey, Carl. Foreword to "Mobilizing America's Resources for the War." *Ann. Am. Ac. of Pol. Sci. and Soc. Sci.* 78 (July 1918): vii-x.

This brief overview discusses the role of education of the public as part of the mobilization process. Kelsey calls for the passage of a law requiring that all immigrants learn English.

1210. Loos, John L. *Oil On Steam!: A History of Interstate Oil Pipe Line Company, 1909-1959.* Baton Rouge: Louisiana State University Press, 1959. 411 pp.

This is a well-researched and well-written study of Interstate Oil Pipe Line Company. During World War I the pipe line's operations became important for the national defense program. Thus, the work on the line was accelerated.

1211. Smith, George Otis. *The Strategy of Minerals: A Study of the Mineral Factor in the World Position of America in War and in Peace.* New York: D. Appleton & Co., 1919. 372 pp.

This interesting volume surveys minerals as an important element in the war and postwar periods. It treats: mineral fuels, shipping, power production, iron, copper, lead and zinc, the minor metals, the chemical industries, and other industrial minerals. In addition the volume examines the position of the United States and Germany.

H. THE ECONOMY

1. General Sources

1212. Ayres, Leonard P. *Business in Two War Periods.* Cleveland, Ohio: Cleveland Trust Co., 1945. 33 pp.

This pamphlet, replete with ten diagrams and sets of tables, illustrates the impact of the two world wars on U.S. business.

1213. Cooling, Benjamin Franklin, ed. *War, Business, and American Society: Historical Perspectives on the Military-Industrial Complex.* Port Washington, N.Y.: Kennikat Press, 1977. 205 pp.

This volume contains several important articles on the military-industrial complex. Several of these articles deal with World War I. They include: "Armor Plate," "Nickel and Steel," "Monopoly and Profit," "Regional Rivalries, Congress, and the MIC," "The Norfolk and Charleston Navy Yards, 1913-20," "The Problem of American Military Supply, 1890-1920," "Development of the Merchants of Death Theory," and "The Naval Military-Industrial Complex, 1918-41."

1214. Culbertson, William Smith. *Commercial Policy in War Time and After: A Study of the Application of Democratic Ideas to International Commercial Relations.* New York: D. Appleton & Co., 1919. 479 pp.

This book examines the permanent changes brought about by World War I on industry and trade. It surveys: the influences of change on U.S. and foreign industrial conditions, national commercial problems, trade practices on an international basis, and proposals for international economic cooperation through the League of Nations. Basically, the author argues for some form of international economic government.

1215. Eddy, Arthur Jerome. *The New Competition*. Chicago: A.C. Mc-Clurg & Co., 1913. 379 pp.

This contemporary work in the pre-World War I period pragmatically examines the economic system in the United States. It deals with competition, cooperation, brutal competition, old competition, new competition, open-price policy, open-price association, harmony, customer relations, seller relations, public relations, vanishing industries, fair price, the trust problem, labor problem, class legislation and discrimination, and constructive legislation. Written in a light vein, the work captures the popular view of economics at the time.

1216. Fabricant, Soloman. *The Output of Manufacturing Industries, 1899-1937*. New York: National Bureau of Economic Research, 1940. 685 pp.

Replete with tables, statistics, reports, and other data, this study chronicles the long-term changes in the production and make-up of American manufacturers between 1899 and 1937. The book documents World War I's impact on the growth of manufacturers.

1217. Hoyt, Homer. "Standardization and Its Relation to Industrial Concentration." *Ann. Am. Ac. of Pol. Sci. and Soc. Sci.* 82 (March 1919): 271-77.

This article argues that standardization leads to concentration of industrial entities.

1218. *Investigation of Economic Power*, Temporary National Economic Power, Monograph No. 22, Technology in Our Economy, U.S. Senate, 76th Congress, 3rd sess., U.S. Govt. Printing Office, 1941. 313 pp.

This monograph produced by a special senate committee examines the impact of technology on the evolution of the concentration of economic power.

1219. Leland, Mrs. Wilfred C., and Millbrook, Minnie Dubbs. *Master of Precision: Henry M. Leland*. Detroit: Wayne State University Press, 1966. 296 pp.

This sympathetic biography examines the career of one of the key leaders in the development of the automotive industry. During World War I, Leland developed the Liberty airplane engine.

1220. Moore, Geoffrey H. *Production of Industrial Materials in World Wars I and II*. New York: National Bureau of Economic Research, 1944. 81 pp.

This brief monograph, filled with graphs and charts, examines industrial production from 1939 to 1944 in comparison
with the record of World War I. The report concludes that
between 1914 and 1917 the rate of industrial expansion was
32% while between 1939 and 1942 the rate was 35%. In both
conflicts the rate of increase decreased after two to three
years.

1221. Nevins, Allan. *Study in Power: John D. Rockefeller, Indus-
trialist and Philanthropist.* New York: Charles Scribner's
Sons, 1953. 2 vols.

This superb study of John D. Rockefeller, based on rich
primary materials including oral interviews, concludes that
without the rapid business growth stimulated by the organizational genius of men like Rockefeller, the United States might
have lost World War II.

1222. ———. and Hill, Frank Ernest. *Ford: Expansion and
Challenge.* New York: Charles Scribner's Sons, 1957. 714 pp.

This second volume of a masterful biography of Henry Ford
contains the experiences of this very important man during
World War I. Ford's plan for a peace ship to end the war,
his war production activity, and his support of Woodrow Wilson
are detailed.

1223. Scheiber, Harry N. "World War I as Entrepreneurial Opportunity:
Willard Straight and the American International Corporation."
Pol. Sci. Quar. 84 (September 1969): 486-511.

This article examines the attempt by the leading officers
of the nation's largest banking and industrial interests to
put the United States among the top nations in world commerce
and finance. In his generally balanced account, Scheiber
concludes that Straight and the AIC saw World War I as a way
to make money and to expand the American market.

2. Profiteering

1224. Berglund, Abraham. "Price Fixing in the Iron and Steel Industry." *Quar. Jour. Econ.* 32 (August 1918): 597-620.

This article treats the rise of iron and steel prices in
1916 and 1917, a comparison with conditions in 1899-1900,
problems involved in government regulation, announcement of
September 1917, other announcements, and prices in early 1918.
Berglund concludes that price fixing did not reduce production.

1225. Engelbrecht, H.C., and Hanighen, F.C. *Merchants of Death: A
Study of the International Armament Industry.* New York:
Dodd, Mead & Co., 1934. 308 pp.

This propaganda work blames the munitions makers for World
War I. The book treats systematically the science and technology of the munitions industry, the organization and sales

methods of the industry, and the history of armaments. It looks at DuPont, Krupp, Seigneur, DeSchnerder, the war in Europe, U.S. intervention, and postwar questions.

1226. Meyers, Eugene, Jr. *War Profiteering: Some Practical Aspects of Its Control.* Washington, D.C., 1917. 17 pp.

This brief essay examines some of the Wilson administration's main areas of concern regarding war profiteering. The work points out that war profiteering must include the possibility of fair profits, and that the policy concerning profiteering must not be radical. The author argues for taxation rather than price-fixing as a means of controlling profiteering.

1227. Morse, Lewis K. "The Price Fixing of Copper." *Quar. Jour. Econ.* 33 (November 1918): 71-106.

This essay deals with the price-fixing of a basic item necessary for war, the uniqueness of the industry, the expanded demand for copper, copper as a "cornered" metal, the cooperative committee on copper, the need for price-fixing, supply sources, risks in expanding production, and increased cost due to the war.

3. Finance

1228. Abrahams, Paul P. "American Bankers and the Economic Tactics of Peace: 1919." *JAH* 56 (December 1969): 572-83.

The Federal Reserve Act and the economic impact of World War I thrust the U.S. banking community into the center of international banking activities. Thus, bankers pushed the government to assume an international role in finance.

1229. Adams, T.S. "Principles of Excess Profit Taxation." *Ann. Am. Ac. of Pol. Sci. and Soc. Sci.* 75 (January 1918): 147-58.

This paper treats excess profits taxation, its scope and the principles on which it must function. The author argues in favor of a valuation of capital assets, and maintains that the excess profits tax must be only temporary.

1230. Blakely, Roy G. "Shifting the War Burden upon the Future." *Ann. Am. Ac. of Pol. Sci. and Soc. Sci.* 75 (January 1917): 90-104.

This article argues against the practice of putting the financial burden of the war on the postwar period. It calls for adequate taxation and proper economization.

1231. Bogort, Ernest Ludlow. *War Costs and Their Financing: A Study of the Financing of the War and the After-War Problems of Debt and Taxation.* New York: D. Appleton & Co., 1921. 510 pp.

This book examines in outline form the procedures used in war finance in the United States, and it treats some of the major financial problems facing the United States and Europe in the period after the war. It concludes that the most significant result of the war was that the United States had become a creditor nation. After analyzing the financing of the war, the work focuses attention on financial reconstruction, inflation, taxation, and the war debt.

1232. Hollander, Jacob H. *War Borrowing: A Study of Treasury Certificates of Indebtedness of the United States.* New York: Macmillan Co., 1919. 215 pp.

This contemporary work treats the question of financing U.S. participation in World War I. The work treats: the background of war borrowing, the present borrowing situation, the role of the Treasury Department, the money market, the price level, and future speculation. Basically, the author sees the methods used for financing the war as successful.

1233. Miller, A.C. "War Finance and Inflation." *Ann. Am. Ac. of Pol. Sci. and Soc. Sci.* 75 (January 1918): 113-34.

Written by a member of the Federal Reserve Board, this essay emphasizes that war finance needs to be concerned less with the dollar than with what it would purchase. Miller argues that the national financial process must produce the wartime needs while encouraging the reduction of consumer goods. This essay reflects well the contemporary feelings of the war period and its propaganda.

1234. Noyes, Alexander D. *The War Period of American Finance, 1908-1925.* New York: G.P. Putnam's Sons, 1926. 459 pp.

A narrative based upon original sources, this study examines in a broad context the economic impact of World War I on the American economy. As a result of the war, the United States emerged as the credit center of the world.

1235. Patten, S.N. "The Fallacy of Price Bidding." *Ann. Am. Ac. of Pol. Sci. and Soc. Sci.* 78 (July 1918): 129-43.

This article explains price bidding and traces its history in the United States to the war's background. Patten argues for price regulation.

1236. ————. "Liquidation Taxes." *Ann. Am. Ac. of Pol. Sci. and Soc. Sci.* 75 (January 1918): 165-81.

This essay argues against the use of large bond issues as a way of financing the war. The author favors a liquidation tax process to bring inflated values in line with physical valuations.

1237. ————. "Problems of War Finance." *Yale Rev.* 7 (October 1917): 73-89.

This essay discusses problems in financing the war and calls for taxes on unearned increment.

1238.   Patterson, E.M. "Some Tendencies in the Federal Reserve Sys-
        tem." *Ann. Am. Ac. of Pol. Sci. and Soc. Sci.* 78 (July
        1918): 118-29.

        This essay discusses the functioning of the Federal Reserve
        System as fiscal agent for the government, as issuer of notes,
        and as loaner to public and private entities. The author recom-
        mends deflationary measures such as tax increases and the
        shifting of the war's financial burden from financial machinery
        to productivity.

1239.   Schiff, Mortimer L. "War Time Borrowing by the Government."
        Ann. Am. Ac. of Pol. Sci. and Soc. Sci. 75 (January 1918):
        38-51.

        This essay discusses borrowing by the government and outlines
        factors to be considered in war finance. It also suggests
        certain principles to ensure a positive public response to
        bond sales. Basically, it concludes that the public should
        be taught to save.

4. Agriculture

1240.   Benedict, Murray R. *Farm Policies of the United States,
        1790-1950.* New York: Twentieth Century Fund, 1953.   548 pp.

        This rather detailed and well-documented survey of American
        farm policies has a well-organized chapter dealing with the
        Wilson administration and reform and war and agricultural poli-
        cies.

1241.   Danborn, David B. "The Agricultural Extension System and the
        First World War." *Historian* 41 (February 1979): 315-31.

        The home and extension agents played an important role
        during World War I in helping to mobilize rural public opinion.
        Agents were given much power as they sat on draft boards and
        treasury boards and were in charge of local distribution of
        seeds, fertilizers, and implements. Even though they were
        basically successful, the agents did have problems because
        they were overworked and treading on unfamiliar ground.

1242.   Pinchot, Gifford. "Essentials to a Food Program for Next Year."
        Ann. Am. Ac. of Pol. Sci. and Soc. Sci. 78 (July 1918): 156-
        63.

        Seeing food as the greatest U.S. contribution to the war
        effort, the author argues that production should be increased
        while usage should be reduced. Pinchot emphasizes that the
        farmer should be brought into the mainstream of planning and
        regulation.

1243.   Shideler, James H. *Farm Crisis, 1919-1923.* Berkeley: Univer-
        sity of California Press, 1957.   345 pp.

        This well-researched work deals with a very frustrating period
        of agricultural history. Basically, it treats farm problems
        which resulted from the World War I period.

1244. Taylor, Alonzo F. "International and National Food Control."
       Ann. Am. Ac. of Pol. Sci. and Soc. Sci. 78 (July 1918):
       149-56.

       The author sees the food problem as a problem of priorities.
       Among those on the priority list are: the Allies, European
       neutrals, hemispheric neutrals, and the United States. He
       calls for the unification of agencies so that there would be
       one export buyer.

1245. Weld, L.D.H. "The Livestock and Meat Situation." *Ann. Am.
       Ac. of Pol. Sci. and Soc. Sci.* 78 (July 1918): 168-75.

       An executive from the meat packing industry examines the
       contribution made by that entity to the war effort. He de-
       fends the interests of the large packer and the practice of
       price speculation. He questions the value of price regulation.

5. Labor

1246. Abell, Aaron I. *American Catholicism and Social Action: A
       Search for Social Justice 1865-1950*. Garden City, N.Y.:
       Hanover House, 1960. 306 pp.

       This survey of the Catholic social reform movement in the
       United States explores the church's attitude toward labor
       during and after World War I. Generally, the church supported
       the labor movement instead of a socialistic approach.

1247. Bing, Alexander M. *War-Time Strikes and Their Adjustment*.
       New York: E.P. Dutton & Co., 1921. 329 pp.

       This older study examines the labor problems of World War I
       as well as the attempts to ameliorate them. Based on the
       author's experiences during the war as well as relevant govern-
       ment documents, the work concludes that the wartime labor prob-
       lems had their roots in prewar problems.

1248. Blackman, John L., Jr. "Navy Policy Toward the Labor Relations
       of Its War Contractors." *Mil. Affairs* 18 (Winter 1954):
       176-87.

       The first half of this article examines the navy's eventual
       emulation during World War I of the army's labor-relations
       sections to provide for industrial harmony.

1249. Brody, David. *Labor in Crisis: The Steel Strike of 1919*.
       Philadelphia: J.B. Lippincott Co., 1965. 208 pp.

       Well-written, this book examines all facets of the steel
       strike of 1919. It contains a good synthesis of labor problems
       during World War I.

1250. Carter, W.S. "Effect of Federal Control on Railway Labor."
       Proc. Acad. Pol. Sci. 8:2 (1920): 64-76.

       The director of the division of labor of the U.S. Railroad
       Administration points out that it was possible to ameliorate

conflicts between labor and management under the wartime structure. He warns that the manipulators of opinion may hurt the cause of peace between labor and management.

1251. Dick, William M. *Labor and Socialism in America: The Gompers Era.* Port Washington, N.Y.: Kennikat Press, 1974. 211 pp.

Dick argues that Gompers was more to the left than most historians have portrayed him. Socialism was factionalized and managed to take an extremely antiwar stand during World War I which hurt it with most people in the United States.

1252. Feiss, Richard A. "Stimulating Labor Efficiency in War Time." *Ann. Am. Ac. of Pol. Sci. and Soc. Sci.* 78 (July 1918): 106-11.

This article argues for public education to improve labor efficiency.

*   Gompers, Samuel. *Seventy Years of Life and Labor.* Cited above as item 881.

1253. Green, Marguerite. *The National Civic Federation and the American Labor Movement, 1900-1925.* Washington, D.C.: Catholic University Press, 1956. 537 pp.

The National Civic Federation served as a forum for the discussion of national affairs. Led by Ralph M. Easly, a Kansas journalist, the Federation influenced the development of progressivism. Generally pro-labor, and with Samuel Gompers serving in a leadership role, the organization became ultra conservative during World War I as it attempted to stamp out radicalism during and after the war. The book is well written and thoroughly documented.

*   Grubbs, Frank L., Jr. *The Struggle for Labor Loyalty: Gompers, the A.F. of L. and the Pacifists, 1917-1920.* Cited above as item 882.

1254. Krivy, Leonard Phillip. "American Organized Labor and the First World War, 1917-1918: A History of Labor Problems and the Development of a Government War Labor Program." Doctoral dissertation, New York University, 1965. 375 pp.

In 1917, as the United States was drawn into World War I, the government discovered that it had no mechanism to pull labor into the mobilization program. This dissertation, based on primary documentation, treats the attempts by the government to deal with labor problems by leaving them in the hands of those who dealt with prewar labor problems. However, their failure led to government intervention by the National War Labor Board and the War Labor Policies Board, which standardized the basic labor policies of all war industries. This centralization with equal standards for all saved much waste.

I. DEMOBILIZATION

1255. Hersey, Harold B. *When the Boys Come Home*. New York: Brittan Publishing Co., 1919. 204 pp.

This interesting volume by a World War I American officer is a kind of memoir and view of what the civilians might expect of the soldiers when they came home. The author emphasizes that the soldiers had undergone a radical physical and psychological change, and that it would be difficult for the soldiers to settle into civilian life. Yet these soldiers have developed a greater appreciation for civilian life. The author emphasizes throughout that the American soldier was a very high type of person. This is a good contemporary view of what the soldiers would be like when they returned home.

1256. Howenstine, E. Jay, Jr. "Lessons of World War I." *Ann. Am. Ac. of Pol. Sci. and Soc. Sci.* 238 (March 1945): 180-87.

This article deals with the lessons learned from World War I concerning rapid demobilization. It concludes that: there was a great demand for rapid demobilization; some special preparations and inducements would be necessary to maintain an occupation army of high morale; a strong public employment service would be needed; and a public works program would be necessary to help provide jobs for the temporarily unemployed.

1257. Mock, James R., and Thruber, Evangeline. *Report on Demobilization*. Norman: University of Oklahoma Press, 1944. 257 pp.

This is a well-written, balanced account of the failure of many postwar reconstruction programs.

1258. Paxson, Frederic L. "The Great Demobilization." *AHR* 44 (January 1939): 237-51.

Paxson's view of demobilization can be summed up with this quotation from his enlightening article: "There are moments in the history of mobilization in which the government of the United States looked like a madhouse; but in demobilization there was lacking even the madhouse in which the crazy might be incarcerated. They were at large."

1259. Rasmussen, John Curtis. "The American Forces in Germany and Civil Affairs, July 1919-January 1923." Doctoral dissertation, University of Georgia, 1972. 266 pp.

This dissertation examines the solid administrative achievements of the American forces that occupied a part of the Rhineland for four years.

1260. Reid, Bill G. "Proposed American Plans for Soldier Settlement During the World War I Period." Doctoral dissertation, University of Oklahoma, 1963. 239 pp.

Faced with the problem of what to do with 450,000 returning soldiers, some in the United States, led by Interior Secretary

Franklin K. Lane, proposed putting the veterans on unused land for development as farm land. Due to the questionable support of reclamators and speculators, the plan was never enacted. Farm colonies were, however, established in six states with preference going to veterans, but the Depression caused these to fail.

1261. Rhodes, Benjamin Dagwell. "The United States and the War Debt Question, 1917-1934." Doctoral dissertation, University of Colorado, 1965. 410 pp.

The focus of this dissertation is on the postwar period, with the author emphasizing the unrealistic nature of American war debt policy.

1262. Shaw, Albert. "The Demobilization of Labor in War Industries and in Military Service." *Proc. Acad. Pol. Sci.* 8:2 (1920): 127-34.

This article surveys the problems concerning the demobilization of the economy at the end of World War I.

1263. Van Meter, Robert Hardin, Jr. "The United States and European Recovery 1918-1923: A Study of Public Policy and Private Finance." Doctoral dissertation, University of Wisconsin, 1971. 491 pp.

This well-researched study treats the efforts of presidents Wilson and Harding in the economic recovery of Europe after World War I. Wilson hoped that postwar political stability would result in increased American private investment in Europe. However, the treaty's rejection, reparations, and hostile feeling in Europe doomed this plan.

1264. Warburg, Paul M. "Same Phases of Financial Reconstruction." *Ann. Am. Ac. of Pol. Sci. and Soc. Sci.* 82 (March 1919): 347-73.

A former member of the Federal Reserve Board examines financial factors in the postwar period. They include: world trade financing, a peace finance corporation, government bonds and inflation, and the financial role of the United States in the world.

1265. Woll, Matthew. "American Labor Readjustment Proposals." *Proc. Acad. Pol. Sci.* 8:2 (1920): 47-58.

The president of a labor organization examines the question of labor and demobilization and offers some suggestions. They include: national control of services and industries vital to national security, mediation and conciliation, and education.

VI. SOCIAL AND INTELLECTUAL IMPACT OF THE WAR

A. GENERAL AND COMPARATIVE SOURCES

* Albrecht-Carrié, René. *The Meaning of the First World War.* Cited above as item 137.

* Ferro, Marc. *The Great War 1914-1918.* Cited above as item 149.

* King, Jere Clemens, ed. *The First World War.* Cited above as item 154.

1266. Marchand, C. Roland. *The American Peace Movement and Social Reform, 1898-1918.* Princeton: Princeton University Press, 1973. 441 pp.

Marchand's study of the peace movement shows how diverse it was. The author successfully illustrates how the various peace groups responded to World War I. This is first-rate social history.

1267. Marwick, Arthur. *Britain in the Century of Total War: War, Peace and Social Change, 1900-1967.* Boston: Atlantic-Little, Brown, 1968. 511 pp.

This exemplary social history is an extension of Marwick's earlier work, *The Deluge*, on the impact of World War I on the British home front. Marwick's research covers a wide variety of printed sources.

1268. ————. *The Deluge: British Society and the First World War.* London: Bodley Head, 1965. 336 pp.

The author, a Scottish historian, has written a first-rate study which offers fresh insight into the impact of war on British society.

1269. ————. *War and Social Change in the Twentieth Century: A Comparative Study of Britain, France, Germany, Russia and the United States.* New York: St. Martin's Press, 1975. 258 pp.

This is a general but stimulating survey of the impact of war on the home fronts of some of the major belligerents in World War I. Among the many sources used in this superior comparative social history are contemporary films.

1270. May, Henry F. *The End of American Innocence: A Study of the*
       First Years of Our Own Time, 1917-1919. New York: Alfred A.
       Knopf, 1959. 413 pp.

       One of the major studies in cultural and intellectual his-
       tory, this work looks at the roots of the cultural revolution
       prior to the war and then analyzes the impact of the conflict
       on the American mind. May concludes that the revolt started
       before the war and that ultimately it involved the loss of
       optimism. This loss of American "innocence" was a tragedy
       but not a disaster.

1271. Mayer, Arno J. *The Persistence of the Old Regime: Europe to*
       the Great War. New York: Pantheon Books, 1981. 368 pp.

       This is a provocative analysis of the perseverance of the
       old regime in the six major European powers. Based on secondary
       sources, it is, in the author's words, "a Marxist history from
       the top down, not the bottom up, with the focus on the upper
       rather than the lower classes."

1272. Shotwell, James T. "The Social History of the War." *Columbia*
       Univ. Quarterly. 21 (October 1919): 284-97.

       In this article, based upon a lecture at the University of
       Paris in 1919, an internationally recognized historian delivers
       a word of advice to historians who will be dealing with the
       social history of the war. He urges that "history must become
       social in outlook and social sciences historical, in order to
       cooperate effectively."

1273. Sullivan, Mark. *Over Here, 1914-1918*, vol. 5: *Our Times: The*
       United States 1900-1925. New York: Charles Scribner's Sons,
       1933. 676 pp.

       This sprightly volume is a narrative social survey of the
       United States from 1914 to 1918. Despite outdated interpre-
       tations, this work captures the spirit of the home front and
       can be used by instructors to enliven their classroom lectures.

1274. Wohl, Robert. *The Generation of 1914.* Cambridge: Harvard
       University Press, 1979. 307 pp.

       Wohl's purpose is a laudable one: "to rescue the generation
       of 1914 from the shadowland of myth and to restore it to the
       realm of history." Utilizing an impressive variety of sources,
       the author assesses the impact of World War I on the French,
       Germans, English, Spanish, and Italians. This is superior
       intellectual history.

B. PRISONERS OF WAR

1275. Dennett, Carl P. *Prisoners of the Great War.* Boston: Houghton
       Mifflin Co., 1919. 236 pp.

Dennett, a deputy Red Cross commissioner who was sent to
Switzerland to provide for the proper care of American prisoners
of war, gives an authoritative statement on conditions in German prison camps.

1276. Glidden, William B. "Internment Camps in America, 1917-1920."
Mil. Affairs 37 (December 1973): 137-41.

The records of the War Department were researched to enable
the author to answer certain questions about the treatment of
alien prisoners in the United States during the war.

1277. Hoffman, Conrad. *In the Prison Camps of Germany.* New York:
Association Press, 1920. 279 pp.

Hoffman provides an insider's view for he served throughout
much of the war as the secretary of the war prisoners' aid
committee of the Y.M.C.A. One chapter is entitled "Visiting
the First American Prisoners."

1278. Isaacs, Edouard V.M. *Prisoner of the U-90.* Boston: Houghton
Mifflin Co., 1919. 184 pp.

This is an interesting account, written by the only U.S.
Navy line officer to be captured during the war. Isaacs,
after a brief stay in German prison camps, escaped to Switzerland.

1279. McCarthy, Daniel J. *The Prisoner of War in Germany: The Care
and Treatment of the Prisoner with a History of the Development of Neutral Inspection and Control.* London: Skeffington,
1918. 256 pp.

McCarthy, a University of Pennsylvania professor, relates
what he discovered about conditions in German prisons as a
representative of the American embassy in Berlin.

1280. O'Brien, Pat. *Outwitting the Hun: My Escape from a German
Prison Camp.* New York: Harper & Brothers, 1918. 283 pp.

This fascinating narrative tells of a U.S. lieutenant's escape from a German prison camp. He was shot down while flying
for the British.

*   Willis, Edward F. *Herbert Hoover and the Russian Prisoners
of World War I: A Study in Diplomacy and Relief, 1918-1919.*
Cited above as item 893.

C. RELIGIOUS AND MORAL ASPECTS

1281. Abrams, Ray H. *Preachers Present Arms: The Role of the Ameri-
can Churches and Clergy in World Wars I and II, with Some
Observations on the War in Vietnam.* Scottdale, Pa.: Herald
Press, 1969. 330 pp.

This is a revised edition of a 1933 thesis which focuses on the Great War. The author, a professor of sociology at the University of Pennsylvania, takes a sociological approach. His research is impressive and his bibliography serves as a good guide to the sources.

1282. Bittle, Celestine N. *Soldiering for Cross and Flag: Impressions of a War Chaplain*. Milwaukee: Bruce Publishing Co., 1929. 331 pp.

Father Bittle served with the AEF in 1918-1919. The story he relates is a very personal one.

1283. Committee on the War and the Religious Outlook. *The Missionary Outlook in the Light of the War*. New York: Associated Press, 1920. 329 pp.

The committee argues that the Great War made missionary work more significant and more urgent. Among other things, Wilson's "new diplomacy" made the foreign efforts of Christians more relevant on a global basis.

1284. ————. *Religion Among American Men, as Revealed by a Study of Conditions in the Army*. New York: Associated Press, 1920. 155 pp.

The committee responsible for the publication of this volume was created by the federal council of the Churches of Christ in America and the general wartime commission of the churches. Based on questionnaires, interviews, letters, articles, and the personal experiences of members of the committee and its secretaries, this work is divided into three parts: "The State of Religion as Revealed in the Army," "The Effect of the War on Religion in the Army," and "Lessons for the Church."

1285. Furniss, Norman F. *The Fundamentalist Controversy, 1918-1931*. Hamden, Conn.: Archon Books, 1963. 199 pp.

This work on fundamentalism in the 1920s traces its roots to World War I. There is a brief discussion of the war's impact on fundamentalism.

1286. Gray, Harold S. *Character "Bad": The Story of a Conscientious Objector, as Told in the Letters of Harold Studley Gray*. Edited by Kenneth I. Brown. New York: Harper & Brothers, 1934. 258 pp.

This volume contains the letters of a conscientious objector to his family. They reveal the everyday affairs of a young man away from home and the influences which caused Gray to learn and live the "will of God in the face of war." Ultimately, Gray's stand caused him to spend time behind bars at Fort Riley, Fort Leavenworth, and Alcatraz before he was given a dishonorable discharge.

1287. Honeywell, Roy J. *Chaplains of the United States Army*. Washington, D.C.: Office of the Chief of Chaplains, Department of the Army, 1958. 376 pp.

This valuable general survey has an extremely thorough bibliography. There are two chapters on World War I.

1288. Hurtzler, J.S. *Mennonites in the World War: Or Nonresistance
       Under Test.* Scottdale, Pa.: Mennonite Publishing House,
       1922. 246 pp.

       This work represents the official Mennonite view of their
       experiences during World War I. It traces the history of
       nonviolence in the Mennonite religion down through World
       War I, describing the Mennonite attempt to present their per-
       spective to the U.S. and Canadian governments. It also treats
       the experiences of some of the conscientious objectors and
       describes the church's relief work.

1289. Jorgensen, Daniel P. *The Service of Chaplains to Army Air
       Units, 1917-1946.* Washington, D.C.: U.S. Office, Chief of
       Air Force Chaplains, 1961. 344 pp.

       The genesis of the air chaplaincy is described in this of-
       ficial history.

1290. McKim, R.H. *For God and Country; Or, the Christian Pulpit
       in War-Time.* New York: E.P. Dutton Co., 1918. 129 pp.

       This volume consists of the wartime addresses of McKim,
       the rector of the Church of the Epiphany, Washington, D.C.,
       most of which were delivered prior to American belligerency.

1291. McMahan, Russell Samuel, Jr. "The Protestant Churches During
       World War I: The Home Front, 1917-1918." Doctoral disser-
       tation, Saint Louis University, 1968. 305 pp.

       This competent study deals with the role of Protestant
       churches in the war effort. It examines the propaganda role
       of Protestant churches in such activities as the Liberty Loans
       and food and fuel conservation. In return for their support
       of the war effort, the churches demanded reforms in prohibi-
       tion, labor, and race relations.

1292. Mathews, Shailer. *Patriotism and Religion.* New York: Mac-
       millan Co., 1918. 161 pp.

       Mathews attempts to reconcile the American military effort
       against Germany with religion in a series of lectures at the
       University of North Carolina in 1918.

1293. Meyer, Ernest L. *"Hey! Yellowbacks!" The War Diary of a Con-
       scientious Objector.* New York: John Day Co., 1930. 209 pp.

       This record of Meyer's experiences during World War I re-
       veals the problems of being a pacifist during war. Meyer was
       a political pacifist of German descent who was expelled from
       the University of Wisconsin for being a draft evader. This
       book details his treatment in the army at Camp Taylor, Camp
       Sherman, Fort Leavenworth, and Fort Riley. He generally re-
       ceived good treatment. Ultimately he was discharged.

1294. Morgan, David T. "The Revivalist as Patriot: Billy Sunday
       and World War I." *Jour. Presby. Hist.* 51 (Summer 1973):
       199-215.

       The Presbyterian evangelist's mixing of patriotism and re-
       ligion is examined in this extremely interesting article.
       Sunday often let himself go in his sermons, once referring
       to Germany's wartime leadership as "Kaiser Bill and his dirty
       bunch of pretzel-chewing, limburger-eating highbinders."

1295. Oxenham, John. *High Altars.* New York: George H. Doran Co.,
       1918. 63 pp.

       An observer who got permission to visit the western front
       writes of the religious attitudes of the soldiers. The sec-
       tions are separated by verse.

1296. Stearns, Gustav. *From Army Camps and Battlefields.* Minneapo-
       lis: Augsburg Publishing House, 1919. 281 pp.

       Stearns took a sabbatical from his church to join American
       troops during the war, writing seventy-six weekly letters to
       his congregation at the Church of Ascension in Milwaukee.
       Numerous illustrations are included.

1297. Stephens, D. Owen. *With Quakers in France.* London: C.W.
       Daniel, 1921. 336 pp.

       Stephens was a Quaker pacifist who helped the French repair
       the destruction caused by the German withdrawal in 1916 to
       their Hindenburg Line.

1298. Stover, Earl F. *The United States Army Chaplaincy,* vol. 3:
       Up from Handymen, 1865-1920. Washington, D.C.: Office of
       the Chief of Chaplains, Department of the Army, 1977. 302
       pp.

       This is a scholarly and enlightening account. About one-
       fourth of this volume focuses on the period of World War I.

1299. *United States Catholic Chaplains in the World War.* New York:
       Army and Navy Chaplains Ordinariate, 1924. 359 pp.

       This is a register of the war records rather than a his-
       torical narrative of the Catholic chaplains, army and navy,
       during the Great War.

1300. U.S. War Department. *Statement Concerning the Treatment of
       Conscientious Objectors in the Army.* Washington, D.C.:
       Government Printing Office, 1919. 71 pp.

       This brief but thorough pamphlet contains much essential
       information concerning the army's official position regarding
       conscientious objectors. The army's position was that con-
       scientious objectors were fairly treated.

D. EDUCATION IN WAR

1301. Gruber, Carol S. *Mars and Minerva: World War I and the Uses of the Higher Learning in America.* Baton Rouge: Louisiana State University Press, 1975. 293 pp.

   This work treats the failures of teachers in higher education to serve the interests of truth, serving instead the interests of power. This well-researched volume critically examines the inadequate defense of academic freedom and the utilization of higher education by the government in propaganda. See also the author's 1968 Columbia University doctoral dissertation.

1302. Howe, M.A. DeWolfe. *Memoirs of the Harvard Dead in the War Against Germany.* Cambridge: Harvard University Press, 1920. 200 pp.

   Howe, the author of several war books, gives the memoirs of thirty Harvard men who died in the war prior to American belligerency. Extracts from letters and diaries are utilized.

1303. Kolbe, Parke R. *The Colleges in War-Time and After: A Contemporary Account of the Effect of the War upon Higher Education in America.* New York: D. Appleton & Co., 1919. 320 pp.

   Kolbe, the president of the Municipal University of Akron, has written a contemporary account of higher education during the Great War. Topics covered include college women and the war, the war's effect on academic conditions and the college curriculum, R.O.T.C., and the Students' Army Training Corps.

1304. Lyons, Gene M., and Masland, John W. "The Origins of the ROTC." *Mil. Affairs* 23 (Spring 1959): 1-12.

   An ROTC program on college campuses was viewed by the general staff during the Great War as a realistic alternative to a greatly expanded military academy.

1305. Nicholas, William Elmer, III. "Academic Dissent in World War I, 1917-1918." Doctoral dissertation, Tulane University, 1970. 264 pp.

   The impact of World War I on the academic community changed the atmosphere of the nation's universities from one of tolerance to a narrow-minded subservience to national purpose. Professors were dismissed for pacifism or disloyal utterances. Despite this "witch hunt," the American Association of University Professors made little attempt to defend academic freedom.

1306. Perry, Ralph Barton. *The Plattsburgh Movement: A Chapter of America's Participation in the World War.* New York: E.P. Dutton and Co., 1921. 275 pp.

   This is a valuable, sympathetic study of the development of the Military Training Campus Association.

1307. Summerscales, William. *Affirmation and Dissent: Columbia's Response to the Crisis of World War I.* New York: Teachers College Press, Teachers College, Columbia University, 1970. 159 pp.

This narrowly focused study examines the impact of World War I on Columbia University. Details of the presidency of Nicholas Murray Butler, faculty dissent, and the hope that the war would advance progressivism are revealed.

1308. *Technology's War Record: An Interpretation of the Contribution Made by the Massachusetts Institute of Technology...in the Great War, 1914-1919.* Cambridge: Alumni Association of Massachusetts Institute of Technology, 1920. 747 pp.

This is an unusually thorough (and valuable) accounting of the contributions made by the staff, students, and alumni of MIT.

1309. Thwing, Charles F. *The American Colleges and Universities in the Great War, 1914-1919: A History.* New York: Macmillan Co., 1920. 276 pp.

According to the preface, Thwing, the president of Western Reserve University, prepared this volume to elucidate the important contributions made by higher education to the war effort.

1310. Todd, Lewis Paul. *Wartime Relations of the Federal Government and the Public Schools, 1917-1918.* New York: Columbia University Teachers College, 1945. 240 pp.

This monograph is concerned with the wartime federal activities in the public elementary and secondary schools. Chapter headings range from "Stimulating Patriotism in the Schools" to "Schoolboys in Uniform."

1311. U.S. War Department. *Committee on Education and Special Training: A Review of Its Work During 1918 by the Advisory Board.* Washington, D.C.: War Department, 1918. 144 pp.

This is an important primary source on the War Department's relationship with educational institutions.

1312. Zimmerman, Norman Allan. "A Triumph for Orthodoxy: The University of Wisconsin During World War I." Doctoral dissertation, University of Minnesota, 1971. 243 pp.

This well-documented study examines the impact of the war on a distinguished state university. Prior to World War I, the University of Wisconsin fostered innovation and experimentation, but during the war hysterical intolerance pervaded the university. This dissertation analyzes why the change occurred on all levels of the university.

E. REPORTING THE WAR

1313. *American Chronicle: The Autobiography of Ray Stannard Baker*.
       New York: Charles Scribner's Sons, 1945. 531 pp.

       This autobiography by a prominent muckraker includes a
       lengthy section on World War I. Baker joined Creel on the
       Committee on Public Information, represented the State Depart-
       ment on a fact-finding mission to Europe in 1918, and headed
       the press department of the American peace commission to Paris.
       He was also an intimate of President Wilson.

1314. Broun, Heywood C. *The A.E.F.: With General Pershing and the
       American Forces*. New York: D. Appleton & Co., 1918. 297 pp.

       This volume contains many of Broun's *New York Tribune*
       columns. Broun was one of seven American journalists who was
       allowed to accompany the First Division into the line. His
       account is full of American firsts in the battle against the
       German army.

1315. Crozier, Emmet. *American Reporters on the Western Front
       1914-1918*. New York: Oxford University Press, 1959. 299 pp.

       Although documentation is lacking, this is a solid piece of
       work on American war correspondents who covered the war in
       France and Flanders, both before and after American interven-
       tion. Pershing is shown as being particularly maladroit in
       his handling of the press. The appendix includes a list of
       the reporters who covered the AEF and the newspapers that they
       represented.

1316. Dorr, Rheta. *Soldier's Mother in France*. Indianapolis: Bobbs-
       Merrill Co., 1918. 248 pp.

       This volume was written by a newspaper correspondent whose
       son was in the AEF to give assurance to other U.S. mothers
       who had sons in France.

1317. Dunn, Robert. *Five Fronts: On the Firing-Lines with English-
       French, Austrian, German and Russian Troops*. New York: Dodd,
       Mead & Co., 1915. 308 pp.

       Some vivid and unbiased glimpses of the war can be found in
       this volume by a reporter for the New York *Evening Post*.

1318. Green, Horace. *The Log of a Noncombatant*. Boston: Houghton
       Mifflin Co., 1915. 169 pp.

       Green relates his experiences and impressions of the first
       year of the war. The alleged German atrocities in Belgium re-
       ceive some attention. The author was the correspondent for
       the New York *Evening Post* and the Boston *Journal*.

1319. Johnson, Walter. *William Allen White's America*. New York:
       Henry Holt & Co., 1947. 621 pp.

       This sympathetic biography of one of the most highly respected
       journalists of the first half of the twentieth century devotes

four chapters to the war as seen through the eyes of a small
town journalist. White traveled to Europe to investigate Red
Cross war work and also covered the peace conference at Paris.
He warned that the German republic was a facade behind which
the militarists would rearm.

1320. McEwen, J.M. "'Brass-Hats' and the British Press During the
       First World War." *Can. Jour. of Hist.* 18 (April 1983):
       43-67.

       This enlightening article examines attempts by generals and
       admirals to use the influential national press as a weapon
       against their civilian masters. Often the military and naval
       leaders who trafficked with Fleet Street discovered to their
       dismay that the use of the press was a double-edged sword.
       Among other sources, the author uses the papers of H.A. Gwynne
       (*Morning Post*) and Leo Maxse (*National Review*).

1321. Mathews, Joseph J. *Reporting the Wars.* Minneapolis: Univer-
       sity of Minnesota Press, 1957. 322 pp.

       This general survey includes some information on the activi-
       ties of war correspondents during the Great War.

1322. Mock, James R. *Censorship, 1917.* Princeton: Princeton Univer-
       sity Press, 1941. 250 pp.

       The author's primary purpose is to emphasize the wartime
       violations of the first amendment of the constitution. It was
       no accident that this volume was published in 1941, only
       months before the United States was drawn into another great
       world war.

1323. Palmer, Frederick. *My Second Year of the War.* New York: Dodd,
       Mead & Co., 1917. 404 pp.

       This is an interesting, though impressionistic, account by
       one of America's most noted war correspondents.

1324. ————. *My Year of the Great War.* New York: Dodd, Mead & Co.,
       1915. 390 pp.

       Palmer was the only accredited American war correspondent
       with the BEF.

1325. ————. *With My Own Eyes: A Personal Story of Battle Years.*
       London: Jarrolds, 1934. 350 pp.

       Palmer gives his firsthand observations of the Great War.

1326. Powell, E. Alexander. *Vive la France!* New York: Charles
       Scribner's Sons, 1915. 254 pp.

       This American reporter describes life in the British and
       French sectors during the mid-years of the war. His account
       of field hospitals is both realistic and noteworthy.

1327. Reed, John. *War in Eastern Europe.* New York: Charles Scrib-
       ner's Sons, 1916. 334 pp.

Reed's unfortunate timing for his tour of Russia and Serbia
prevented him from seeing much of the actual fighting, but his
views of life behind the lines are valuable nonetheless. Cartoons by Boardman Robinson are included.

1328. Ruhl, Arthur. *Antwerp to Gallipoli: A Year of War on Many
Fronts--and Behind Them.* New York: Charles Scribner's Sons,
1916. 304 pp.

The views of an American reporter, based upon travel on both
sides of the front, are given in this illustrated volume. Ruhl
covered the war from many vantage points, including Paris, the
Russian front, the Dardanelles, and German prison camps.

*   *Stars and Stripes.* Cited above as item 436.

1329. Sweetser, Arthur. *Roadside Glimpses of the Great War.* New
York: Macmillan Co., 1916. 272 pp.

This work concerns the experiences of a Boston reporter who
covered the opening battles of the war on a bicycle in Belgium.
Sweetser was at different times the prisoner of the French and
the Germans.

1330. Waldo, Fullerton L. *America at the Front.* New York: E.P.
Dutton & Co., 1918. 170 pp.

Written by a Philadelphia reporter, this narrative tells of
Waldo's observations of the AEF. This illustrated narrative
begins in June 1918.

1331. Wile, Frederic William. *Assault: Germany Before the Outbreak
and England in War-Time.* Indianapolis: Bobbs-Merrill Co.,
1916. 413 pp.

Wile had been reporting on events in Germany for thirteen
years when the war came. Accused of being a spy, he was forced
to leave Berlin. He then covered the war from London.

1332. Williams, Wythe. *Passed by the Censor.* New York: E.P. Dutton
& Co., 1916. 270 pp.

Williams, a New York *Times* reporter, joined the Red Cross in
1914 in order to cover the war in the front lines. By 1915 he
was allowed by the French to visit the front as a reporter.

F. WOMEN AND THE WAR

1333. Addams, Jane. *Peace and Bread in Time of War.* New York: Macmillan Co., 1922. 257 pp.

This volume is a brief history of the women's peace movement
during World War I. It is basically an autobiographical account
of the role of Jane Addams in that movement. It treats the
war's beginning, the neutral conference and the Ford Peace Ship,

Wilson's policies and the Woman's Peace Party, the bread
rations and women's tradition, a speculation on bread labor
and war slogans, the U.S. entry into the war, Addams's reactions to the war, the armistice, and the aftermath of war.

1334.   ————; Balch, Emily G.; and Hamilton, Alice. *Women at the
        Hague: The International Congress of Women and Its Results*.
        New York: Macmillan Co., 1915. 171 pp.

        Written by three American delegates, this volume presents
        the story of the International Congress of Women in 1915. It
        is a good and somewhat journalistic account of European peace
        sentiment in 1915. The impressions of the war from the war
        capitals are especially interesting. In addition to examining
        antiwar sentiment as well as the reasons for the continuation
        of the war, this work reveals the growing political importance
        of women.

1335.   Braybon, Gail. *Women Workers in the First World War*. London:
        Croom Helm, 1981. 244 pp.

        This examination of attitudes toward working-class women in
        British industry during World War I will be valuable to anyone
        interested in comparing American and British women factory
        workers.

1336.   Falconer, Martha P. "The Segregation of Delinquent Women and
        Girls as a War Problem." *Ann. Am. Ac. of Pol. Sci. and Soc.
        Sci.* 79 (September 1918): 160-67.

        This article concerns the problem of the treatment of female
        delinquents. It deals with the question of institutional
        treatment and calls for the development of modern reformatories
        for girls and women.

1337.   Greenwald, Maurine Weiner. *Women, War, and Work: The Impact
        of World War I on Women Workers in the United States*. West-
        port, Conn.: Greenwood Press, 1980. 309 pp.

        A thoroughly documented analysis of World War I women street-
        car workers, railroad workers, and telephone operators, this
        study concludes that even though the war failed to liberate
        women, it did provide the opportunity for advancement. Green-
        wald points out that unions tended to oppose women's taking
        non-traditional jobs.

1338.   Hitchcock, Nevada D. "The Mobilization of Women." *Ann. Am.
        Ac. of Pol. Sci. and Soc. Sci.* 78 (July 1918): 24-31.

        This interesting article by an official of the National
        League for Woman's Service surveys the role of women during
        the war.

1339.   Lane, W.D. "Girls and Khaki." *Survey*, 1 December 1917, pp.
        236-40.

        This article, based upon the findings of an institute conduc-
        ted at the New York School of Philanthropy, outlines a program
        for protecting young women during the war. The program includes:

the formation of a girls' protective bureau, a house of deten-
tion, a female probation officer, better laws for the protection of girls, and the promotion of educational work.

1340. McGovern, James R. "The American Woman's Pre-World War I
Freedom in Manners and Morals." *JAH* 55 (September 1968):
315-33.

McGovern argues in this interesting article that the changes
in manners and morals often attributed to World War I were
actually under way by 1910.

1341. Morgan, David. *Suffragists and Democrats: The Politics of
Woman Suffrage in America.* East Lansing: Michigan State
University Press, 1972. 225 pp.

This is a valuable synthesis by an English political scientist of the political struggle of American women for the right
to vote from 1912 to 1920. The excellent bibliography includes
the manuscript collections of the leading suffragists.

1342. Pegen, Mary Louise. *The History of the Woman's Peace Party.*
Baltimore, Md.: Johns Hopkins Press, 1939. 266 pp.

This important monograph treats the development of the
Woman's Peace Party, giving particular attention to the part
played by Jane Addams. Henry Ford's role in the peace movement, wartime pacifism, and the attempts to influence the
peace treaties are also examined.

1343. Steinson, Barbara J. *America's Women's Activism in World
War I.* New York: Garland Publishing, 1982. 440 pp.

This study examines the various women's relief, military
preparedness, and peace organizations of World War I. Based
on primary sources, it treats the methods employed by the
groups to achieve their goals as well as how the groups reacted
to the suffrage movement.

1344. Van Kleeck, Mary. "Women's Invasion of Industry and Changes
in Protective Standards." *Proc. Acad. Pol. Sci.* 8 (1918-
1920): 141-46.

This article treats the new occupations which opened to women
during the war. It argues that women should play a role in
production after the war, and it examines the question of protective standards for female workers.

1345. Van Rensselaer, Mrs. Coffin. "The National League for Woman's
Service." *Ann. Am. Ac. of Pol. Sci. and Soc. Sci.* 79 (September 1918): 275-82.

This article discusses the work of the National League for
Woman's Service, which cooperated with many other service organizations.

G. WAR RELIEF: RED CROSS, YMCA,
AMERICAN FIELD SERVICE, AMERICAN RELIEF
ADMINISTRATION, AND CIVILIAN RELIEF

1346. *American Catholics in the War: National Catholic War Council,*
1917-1921. New York: Macmillan Co., 1921. 467 pp.

This book surveys the work of the Catholic war council,
made up of fourteen archbishops. The work focuses attention
on the activities of the committee on special war activities,
which was a subcommittee of the war council.

1347. *An American in the Army and YMCA, 1917-1920: The Diary of*
David Lee Shillinglaw. Edited by Glen E. Holt. Chicago:
University of Chicago Press, 1971. 219 pp.

This volume tells of the war experiences of the head of
the construction services for the YMCA. Shillinglaw presents
an interesting portrait of U.S. attitudes toward France
during the war.

1348. Bane, Suda Lorena, and Lutz, Ralph Haswell, eds. *Organization*
of American Relief in Europe, 1918-1919, Including Negotia-
tions Leading up to the Establishment of the Office of Direc-
tor General of Relief at Paris by the Allied and Associated
Powers. Stanford, Calif.: Stanford University Press, 1943.
745 pp.

This is a valuable documentary history despite the absence
of any explanatory notes or commentary with the exception of
Hoover's brief introduction.

1349. Brooks, Sidney. *America and Germany, 1918-1925.* New York:
Macmillan Co., 1925. 191 pp.

This work contains some interesting material on American and
Allied efforts to get food to the starving German population
after the war. There is no index.

1350. Bryan, Julien H. *Ambulance 464: Encore des Blessés.* New
York: Macmillan Co., 1918. 220 pp.

This is an interesting account by a seventeen-year-old
Princeton student who drove an ambulance in the French sector
of the western front.

1351. Byington, Margaret F. "The Scope and Organization of the Department of Civilian Relief." *Ann. Am. Ac. of Pol. Sci. and*
Soc. Sci. 79 (September 1918): 88-96.

This brief article explains in general the operation of the
department of civilian relief. Basically, this department
attempted to help servicemen's families maintain their normal
standard of living.

1352. Cornebise, Alfred E. *Typhus and Doughboys: The American Polish*
Typhus Relief Expedition, 1919-1921. Newark: University of
Delaware Press, 1982. 192 pp.

Some five hundred men and thirty officers commanded by
Colonel Harry L. Gilchrist were sent to Poland to contain a
terrible typhus epidemic. This is their story.

1353. Coyle, Edward R. *Ambulancing on the French Front.* New York:
Britton Publishing Co., 1918. 243 pp.

An American ambulance volunteer gives his experiences
serving in the Verdun sector. His views of trench warfare
are realistic.

1354. Davis, Donald E., and Trani, Eugene P. "The American YMCA and
the Russian Revolution." *Slav. Rev.* 33 (September 1974):
469-91.

The YMCA's difficulties with both the Red and White factions
are examined. Its Christian purpose and foreign roots made it
impossible for it to continue in Russia once the Bolsheviks
had consolidated their position.

1355. Davison, Henry P. *The American Red Cross in the Great War.*
New York: Macmillan Co., 1919. 303 pp.

Utilizing the files of the national headquarters, Davison,
who directed the activities of the Red Cross during the conflict, surveys all aspects of the work of that organization.
The article is strong in describing relief work, but is weak
in including too many anecdotes and commendations for workers.

1356. Douglas, Paul H. "The War Risk Insurance Act." *Jour. Pol.
Econ.* 26 (May 1918): 461-83.

This excellent analysis of the War Risk Insurance Act reveals that it was the most comprehensive of any of the acts
passed by the warring countries to protect the soldier and his
family through a plan of compensation.

1357. Dulles, Foster Rhea. *The American Red Cross: A History.* New
York: Harper & Brothers, 1950. 554 pp.

The activities of the American Red Cross in both world wars
are chronicled in this work. There is a bibliographical
essay but no footnotes.

1358. Egan, Maurice F., and Kennedy, John B. *Knights of Columbus
in Peace and War.* New Haven: Knights of Columbus, 1920.
2 vols.

This two-volume work details the activities of the Knights
of Columbus during World War I. It treats the relief work
at the front, which included hospital work and letter writing.
Moreover, this monograph examines the war fund campaign, home
work, and the activities of some front line priests. Vol. 2
is filled with commendations and the honor roll.

1359. *Friends of France: The Field Service of the American Ambulance
Described by Its Members.* Boston: Houghton Mifflin Co.,
1916. 297 pp.

Three more volumes were later published to fill in the gaps
left by these firsthand accounts. See *History of the American
Field Service in France: Friends of France, 1914-1917.*

1360. Glenn, Mary W. "Purpose and Methods of a Home Service Section." *Ann. Am. Ac. of Pol. Sci. and Soc. Sci.* 79 (September 1918): 97-105.

This facet of Red Cross activities is treated in this article, which explains how the home service section attempted
to help preserve the homes which the soldiers left behind.

1361. Gray, Andrew. "The American Field Service." *Amer. Heritage*
26 (December 1974): 58-63, 88-92.

This is a well-written and succinct account of the American
Field Service in the Great War.

1362. Gulick, Luther H. *Morals and Morale.* New York: Association
Press, 1919. 192 pp.

This study of the factors which influenced the morale of
the U.S. Army during the war focuses attention on the work
of the Young Men's Christian Association. This is basically
a firsthand account by a physician who was quite concerned
with morals and morale. It also attempts to put forth an
educational program for morale and morals after the war.

1363. Harding, Priscilla M. "An American Red Cross Nurse in Belgrade."
Amer. Hist. Ill. 17 (March 1982): 41-47.

The diary of Mary Gladwin was used to describe her work as
a Red Cross nurse in the American Military Hospital in Belgrade.

1364. *History of the American Field Service in France: Friends of
France, 1914-1917.* Boston: Houghton Mifflin Co., 1920.
3 vols.

The story of the American Field Service, which was organized
and paid for by Americans prior to American entry into the
war, is told by its members in articles, diaries, home letters,
verse, and frequently humorous sketches. Many of the accounts
found in the 1916 volume, entitled *Friends of France*, are here
reproduced.

1365. Hopkins, C. Howard. *John R. Mott, 1865-1955: A Biography.*
Grand Rapids, Mich.: William B. Eerdmans Publishing Co.,
1980. 816 pp.

This biography of a lay minister who played a major role in
the development of the YMCA and other Christian organizations
sheds light on the humanitarian side of World War I. Woodrow
Wilson utilized Mott's advice in humanitarian affairs, and
Mott raised huge sums of money for relief activities.

1366. Howe, Mark Anthony De Wolfe, ed. *The Harvard Volunteers in
France: Personal Records of Experience in Military, Ambulance,
and Hospital Service.* Cambridge: Harvard University Press,
1916. 263 pp.

This volume is made up of letters of Harvard men who served abroad in military and relief capacities.

1367. Hunton, Addie D., and Johnson, Kathryn M. *Two Colored Women with the American Expeditionary Forces*. New York: Brooklyn Eagle Press, 1920. 256 pp.

Two black women with the YMCA in France tell their story.

1368. Kellogg, Paul U. "The Expanding Demands for War Relief in Europe." *Ann. Am. Ac. of Pol. Sci. and Soc. Sci.* 79 (September 1918): 9-23.

This article treats the expanded need to provide relief for Europeans after the war. It emphasizes the activities of the Red Cross, as well as the role it would be called upon to play.

1369. Keough, Frederic W. "The Employment of Disabled Service Men." *Ann. Am. Ac. of Pol. Sci. and Soc. Sci.* 80 (November 1918): 84-94.

This essay sees the problem of the employment of the handicapped as an individual problem. It surveys industries where the disabled veteran can be employed and emphasizes that it is up to the individual veteran to find and be successful at employment.

1370. Lakeman, Curtis E. "The After-Care of Our Disabled Soldiers and Sailors." *Ann. Am. Ac. of Pol. Sci. and Soc. Sci.* 79 (September 1918): 114-29.

This informative article examines factors which would affect the treatment of disabled veterans. They include: the vocational rehabilitation law, psychological factors, family influence, financial provisions, and special problems.

1371. Lathrop, Julia C. "Provisions for the Care of the Families and Dependents of Soldiers and Sailors." *Proc. Acad. Pol. Sci.* 7 (February 1918): 140-51.

The chief of the United States Children's Bureau explains the provisions of the Military and Naval Insurance Act relating to care of families and dependents of soldiers and sailors.

1372. Mock, Harry E. "Reclamation of the Disabled from the Industrial Army." *Ann. Am. Ac. of Pol. Sci. and Soc. Sci.* 80 (November 1918): 29-34.

This essay argues for a program of rehabilitation for those who have become handicapped as a result of industrial accidents.

1373. Orcutt, Philip D. *The White Road of Mystery*. New York: John Lane Co., 1918. 173 pp.

This personal record of an American who served with the ambulance field service is of a high literary quality. There are photographs and a glossary of war terms in this volume.

1374. Persons, W. Frank. "The Soldiers' and Sailors' Families."
       Ann. Am. Ac. of Pol. Sci. and Soc. Sci. 77 (May 1918): 171-
       84.

       Written by the director of civilian relief for the American
       Red Cross, this essay explains how the home service operates.

1375. Smith, Paul M. "The Famous and the Extraordinary." *Der
       Angriff* (July 1982): 23-27.

       This article discusses famous Americans such as Walt Disney
       and Ernest Hemingway who served in the American Field Service.

1376. ————. "Swift Evacuation: Ambulances and Drivers from
       America." *Der Angriff* (July 1982): 11-23.

       This is a well-illustrated and solidly researched article.

1377. Toland, Edward D. *The Aftermath of Battle: With the Red Cross
       in France.* New York: Macmillan Co., 1916. 175 pp.

       This is the diary of a Princeton graduate who went to France
       and worked in a French hospital before joining a unit of the
       American Field Service.

1378. Zinsser, William H. "Working with Men Outside the Camps."
       Ann. Am. Ac. of Pol. Sci. and Soc. Sci. 79 (September 1918):
       194-203.

       This article discusses the attempts to keep civilian young
       men away from the evils of alcohol and prostitution.

                  H. WAR SONGS, POETRY, BALLADS, AND SLANG

1379. Braley, Berton. *In Camp and Trench: Songs of the Fighting
       Forces.* New York: George H. Doran Co., 1918. 84 pp.

       This volume includes songs of national guardsmen, "Platts-
       burgers," draftees in training camps and at the front, and
       sailors.

1380. Brophy, John, and Partridge, Eric. *The Long Trail: What the
       British Soldier Sang and Said in the Great War of 1914-1918.*
       London: Andre Deutsch, 1965. 239 pp.

       This is a revision of the 1931 edition entitled *Songs and
       Slang of the British Soldier 1914-1918.* It gives songs, chants,
       sayings, and the slang of the British soldier. The extensive
       "Glossary of Soldiers' Slang," one of the best of its kind, is
       especially useful for a study of the AEF because the doughboy
       adopted some of the slang of his British counterpart.

1381. Cary, Melbert B., Jr. *Mademoiselle from Armentières.* New
       York: Press of the Woolly Wale, 1930-1935. 2 vols.

       It took two slim volumes to collect the frequently ribald
       verses of this popular song sung by both American and British

soldiers. The volumes are nicely illustrated by Alban B. Butler, Jr.

1382. Garrett, Erwin Clarkson. *Trench Ballads and Other Verses.* Philadelphia: John C. Winston Co., 1919. 134 pp.

Part one consists of forty doughboy ballads, most of them composed in France. The compiler was a private in the 16th Infantry, First Division.

1383. Gibbons, Herbert Adams, comp. *Songs from the Trenches: The Soul of the A.E.F.* New York: Harper & Brothers, 1918. 207 pp.

This collection by Gibbons consists of verses submitted to the *New York Herald*'s literary competition. It was intended to be "a message from the American soldiers abroad to the home folks, written on the decks of transports, in French villages, in muddy camps, in the trenches, beside cannon or camion, in hospitals."

1384. Lighter, Jonathan. "The Slang of the American Expeditionary Forces in Europe, 1917-1919: An Historical Glossary." *Amer. Speech* 47 (Spring-Summer 1972): 5-143.

This lengthy and scholarly article gives army and marine slang used during World War I. An impressive bibliography of over twenty pages is included.

1385. McCollum, L.C. *History and Rhymes of the Lost Battalion.* New York: Bucklee Publishers, 1919. 140 pp.

The work of a private in the "Lost Battalion," this collection of McCollum's poems, usually humorous, and accounts contributed by others went through several editions and is claimed to have sold some 600,000 copies.

1386. Niles, John Jacob, ed. *Singing Soldiers.* Detroit, Mich.: Singing Tree Press, 1968. 171 pp.

This is a reissue of the 1927 edition of the songs and anecdotes of black soldiers which was published by Charles Scribner's Sons. Illustrations were produced by Margaret Thorniley and a new introduction was written by Leslie Shepard. Niles, a Kentuckian, was already a considerable authority on American folk song before serving as a ferry pilot in the U.S. Air Service in France.

1387. ———; Moore, Douglas S.; and Wallgren, A.A. *The Songs My Mother Never Taught Me.* New York: Macaulay Co., 1929. 227 pp.

This standard work is an important collection of many of the songs sung on land and at sea by U.S. servicemen. Some of the songs submitted to the compilers, however, were not included because they "were so hot they melted the type every time the linotypers set 'em up." "Wally" Wallgren, the official cartoonist of the *Stars and Stripes*, illustrated this work.

1388. *Pack Up Your Troubles--Songs of Two World Wars.* RCA.

Many of the popular songs of the Great War are sung in this recording by the Carl Tapscott Male Chorus.

1389. *Quips and Memories of the Corps.* Q.M.C. Souvenir Book Committee, 1919. 256 pp.

This illustrated work, which includes a good deal of verse, was prepared by a committee of the Q.M.C. Some of the subject matter concerns service in the Q.M.C. "over here."

1390. Silken, Jon, ed. *The Penguin Book of First World War Poetry.* New York: Penguin Books, 1982. 270 pp.

This handy collection brings together the works of thirty-eight British, American, and European writers.

1391. Spaeth, Sigmund. *A History of Popular Music in America.* New York: Random House, 1948. 729 pp.

This survey of popular music contains a very extensive list of popular music, which reflects the beliefs and emotions of the majority of the American people. This volume shows how the popular music of the war period captured the feelings of the American public and it analyzes the song "Over There."

1392. Stokes, Will. *Songs of the Services: Army, Navy and Marine Corps.* New York: Frederick A. Stokes Co., 1919. 235 pp.

Many long-forgotten poems are included in this collection by a chief yeoman of the U.S. Navy.

1393. *Yanks: A.E.F. Verse.* New York: Knickerbocker Press, 1919. 157 pp.

This volume consists entirely of selections from the *Stars and Stripes.*

I. HUMOR AND CARICATURE

1394. Graves, Charles Larcom. *Mr. Punch's History of the Great War.* New York: Frederick A. Stokes Co., 1919. 303 pp.

This is a volume of selected cartoons and commentary from the important British publication *Punch.* Despite its humorous vein, *Punch* had the serious purpose of keeping the British public behind the war.

1395. Hecht, George J., comp. and ed. *The War in Cartoons: A History of the War in 100 Cartoons by 27 of the Most Prominent American Cartoonists.* New York: E.P. Dutton & Co., 1919. 207 pp.

Hecht was the founder of the bureau of cartoons, Committee on Public Information, which suggested subject matter to

American cartoonists in 1918. A review of this collection of cartoons from the American press demonstrates that the pen in the hand of a cartoonist was a potent weapon against the Central Powers. Each cartoon is accompanied by quotations from war leaders to describe the events drawn by the cartoonist.

1396. Raemaekers, Louis. *America in the War*. New York: Century Co., 1918. 207 pp.

Each cartoon is accompanied by a page of comment from such American notables as William Jennings Bryan and Albert Bushnell Hart.

1397. *Raemaekers' Cartoons: With Accompanying Notes by Well-Known English Writers*. Garden City, N.Y.: Doubleday, Page & Co., 1916. 305 pp.

A German newspaper once proclaimed that the Dutch cartoonist Louis Raemaekers's work was "worth at least two Army Corps to the Allies." This was no doubt hyperbole. Nevertheless, many of his cartoons from the Amsterdam *Telegraaf* are truly devastating in their treatment of German words and actions.

1398. Reinert, Frederick George. *With the 332 Reg. in Italy 1918*. N.p., 1919.

There are some quite good comics and sketches in this privately published volume with no pagination.

1399. Rogers, W.A., ed. *America's Black and White Book: One Hundred Pictured Reasons Why We Are at War*. New York: Cupples & Leon Co., 1917. 100 pp.

The title is a play on words and refers to the so-called colored books issued by the European belligerents to justify their participation in the war. These often powerful cartoons are a reflection of the growing importance of political cartoons in the U.S. press and their effectiveness as propaganda. There is a brief explanation of each cartoon.

1400. Streeter, Edward. *Dere Mable: Love Letters of a Rookie*. New York: Frederick A. Stokes Co., 1918. 61 pp.

Streeter, a lieutenant in the 27th Division, composed humorous letters from a fictitious "Bill" to his girl Mable describing his strange new life in uniform. This pocket-size book sold an astonishing 550,000 copies in eight months, prompting the author to publish more letters from "Bill." G. William Breck provided thirty-five black-and-white illustrations.

1401. ————. *Same old Bill, eh Mable!* New York: Frederick A. Stokes Co., 1919. 120 pp.

"Bill" finally makes it to the trenches to send his impressions home to Mable. G. William Breck provided twenty-seven black-and-white illustrations.

1402. ———. *That's me all over, Mable*. New York: Frederick A.
       Stokes Co., 1919. 69 pp.

       This "simple" soldier continues to write his girl back home
       as he finishes his basic training and departs for Europe.
       G. William Breck drew twenty-five black-and-white illustra-
       tions.

1403. Wallgren, A.A. *Wally: His Cartoons of the A.E.F.* N.p., n.d.

       The famous cartoons of a USMC private ("Wally") are reprinted
       from the *Stars and Stripes*. This booklet was sold in France
       for five francs, with the profits going to the Stars and
       Stripes French War Orphans' Fund.

                            J. WAR POSTERS

1404. Darracott, Joseph, and Loftus, Belinda, eds. *First World War
       Posters*. London: H.M. Stationery Office, 1972. 72 pp.

       This beautifully illustrated survey of World War I posters
       includes a brief but excellent introduction and a select bib-
       liography. Information on each artist is provided. The com-
       pilers were members of the art department at the Imperial War
       Museum. The two best collections of American war posters are
       at the National Archives and the Hoover Institution of War,
       Revolution and Peace.

1405. Hardie, Martin, and Sabin, Arthur K., eds. *War Posters Issued
       by Belligerent and Neutral Nations, 1914-1919*. New York:
       Macmillan Co., 1920. 275 pp.

       This volume reproduces many of the important war posters,
       and includes an artist index. The circumstances behind some
       of the war posters are given.

1406. Pennell, Joseph. *Joseph Pennell's Liberty-Loan Poster*. Phila-
       delphia: J.B. Lippincott Co., 1918. 47 pp.

       This fascinating little volume traces the artistic and
       graphic evolution of the Liberty Loan poster. It contains a
       description of the poster's development and five illustrations
       showing how the poster began as a sketch and ended as a
       printed poster.

1407. *Recruiting Posters Issued by the U.S. Navy Since the Declara-
       tion of the War*. Washington, D.C.: U.S. Navy Recruiting
       Bureau, 1918.

       This booklet of thirty posters has no pagination. One of
       the most-used posters was by Howard Chandler Christy, who
       simply portrayed a pretty girl in a CPO uniform without any
       accompanying message.

1408. "Recruiting Posters WW I." *U.S. Naval Inst., Proc.* 98 (Feb-
       ruary 1972): 68-82.

This pictorial includes the most popular U.S. Navy recruiting posters in the war.

1409. Rickards, Maurice, ed. *Posters of the First World War.* New York: Walker & Co., 1968. 32 pp.

This volume contains a representative selection of the over 30,000 posters and proclamations issued during the Great War.

1410. Roetter, Charles. *The Art of Psychological Warfare 1914-1945.* New York: Stein & Day, 1974. 199 pp.

Part one, "First World War 1914-1918," includes the chapter "Courting the United States." Some of the best-known propaganda posters are included in this undocumented work.

K. LITERATURE AND THE WAR

1411. Aichinger, Peter. *The American Soldier in Fiction, 1880-1963: A History of Attitudes Toward Warfare and the Military Establishment.* Ames: Iowa State University Press, 1975. 143 pp.

This work surveys the views of war and the military reflected in American war novels written between 1880 and 1963. Besides looking at the World War I novels, Aichinger examines various themes reflected in the novels.

1412. Barbusse, Henri. *Under Fire: The Story of a Squad.* London: J.M. Dent & Sons, 1917. 344 pp.

This powerful indictment of the war by a Frenchman was a best seller in France. Although not of the same literary quality as *All Quiet on the Western Front*, its impact was similar. The English translation is by Fitzwater Wray.

1413. Binding, Rudolf. *A Fatalist at War.* London: Allen & Unwin, 1928. 246 pp.

The reminiscences of this famous German literary figure constitute one of the most important firsthand accounts of the war on the German side of the trenches.

1414. Binns, Archie. *The Laurels Are Cut Down.* New York: Reynal & Hitchcock, 1937. 332 pp.

This novel is about a young man's service with his brother in Siberia and his resultant disillusionment with the war.

1415. Blunden, Edmund. *Undertones of War.* London: Oxford University Press, 1956. 366 pp.

This classic work by a British poet is divided into two sections: first a narrative and then the author's poems. This reprint of the 1928 edition has a new preface.

1416. Boyd, Thomas A. *Through the Wheat.* New York: Charles Scrib-
       ner's Sons, 1926. 266 pp.

       William Hicks, the central figure in the novel, is a good
       soldier who performs his duty well. Yet in a heavy attack
       his experiences during war render him zombie-like. The horror
       of war is vividly portrayed in this novel.

1417. Cather, Willa S. *One of Ours.* New York: Alfred A. Knopf,
       1922. 459 pp.

       This Pulitzer Prize-winning novel describes the experiences
       of a young man who leaves a narrow-minded small town atmosphere
       to expand his horizons through his activities in France during
       World War I.

1418. Cobb, Humphrey. *Paths of Glory.* New York: Viking Press,
       1935. 265 pp.

       This important World War I novel, replete with all the typi-
       cal battlefront experiences, concentrates on the unbridgeable
       class differences between French officers and men on the
       western front.

1419. Conner, James Richard. "Pen and Sword, World War I Novels in
       America 1916-1941." Doctoral dissertation, University of
       Wisconsin, 1961. 415 pp.

       Connor analyzes several hundred novels written about World
       War I, dividing them into three categories. The first category
       concerns the attempt to treat the war in the early 1920s as a
       "great crusade" to save the oppressed. The second category
       examines the view in the mid-1920s that the war was a "great
       tragedy." The final category is concerned with novels that
       view the war as a "great adventure."

1420. Cooperman, Stanley R. *World War I and the American Novel.*
       Baltimore, Md.: Johns Hopkins Press, 1967. 273 pp.

       This work argues that the World War I experience influenced
       a generation of American literature through its emotional
       effects on American soldiers and writers of war novels.

1421. Cummings, E.E. *The Enormous Room.* New York: Boni & Liveright,
       1922. 271 pp.

       The "enormous room" of the title refers to a French prison
       camp in which the author was unjustly confined. Cummings
       served with the Norton-Harjes ambulance corps. This volume
       is one of the greatest World War I narratives produced by an
       American writer.

1422. Dos Passos, John R. *First Encounter.* New York: Philosophical
       Library, 1945. 160 pp.

       This novel about an ambulance driver was partially based
       upon the author's World War I experiences. It reflects his
       generation's disillusionment with the war.

1423. ————. *1919*. New York: Harcourt, Brace & Co., 1932. 473 pp.

This second novel in the trilogy *U.S.A.* focuses attention on the decay of American civilization which was based on commercialism and exploitation. Numerous historical events of the war period provide the backdrop for episodes involving various characters.

1424. ————. *Three Soldiers*. New York: George H. Doran Co., 1921. 433 pp.

World War I's impact on the lives of three ordinary American privates is the focus of this work, which shows how each reacted to the war and reflects the tragic way the war influenced the lives of individuals.

1425. Edmonds, Charles. *A Subaltern's War*. London: Peter Davies, 1929. 224 pp.

This classic account of war in the trenches by Charles Carrington (who used the nom de plume of Charles Edmonds) demonstrates that war can bring out both the best and the worst in men. The diarist takes the commonsense position that one should expect modern war to be horrible. His experiences during the Somme and Third Ypres battles certainly strengthened this conviction.

1426. Eksteins, Modris. "All Quiet on the Western Front and the Fate of a War." *Jour. Contemp. Hist.* 15 (April 1980): 345-66.

This is an enlightening article on both Erich Remarque and the reaction to his famous antiwar novel, *All Quiet on the Western Front*. Eksteins notes: "*All Quiet* was not 'the truth about the war': it was, first and foremost, the truth about Erich Maria Remarque in 1928. But equally, most of his critics were no nearer 'the truth about the war.' They expressed merely the tenor of their own endeavors."

1427. Faulkner, William. *Soldiers' Pay*. New York: Boni & Liveright, 1926. 319 pp.

This first novel by Faulkner concerns the homecoming of a dying soldier. It offers a good example of the postwar disillusionment with World War I.

1428. Fenton, Charles A. "Ambulance Drivers in France and Italy, 1914-1918." *Amer. Quarterly* 3 (Winter 1951): 326-43.

Fenton probes the motives and reactions of the members of the American Ambulance Field Service. He argues that disillusioned writers such as Dos Passos and Hemingway have distorted the way in which the typical American ambulance driver viewed his wartime experiences.

1429. Fisher, Dorothea Canfield. *Home Fires in France*. New York: Henry Holt & Co., 1918. 306 pp.

The author's eleven short stories about life behind the lines in France have been described as "fiction in form, but fact in essence."

1430. Fussell, Paul. *The Great War and Modern Memory*. New York: Oxford University Press, 1975. 363 pp.

This is a masterful analysis of the British experience on the western front as expressed in British literature. The great war memoirs by Sassoon, Graves, and Blunden as well as the memoirs of ordinary soldiers are effectively utilized to portray the horrors of trench warfare.

1431. Graves, Robert. *Good-Bye to All That*. London: J. Cape, 1929. 446 pp.

Graves must be included among the great war memoirists. An officer in the BEF, he gives a vivid representation of combat on the western front.

*   Hager, Philip E., and Taylor, Desmond. *The Novels of World War I: An Annotated Bibliography*. Cited above as item 29.

1432. Hašek, Jaroslav. *The Good Soldier Švejk and His Fortunes in the World War*. New York: Thomas Y. Crowell Co., 1974. 752 pp.

This novel concerning a Czech soldier in the Austro-Hungarian army has become a classic. It has been used somewhat unfairly by some to characterize the multi-national Austro-Hungarian army. Cecil Parrott provides a new and unabridged translation, and there are many original illustrations by Jesef Lada in this edition.

1433. Hemingway, Ernest. *A Farewell to Arms*. New York: Charles Scribner's Sons, 1919. 355 pp.

This poignant novel deals with the love between Frederic Henry, an American national in the Italian ambulance service, and Catherine Barkley, an English nurse. Their affair leads to Catherine's pregnancy and Henry's desertion to be with her. Ultimately, the affair ends tragically. An ambulance driver on the Piave front, Hemingway was the first American to be wounded in Italy. This novel was based upon his Italian experiences.

1434. Joyner, Charles Winston. "John Dos Passos and World War I: The Literary Use of Historical Experience." Doctoral dissertation, University of South Carolina, 1968. 312 pp.

Dos Passos's three novels about World War I reflect his theme of revolt against the established order. This dissertation attempts to explain how his World War I experiences helped influence Dos Passos's writings and social attitudes.

1435. Klein, Holger, ed. *The First World War in Fiction: A Collection of Critical Essays*. London: Macmillan & Co., 1976. 246 pp.

This series of eighteen essays analyzes a work or group of works dealing with World War I. Utilizing the comparative approach, the contributors to this collection examine literature from Britain, France, Germany, Italy, Austria-Hungary, and the United States. For those interested in understanding the impact of the war on literature, this work is a must.

1436. Paul, Elliot. *Impromptu: A Novel in Four Movements*. New York: Alfred A. Knopf, 1924. 356 pp.

Written by an expatriate, this novel deals with how World War I changed a young couple's lives.

1437. Remarque, Erich Maria. *All Quiet on the Western Front*. Boston: Little, Brown & Co., 1929. 291 pp.

When published in German in 1928, this powerful antiwar novel became an instant best seller, with some 1.2 million copies being sold in Germany alone. This work by a five-times-wounded German veteran remains the best known of the antiwar novels concerning World War I.

1438. Sassoon, Siegfried. *The Memoirs of an Infantry Officer*. New York: Doubleday, Doran & Co., 1938. 334 pp.

This is widely recognized as one of the greatest memoirs produced by a participant in the Great War.

1439. ———. *Sherston's Progress*. New York: Doubleday, Doran & Co., 1936. 245 pp.

This is the concluding volume of Sassoon's biographical trilogy, the last two volumes being primarily concerned with Sassoon's combat experiences and recovery from "shell-shock."

1440. Sinclair, Upton. *Jimmie Higgins*. New York: Boni & Liveright, 1919. 282 pp.

This is a socialistic novel with pacifistic overtones.

1441. Stallings, Laurence. *Plumes*. New York: Harcourt, Brace & Co., 1924. 348 pp.

This Georgia-born author writes a personal indictment of war as seen through the eyes of Richard Plume, a southerner whose misguided patriotism resulted in a painfully crippling injury during the war.

1442. Stevens, James. *Mattock*. New York: Alfred A. Knopf, 1927. 320 pp.

Best known for his Paul Bunyan tales, Stevens also wrote this semi-autobiographical novel about the wartime experiences of a midwestern farmer, Marvin Mattock.

1443. Train, Arthur. *Earthquake*. New York: Charles Scribner's Sons, 1918. 307 pp.

Nationalistic in tone, this work focuses attention on the war's impact on an American family.

1444. Trumbo, Dalton. *Johnny Got His Gun*. Philadelphia: J.B. Lip-
       pincott Co., 1939. 309 pp.

       This novel, which was published two days after World War II
       began, tells the story of Joe Bonham, a soldier who lost his
       arms, legs, and face. Joe discovers that the only thing he
       can do is think, and he survives by using his mind to keep him
       in touch with reality. The novel is depressing and antiwar in
       flavor.

1445. Wharton, Edith. *The Marne: A Story of the War*. New York: D.
       Appleton & Co., 1918. 128 pp.

       This novel focuses attention on Troy Belknap, a Francophile,
       and how he managed to get into the war. He is wounded and
       believes he is saved from death by the spirit of his French
       tutor who was buried close to the Marne battlefield.

1446. ———. *A Son at the Front*. New York: Charles Scribner's
       Sons, 1923. 426 pp.

       This rather weak novel deals with an American painter's son
       who serves in the French Army. Basically, the work addresses
       the question of American participation in the war. Ultimately
       the son is killed.

1447. Zweig, Arnold. *The Case of Sergeant Grischa*. New York: Viking
       Press, 1928. 449 pp.

       This German novel was quickly proclaimed by critics as one
       of the best European war novels. The central character is a
       peasant in the Tsarist army who is captured by the Germans and
       then escapes. Man's inhumanity to man emerges from the pages
       of this well-written book. Eric Sutton translated this work
       into English.

                                L. FILM

1448. *All Quiet on the Western Front*. Universal, 1930.

       This is perhaps the most important film about World War I.
       Based upon the pacifistic novel by Erich Maria Remarque, the
       movie realistically portrays war in all its brutality. Directed
       by Lewis Milestone, Lew Ayres gave an excellent performance
       as the film's lead. This film portrays the efficiency of
       killing machines such as the machine gun with depressing vivid-
       ness. Nazis demonstrated outside German theaters when this
       film was first shown in Germany.

1449. *America's Answer*. Committee on Public Information, 1918.

       This Creel Committee film is one of the best examples of an
       American feature propaganda film. Germany is depicted as the
       aggressor and the AEF led by Pershing as the savior of western
       civilization. This documentary attempts to inspire war workers
       to increase their production.

1450. Bauer, K. Jack. *List of World War I Signal Corps Films*. Wash-
      ington, D.C.: The National Archives, 1957. 68 pp.

    This excellent guide describes the films under the control
of the Signal Corps, and contains an excellent pictorial history of the war. Most of the films indexed are available for
use at the archives. The films are not confined to military
operations; a good collection of films on civilian activities
are also listed.

1451. *The Big Parade*. MGM, 1925.

    Based upon a Laurence Stallings story, the film realistically
deals with the standard war themes. The battle scenes are
first rate. An upper-class youth joins the army and becomes
friendly with two working-class comrades. The hero avenges
the death of one of his friends, is wounded, and falls in love
with a French girl. The film was directed by King Vidor and
produced by Irving Thalberg.

1452. *Dealers in Death*. Topical Films, 1934.

    This semi-documentary film, reflecting the isolationism of
the between-the-war period, blames the munitions makers for
World War I.

1453. *The Fighting 69th*. Warner Brothers, 1940.

    Featuring James Cagney and Pat O'Brien, this movie focuses
attention on the exploits of a New York city unit. Patriotism
is emphasized throughout.

1454. *The First World War*. Fox, 1934.

    Utilizing some Signal Corps footage, this film stresses the
horror of war while projecting an Allied bias.

1455. *Gallipoli*. Paramount, 1981.

    This powerful antiwar film focuses on the part played by
Australians in the 1915 Gallipoli campaign. The director is
Peter Weir.

1456. *Goodbye Billy--America Goes to War, 1917-1918*. Churchill Films,
      1972.

    A historian uses music and film footage to contrast the views
of combatants and noncombatants.

1457. *The Guns of August*. Universal, 1965.

    This documentary was based on Barbara Tuchman's book on pre-
war society and the opening battles of World War I.

1458. *Hell's Angels*. United Artists, 1930.

    With its air scenes directed by Howard Hughes, this film
stands as one of the very best at portraying the glory of the
air war. Hughes used his own stunt pilots. This movie, featuring
Jean Harlow, became a sound film although it started production
in the silent era.

1459.   Isenberg, Michael T. *War on Film: The American Cinema and
        World War I, 1914-1941.* Rutherford, N.J.: Fairleigh Dickin-
        son University Press, 1981. 273 pp.

        This is an important survey of how a major war was presented
        on film. It attempts to show that film is an important source
        for understanding American history. Film was often used for
        promotion and propaganda as well as for entertainment. Well
        written and researched, this volume should be the starting
        point for anyone interested in the war on film.

1460.   *Men of Bronze.* Killiam Shows/Films Inc., 1977.

        This color film portrays the experiences of the black 369th
        Regiment which fought with a French division.

1461.   *The Moving Picture Boys in the Great War.* Black Hawk Films,
        1975.

        Hollywood's part in the Great War is the theme of this film
        which makes use of some excellent contemporary footage.

1462.   *Nicholas and Alexandra.* Columbia Pictures Corp., 1972.

        The origins and course of the Russian Revolution can be
        followed in this color film.

1463.   *The Ordeal of Woodrow Wilson.* NBC/Encyclopaedia Britannica,
        1965.

        This black-and-white film is excellent for classroom use.

1464.   *Paths of Glory.* United Artists, 1957.

        Kirk Douglas stars in this Stanley Kubrick film, which is
        critical of French military leadership.

1465.   Reeves, Nicholas. "Film Propaganda and Its Audience: The Ex-
        ample of Britain's Official Films During the First World
        War." *Jour. Contemp. Hist.* 18 (July 1983): 463-94.

        Reeves suggests that film propaganda was "better suited in
        every way to strengthening and reinforcing existing attitudes
        than to creating new ones."

1466.   *Sergeant York.* Warner Brothers, 1941.

        A Hollywood classic starring Gary Cooper, this film examines
        the life of a Tennessee mountaineer who captured 132 German
        soldiers in 1918. It emphasizes the heroic exploits of a rural
        American who had pacifist leanings.

1467.   Soderbergh, Peter A. "'Aux Armes!': The Rise of the Hollywood
        War Film, 1916-1930." *So. Atl. Quar.* 65 (Autumn 1966):
        509-22.

        This interesting article surveys the birth and rise of the
        Hollywood war film from 1916 to 1930. Initially Hollywood had
        a restricted view of the war, but the Creel Committee saw film
        as a tool to sell the war. Nonetheless, Hollywood remained

generally indifferent. However, between 1925 and 1930 several superior war films were produced, including *The Big Parade* and *All Quiet on the Western Front*. War was pictured as being a result more of destructive "forces" than of the aggressive Hun.

1468. *The Soviet Union, 1918-1920: The Civil War and Allied Intervention*. CBS/Films Inc., 1961.

This seventeen-minute film is part of the "World in Turmoil" series.

1469. *The Unbeliever*. Edison, 1918.

This film portrays Germans as Huns and barbarians. Eric Von Stroheim plays the typical German.

1470. *Versailles: The Lost Peace*. Allan Landsburg Productions, 1978.

This twenty-two-minute film is part of the "Between the Wars" series.

1471. Ward, Larry W. "The Motion Picture Goes to War: A Political History of the U.S. Government's Film Effort in the World War, 1914-1918." Doctoral dissertation, University of Iowa, 1981. 303 pp.

This study analyzes the wartime collaboration between filmmakers and the government. Ward, however, does not attempt "to assess the effectiveness of film propaganda." U.S. Army Signal Corps films, CPI films, and privately produced films are discussed.

1472. *Wings*. Paramount, 1927.

The strength of this film is the classic aerial footage. Two American heroes take on a German "flying circus." Medieval chivalry lives in the aerial dueling which is prominent in the film. William Wellman directed this significant movie.

M. BLACKS AND THE WAR

1473. Contee, Clarence G. "Du Bois, the NAACP, and the Pan-African Congress of 1919." *Jour. Negro Hist.* 57 (January 1972): 13-28.

This article focuses attention on Du Bois's role in the 1919 Pan-African independence movement. Du Bois pressured Woodrow Wilson and marshalled the power of the NAACP to see that the Pan-African Conference of 1919 was held.

1474. Cronon, Edmund David. *Black Moses: The Story of Marcus Garvey and the Universal Negro Improvement Association*. Madison: University of Wisconsin Press, 1955. 278 pp.

This first-rate work traces the career of Marcus Garvey and his impact on blacks during and after World War I. Garvey

worked hard to uplift blacks and improve their image. His re-
ward was deportation.

1475. Finney, John Dustin. "A Study of Negro Labor During and After
World War I." Doctoral dissertation, Georgetown University,
1967. 425 pp.

This study examines the Negro migration northward to work in
the northern industrial labor market. The government's role,
the attitude of the American Federation of Labor, and black
leadership are scrutinized. Finney points out that blacks
entered the market under temporary circumstances and that the
government failed to protect them. Moreover, organized labor
did not welcome them and they failed to achieve strong unioni-
zation for their own interests.

1476. Haynes, George E. "The Effect of War Conditions on Negro
Labor." *Proc. Acad. Pol. Sci.* 8 (February 1919): 165-78.

This important article surveys the impact of the war on
black labor. Blacks wanted fair pay, education, an end to
racial discrimination, and the right to participate in the
political process.

1477. Haynes, Robert V. *A Night of Violence: The Houston Riot of
1917*. Baton Rouge: Louisiana State University Press, 1976.
338 pp.

This detailed study examines the reaction of the black 24th
Infantry to the racism which led to the Houston riot of
August 23, 1917. Nineteen soldiers were hanged.

1478. Miller, Sally M. "The Socialist Party and the Negro, 1901-20."
Jour. Negro Hist. 56 (July 1971): 222-29.

This article deals with the treatment of Negroes by the
Socialist Party from 1901 to 1920. Even though the Socialist
Party never downgraded the Negro, it never admitted that the
black was an equal. Some Socialists fought to gain equal
rights for the Negro, but failed in their attempts.

1479. Newby, I.A. *Jim Crow's Defense: Anti-Negro Thought in America
1900-1930*. Baton Rouge: Louisiana State University Press,
1965.

This study concentrates on the body of ideas which argued for
the racial inferiority of the Negro. Newby concludes that
World War I led to a racial migration to northern cities, more
opportunities, and a concern about these changes.

1480. Ross, B. Joyce. *J.E. Spingarn and the Rise of the NAACP, 1911-
1939*. New York: Atheneum, 1972. 305 pp.

This study focuses attention on a white liberal who played a
leadership role in a minority-group organization for twenty-
eight years. Based on primary sources and topically organized,
this work deals with the problems of the organization and how
it dealt with those problems. During World War I, the NAACP
fought successfully for a Negro officers' training camp.

1481. Rudwick, Elliott M. *Race Riot at East St. Louis, July 2, 1917.* Carbondale: Southern Illinois University Press, 1964. 300 pp.

This volume treats the background and events of the East St. Louis riots of 1917.

1482. Scheiber, Jane Lang and Harry N. "The Wilson Administration and the Wartime Mobilization of Black Americans, 1917-18." *Labor Hist.* 10 (Summer 1969): 433-58.

This article examines the wartime mobilization of blacks to see if Wilson used them or took advantage of their situation. Before the war Wilson had failed to live up to many of his promises to blacks. After the war began, however, Wilson catered to blacks and they made many contributions to the war effort. Yet Wilson refused to ally himself with black leaders for fear that this would identify him with their demands for equality in exchange for their war efforts.

1483. Scott, Emmett J. *Negro Migration During the War.* New York: Arno Press and the New York Times, 1969. 189 pp.

First published in 1920 with funding by the Carnegie Endowment for Peace, this study traces the migration of over 400,000 Negroes northward during World War I. The exodus, basically economic, depopulated some southern areas. Scott looks at the causes and at the cities where the impact was the greatest, St. Louis and Chicago. This important work is a must for a study of the war's impact on the social fabric of the country.

1484. Sochen, June. *The Unbridgeable Gap: Blacks and Their Quest for the American Dream, 1900-1930.* Chicago: Rand McNally College Publishing Co., 1972. 136 pp.

Sochen surveys the intellectual history of blacks from 1900 to 1930 and attempts to bring together myth and fact as treated by black intellectuals. Even though the study is well researched and written, it focuses little attention on the impact of World War I on the thought of black intellectuals.

1485. Speer, Allan H. *Black Chicago: The Making of a Negro Ghetto 1890-1920.* Chicago: University of Chicago Press, 1967. 254 pp.

Speer, in this well-documented and well-written book illustrates in fine fashion the great migration of blacks from the south to Chicago during World War I. The blacks who arrived to work in war-related industries found a well-developed black ghetto. Considerable attention is given to the resultant racial tensions.

N. RADICALISM

1486. Bindler, Norman. "American Socialism and the First World War." Doctoral dissertation, New York University, 1970. 181 pp.

This well-researched study analyzes the motives, ideology, and influences which determined the role of the American Socialist movement from 1914 to 1918. The socialists responded to the European war by calling for U.S. mediation as well as an embargo. During the war the socialists split into pro- and antiwar factions. The general public and the government harassed the socialists, and several leaders ended up in jail for violating the Espionage and Sedition acts.

1487. Brissenden, Paul F. *The I.W.W.: A Study of American Syndicalism.* New York: Russell & Russell, 1957. 438 pp.

An early survey of the Industrial Workers of the World, this book seeks to put the movement in perspective as it downplays the more radical side of this radical labor force. A brief discussion of the war's negative impact on the I.W.W. is included.

1488. Carsten, F.L. *War Against War: British and German Radical Movements in the First World War.* Berkeley: University of California Press, 1982. 285 pp.

Much familiar ground is covered in this monograph, but it is valuable because it offers a comparative view of antiwar activities of the socialist left in Britain and Germany.

1489. Coben, Stanley. "A Study in Nativism: The American Red Scare of 1919-20." *Pol. Sci. Quar.* 74 (March 1964): 52-75.

Coben examines the roots of the U.S. fears of Communism as well as the fears themselves. Many psychologists felt that many Americans were insecure and that they sought security in the nation. Thus, they perceived Communism as an outside threat to their own security and they resorted to violence. Politicians such as A. Mitchell Palmer inflamed the public even more. Coben concludes that Communism was a threat, but that postwar America overreacted to that threat.

1490. Conlin, Joseph R. *Big Bill Haywood and the Radical Union Movement.* Syracuse, N.Y.: Syracuse University Press, 1969. 244 pp.

This book, which is not based on manuscript collections, examines Haywood's relationship to the I.W.W. and socialism. Conlin argues that the socialistic split with the I.W.W. in 1912 ruined Socialism in America. World War I and the resulting repression destroyed the I.W.W. Haywood was exiled to Russia, where he lived until 1928.

1491. ———, ed. *The American Radical Press, 1880-1960.* Westport, Conn.: Greenwood Press, 1974. 2 vols.

This collection of 100 essays (with elaborate notes) on 119 periodicals provides a thorough look at the U.S. radical press. Several essays reflect the reaction of the radical press to the Great War.

1492. Dewitt, Howard A. *Images of Ethnic and Radical Violence in California Politics, 1917-1930: A Survey*. San Francisco: R and E Research Associates, 1975. 136 pp.

This is an important, well-documented case study of anti-radicalism coming out of the World War I experience.

1493. Draper, Theodore. *The Roots of American Communism*. New York: Viking Press, 1963. 498 pp.

This work reconstructs the birth and early years of American Communism. It is especially good at examining the impact of World War I on the movement, which actually led to the real birth of American Communism as it became an arm of the Russian movement.

1494. Jaffe, Julian F. *Crusade Against Radicalism: New York During the Red Scare*. Port Washington, N.Y.: Kennikat Press, 1972. 265 pp.

In this completely researched volume, Jaffe examines the main aspects of the Red Scare in New York. The major radical groups are discussed and anti-radical activities are analyzed. Jaffe concludes that the harassment of radicals provided a training ground for postwar anti-radicalism activities.

1495. Miller, Sally M. *Victor Berger and the Promise of Constructive Socialism, 1910-1920*. Westport, Conn.: Greenwood Press, 1973. 274 pp.

This superior study examines how Victor Berger attempted to achieve socialist principles by working within the system through political action. Miller focuses much attention on the war's impact on Socialism in the United States.

1496. Murray, Robert K. *Red Scare: A Study of National Hysteria, 1919-1920*. New York: McGraw-Hill Book Co., 1955. 337 pp.

Murray sees the Red Scare as a phenomenon with roots in World War I and the Bolshevik Revolution.

1497. Shannon, David A. *The Socialist Party of America: A History*. New York: Macmillan Co., 1955. 320 pp.

Objective and well researched, this volume argues that the socialists in World War I hoped to gain power by working within the political system. The failure to work out its internal differences caused the party to change from being pragmatic to doctrinaire. Shannon's approach is institutional, and he treats the decline of American Socialism in the context of its failure to adapt to the two-party system.

1498. Shepperson, Wilbur S., and Folkes, John G. *Retreat to Nevada: A Socialist Colony of World War I*. Reno: University of Nevada Press, 1966. 244 pp.

This study examines a socialist experiment in cooperative living in the Lahonton Valley in Nevada. Midwestern society saw the colony as a way of avoiding both the consequences of

American participation in World War I and the decaying capital-
istic system.

1499. Szajkowski, Zosa. *Jews, Wars, and Communism.* New York: KTAV,
       1973-1974. 2 vols.

       This is the first attempt to document the attitude of American
       Jews in the World War I period. The second volume emphasizes
       the impact of the Red Scare on American Jewish life.

1500. Weinstein, James. "Anti-War Sentiment and the Socialist Party,
       1917-1918." *Pol. Sci. Quar.* 74 (June 1959): 215-39.

       The belief that President Wilson could keep America out of
       the war contributed to his reelection in 1916. Only five months
       after the election, however, the United States was at war. The
       American Socialist Party's antiwar push led to verbal attacks,
       physical violence, and combat with U.S. troops.

1501. ———. *The Decline of Socialism in America, 1912-1925.* New
       York: Monthly Review Press, 1967. 367 pp.

       Weinstein examines the socialist movement in the United
       States before, during, and after World War I. He concludes
       that repression and division resulting from the war and the
       Russian Revolution caused the decline of Socialism in America.

                          O. CIVIL LIBERTIES

1502. Dunning, W.A. "Disloyalty in Two Wars." *AHR* 24 (July 1919):
       625-30.

       This essay compares the treatment of disloyal citizens in
       World War I and the American Civil War.

1503. Johnson, Donald. *Challenge to American Freedoms: World War I
       and the Rise of American Civil Liberties Union.* Lexington:
       University Press of Kentucky, 1963. 243 pp.

       This important work, the winner of the 1962 M.V.H.A. award,
       focuses on the A.C.L.U. and its predecessor, the National Civil
       Liberties Bureau. Johnson argues that the hysteria generated
       by the war was responsible for the start of a true civil liber-
       ties movement in the United States.

*   Mock, James R. *Censorship, 1917.* Cited above as item 1322.

1504. Murphy, Paul L. *The Meaning of Freedom of Speech: First Amend-
       ment Freedoms from Wilson to FDR.* Westport, Conn.: Greenwood
       Publishing Co., 1972. 401 pp.

       Murphy's legalistic examination of free speech during World
       War I shows that the government restricted many basic freedoms
       and attempted to propagandize the American people. This cir-
       cumstance developed without any major protest, and represented
       a sharp break with past traditions.

1505. ————. *World War I and the Origin of Civil Liberties in the
       United States*. New York: W.W. Norton & Co., 1979. 285 pp.

       This work attempts to examine why serious violations of civil
       liberties occurred during the war. Murphy concludes that the
       roots of the problem can be found in progressivism which em-
       phasized the strengthening of the government and the failure
       of the administration to see the need of preserving civil liber-
       ties. Moreover, Murphy feels that Americans saw nothing wrong
       in harassing dissenters.

1506. Scheiber, Harry N. *The Wilson Administration and Civil Liber-
       ties 1917-1921*. Ithaca, N.Y.: Cornell University Press,
       1960. 69 pp.

       This slim monograph, which is based on an M.A. thesis, ex-
       amines the period from 1917 to 1921. Scheiber concludes that
       civil liberties were sacrificed heavily during the war, par-
       ticularly with the passage of the Sedition Act. Government
       officials and vigilantes were enthusiastic about enforcing
       conformity. Wilson is criticized for not attempting to moder-
       ate public opinion.

VII. DIPLOMACY OF THE WAR

A. GENERAL SOURCES

1507. Anderson, George L., ed. *Issues and Conflicts: Studies in Twentieth Century American Diplomacy.* Lawrence: University of Kansas Press, 1959. 374 pp.

Included in this collection are essays by Stromberg on collective security, 1916-1920; by Ferrell on Wilson's views of open diplomacy; and by Lilienthal on the Balfour Declaration.

1508. Bailey, Thomas A. *The Policy of the United States Toward the Neutrals, 1917-1918.* Baltimore, Md.: Johns Hopkins University Press, 1942. 520 pp.

After entering the war, Bailey points out, the United States drove a hard bargain with the neutrals. This policy of limiting neutral goods to the Central Powers shortened the war. Bailey argues that the United States did not violate international law in a sweeping way.

1509. Buehrig, Edward H., ed. *Wilson's Foreign Policy in Perspective.* Bloomington: Indiana University Press, 1957. 176 pp.

This is a collection of lectures given at Indiana University during the Wilson centennial year. Some of the topics covered by distinguished scholars are the role that House played in Wilson's diplomacy, the origins of Wilson's views on collective security, Wilson's regional policies, and an evaluation of Keynes's hostile portrayal of Wilson.

1510. Curry, Roy Watson. *Woodrow Wilson and Far Eastern Policy, 1913-1921.* New York: Bookman Associates, 1957. 411 pp.

This important piece of scholarship emphasizes three aspects of Wilson's Far Eastern policy: "Wilson himself, the particular situation, and the tradition of American policy." There is an especially thorough bibliography.

1511. Edwards, Warrick Ridgely, III. "United States-Mexican Relations 1913-1916: Revolution, Oil and Intervention." Doctoral dissertation, Louisiana State University, 1971. 628 pp.

Based largely on State Department records, this dissertation treats Wilson's attempt to interfere with the internal affairs of Mexico from 1913 to 1916. It examines Wilson's attempts to arrange a Pan-American intervention so the United States could disengage and face its problems created by the European war.

1512. Ershkowitz, Herbert. *The Attitude of Business Toward American
       Foreign Policy, 1900-1916.* University Park: Pennsylvania
       State University, 1967. 77 pp.

       In the early part of the twentieth century, some U.S. intel-
       lectual and commercial leaders concluded that the country was
       overproducing. Thus, in order to prevent potential economic
       problems, business leaders looked to new markets in the Far
       East and Latin America. The author concludes that this con-
       cern over overproduction was groundless and the China market
       proved to be a dream. Yet the United States did develop an
       important market in Latin America.

1513. Griswold, A. Whitney. *The Far Eastern Policy of the United
       States.* New Haven: Yale University Press, 1962. 530 pp.

       First published in 1938, this volume has become a classic
       even though the archives of the State Department beyond 1906
       were not available to the author at the time of his research.
       This work provides a sound introduction to American policy in
       Asia prior to World War I. Chapters 5, 6, and 7 cover the
       period of the Great War and the peace settlement.

1514. Herman, Sondra. *Eleven Against War: Studies in American Inter-
       nationalist Thought, 1898-1921.* Stanford, Calif.: Hoover
       Institution Press, Stanford University, 1969. 264 pp.

       This is an interesting study of Americans who wished to
       launch a new era in international politics. Some, such as
       Elihu Root and Hamilton Holt, saw a world court or a league of
       nations as the answer. Still others, for example, Thorstein
       Veblen, placed their hopes in a new world economic and social
       order.

1515. Hill, Larry D. *Emissaries to a Revolution: Woodrow Wilson's
       Executive Agents in Mexico.* Baton Rouge: Louisiana State
       University Press, 1974. 394 pp.

       Based primarily on materials in the state archives and manu-
       script collections in the United States and Mexico, this study
       focuses attention on the relations of the United States and
       Mexico from 1913 to the U.S. recognition of the Carranza govern-
       ment. Wilson's actions prior to Carranza's recognition created
       bad relations between the two countries. See also Hill's 1971
       Louisiana State University dissertation.

1516. Johnson, Robert Bruce. "The Punitive Expedition: A Military,
       Diplomatic, and Political History of Pershing's Chase After
       Pancho Villa, 1916-1917." Doctoral dissertation, University
       of Southern California, 1964. 912 pp.

       This study describes the U.S. expedition under General John
       J. Pershing to punish the Mexican bandit Pancho Villa for his
       raid in New Mexico. Carranza, the head of the Mexican govern-
       ment, did not want the U.S. forces on Mexican soil. Pershing
       failed to catch Villa and there were several altercations with
       Carranza's forces. When the United States entered World War I,
       American forces were withdrawn from Mexico.

1517. Kennan, George F. *American Diplomacy 1900-1950*. Chicago: University of Chicago Press, 1951. 154 pp.

One of the six lectures published in this collection concerns American involvement in World War I. Wilson and other American leaders are faulted for their moralistic slogans and their determination to make the American military and diplomatic effort a crusade.

1518. Komarnicki, Titus. *Rebirth of the Polish Republic: A Study in the Diplomatic History of Europe, 1914-1920*. London: W. Heinemann, 1957. 776 pp.

This massively documented study is still useful for the study of both wartime diplomacy and the Paris Peace Conference. The author, however, does give a highly Polish view of events.

1519. Leuchtenburg, William E. "Progressivism and Imperialism: The Progressive Movement and American Foreign Policy, 1898-1916." *MVHR* 39 (December 1952): 483-504.

Leuchtenburg argues that progressives generally supported U.S. imperialism and preparedness.

1520. Levin, N. Gordon, Jr. *Woodrow Wilson and World Politics: America's Response to War and Revolution*. New York: Oxford University Press, 1968. 340 pp.

In this well-researched and balanced study, Levin examines the theory and practice of Wilsonian diplomacy during American belligerency, intervention in Russia, and the peace settlement. He argues that the primary objective of Wilson's diplomacy was to make the world safe for liberal capitalism. This made Wilson an opponent of both traditional imperialism and revolutionary socialism. Although the American people rejected the League of Nations, Wilson's world view eventually came to dominate American foreign policy.

1521. Lewis, Cleona. *America's Stake in International Investments*. Washington, D.C.: Brookings Institution, 1938. 710 pp.

This study traces America's transition from a debtor to a creditor country. The author's purpose is to show "the complex character of lending and investment transactions by which American capital moves abroad while foreign capital in large amounts comes into the United States." Karl T. Schlotterbeck assisted the author. Numerous charts and statistical tables are included.

1522. Link, Arthur S. *Wilson the Diplomatist: A Look at His Major Foreign Policies*. Baltimore, Md.: Johns Hopkins Press, 1957. 165 pp.

Link's Albert Shaw Lectures on Diplomatic History are published herein. Link contends that Wilson was genuinely committed to neutrality, 1914-1917, but that the German decision to embark on a policy of unrestricted warfare forced his hand. Concern about the German threat to his world order, according to Link, influenced Wilson to choose full belligerency instead

of armed neutrality or a maritime strategy. It should also be
noted that Link made several changes, some of them major, in
the second edition, which appeared in 1963.

1523. ————, ed. *Woodrow Wilson and a Revolutionary World, 1913-
        1921*. Chapel Hill: University of North Carolina Press,
        1982. 241 pp.

        This collection reflects the most current research on various
        aspects of Wilson's diplomacy by scholars such as Lloyd C.
        Gardner, Betty Miller Unterberger, Jay Lundgreen-Nielsen, Inga
        Floto, Kurt Wimer, Herbert G. Nichols, and Whittle Johnston.
        Among the topics covered are Wilson's approach to revolution
        in Mexico and Russia, his policy toward Poland, and his efforts
        to construct a new world order.

1524. Lippmann, Walter. *United States Foreign Policy: Shield of the
        Republic*. Boston: Little, Brown & Co., 1943. 177 pp.

        This noted American journalist argues that the continuation
        of nineteenth-century American diplomacy into the twentieth
        century ill served the nation and was "dangerously inadequate."
        Lippmann also argues that national self-interest rather than
        Wilson's idealistic explanations was the best justification
        for American belligerency.

1525. Lowe, Cedric James, and Marzari, F. *Italian Foreign Policy,
        1870-1940*. London: Routledge & Kegan Paul, 1975. 476 pp.

        This valuable and clearly written work surveys British dip-
        lomacy from 1902 to 1922. Vol. 2 covers the war and the peace
        conference. Vol. 3 is a collection of documents, some of
        which concern Anglo-American relations.

1526. ————, and Marzari, F. *Italian Foreign Policy, 1870-1940*.
        London: Routledge & Kegan Paul, 1975. 476 pp.

        This general survey fills a void in English-language litera-
        ture on Italian diplomacy. Chapter 8 concerns Italy at the
        Paris Peace Conference.

1527. Martin, Percy Alvin. *Latin America and the War*. Baltimore,
        Md.: Johns Hopkins Press, 1925. 582 pp.

        This highly interpretative volume examines how the twenty
        Latin American nations reacted to the Great War.

1528. Mason, Herbert Molloy, Jr. *The Great Pursuit*. New York: Ran-
        dom House, 1970. 269 pp.

        This is a sound though nonscholarly day-by-day account of
        Pershing's pursuit of Villa which exacerbated U.S.-Mexican re-
        lations.

1529. Morgenthau, Hans J. *In Defense of the National Interest: A
        Critical Examination of American Foreign Policy*. New York:
        Alfred A. Knopf, 1951. 283 pp.

        Morgenthau, a political scientist, has prepared a standard
        brief in support of the "realist" as opposed to the "idealist"

approach to international relations. Although concerned more with Cold War politics, this work also attempts to serve as a corrective to Wilsonian diplomacy.

1530. Munro, Dana G. *Intervention and Dollar Diplomacy in the Caribbean, 1900-1921.* Princeton: Princeton University Press, 1964. 553 pp.

Based primarily on State Department records, this detailed study of U.S. policy in the Caribbean treats how the intervention policy developed and why the United States acted as it did. The interventions seemed to have been motivated by the feeling that the United States had a responsibility to help its neighbors and the fear of possible European intervention. American interventionist policy served to undermine the U.S. position in the area.

1531. Osgood, Robert E. *Ideals and Self-Interest in American Foreign Relations.* Chicago: University of Chicago Press, 1953. 491 pp.

A revision of the author's thesis, this important work is critical of President Wilson for allowing abstract moral and idealistic considerations to shape his views of world politics. A basic problem examined by Osgood is the conflict between what is ideal and what is practical in international affairs. There are chapter notes but no bibliography.

1532. Renouvin, Pierre. *War and Aftermath: 1914-1929.* New York: Harper & Row, 1968. 369 pp.

This volume is a major contribution to diplomatic history by one of France's foremost historians. The French edition was published in 1957.

1533. Schmidt, Hans. *The United States Occupation of Haiti, 1915-1934.* New Brunswick, N.J.: Rutgers University Press, 1971. 303 pp.

This well-written and well-documented study examines U.S. policy in regard to Haiti. Ironically, intervention came when American policy emphasized human rights and respect for smaller countries. The occupation emphasized the materialistic rather than the idealistic. The realities of World War I, fear of the Germans, and the strategic importance of Haiti to the United States prompted the intervention.

1534. Schulz, Gerhard. *Revolutions and Peace Treaties, 1917-1920.* London: Methuen & Co., 1972. 258 pp.

This is the translation of the German edition which was published in 1967. Schulz's purpose is to examine the diplomacy and revolutions of World War I and their effects as part of the history of the world. President Wilson, who is pictured as a well-meaning victim of circumstances, receives sympathetic treatment.

1535. Seymour, Charles. *American Diplomacy During the World War.* Hamden, Conn.: Archon Books, 1964. 417 pp.

Between the wars Seymour emerged as Wilson's most important
defender among professional historians. He stressed American
determination to protect life and property against Germany's
undersea assault and argued that the political and economic
factors stressed by the revisionists were secondary considerations for Wilson and his advisors. This well-documented work,
which has an extensive bibliography, is a reprint of the 1934
edition.

1536. Silberstein, Gerard E. *The Troubled Alliance: German-Austrian
      Relations, 1914-1917*. Lexington: University Press of Ken-
      tucky, 1970. 366 pp.

      This work includes an analysis of the relationship between
      the German and Austrian high commands, with the conflict be-
      tween Falkenhayn and Conrad von Hötzendorff being highlighted.
      There is also a comprehensive account of the Dual Alliance's
      attempts to win Balkan allies. The research in German and
      Austrian sources is thorough and there is extensive documenta-
      tion.

1537. Smith, Daniel M. *The Great Departure: The United States and
      World War I, 1914-1920*. New York: John Wiley & Sons, 1965.
      221 pp.

      This is a scholarly synthesis of American neutrality, bel-
      ligerency, and peacemaking based on extensive research in un-
      published sources and the latest literature. Wilson's diplomacy
      is treated with sympathy and understanding.

1538. Surface, Frank M. *The Grain Trade During the World War*. New
      York: Macmillan Co., 1928. 679 pp.

      The roles of the Food Administration Grain Corporation and
      the United States Grain Corporation receive detailed treatment.
      The humanitarian effort to feed the starving people of Europe
      is also covered. Relevant documents are included in the lengthy
      appendices and there are numerous statistics and graphs in the
      text.

*   Taylor, A.J.P. *The Struggle for Mastery in Europe 1848-1918*.
      Cited above as item 131.

1539. Trow, Clifford W. "Woodrow Wilson and the Mexican Interven-
      tionist Movement of 1919." *JAH* 58 (June 1971): 46-72.

      This article examines the 1919 Mexican interventionist move-
      ment headed by Republican Senator Albert Fall of New Mexico.
      Motivated by oil interests and other investments, Fall, backed
      by Senator Henry Cabot Lodge, urged President Wilson to estab-
      lish a protectorate over Mexico. Wilson, however, refused to
      go along and reasserted his control over foreign affairs by
      forcing Secretary of State Lansing to resign. Trow defends
      Wilson's actions throughout.

1540. Tulchin, Joseph S. *The Aftermath of War: World War I and U.S.
      Policy Toward Latin America*. New York: New York University
      Press, 1971. 287 pp.

This well-written and competently researched volume argues
that U.S. Latin American policy, 1918-1919, was determined by
U.S. experiences during World War I. Disillusioned Americans
lost interest in interfering in the affairs of other nations
and were little inclined to get involved in hemispheric disputes. U.S. policy was formulated without regard to hemispheric
government.

1541. United States Department of State. *Papers Relating to the
Foreign Relations of the United States, 1914-1918: Supple-
ment, The World War*. Washington, D.C.: Government Printing
Office, 1928-1933. 9 vols.

This collection of State Department papers covers a wide
range of subjects from prisoners of war to neutral rights.

1542. Vagts, Alfred. *Defense and Diplomacy: The Soldier and the
Conduct of Foreign Relations*. New York: King's Crown Press,
1956. 547 pp.

This series of essays sheds light on the role of the military
expert in formulating and conducting foreign relations. The
author's organization is thematic rather than chronological.

1543. Ward, Alan J. *Ireland and Anglo-American Relations, 1899-1921*.
Toronto: University of Toronto Press, 1969. 291 pp.

Ward examines the role played by Ireland in driving a wedge
between Britain and the United States during World War I.
He also delineates the part played by Irish-Americans in de-
feating the Treaty of Versailles.

1544. West, Rachel. *The Department of State on the Eve of the First
World War*. Athens: University of Georgia Press, 1978. 183
pp.

This study shows that the State Department was unprepared to
deal with the crisis of World War I. Critical of Bryan and
Wilson, the author feels that the department had Europe at
too low a priority. See also her 1972 Indiana University doctoral dissertation.

1545. Williams, Benjamin H. *Economic Foreign Policy of the United
States*. New York: Howard Fertig, 1967. 426 pp.

This book, originally published in 1927, examines U.S. eco-
nomic foreign policy from its prewar roots into the mid-1920s.
Williams examines basic U.S. cornerstone policies, such as the
Open Door Policy, in light of economics. This study shows how
World War I transformed the United States from a debtor into a
creditor nation.

1546. Zeman, Z.A.B. *The Gentleman Negotiators: A Diplomatic History
of World War I*. New York: Macmillan Co., 1971. 402 pp.

An attempt at a general diplomatic history of World War I,
this volume relates the strategy of the war to diplomacy.
Zeman moves from capital to capital of the belligerents as he

describes the formulation of war aims and the attempts to en-
list allies or detach members of the enemy coalition. Chapter
5, "Washington," examines America's road to war.

B. DIPLOMATS (INCLUDING MANUSCRIPT COLLECTIONS)

1. United States

Bryan

1547. Bryan, William Jennings. Collection in the National Archives.

This collection consists of four volumes of Bryan's correspondence. Many of Wilson's letters are included.

1548. ———. Collection in the Division of Manuscripts, Library
of Congress.

Bryan's generally disappointing papers are arranged chronologically. It has been alleged that Bryan destroyed many important papers.

1549. ——— and Mary B. *The Memoirs of William Jennings Bryan*.
Philadelphia: John C. Winston Co., 1925. 560 pp.

These memoirs unfortunately close with an account of the
1912 convention in Baltimore.

1550. Challener, Richard. "William Jennings Bryan (1913-1915)."
In *An Uncertain Tradition*, edited by Norman A. Graebner,
pp. 79-100. New York: McGraw-Hill Book Co., 1961.

Challener examines the successes and failures of Bryan's
diplomacy and the values he represented.

1551. Coletta, Paolo E. *William Jennings Bryan*, vol. 2: *Progressive
Politician and Moral Statesman, 1909-1915*. Lincoln: University of Nebraska Press, 1969. 380 pp.

This second volume of Coletta's three-volume biography of
Bryan devotes most of its attention to his career in the
Wilson administration. The author concludes that Bryan was
not a great secretary of state, but that his peace proposals
influenced the League Covenant, the Kellogg-Briand pact, and
the United Nations.

1552. Curti, Merle Eugene. *Bryan and World Peace*. Smith College
Studies in History, 16, nos. 3-4 (April-July 1931): 113-260.

Bryan's peace efforts during World War I receive attention
in this solid study.

1553. Levine, Lawrence W. *Defender of the Faith. William Jennings
Bryan: The Last Decade, 1915-1925*. New York: Oxford University Press, 1965. 386 pp.

This scholarly biography is a masterful reinterpretation of Bryan's final years. Although it is not a study of Bryan's World War I diplomacy, it sheds light on Bryan's fundamental beliefs.

Bullitt

1554. Bullitt, William Christian. Collection in Yale University Library.

This collection of 750 items includes materials concerning Germany in World War I, the Paris Peace Conference, and Bullitt's mission to Russia in 1919. It also includes Bullitt's correspondence with President Wilson.

1555. ———. *The Bullitt Mission to Russia: Testimony Before the Committee on Foreign Relations, United States Senate.* New York: B.W. Heubsch, 1919. 151 pp.

Bullitt used the committee on foreign relations in September 1919 as a forum to attack President Wilson's Russian policy. Bullitt mistakenly believed that Wilson had thrown away the opportunity to end the civil war in Russia.

1556. Farnsworth, Beatrice. *William C. Bullitt and the Soviet Union.* Bloomington: Indiana University Press, 1967. 244 pp.

This volume, based on some hitherto unavailable sources, sheds new light on Bullitt's role at the Paris Peace Conference and his controversial mission to Russia to negotiate with the Soviet leaders. Bullitt's sympathetic attitude toward the Soviet regime during the Wilson presidency was not to survive his ambassadorship in the USSR during the 1930s.

Egan

1557. Egan, Maurice Francis. *Ten Years Near the German Frontier: A Retrospect and a Warning.* New York: George H. Doran Co., 1919. 364 pp.

Egan was the U.S. minister to Denmark from 1907 until 1918. His book is a lively discussion of the German threat to Europe.

Francis

1558. Francis, David Rowland. Collection in Missouri Historical Society Library.

Francis's ambassadorship in Russia is well covered in this collection of some 50,000 items.

1559. ———. *Russia from the American Embassy, April 1916-November 1918.* New York: Charles Scribner's Sons, 1921. 361 pp.

This rambling and often disappointing account by the American ambassador in Petrograd who succeeded Marye is still useful for any examination of Russo-American relations during the Great War. Francis, however, played little role in American intervention.

1560. *Dollars and Diplomacy: Ambassador David Rowland Francis and*
       the Fall of Tsarism, 1916-1917. Edited by Jamie H. Cock-
       field. Durham, N.C.: Duke University Press, 1981. 149 pp.

       The correspondence, personal and official, of Francis,
       largely from his papers held by the Missouri Historical Society,
       but also including documents from the National Archives, is
       arranged in chronological order. Cockfield covers the period
       before the abdication of Nicholas II. Francis's correspondence
       after the February (or March) Revolution is excluded because
       Kennan made extensive use of it in his study. Commentary and
       footnotes are included.

1561. Kohlenberg, Gilbert C. "David Rowland Francis: American
       Business Man in Russia." *Mid-Amer.* 40 (October 1958):
       195-217.

       Francis aggressively pursued American economic interests in
       Russia, but he was clearly a failure when it came to diplomacy.

       Gerard

1562. Gerard, James W. Collection in University of Montana Library.

       These papers include Gerard's general correspondence. Access
       is restricted.

1563. ————. *My Four Years in Germany.* New York: George H. Doran
       Co., 1917. 448 pp.

       This is an interesting account by the American ambassador
       in Berlin. Gerard, who had been a Tammany politician, often
       displeased President Wilson who thought little of his advice
       and once minuted one of his dispatches: "Who can fathom this?
       I wish they would hand this idiot his passports!" There is
       much of interest in Gerard's reminiscences, but the volume
       does not live up to its advertisement as "the most important
       contribution to the literature of great present-day events."

1564. Barthold, Theodore Richard. "Assignment to Berlin: The Em-
       bassy of James W. Gerard, 1913-1917." Doctoral dissertation,
       Temple University, 1981. 445 pp.

       The newly available papers of Gerard were used in this dip-
       lomatic biography of Gerard's years in Berlin. The author
       contends that Gerard was a more able representative of American
       interests than is usually thought.

       Gibson

1565. Gibson, Hugh. *A Journal from Our Legation in Belgium.* Garden
       City, N.Y.: Doubleday, Page & Co., 1917. 362 pp.

       Written by the first secretary of the American legation in
       Brussels, this diary chronicles the first three months (July 4
       to December 31) of the war. There are numerous illustrations,
       including a portrait of Miss Cavell.

Grew

1566. Grew, Joseph C. *Turbulent Era: A Diplomatic Record of Forty Years, 1904-1945*. Boston: Houghton Mifflin Co., 1982. 2 vols.

These memoirs contain some information on Grew's service in the American embassy in Berlin from 1912 to 1917.

1567. Heinrichs, Waldo H., Jr. *American Ambassador Joseph C. Grew and the Development of the United States Diplomatic Tradition*. Boston: Little, Brown and Co., 1966. 460 pp.

This biography of Grew examines the development of the professional diplomatic corps in the United States. During World War I, Grew served as executive officer for the American embassy in Berlin; he also played a minor role at the Paris Peace Conference.

House

1568. House, Edward M. Collection in Yale University Library.

The Wilson-House correspondence is bound separately in this important manuscript collection. Many of the key documents have been published in Seymour's *Intimate Papers of Colonel House*.

1569. *The Intimate Papers of Colonel House*. Edited by Charles Seymour. Boston: Houghton Mifflin Co., 1926-1928. 4 vols.

The papers of House are arranged in a historical narrative by a distinguished professor of history. This is an indispensable source because of House's close relationship with President Wilson and his important role in formulating American diplomatic policy. House was a historian's dream because he kept extensive and careful records, including a daily journal. His views of events, however, must often be examined with a critical eye. Moreover, Seymour is biased in his favor. Vols. 3 and 4 cover the period of American belligerency and the peace conference.

1570. Floto, Inga. *Colonel House in Paris: A Study of American Policy at the Paris Peace Conference, 1919*. Princeton: Princeton University Press, 1981. 374 pp.

This is a superior analysis of House's influence and activities at the peace conference. House is blamed for some of Wilson's shortcomings during the peace negotiations. Floto argues that House pushed upon Wilson policies which he could not accept, thus causing the break between the two men.

1571. George, Alexander L. and Juliette L. *Woodrow Wilson and Colonel House: A Personality Study*. New York: J. Day Co., 1956. 362 pp.

Extensive research went into this psychological study of what one biographer has called the "perfect friendship" between President Wilson and his friend and advisor Colonel House. The two authors are political scientists.

1572. Smith, A.D.H. *Mr. House of Texas*. New York: Funk & Wagnalls
       Co., 1940. 381 pp.

       This sympathetic biography has much to say about House's
       part in the politics and international diplomacy of the Great
       War and the Paris Peace Conference. Smith, a close friend of
       House, would not publish this work while House still lived.

1573. Williams, Joyce Ellen Grigsby. "Colonel House and Sir Edward
       Grey, A Study in Anglo-American Diplomacy." Doctoral dis-
       sertation, Indiana University, 1971. 235 pp.

       Anglo-American relations, 1913-1919, are studied through the
       relationship of House and Grey. The House-Grey Memorandum and
       the development of the League of Nations receive particular
       attention.

       Lansing

1574. Lansing, Robert. Collection in the Division of Mansucripts,
       Library of Congress.

       Lansing's official correspondence in the records of the
       State Department should be used in conjunction with this col-
       lection. These papers include Lansing's personal diary and
       his appointment or desk diary. The papers are arranged chrono-
       logically.

1575. ————. *The Peace Negotiations: A Personal Narrative*. Boston:
       Houghton Mifflin Co., 1921. 328 pp.

       Lansing tries to give his side of his numerous differences
       with President Wilson at the Paris Peace Conference. Photo-
       graphs and excerpts from previously unpublished documents are
       included.

1576. ————. *War Memoirs of Robert Lansing, Secretary of State*.
       Indianapolis: Bobbs-Merrill Co., 1935. 383 pp.

       The title of this work is rather misleading. Lansing begins
       his memoirs when he becomes Secretary of State in 1915 and con-
       cludes shortly after American intervention in the war. Lansing
       readily admits his pro-British sympathies and attempts to ex-
       plain why Wilson waited so long before going to war with Ger-
       many. There are excerpts from the Lansing diaries and war
       memoranda.

1577. United States Department of State. *Papers Relating to the
       Foreign Relations of the United States: The Lansing Papers,
       1914-1920*. Washington, D.C.: Government Printing Office,
       1940. 2 vols.

       The papers of the Secretary of State reveal, among other
       things, that there was no coherent American policy toward
       Russia and that decisions were made essentially on a day-to-day
       basis.

1578. Barany, George. "Wilsonian Central Europe: Lansing's Contribu-
       tion." *Historian* 28 (February 1966): 224-51.

Barany examines Lansing's influence on American policy toward Central Europe.

1579. Beers, Burton F. *Vain Endeavor: Robert Lansing's Attempts to End the American-Japanese Rivalry*. Durham, N.C.: Duke University Press, 1962. 207 pp.

This study highlights the often differing approaches of Wilson and Lansing to Far Eastern problems, which were especially prominent at the Paris Peace Conference. Beers seems to suggest that if Wilson had accepted Lansing's position on several critical issues, America's relations with Japan might have been better.

1580. Smith, Daniel M. *Robert Lansing and American Neutrality, 1914-1917*. Berkeley: University of California Press, 1958. 241 pp.

This well-documented study highlights the differences between Wilson and Lansing on American neutrality. Lansing, more conscious of national security concerns than Wilson, concluded before Wilson that war against Germany was inevitable.

1581. ————. "Robert Lansing and the Formulation of American Neutrality Policies, 1914-1915." *MVHR* 43 (June 1956): 59-81.

Smith concludes that Lansing was one of the "principal architects of the 1914-1917 neutrality structure."

1582. ————. "Robert Lansing (1915-1920)." In *An Uncertain Tradition*, edited by Norman A. Graebner, pp. 101-27. New York: McGraw-Hill Book Co., 1961.

Smith offers a solid and succinct account of Lansing's tenure as Secretary of State, emphasizing his important contributions to U.S. diplomacy. "In retrospect," Smith asserts, "one of the many tragedies of the Wilson years was the President's failure to avail himself more fully of Lansing's talents."

1583. Živojinović, Dragan. "Robert Lansing's Comments on the Pontifical Peace Note of August 1, 1917." *JAH* 56 (December 1969): 556-71.

This Yugoslavian historian reproduces Lansing's comments in full and analyzes the views of the Secretary of State who believed that the Vatican desired the survival of Austria-Hungary as a great state.

Long

1584. Long, Breckinridge. Collection in the Division of Manuscripts, Library of Congress.

Long was an assistant secretary of state in charge of Far Eastern Affairs from 1917 to 1920. His papers are especially useful for any examination of American intervention in Siberia.

Marye

1585.   Marye, George T. *Nearing the End in Imperial Russia.* Phila-
        delphia: Dorrance & Co., 1929. 479 pp.

        Marye kept a journal of his daily activities and impressions
        during his sixteen months as the American ambassador to Russia.

Meriwether

1586.   Meriwether, Lee. *The War Diary of a Diplomat.* New York: Dodd,
        Mead & Co., 1919. 303 pp.

        Meriwether was the special assistant to the U.S. ambassador
        to France from 1916 to 1918. One of his responsibilities was
        to inspect prison camps.

Morgenthau

1587.   Morgenthau, Henry. Collection in the Division of Manuscripts,
        Library of Congress.

        These papers include materials relating to Morgenthau's
        service as U.S. ambassador to Turkey during the Great War.

1588.   ————. *Ambassador Morgenthau's Story.* Garden City, N.Y.:
        Doubleday, Page & Co., 1919. 407 pp.

        Assisted by Burton J. Hendrick, Morgenthau, the former
        American ambassador to Turkey, has written an interesting
        account which is revealing on Turkish and German diplomacy.
        Many illustrations are included.

1589.   ————. *Secrets of the Bosphorus.* London: Hutchinson & Co.,
        1918. 275 pp.

        Morgenthau was the American ambassador to Turkey, 1913-1916.
        He has written an account of the Turkish capital in the throes
        of war. Particular attention is given to the Allied land and
        naval campaign at the Straits in 1915.

Page, Thomas Nelson

1590.   Page, Thomas Nelson. Collection in Duke University Library.

        This collection includes copies of Page's diplomatic corres-
        pondence with the State Department and President Wilson. Page
        was the U.S. ambassador to Italy during the Great War.

*   ————. *Italy and the World War.* Cited above as item 1041.

Page, Walter Hines

1591.   Page, Walter Hines. Collection in Houghton Library, Harvard
        University.

        Most of the important material in these papers has been pub-
        lished in the books of Hendrick, Gregory, and Cooper.

1592.   Cooper, John Milton. *Walter Hines Page: The Southerner as
        American, 1855-1918.* Chapel Hill: University of North Caro-
        lina Press, 1977. 457 pp.

Cooper consulted many private papers in the United States and Great Britain in preparing this excellent biography of Page, who was appointed U.S. ambassador to the Court of St. James's in 1913. Cooper makes a persuasive case that Page's southern roots ("southerner as American on the international scene") had a dominating influence on his perceptions of Anglo-American relations. This led to misunderstandings with both Wilson and the British.

1593. Gregory, Ross. *Walter Hines Page: Ambassador to the Court of St. James's.* Lexington: University Press of Kentucky, 1970. 236 pp.

Anglo-American relations prior to American intervention as well as the pro-British diplomacy of Page are analyzed in this well-researched monograph.

1594. Hendrick, Burton J. *The Life and Letters of Walter Hines Page.* Garden City, N.Y.: Doubleday, Page & Co., 1923-1926. 3 vols.

This biography of the pro-British U.S. ambassador to Britain in World War I was a tremendous publishing success. The two-volume edition in 1923 was the third biggest American nonfiction best seller of that year. A third volume, which contained letters to President Wilson, was almost as well received. These volumes remain a valuable source for studying Anglo-American relations during the war despite Wilson's and House's tendency to ignore the advice offered by Page. The studies by Gregory and Cooper serve as a corrective to some of Hendrick's conclusions.

1595. Kihl, Mary R. "A Failure of Ambassadorial Diplomacy." *JAH* 57 (December 1970): 636-53.

Kihl concludes that House's influence in foreign affairs and his low opinion of British Ambassador Spring-Rice in Washington and U.S. Ambassador Page in London helps explain why both ambassadors were generally ineffective in serving American policymakers. See also her 1968 Pennsylvania State University doctoral dissertation.

Polk

1596. Polk, Frank L. Collection in Yale University Library.

Polk was under secretary of state, 1919, and secretary of state ad interim, 1920. His diary and letters provide insight into some of the views of the State Department.

1597. Mitchell, Kell, Jr. "Frank L. Polk and the Paris Peace Conference, 1919." Doctoral dissertation, University of Georgia, 1966. 312 pp.

Mitchell analyzes Polk's activities and influence as the head of the U.S. delegation to the Paris Peace Conference, concluding that he had little influence in shaping U.S. policy, in part because of his lack of confidence in his own views.

Sharp

1598. Sharp, William Graves. *The War Memoirs of William Graves Sharp, American Minister to France, 1914-1919.* London: Constable & Co., 1931. 431 pp.

The preface of this volume was written by Marshal Joffre.

Van Dyke

1599. Van Dyke, Henry. *Fighting for Peace.* New York: Charles Scribner's Sons, 1917. 256 pp.

Written by the U.S. ambassador to Holland, this volume portrays the Great War as a morality play.

Whitlock

1600. Whitlock, Brand. Collection in the Division of Manuscripts, Library of Congress.

This large collection of some 40,000 items contains extensive materials on wartime conditions in Belgium and American relief work there. Whitlock was U.S. minister and ambassador to Belgium, 1913-1922.

1601. ————. *Belgium: A Personal Narrative.* New York: D Appleton & Co., 1919. 2 vols.

Whitlock's experiences in Belgium during the German invasion in 1914 and the subsequent harsh occupation period are described in this interesting personal narrative.

1602. Crunden, Robert M. *A Hero in Spite of Himself: Brand Whitlock in Art, Politics, & War.* New York: Alfred A. Knopf, 1969. 479 pp.

The value of this biography to those interested in World War I is its treatment of Whitlock as U.S. minister to Belgium during the Great War.

Wood

1603. Wood, Eric Fisher. *The Note-Book of an Attaché: Seven Months in the War Zone.* New York: Century Co., 1915. 345 pp.

Fifteen of the author's photographs illustrate this narrative by a member of the U.S. embassy staff in Paris.

2. Foreign

Andrássy

1604. Andrássy, Count Julius. *Diplomacy and War.* London: John Bale, Sons & Danielsson, 1921. 323 pp.

This work is especially valuable for its treatment of the collapse of the Dual Monarchy in 1918 and Austro-Hungarian efforts to sign a separate peace with the Allies. Andrássy was the Austro-Hungarian foreign minister. The English translation is by J.H. Reece.

Balfour

1605. Balfour, Arthur James (later first earl). Collection in
FO 800, Public Record Office, Kew.

Balfour was foreign secretary during the last half of the
war and headed a British mission to the United States shortly
after the United States came into the war.

1606. ————. Collection in the Department of Manuscripts, The
British Library, London.

These papers shed light on Anglo-American relations.

1607. Dugdale, Blanche E.C. *Arthur James Balfour, First Earl of
Balfour, K.G., O.M., F.R.S.* Westport, Conn.: Greenwood
Press, 1970. Vol. 2, 450 pp.

This is a reprint of the 1936 edition. The author was Balfour's niece. The chapters "Enter the United States, 1917"
and "Treaty Making" are especially relevant to Anglo-American
relations during the era of the Great War. This volume is
based to a large degree on Balfour's voluminous papers.

1608. Young, Kenneth. *Arthur James Balfour: The Happy Life of the
Politician, Prime Minister, Statesman and Philosopher, 1848-
1930.* London: G. Bell & Sons, 1963.

This was the first biography to appear on Balfour since
1936. It generally does justice to his long and distinguished
career. In 1917 Balfour was the first member of Lloyd George's
ministry to meet Wilson.

1609. Zebel, Sydney H. *Balfour: A Political Biography.* Cambridge,
England: Cambridge University Press, 1973. 312 pp.

This biography includes unpublished materials that had been
unavailable to previous biographers.

Bernstorff

1610. Bernstorff, Count. *My Three Years in America.* New York:
Charles Scribner's Sons, 1920. 428 pp.

This volume is an important source for the study of Wilson's
efforts to mediate the war. It also includes an effective
statement of the German case against what was considered
America's double standard toward Germany. British violations
of American neutrality were generally accepted while Germany's
were resisted. The former German ambassador to the United
States, however, is not as convincing in defending the German
embassy from charges of illegal acts during the war.

Cecil

1611. Cecil, Lord Robert (later first viscount). Collection in the
Department of Manuscripts, The British Library, London.

These papers are useful in any study of civil-military relations and British diplomacy during the war and at the Paris
Peace Conference.

1612. ————. Collection in FO 800, Public Record Office, Kew.

Cecil was a key member of the British Foreign Office, serving as minister of blockade, February 1916 to July 1918.

1613. ————. *A Great Experiment*. New York: Oxford University Press, 1941. 390 pp.

Cecil, a prominent Foreign Office official, was one of Britain's leading advocates of the League of Nations, and his autobiography gives a revealing glimpse of his happy working relationship with House and President Wilson during the drafting of the Covenant.

Czernin

1614. Czernin, Count Ottokar. *In the World War*. London: Cassell & Co., 1919. 387 pp.

This is an extremely valuable source for the study of war aims and peace diplomacy during the Great War. Czernin was the Austro–Hungarian foreign minister, 1916–1918. Some extracts from the author's diary are published here.

Drummond

1615. Drummond, Sir Eric (later sixteenth earl of Perth). Collection in FO 800, Public Record Office, Kew.

This influential diplomat was successively private secretary to Asquith, Grey, and Balfour.

Dumba

1616. Dumba, Constantin. *Memoirs of a Diplomat*. Boston: Little, Brown & Co., 1932. 347 pp.

Dumba, the Austrian ambassador, was forced to hand in his passport because of acts of sabotage. In this volume, he attempts to defend the legality of his position. His comments on official Washington during the first years of the war are of interest.

Grey

1617. Grey, Sir Edward (later first viscount). Collection in FO 800, Public Record Office, Kew.

The prospector can find some nuggets on Anglo–American relations in these papers, including material on Grey's view of Wilson's efforts to mediate the war.

1618. ————. *Twenty-Five Years, 1892-1916*. New York: Frederick A. Stokes Co., 1925. 2 vols.

Vol. 2 covers the period of Grey's wartime tenure as Foreign Secretary and is still useful to any study of Anglo–American relations.

1619. Robbins, Keith. *Sir Edward Grey: A Biography of Lord Grey of Fallodon*. London: Cassell & Co., 1971. 438 pp.

The opening of official sources enabled Robbins to improve
in some respects on previous treatments of Grey's diplomacy
during the Great War. This most thorough accounting of Grey's
wartime diplomacy, however, is found in the collection of
articles in F.H. Hinsky, ed., *British Foreign Policy under
Sir Edward Grey* (1977).

1620. Trevelyan, George Macaulay. *Grey of Fallodon: The Life and
      Letters of Sir Edward Grey, Afterwards Viscount Grey of
      Fallodon.* Boston: Houghton Mifflin Co., 1937. 433 pp.

      This sympathetic examination of Grey's diplomacy emphasizes
      that the British Foreign Secretary believed that his country's
      "most vital interest of all" was to stay on good terms with the
      United States.

Murray

1621. Murray, Arthur Cecil (later third viscount Elibank). Collec-
      tion in the Department of Manuscripts, National Library of
      Scotland, Edinburgh.

      Murray was assistant military attaché in Washington, 1917–
      1918. This collection consists of his correspondence and
      papers.

1622. ———. *At Close Quarters, A Sidelight on Anglo-American Re-
      lations.* London: J. Murray, 1946. 106 pp.

      Murray served as one of Wiseman's contacts.

Reading

1623. Isaacs, Rufus Daniel (later first marquess of Reading). Collec-
      tion in European Manuscripts, India Office Library and India
      Office Records, London.

      This collection includes papers relating to his U.S. mission,
      correspondence with Lloyd George, and British competition with
      the French over the use of U.S. troops.

1624. ———. Collection in FO 800, Public Record Office, Kew.

      Reading served as High Commissioner and special ambassador
      to the United States in 1918. He and Wiseman had much closer
      relations with Wilson than Spring-Rice had had.

Spring-Rice

1625. Spring-Rice, Sir Cecil. Collection in FO 800, Public Record
      Office, Kew.

      Spring-Rice was the British ambassador to Washington from
      1912 to 1918, but was never able to win the confidence of
      President Wilson.

1626. ———. *The Letters and Friendships of Sir Cecil Spring-Rice:
      A Record.* Edited by Stephen Gwynn. Boston: Houghton Mifflin
      Co., 1929. 2 vols.

      Spring-Rice, a career diplomat, was replaced by Lord Reading
      in early 1918 because of failing health and mental instability.
      Although little of his official correspondence is printed, his

informal and private letters constitute a valuable primary
source for Anglo-American relations both before and after
America entered the war.

Wiseman

1627. Wiseman, Sir William George Eden. Collection in Yale Univer-
       sity Library.

       This important collection of 131 folders on the period 1917-
       1919 includes Wiseman's official telegrams to the British
       Foreign Office and his correspondence with Colonel House.
       Wiseman's papers are especially helpful for any study of Anglo-
       American relations and U.S. intervention in Russia.

1628. Fowler, Wilton B. *British-American Relations, 1917-1918: The
       Role of Sir William Wiseman.* Princeton: Princeton University
       Press, 1969. 334 pp.

       This is a revision of a 1966 Yale dissertation. Wiseman was
       a liaison between his government and Wilson and House. Fowler
       makes extensive use of the Wiseman papers in this superior
       study. Many of Wiseman's notes on interviews with the president
       and his impressions of Wilson's views are included in the
       appendix. There is an excellent chapter dealing with inter-
       vention in Russia.

C. AMERICAN NEUTRALITY AND ORIGINS OF AMERICAN BELLIGERENCY
(*SEE ALSO* IV:D:3:c, THE WAR BENEATH THE SEA;
IV:D:3:d, BLOCKADE OF THE CENTRAL POWERS;
VII:D, PROPAGANDA AND U.S. PUBLIC OPINION;
VII:E, HYPHENATED AMERICANS AND FOREIGN POLICY)

1629. Auerbach, Jerold S. "Woodrow Wilson's 'Prediction' to Cobb:
       Words Historians Should Doubt Ever Got Spoken." *JAH* 54
       (December 1967): 608-17.

       Prior to his speech to Congress to ask for a war declaration,
       President Wilson supposedly discussed his fears about the war's
       impact on the United States with Frank Cobb of the New York
       World. Auerbach, however, argues that the conversation never
       took place and that it was created by Maxwell Anderson and
       Laurence Stallings in 1924.

1630. Bailey, Thomas A. "German Documents Relating to the 'Lusi-
       tania.'" *Jour. Mod. Hist.* 8 (September 1936): 320-37.

       Bailey reproduces in the original German excerpts from the
       diary of Fregattenkapitän Bauer, the commander of the high
       seas U-boat fleet, and the diary of Schwieger, the captain of
       the U-boat which sank the *Lusitania*.

1631. ————. "The Sinking of the Lusitania." *AHR* 41 (October 1935):
       54-73.

The debate over the sinking of the *Lusitania* is examined in this article. Bailey rejects most of the German arguments.

1632.   ————. "The United States and the Blacklist During the Great War." *Jour. Mod. Hist.* 6 (March 1934): 14-35.

This is a brief survey of the American reaction to the use of a blacklist during World War I. Although the British blacklist caused considerable friction between Washington and London, the United States quickly adopted this form of economic warfare when it joined the anti-German coalition.

1633.   ————. "World War Analogues of the Trent Affair." *AHR* 38 (January 1933): 286-90.

Bailey points out that the principles of the Trent case were not in all cases being accepted by the belligerents between 1914 and 1917.

1634.   ————, and Ryan, Paul B. *The Lusitania Disaster: An Episode in Modern Warfare and Diplomacy.* New York: Free Press, 1975. 383 pp.

The British journalist Colin Simpson's conspiracy thesis concerning the sinking of the *Lusitania* is challenged in this cogently argued and well-researched work by Bailey, one of America's best-known diplomatic historians, and Ryan, a retired U.S. Navy captain. Winston Churchill, then the First Lord of the Admiralty, is cleared of Simpson's charge that he attempted to create an incident that would bring the United States into the war. Many other myths concerning the *Lusitania* affair are also demolished.

1635.   Baker, Newton D. *Why We Went to War.* New York: Harper & Brothers, 1936. 199 pp.

Baker attempts to set the record straight according to his lights in this thinly researched and generally disappointing volume.

*   Barnes, Harry Elmer. *The Genesis of the World War: An Introduction to the Problem of War Guilt.* Cited above as item 102.

1636.   Beard, Charles A. *The Devil Theory of War: An Inquiry into the Nature of History and the Possibility of Keeping Out of War.* New York: Greenwood Press, 1969. 1,244 pp.

Beard debunks the "devil theory" or the theory that wicked men make war in this discussion of causation. Economic factors receive primary attention in his discussion of America's involvement in World War I. The first edition appeared in 1935 during the renewed debate over American intervention brought on by the approaching war in Europe.

1637.   Birnbaum, Karl E. *Peace Moves and U-Boat Warfare: A Study of Imperial Germany's Policy Toward the United States, April 18, 1916-January 9, 1917.* Stockholm: Almquist & Wiksell, 1958. 388 pp.

The tug-of-war between Chancellor Bethmann Hollweg and the military "experts" over the unrestricted use of U-boats is described. Based on extensive archival research, this study concludes that profound German skepticism about Wilson's motives and the ascendancy of Ludendorff and Hindenburg in late 1916 brought American-German relations to the breaking point at the beginning of 1917.

1638.   Borchard, Edwin M., and Lage, William P. *Neutrality for the United States*. New Haven: Yale University Press, 1937. 380 pp.

The authors trace the history of neutrality prior to World War I and then concentrate on the "errors in the administration of American neutrality" from 1914 to 1917. A concluding section treats postwar developments concerning American neutrality. President Wilson is criticized for his lack of concern with maintaining U.S. neutrality.

1639.   Brunauer, Esther C. "The Peace Proposals of December 1916-January 1917." *Jour. Mod. Hist.* 4 (December 1932): 544-71.

Brunauer analyzes the part played by Berlin's December 12, 1916, peace proposal and Wilson's mediation efforts in bringing about U.S. entry into the war.

1640.   Buchanan, A. Russell. "Theodore Roosevelt and American Neutrality, 1914-1917." *AHR* 43 (July 1938): 775-90.

Buchanan surveys the speeches and personal letters of Theodore Roosevelt and concludes that this influential American statesman decided very early that the United States should stand with the Allies in World War I and that he attempted to influence American opinion in this direction.

1641.   Buehrig, Edward H. *Woodrow Wilson and the Balance of Power*. Gloucester, Mass.: Peter Smith, 1968. 325 pp.

The author, a political scientist, examines Wilson's policies and concludes that he and his circle of advisers were motivated to a degree by concern that a victory by the Central Powers would be against American national interests. Buehrig, however, puts Wilson's idealism and world view ahead of national security as reasons for American belligerency. This work is documented but there is no bibliography.

1642.   Chatfield, Charles. *For Peace and Justice: Pacifism in America, 1914-1941*. Knoxville: University of Tennessee Press, 1971. 447 pp.

This excellently researched survey of the American peace movement details how all types of pacifists failed to keep the United States out of World War I and how the movement suffered great repression until 1920. By the 1930s the movement had reached its strong point. This work is important for those interested in understanding pacifism in the United States during World War I.

1643.   Cohen, Warren I. *The American Revisionists: The Lessons of Intervention in World War I.* Chicago: University of Chicago Press, 1967. 252 pp.

The evolution of revisionist thinking is described in this informative book which focuses on five American historians, Barnes, Grattan, Beard, Millis, and Tansill. These historians attempted to use their views of the past to influence contemporary foreign policy. Cohen's research concentrates on books, articles, speeches, and book reviews.

1644.   ————, ed. *Intervention, 1917: Why America Fought.* Lexington, Mass.: D.C. Heath & Co., 1966. 118 pp.

This volume in the "Problems in American Civilization" series is a collection of differing views on American intervention. It includes, among others, excerpts from the works of "revisionists" such as Barnes and Grattan and the proponents of the submarine thesis such as Seymour and Baker. There is a short essay on suggestions for additional reading.

1645.   Coogan, John W. *The End of Neutrality: The United States, Britain and Maritime Rights, 1899-1915.* Ithaca, N.Y.: Cornell University Press, 1981. 284 pp.

This solid work of scholarship offers a provocative challenge to the standard interpretations of Anglo-American difficulties over maritime rights. Coogan contends that American policymakers, most notably President Wilson, went beyond British expectations in acquiescing to British blockade measures. In sum, America's policy clearly violated her professed neutrality. See also Coogan's 1976 Yale University dissertation of the same title.

1646.   Cooper, John Milton, Jr. *Causes and Consequences of World War I.* New York: Quadrangle Books, 1972. 360 pp.

This excellent collection of articles by distinguished historians concerns America's entry into the war and its consequences. Cooper contributes a valuable historiographical essay.

1647.   ————. *The Vanity of Power: American Isolation and the First World War, 1914-1917.* Westport, Conn.: Greenwood Publishing Corporation, 1969. 271 pp.

This study provides a fuller insight into American "isolationiam" by examining its neglected period, the years just prior to American belligerency in World War I. The author asserts that the isolationist position that emerged during this period "remained intact over the next twenty-five years." This is a well-documented study with an annotated bibliography.

1648.   Davis, Gerald H. "The *Ancona* Affair: A Case of Preventive Diplomacy." *Jour. Mod. Hist.* 38 (September 1966): 267-77.

This article reveals that Austria-Hungary falsely accepted the responsibility for the German sinking of an Italian passenger ship (with the loss of nine American lives) in late 1915.

1649. ———. "The Diplomatic Relations Between the United States
       and Austria-Hungary, 1913-1917." Doctoral dissertation,
       Vanderbilt University, 1958. 301 pp.

       The emerging conflict between two unlikely rivals is ex-
       amined through, among other sources, the diplomatic files of
       both nations.

1650. DeBennetti, Charles. *The Peace Reform in American History.*
       Bloomington: Indiana University Press, 1980. 245 pp.

       This first-rate survey of the American peace reform movement
       traces it from 1620 through the 1970s. The author sees the
       period from 1901 to 1914 as an era of practical reform, but
       World War I ruined the hopes concerning the effectiveness of
       a peacemaking machinery. During and after World War I the
       multifaceted movement turned to preventing another war.

1651. Devlin, Patrick. *Too Proud to Fight: Woodrow Wilson's Neu-
       trality.* New York: Oxford University Press, 1975. 731 pp.

       This British jurist focuses on how Wilson's character shaped
       American policy toward the Allies and Central Powers. Well
       written, with flashes of insight, this work is flawed by too
       much reliance on published sources. The same subject is
       better covered by Link's multi-volume biography of Wilson, a
       work of immense scholarship.

1652. Doerries, Reinhard R. "Imperial Berlin and Washington: New
       Light on Germany's Foreign Policy and America's Entry into
       World War I." *Central Eur. Hist.* 11 (March 1978): 23-49.

       Doerries argues that Germany's diplomatic stance during the
       war "left the United States with no other alterantive but to
       enter the conflict on the side of the Entente."

1653. Fenwick, Charles G. *American Neutrality: Trial and Failure.*
       New York: New York University Press, 1940. 190 pp.

       This professor of political science argues that any neutrality
       policy is "an inherently illogical and paradoxical system which
       had neither the facts of history to justify it nor the logic
       of practical politics." American neutrality during World War I
       receives considerable attention.

*   Frost, Wesley. *German Submarine Warfare: A Study of Its
       Methods and Spirit, Including the Crime of the Lusitania.*
       Cited above as item 788.

1654. Frothingham, Thomas G. "The Entrance of the United States into
       the First World War." *U.S. Naval Inst., Proc.* 53 (April
       1927): 399-402.

       Frothingham takes on the revisionists with considerable zeal,
       asserting that "there can be no question of the fact that the
       United States was driven into the war by the hostile acts of
       the German Imperial Government."

1655. Fuller, Joseph V. "The Genesis of the Munitions Traffic."
       Jour. Mod. Hist. 6 (September 1934): 280-93.

       Fuller asserts that Wilson's failure to restrict arms ship-
       ments opened the way to American belligerency.

1656. Garner, James Wilford. *International Law and the World War.*
       New York: Longmans, Green, & Co., 1920. 2 vols.

       This is a comprehensive and balanced legal history of World
       War I by an American political scientist. Undersea assault
       against merchant ships is one of many topics covered.

1657. Giffin, Frederick C. *Six Who Protested: Radical Opposition to
       the First World War.* Port Washington, N.Y.: Kennikat Press,
       1977. 158 pp.

       The radicals, Eugene V. Debs, Morris Hillquit, Max Eastman,
       John Reed, Emma Goldman, and William D. Haywood, are the sub-
       ject of this book because they opposed World War I. The back-
       ground and rationale for war opposition come under the author's
       scrutiny. This volume captures well the different positions
       taken by six radicals.

1658. Goddard, Arthur, ed. *Harry Elmer Barnes, Learned Crusader:
       The New History in Action.* Colorado Springs, Colo.: Ralph
       Myles Publisher, 1968. 884 pp.

       This Festschrift includes a chapter by William Neumann on
       Barnes as a World War I revisionist.

1659. Graham, Otis L., Jr. *The Great Campaigns: Reform and War in
       America, 1900-1928.* Englewood Cliffs, N.J.: Prentice-Hall,
       1971. 386 pp.

       A central part of this interpretative synthesis is the
       neutral rights policy of President Wilson. Graham believes
       that Wilson could have kept the United States out of the war.

1660. Grattan, C. Hartley. *Why We Fought.* New York: Vanguard Press,
       1929. 453 pp.

       This pioneer revisionist work supports Barnes's view that
       America was not forced into the war by German actions. Atten-
       tion is given to America's economic stake in an Allied victory
       and to the effectiveness of Allied propaganda on American public
       opinion. This study is documented and contains a bibliography.

1661. Gregory, Ross. "A New Look at the Case of the Dacia." *JAH* 55
       (September 1968): 292-96.

       It has been thought that the French, encouraged by the
       British and Walter Hines Page, the U.S. ambassador in London,
       intercepted the German merchant ship *Dacia* to avoid a shock to
       Anglo-American relations. Gregory demonstrates, however, that
       the interception was done routinely by the French.

1662. ————. *The Origins of the American Intervention in the First
       World War.* New York: W.W. Norton, 1971. 162 pp.

Designed largely for classroom use, this work traces Wilson's unsuccessful effort to keep America out of the war, concluding that American intervention was a result more of American than of German policies. There is a useful annotated bibliography which in 1971 was generally up to date. During the last decade, however, much new light has been shed on, among other subjects, the diplomacy and politics of the major European states.

1663. Harbaugh, William H. "Wilson, Roosevelt, and Interventionism, 1914-1917: A Study of Domestic Influence on the Formulation of American Foreign Policy." Doctoral dissertation, Northwestern University, 1954. 335 pp.

Harbaugh focuses on the influence of isolationist, nationalist, and interventionist factions on U.S. foreign policy prior to belligerency. He utilized manuscripts, the contemporary press, the *Congressional Record*, and relevant secondary sources.

1664. Hershey, Burnet. *The Odyssey of Henry Ford and the Great Peace Ship*. New York: Taplinger, 1967. 212 pp.

This illustrated work is based primarily upon the memory of the author, who covered the peace voyage of the *Oscar II* as a young reporter. Handled in a light manner, this adventure in peace making is characterized by the author as foolish.

1665. Hoehling, A.A. and Mary. *The Last Voyage of the Lusitania*. New York: Holt, 1956. 255 pp.

This popular history of the sinking of the *Lusitania* focuses on life aboard the ill-fated ocean liner. Photographs are included.

*   Link, Arthur S. *Wilson the Diplomatist: A Look at His Major Foreign Policies*. Cited above as item 1522.

1666. Lochner, Louis P. *America's Don Quixote: Henry Ford's Attempt to Save Europe*. London: K. Paul, Trench, Trübner & Co., 1924. 240 pp.

This is a sympathetic, detailed, illustrated account of the Ford Peace Ship in 1915. The author was the secretary of the expedition. Maxim Gorki contributed a preface.

1667. Lowitt, Richard. "The Armed-Ship Bill Controversy: A Legislative View." *Mid-Amer.* 46 (January 1964): 38-47.

This article gives a new perspective on the Senate filibuster on Wilson's request for the authority to arm American merchant ships. Lowitt contends that many congressmen, not just the so-called eleven willful men in the Senate, were concerned about the direction of Wilson's policies and desired a special session of Congress to check his actions.

1668. Martin, Edward S. *Diary of a Nation: The War and How We Got Into It*. Garden City, N.Y.: Doubleday, Page & Co., 1917. 407 pp.

This volume of *Life* editorials covers a three-year period during the war. It reflects the changing attitudes and moods of the American people as they were forced into war.

1669. May, Ernest Richard. *The World War and American Isolation, 1914-1917.* Cambridge: Harvard University Press, 1959. 482 pp.

May's impressive multi-archival approach has produced the best one-volume examination of American neutrality and the decision for war. There is much enlightening material on German policy, with May concluding that Berlin's actions made American intervention inevitable.

1670. Millis, Walter. *Road to War: America 1914-1917.* Boston: Houghton Mifflin Co., 1935. 466 pp.

The author makes his intention clear in his preface when he writes that this volume "was designedly undertaken as an effort in interpretation rather than research." Agreeing with the pioneer revisionist Grattan, Millis concludes that pro-Allied sentiment and economic factors drew America into the war. There is a brief discussion of sources but no documentation.

1671. Morrissey, Alice M. *The American Defense of Neutral Rights, 1914-1917.* Cambridge: Harvard University Press, 1939. 230 pp.

This narrative falls generally in the camp of the revisionists Grattan, Millis, Tansill, and others. Morrissey contrasts the soft executive response to British violations of American neutrality to the hard and unyielding approach to Germany.

1672. Patterson, David S. *Toward a Warless World: The Travail of the American Peace Movement, 1887-1914.* Bloomington: Indiana University Press, 1976. 339 pp.

Filled with detailed information, this work treats the evolution of the American peace movement as part of the general reform impulses of the late nineteenth century. Patterson is concerned with the Olney-Pauncefote arbitration treaty, the Spanish-American War, the National Arbitration Conference, and the role of Andrew Carnegie.

1673. Rappaport, Armin. *The British Press and Wilsonian Neutrality.* Stanford, Calif.: Stanford University Press, 1951. 162 pp.

Rappaport has thoroughly researched the British press, 1914-1917, to give the British view of Wilsonian neutrality.

1674. Robinson, Edgar E., and West, Victor J. *The Foreign Policy of Woodrow Wilson, 1913-1917.* New York: Macmillan Co., 1917. 428 pp.

The authors' attempts to interpret Wilson's foreign policy during the first years of the war are unsatisfactory. The collection of almost every significant public statement by Wilson on foreign policy, which makes up one-half of this book is valuable, however.

1675. Ryan, Paul B. "The Great Lusitania Whitewash." *American Nep-tune* 35 (January 1975): 36-48.

Ryan examines the motives of the official British court of inquiry in covering up the incompetence of the master of the *Lusitania*.

1676. Seymour, Charles. *American Neutrality 1914-1917: Essays on the Causes of American Intervention in the World War.* Hamden, Conn.: Archon Books, 1967.

This is a reprint of a work which was published in 1935 by the Yale University Press. In seven interpretative essays Seymour defends Wilson's diplomacy against revisionist attacks, arguing that the submarine was the primary cause for intervention. There is scanty documentation and no bibliography.

1677. Simpson, Colin. *Lusitania.* Boston: Little, Brown & Co., 1973. 303 pp.

The author of this controversial work attempts to implicate the British government in the sinking of the *Lusitania*. His evidence is circumstantial and his conclusions are most questionable. See the work by Bailey and Ryan, which challenges Simpson's findings.

*   Smith, Daniel M. "National Interest and American Intervention, 1917: An Historiographical Appraisal." Cited above as item 42.

*   ————. *Robert Lansing and American Neutrality, 1914-1917.* Cited above as item 1580.

*   ————. "Robert Lansing and the Formulation of American Neutrality Policies, 1914-1915." Cited above as item 1581.

1678. ————, ed. *American Intervention, 1917: Sentiment, Self-Interest, or Ideals?* Boston: Houghton Mifflin Co., 1966. 260 pp.

This is a collection of documents and interpretative secondary sources which would be especially valuable to a graduate student seeking knowledge of the debate over American intervention in the war. Smith provides a three-page guide to further reading.

1679. Smith, Dean. "The Zimmermann Telegram, 1917." *Amer. Hist. Ill.* 13 (June 1978): 28-37.

Smith argues that the Zimmermann note, although not the primary cause of U.S. belligerency, did provide the "last fateful push over the precipice."

1680. Smith, Gaddis. *Britain's Clandestine Submarines, 1914-1915.* New Haven: Yale University Press, 1964. 155 pp.

This volume concerns the manufacture of ten submarines by Charles M. Schwab of the Bethlehem Steel Corporation under contract with the British Admiralty in a Canadian plant. This is a solidly researched monograph concerning a little-known episode in Anglo-American-Canadian relations.

1681. Spencer, Samuel J., Jr. *Decision for War, 1917: The Laconia Sinking and the Zimmermann Telegram as Key Factors in the Public Reaction Against Germany.* Rindge, N.H.: Richard R. Smith, 1953. 109 pp.

In this brief tome, Spencer argues that the sinking of the *Laconia* and the publishing of the Zimmermann telegram were the major factors in causing the United States to go to war.

1682. Syrett, Harold C. "The Business Press and American Neutrality, 1914-1917." *MVHR* 32 (September 1945): 215-30.

After surveying the business press from 1914 to 1917, the author concludes that businessmen could not be charged with "war mongering before 1917." The U.S. businessman made up his mind with the profit motive as his guide.

1683. Tansill, Charles Callan. *America Goes to War.* Boston: Little, Brown & Co., 1938. 731 pp.

This is an exhaustively researched study of the reasons why America entered the war. Tansill writes that he "has no thesis to prove nor any viewpoint to exploit." However, he clearly sides with the revisionists, portraying American entrance into the war as an avoidable tragedy. Tansill is especially harsh in his treatment of House and Lansing.

1684. Trotter, Agnes Anne. "The Development of Merchants of Death Theory of American Intervention in the First World War, 1914-1917." Doctoral dissertation, Duke University, 1966. 374 pp.

The public accepted the "merchants of death" theory largely because of its timing. For some time congressmen and peace societies had been blaming the munitions industry for U.S. entrance into the war. The Nye Committee exploited this atmosphere of suspicion around the munitions industry.

1685. Tuchman, Barbara W. *The Zimmermann Telegram.* New York: Macmillan Co., 1966. 244 pp.

This account of the Zimmermann Telegram reads like a detective novel. Tuchman demonstrates that it is possible to be scholarly and entertaining at the same time. A bibliography and notes are included. The 1966 edition includes a short essay on new facts that had come to light since the first edition in 1958.

1686. Tuttle, Peter Guertin. "The Ford Peace Ship: Volunteer Diplomacy in the Twentieth Century." Doctoral dissertation, Yale University, 1958. 257 pp.

This dissertation covers the development of a scheme to end the war through a neutral conference, the voyage of the Ford

Peace Ship, the journey through Scandinavia, and the establishment of the unsuccessful neutral peace conference.

1687. Vagts, Alfred. "Hopes and Fears of an American-German War, 1870-1915." *Pol. Sci. Quar.* 54 (December 1939): 514-35; (March 1940): 53-76.

Vagts examines world opinion and the emerging German-American conflict.

1688. Van Alstyne, Richard W. "The Policy of the United States Regarding the Declaration of London at the Outbreak of the Great War." *Jour. Mod. Hist.* 7 (December 1935): 434-47.

This article examines the British blockade of the North Sea during the early stages of World War I and the British seizure of contraband of war. The United States wanted a firm commitment from the British concerning seizures in line with the 1909 Declaration of London, which the United States had not yet ratified. Although Walter H. Page received credit for the successful negotiations, Robert Lansing deserves most of the credit.

1689. Wreszin, Michael. *Oswald Garrison Villard: Pacifist at War.* Bloomington: Indiana University Press, 1965. 342 pp.

Editor of *The Nation*, Villard was the leading liberal spokesman of the twenties and thirties. Feeling that liberalism and war were incompatible, he spoke out strongly against U.S. participation in World War I. After he opposed the preparedness program, Villard, although friendly with Wilson, was shut out of the administration. Villard also opposed the Treaty of Versailles.

D. PROPAGANDA AND U.S. PUBLIC OPINION
(*SEE ALSO* VI:I, HUMOR AND CARICATURE;
VI:J, WAR POSTERS; AND VI:L, FILM)

1690. Bailey, Thomas A. *The Man in the Street: The Impact of American Public Opinion on Foreign Policy.* New York: Macmillan Co., 1948. 334 pp.

This classic work examines the role of public opinion in the formation of American foreign policy. It looks at a wide variety of factors which have influenced American public opinion including: tradition, religion, xenophobia, isolationism, propaganda, apathy, and democracy.

1691. Blakey, George T. *Historians on the Homefront: American Propagandists for the Great War.* Lexington: University Press of Kentucky, 1970. 168 pp.

Blakey, in a well-written book, examines whether a historian during a national crisis can serve his country as well as his profession. J. Franklin Jameson, a leading historian, receives particular attention. The war work of historians represented a major break with previous scholarly standards.

1692. Bonadio, Felice A. "The Failure of German Propaganda in the United States, 1914-1917." *Mid-Amer.* 41 (January 1959): 40-57.

Bonadio explains why German propaganda had little impact on American public opinion.

1693. Bruntz, George G. *Allied Propaganda and the Collapse of the German Empire in 1918.* Stanford, Calif.: Stanford University Press, 1938. 246 pp.

The impact on Germany of "paper bullets" or propaganda is analyzed in this balanced study. The author carefully avoids claiming too much for the part played by propaganda in Germany's collapse, but he argues that it was a factor that historians must take into account.

* Creel, George. *How We Advertised America.* Cited above as item 872.

* ————. "Public Opinion in War Time." Cited above as item 873.

1694. Crighton, John Clark. *Missouri and the World War, 1914-1917: A Study in Public Opinion.* Columbia: University of Missouri, 1947. 199 pp.

This monograph is an analysis of middle western opinion during World War I with Missouri as its focus. Anglo-Saxon ties, economic considerations, propaganda, and the nature of the war itself were major factors in persuading the people of Missouri to favor American participation.

1695. Cummins, Cedric C. *Indiana Public Opinion and the World War, 1914-1917.* Indianapolis: Indiana Historical Bureau, 1945. 254 pp.

This well-written volume surveys Indiana public opinion until the United States intervened in World War I. Ultimately Indiana was converted to the cause by a fear that the war would spread beyond Europe.

1696. Curti, Merle. *The Roots of American Loyalty.* New York: Columbia University Press, 1946. 267 pp.

This history of American patriotism, based on primary sources, examines with broad strokes the various facets of American loyalty. Curti concludes that patriotic thought and feeling during the war were heightened by hatred of an external foe, the coupling of military power and loyalty, and an increased emotional insistence on unity.

1697. Hazen, Charles D. *The Government of Germany.* Washington, D.C.: Government Printing Office, 1917. 16 pp.

This propaganda piece places a great deal of emphasis on the fact that the German government was not democratic in nature.

1698. Hirst, David Wayne. "German Propaganda in the United States, 1914-1917." Doctoral dissertation, Northwestern University, 1962. 281 pp.

This propaganda piece places a great deal of emphasis on the German propagandists, their varied activities in the United States, and the propaganda message they delivered are examined in this dissertation directed by Arthur Link. The magnitude of the German propaganda is fully developed.

1699. Hutchinson, William T. "The American Historian in Wartime." *MVHR* 29 (September 1942): 163-86.

This article examines the historian as a professional man, as a businessman, and as a citizen during war. Hutchinson focuses attention on the World War I experience and treats the dilemma faced by scholars as they attempted to play out their roles under the pressure of war.

1700. Lansing, Robert, and Post, Louis F. *A War of Self-Defense*. Washington, D.C.: Government Printing Office, 1917. 22 pp.

This government publication contains two short essays. The one by Secretary of State Lansing, entitled "America's Future at Stake," argues that the future of American democracy is at peril. The other, by the assistant secretary of labor, entitled "The German Attack," points out that the United States is fighting for self-defense.

1701. Lasswell, Harold D. *Propaganda Technique in the World War*. New York: Alfred A. Knopf, 1927. 239 pp.

This judicious, solid study by an American political scientist concerns the propaganda conducted at home and abroad by the major belligerents. The author's combination of common sense and exhaustive research makes this book a classic.

1702. Lutter, Martin Henry. "Oklahoma and the World War, 1914-1917: A Study in Public Opinion." Doctoral dissertation, University of Oklahoma, 1961. 595 pp.

Lutter analyzes the impact of World War I on Oklahoma and the factionalism that resulted from it. He points out that the state boasted the largest Indian and socialist population in the country. Lutter states that Oklahoma reflected the rural and isolationist policies of the West and reacted in much the same manner as its neighboring states.

1703. McLaughlin, Andrew C. *The Great War: From Spectator to Participant*. Washington, D.C.: Government Printing Office, 1917. 16 pp.

This propaganda piece portrays the Germans as militarists who caused World War I.

1704. Military Intelligence Branch. U.S. General Staff. *Propaganda*

in Its Military and Legal Aspects. Military Intelligence
Branch, n.d. 187 pp.

Chapter 4 is entitled "German Propaganda in America." Numerous illustrations of propaganda, from both the Allies and
Central Powers, are included.

1705. Mock, James R., and Larson, Cedric. *Words That Won the War:
The Story of the Committee on Public Information, 1917-
1919.* Princeton: Princeton University Press, 1939. 372 pp.

Records in the National Archives are utilized to tell the
story of the Committee on Public Information, which was established in 1917 to mobilize the American people for war. All
in all, the American propaganda effort, directed by George
Creel, was a great success in creating a collective enthusiasm
for war. As the war continued, the CPI also played an important
role in influencing worldwide opinion in favor of Wilson's
world view.

1706. Peterson, H.C. *Propaganda for War: The Campaign Against
American Neutrality, 1914-1917.* Norman: University of
Oklahoma Press, 1939. 357 pp.

This volume traces the impact of British propaganda on
American public opinion during the neutrality period. In the
author's lights, British propaganda had a decisive influence
in moving America away from true neutrality. This work is extensively documented and contains appendices and a bibliography.

1707. Read, James Morgan. *Atrocity Propaganda, 1914-1919.* New
Haven: Yale University Press, 1941. 319 pp.

The author gives comprehensive treatment to the use of
atrocities in war propaganda and attempts to separate atrocities from atrocity stories. Read also shows how atrocity
propaganda had an impact on the peace conference by provoking
the effort to punish those who engaged in atrocities.

*   Roetter, Charles. *The Art of Psychological Warfare 1914-1945.*
Cited above as item 1410.

1708. Sanders, M.L., and Taylor, Philip M. *British Propaganda
During the First World War, 1914-1918.* London: Macmillan
Press, 1982. 320 pp.

This scholarly and detailed work has some important things
to say about British propaganda in the United States.

1709. Scott, Jonathan French. *Five Weeks: The Surge of Public
Opinion on the Eve of the Great War.* New York: John Day
Co., 1921. 305 pp.

Utilizing a wide survey of newspapers representing all shades
of opinion, Scott analyzes the public's reaction to the European war from the assassination of Archduke Ferdinand to the
entry of Great Britain into the war. Scott concludes that

public opinion forced the governments to take the actions
they did. However, he fails to deal with the question of
governmental manipulation of public opinion.

1710. Squires, James Duane. *British Propaganda at Home and in the
        United States from 1914-1917.* Cambridge: Harvard University
        Press, 1935. 113 pp.

        This slim but admirable volume focuses on the activities
        of the British propaganda bureau, which was headed by Charles
        F.G. Masterman, and its agents in the United States. Squires
        gives very high marks to the effectiveness of British propa-
        ganda, arguing that propaganda was one of the most important
        reasons for the involvement of the United States in the war.

1711. Stuart, Sir Campbell. *Secrets of Crewe House: The Story of a
        Famous Campaign.* London: Hodder & Stoughton, 1920. 240 pp.

        Stuart was second in command in Lord Northcliffe's propaganda
        department at Crewe House. He provides a history of the
        British propaganda offensive in enemy countries from February
        1918 until the end of the war.

1712. Tatlock, John S.P. *Why America Fights Germany.* Washington,
        D.C.: Government Printing Office, 1918. 16 pp.

        In this propaganda pamphlet issued by the Committee on Public
        Information, the author argues that the United States went to
        war because Germany aggressively attacked the United States.
        War is seen as being necessary to preserve democracy.

1713. U.S. Committee on Public Information. *Complete Report of the
        Chairman of the Committee on Public Information.* Washington,
        D.C.: Government Printing Office, 1920. 290 pp.

        This report on the activities of the Creel Committee is a
        must for those interested in the work of the CPI. It is the
        starting point for any study of U.S. propaganda activities
        during the war. This report reveals that the committee touched
        every area of American life and employed all possible methods
        to sell the war. It also sums up the committee's work in
        other countries.

1714. Vaughn, Stephen. *Holding Fast the Inner Lines: Democracy,
        Nationalism, and the Committee on Public Information.* Chapel
        Hill: University of North Carolina Press, 1980. 397 pp.

        This well-researched monograph examines this important World
        War I propaganda agency. Vaughn concludes that Creel engaged
        in some censorship, but that his record was generally good in
        the area of civil liberties. This is a solid assessment of the
        record of the CPI in selling the war to the American people.

1715. Ventry, Lance T. "The Impact of the United States Committee
        on Public Information on Italian Participation in the First
        World War." Doctoral dissertation, Catholic University of
        America, 1968. 164 pp.

Ventry argues that the Committee on Public Information drove a wedge between Italy and the United States because of its advocacy of liberal war objectives.

1716. Viereck, George Sylvester. *Spreading Germs of Hate.* New York: Horace Liveright, 1930. 327 pp.

Viereck interviewed Allied propagandists in researching this study which focuses on propaganda in the United States. Colonel House has written the foreword.

E. HYPHENATED AMERICANS AND FOREIGN POLICY

1717. Capps, Finis Herbert. *From Isolationism to Involvement: The Swedish Immigrant Press in America, 1914-1945.* Chicago: Swedish Pioneer Historical Society, 1968. 338 pp.

This volume surveys the opinion of an important immigrant group from 1914 to 1945. The Swedish press distrusted Russia and was critical of Great Britain and France.

1718. Carroll, F.M. *American Opinion and the Irish Question, 1910-1923: A Study in Opinion and Policy.* New York: St. Martin's, 1978. 319 pp.

This monograph concerns U.S. opinion and the Irish question during the period of World War I. Utilizing sources in the United States and Great Britain, Carroll concludes that various Irish-American groups took positions after 1914 which would lead to Irish independence. Ultimately, Irish-American opinion concluded that the United States would intervene on Ireland's behalf. The United States, however, would not let the Irish question upset the peace conference and U.S. relations with Britain.

1719. Child, Clifton James. *The German-Americans in Politics, 1914-1917.* Madison: University of Wisconsin Press, 1939. 193 pp.

Based upon wide use of the German-language press as well as other primary sources, this monograph examines the German-American reaction to the war in Europe. It focuses attention on the National German-American Alliance as it denounced the "pro-British policy" of the American government, protested loans to the Allies, attempted to prevent the loss of German culture, opposed Wilson in 1916, and fell in influence as the United States entered the war.

1720. Gerson, Louis L. *Woodrow Wilson and the Rebirth of Poland, 1914-1920: A Study in the Influence on American Policy of Minority Groups of Foreign Origin.* New Haven: Yale University Press, 1953. 166 pp.

This well-documented work discusses the political pressure brought by Polish-Americans for an independent Poland. There is a superior bibliographical essay.

1721. Johnson, Niel M. *George Sylvester Viereck: German-American Propagandist*. Urbana: University of Illinois Press, 1972. 282 pp.

This biography of a German-American propagandist contains two chapters on World War I. Johnson concludes that Viereck did not have much influence on U.S. opinion.

1722. Keller, Phyllis. *States of Belonging: German-American Intellectuals and the First World War*. Cambridge: Harvard University Press, 1979. 324 pp.

This volume is a comparative biography of three German-American intellectuals during World War I. Based on manuscript sources and utilizing psychology, this work shows that the three reacted in different ways to the stress of war; one attempted to mediate conflicting loyalties, another advocated the German cause, and the third became a super patriot. Also see Keller's 1969 University of Pennsylvania doctoral dissertation.

1723. Kerr, Thomas J. "German-Americans and Neutrality in the 1916 Elections." *Mid-Amer*. 43 (April 1961): 95-105.

The election of 1916 is examined to show how Berlin's efforts to manipulate German-Americans backfired.

1724. Leary, William M., Jr. "Woodrow Wilson, Irish-Americans, and the Election of 1916." *JAH* 54 (June 1967): 57-72.

Leary argues that the Irish, despite the influence of international questions which should have caused them to oppose Wilson's election in 1916, paid more attention to American issues and thus voted for Wilson.

1725. Luebke, Frederick C. *Bonds of Loyalty: German Americans and World War I*. Dekalb: Northern Illinois University Press, 1974. 366 pp.

A volume in a series on minorities in American history, this narrative history attempts to explain why many Americans reacted so violently against the German element in American society. There is a useful annotated bibliography.

1726. Nelson, Clifford L. *German American Political Behavior in Nebraska and Wisconsin 1916-1920*. Lincoln: University of Nebraska-Lincoln Publication, 1972. 114 pp.

This study, which focuses on the reaction of German-Americans in two states to World War I, concludes that those sections which tended to vote Democratic turned against Wilson in 1916 and 1918 because of his stand on the war. Based on rich primary materials, this study is limited by the narrow approach used.

1727. O'Grady, Joseph P., ed. *The Immigrants' Influence on Wilson's Peace Policies*. Lexington: University Press of Kentucky, 1967. 329 pp.

This is an important collection of essays by authorities on
the influence of ten "hyphenated" American groups. Many
foreign-language papers have been researched to increase our
understanding of ethnic politics during World War I. O'Grady
concludes that only the Poles and Jews were able to influence
Wilson.

1728. Wittke, Carl. *German-Americans in the World War, with Special
       Emphasis on Ohio's German-Language Press*. Columbus: Ohio
       State Archaeological and Historical Society, 1936. 223 pp.

       Based to a great degree on the German-language press in
       Ohio, this book deals with the way German-Americans responded
       to the war as well as the way they were treated by Americans.
       It is especially good at giving examples of harassment of
       German-Americans. There is thorough documentation.

1729. ———. *The German-Language Press in America*. Lexington:
       University Press of Kentucky, 1957. 311 pp.

       This survey of the American German-language press begins
       in 1732 and goes through the mid-1950s. The German press was
       allowed to develop in its own way until World War I. Wittke
       sees the German-language press as a way of keeping in contact
       with the old country. Its most acute crisis came during
       World War I when it opposed U.S. intervention. When the
       United States became a belligerent, the German-language press
       had to withstand charges of being unpatriotic.

       F. WAR OBJECTIVES AND PEACE DIPLOMACY, 1914-1918
          (*SEE ALSO* VIII:E, LEAGUE OF NATIONS
          AND ITS REJECTION BY UNITED STATES)

          1. General and Comparative Sources

1730. Dahlin, Ebba. *French and German Public Opinion on Declared
       War Aims, 1914-1918*. New York: AMS Press, 1971. 168 pp.

       The research in the contemporary press of France and Germany
       is thorough and still useful to the historian. Dahlin argues
       that the people of France and Germany wanted peace, but that
       their imperialistic governments prevented any negotiated
       settlement.

1731. Elke, Frank W. "Japanese-German Peace Negotiations During
       World War I." *AHR* 71 (October 1965): 62-76.

       This examination of this little-known episode reveals that
       the Japanese leaked news of their negotiations with the Germans
       to gain concessions from their allies.

1732. Forster, Kent. *The Failures of Peace: The Search for a Nego-
       tiated Peace During the First World War*. Washington, D.C.:
       American Council on Public Affairs, 1941. 159 pp.

This solid work is now dated, but it still provides a valuable outline of attempts at a negotiated peace. See also Forster's 1941 University of Pennsylvania Ph.D. dissertation.

1733. Gifford, Prosser, and Louis, Wm. Roger, eds. *Britain and Germany in Africa: Imperial Rivalry and Colonial Rule*. New Haven: Yale University Press, 1967. 825 pp.

This collection of papers delivered at a Yale University conference in 1965 examines both the diplomatic and administrative policies of Germany and Great Britain. Alison Smith assisted the editors.

1734. Gottlieb, W.W. *Studies in Secret Diplomacy During the First World War*. London: Allen & Unwin, 1957. 430 pp.

This work focuses on the most important "secret treaties" of the Great War. Turkey's intervention in the war, Allied plans to partition that state, and competition between the Allies and Central Powers for Italisn support are examined in detail. The author used published collections of official documents in English, Italian, Russian, and German and researched extensively the records of the German foreign ministry which were captured during World War II. This remains an important study, although recently opened papers and archives and more current research have dated it in some respects.

1735. Howard, Harry N. *The Partition of Turkey: A Diplomatic History, 1913-1923*. Norman: University of Oklahoma Press, 1931. 486 pp.

This is a pioneer work of considerable scholarly merit on war and peace objectives.

1736. Kent, Marian, ed. *The Great Powers and the End of the Ottoman Empire*. London: Allen & Unwin, 1984. 240 pp.

This collection of seven essays assesses the role of the Great Powers in the demise of the Ottoman Empire.

1737. La Fargue, Thomas Edward. *China and the World War*. Stanford, Calif.: Stanford University Press, 1937. 278 pp.

American-Japanese rivalry over China during the war and at the Paris Peace Conference is a central theme in this scholarly account.

1738. Martin, Laurence W. *Peace Without Victory: Woodrow Wilson and the British Liberals*. New Haven: Yale University Press, 1958. 230 pp.

A revision of a Yale dissertation (1955), this volume, now dated by the availability of many primary sources, examines the similarities between the peace program of British radicals such as Norman Angell and E.D. Morel and that of President Wilson. The British press, with emphasis on the *Nation*, is surveyed.

1739. ———. "Woodrow Wilson's Appeals to the People of Europe: British Radical Influence on the President's Strategy." *Pol. Sci. Quar.* 74 (December 1959): 498-516.

The interchange between Wilson and British liberals during World War I is examined in detail.

1740. Mayer, Arno J. *Political Origins of the New Diplomacy, 1917-1918*. New Haven: Yale University Press, 1959. 435 pp.

This interpretative study examines how the war objectives of the belligerents were affected by pressures from the left. The period covered is from March 1917 to January 1918 when the continued stalemate in the trenches, the Russian Revolution, and American intervention changed the shape of the war. This volume is especially valuable in its treatment of Wilson's competition with Lenin's peace program. A weakness is that many important public and private papers became available after its publication.

2. United States

*   Barany, George. "Wilsonian Central Europe: Lansing's Contribution." Cited above as item 1578.

1741. Bell, Sidney. *Righteous Conquest: Woodrow Wilson and the Evolution of the New Diplomacy*. Port Washington, N.Y.: Kennikat Press, 1972. 209 pp.

Bell, a professor of history at Concord College in West Virginia, treats Wilson as a pragmatic politician attempting to expand American global economic interests. In sum, American economic self-interest shaped Wilson's world view to a great degree. See also his 1969 University of Wisconsin dissertation.

1742. Boothe, Leon E. "Anglo-Ameican Pro-League Groups Lead Wilson 1915-1918." *Mid-Amer.* 51 (April 1969): 92-107.

Boothe maintains that President Wilson initially was not a whole-hearted supporter of a world organization.

1743. Burns, Richard Dean, and Urquidi, Donald. "Woodrow Wilson and Disarmament: Ideas vs. Realities." *Aerospace Hist.* 18 (December 1971): 186-94.

Wilson pushed disarmament to prevent war but "he did implicitly accord to it a lower, more distant priority than to other political mechanisms intended to promote international stability and security."

1744. Civitello, Maryann. "The State Department and Peacemaking, 1917-1920: Attitudes of State Department Officials Toward Wilson's Peacemaking Efforts." Doctoral dissertation, Fordham University, 1981. 381 pp.

This dissertation focuses on the reaction to Wilson's peace program of six important State Department officials: Lansing,

Polk, Phillips, Adee, Long, and Carr. Civitello asserts that it is tragic that the State Department's desire for compromise in the debate over the League of Nations was ignored by Wilson.

1745. Daniel, Robert L. "The Armenian Question and American-Turkish Relations, 1914-1927." *MVHR* 46 (September 1959): 252-75.

Daniel, with emphasis on the Armenian question, examines the evolution of American policy toward Turkey as that nation emerged as a modern political state.

1746. Devasia, Arackal Thomas. "The United States and the Formation of Greater Romania, 1914-1918: A Study in Diplomacy and Propaganda." Doctoral dissertation, Boston College, 1970. 432 pp.

The author's purpose is "to analyze the changing American attitude toward the Greater Romania problem and to study the forces and events that made the change possible."

1747. Evans, Laurence. *United States Policy and the Partition of Turkey, 1914-1924*. Baltimore, Md.: Johns Hopkins Press, 1965. 437 pp.

This is a thoroughly researched and detailed treatment of the evolution of U.S. policy toward Turkey from 1914 to 1924. American policy went full circle from nonintervention to involvement to nonintervention.

1748. Fike, Claude E. "The United States and Russian Territorial Problems, 1917-1920." *Historian* 24 (May 1962): 331-46.

Fike emphasizes Washington's efforts to protect the territorial integrity of Russia.

1749. Fusco, Jeremiah Nicholas. "Diplomatic Relations Between Italy and the United States, 1913-1917." Doctoral dissertation, George Washington University, 1969. 403 pp.

Based on documents in the United States and Italian foreign ministry archives, this work examines U.S.-Italian relations from 1913 to 1917. Initially relations were poor because of American opposition to Italian war aims. Relations improved dramatically when the United States declared war on Austria-Hungary, Italy's traditional enemy.

1750. Gelfand, Lawrence E. *The Inquiry: American Preparations for Peace, 1917-1919*. New Haven: Yale University Press, 1963. 387 pp.

This is a first-rate and impressively researched account of the work and influence of the body of scholars and publicists of the Inquiry who attempted to give President Wilson the depth and knowledge of global affairs to establish a just peace. Private papers, the files of the State Department, and records of the Inquiry are researched.

1751. Gould, John Wells. "Italy and the United States, 1914-1918: Background to Confrontation." Doctoral dissertation, Yale University, 1969. 445 pp.

Gould rejects the framework of idealism vs. realism in his study of American-Italian relations. Wilson, he argues, was actually more prepared and realistic about Italian objectives than were the Italians.

1752. Howard, Harry N. *Turkey, the Straits and U.S. Policy*. Baltimore, Md.: Johns Hopkins University Press, 1974. 337 pp.

Chapters 2, "The Turkish Problem During World War I (1914-1918)," and 3, "The Question of Constantinople and the Straits at the Paris Peace Conference (1919)," are of interest to the World War I scholar.

1753. Lebow, Richard Ned. "Woodrow Wilson and the Balfour Declaration." *Jour. Mod. Hist.* 40 (December 1968): 501-23.

Lebow discusses the reasons for Wilson's decision to acquiesce in this famous British proclamation, in the process challenging the views of such scholars as Selig Adler who have written on the subject.

1754. Mamatey, Victor S. "The United States and Bulgaria in World War I." *Amer. Slavic and East Eur. Rev.* 12 (1953): 233-57.

Mamatey examines the curious state of affairs that existed between the United States and Bulgaria. Although on opposite sides, the two countries maintained normal relations. Wilson hoped to detach Bulgaria from the Central Powers by treating her as a "victim" rather than as an "accomplice" of Germany. This policy of expediency failed.

1755. ———. *The United States and East Central Europe, 1914-1918: A Study in Wilsonian Diplomacy and Propaganda*. Princeton: Princeton University Press, 1957. 431 pp.

This is a meticulous, scholarly, and balanced examination of how the United States came to support independence for the subject minorities of the Austro-Hungarian Dual Monarchy. Wilson's influence on Allied policy toward Southeastern Europe is also assessed. Many non-English sources have been utilized.

1756. ———. "The United States and the Dissolution of Austria-Hungary." *Jour. of Central Eur. Affairs* 10 (October 1950): 256-70.

Mamatey examines this question from the American side, focusing on the declaration of May 29, 1918. He takes exception with the conventional interpretation of T.G. Masaryk's influence on President Wilson.

1757. May, Ernest R. "American Policy and Japan's Entrance into World War I." *MVHR* 40 (September 1953): 279-90.

May shows that Washington's concern for China was central to its response to Japan's joining the anti-German coalition. He also suggests that the future balance of power and strategic considerations of the situation were not always understood by U.S. policymakers.

*   O'Grady, Joseph P., ed. *The Immigrants' Influence on Wilson's
         Peace Policies.* Cited above as item 1727.

1758.   Patterson, David S. "Woodrow Wilson and the Mediation Move-
         ment, 1914-1917." *Historian* 33 (August 1971): 535-56.

         Patterson focuses on the efforts of "peace workers outside
         the administration" who put pressure on President Wilson to
         mediate the war. Wilson handled these peace advocates with
         tact but thought little of their understanding of questions
         concerning war and peace.

1759.   Stafford, Jeffrey J. "Edward Hurley and American Shipping
         Policy: An Elaboration on Wilsonian Diplomacy, 1918-1919."
         Historian 35 (August 1973): 568-86.

         Stafford contends that Hurley, the head of the shipping
         board, generally supported President Wilson's "plan to recon-
         struct and reorganize the post-war world along lines of a moral
         and market-oriented capitalistic" order.

1760.   ———. *Wilsonian Maritime Diplomacy 1913-1921.* New Bruns-
         wick, N.J.: Rutgers University Press, 1978. 282 pp.

         Stafford's theme is that Wilson used the dramatic expansion
         of the American merchant fleet during the war to challenge
         British commercial supremacy on the seas and to help him lobby
         for a Wilsonian peace. Stafford's use of American sources is
         impressive, but he would have been even more persuasive in his
         conclusions if he had ventured across the Atlantic to consult
         archival sources in Great Britain.

*   Živojinović, Dragan. "Robert Lansing's Comments on the Pontifi-
         cal Peace Note of August 1, 1917." Cited above as item 1583.

1761.   ———. "The United States and Italy, April 1917-April 1919,
         with Special Reference to the Creation of the Yugoslav State."
         Doctoral dissertation, University of Pennsylvania, 1966.
         610 pp.

         The author argues that the differences between the United
         States and Italy were "irreconcilable." The Adriatic, rather
         than the Paris Peace Conference, is the focus of this study.

1762.   ———. "The Vatican, Woodrow Wilson and the Dissolution of
         the Hapsburg Monarchy 1914-1918." *East European Quarterly* 3
         (March 1969): 31-70.

         The author gives a detailed treatment of this little-known
         episode.

                              3. Entente

1763.   Andrew, Christopher M., and Kanya-Forstner, A.S. *France Over-
         seas: The Great War and the Climax of French Imperial Expan-
         sion.* London: Thames & Hudson, 1981. 302 pp.

The authors fill a void by focusing on the neglected topic
of French imperialism during the war years. There is also a
chapter on the Paris Peace Conference. A multi-archival approach is taken, with extensive research having been conducted
in British and French depositories. There is extensive documentation and a lengthy bibliography.

1764. Brand, Carl F. "The Reaction of British Labor to the Policies
of President Wilson During the World War." *AHR* 38 (January
1933): 263-85.

The materials utilized by the author are in the Hoover War
Library. His survey of the British press, especially the pro-
labor organs, constitutes his most valuable contribution.

1765. Cooper, John Milton, Jr. "The British Response to the House-
Grey Memorandum: New Evidence and New Questions." *JAH* 59
(March 1973): 958-71.

Published as a "note," this valuable examination of British
motives for rejecting the so-called House-Grey Memorandum
includes the minutes of the War Committee of March 21, 1916,
which are reprinted in full with Grey's deletions and inser-
tions. For a further discussion of Grey's motives based on
his papers, see Woodward's article in this section (item 1784).

1766. Davis, Rodney Oliver. "British Policy and Opinion of War
Aims and Peace Proposals, 1914-1918." Doctoral dissertation,
Duke University, 1958. 400 pp.

For more recent accounts on public pressures on the British
government concerning war aims and a negotiated peace, see
the works by Martin (item 1738) and Swartz (item 1781).

1767. Fry, Michael G. *Lloyd George and Foreign Policy*, vol. 1: *The
Education of a Statesman, 1890-1916*. Montreal: McGill-
Queen's University Press, 1977. 314 pp.

This is the first volume of a projected two-volume examination of the foreign policy views and actions of Lloyd George.
The research in manuscript and official sources is extensive.
Students of American diplomacy will be interested in Fry's
treatment of the British rejection of the House-Grey Memorandum.

*   Guinn, Paul. *British Strategy and Politics 1914-1918*. Cited
above as item 346.

1768. Hanak, Harry. *Great Britain and Austria-Hungary During the
First World War: A Study in the Formation of Public Opinion*.
New York: Oxford University Press, 1962. 312 pp.

This volume traces the ultimate triumph in Britain of those
who believed that the Dual Monarchy was doomed because of the
strength of Slav nationalism.

1769. Kernek, Sterling J. "The British Government's Reaction to
President Wilson's 'Peace' Note of December, 1917." *Hist.
Jour.* 13 (December 1970): 721-66.

Kernek argues that Link has exaggerated Lloyd George's willingness to consider a compromise peace in late 1916.

1770. ———. *Distractions of Peace During War: The Lloyd George Government's Reactions to Woodrow Wilson December, 1916-November, 1918*. Philadelphia: American Philosophical Society, 1975. 117 pp.

Kernek has made a painstaking examination of the reaction of Lloyd George's ministry to Wilson's peace moves and war objectives. The research in American and British archival sources is impressive. Kernek makes the point that "the basic similarity between British and American attitudes toward peace terms in one sense aggravated antagonism because it set the stage for a contest between two powers who wanted to preside over their common values."

1771. Lederer, Ivo J., ed. *Russian Foreign Policy: Essays in Historical Perspective*. New Haven: Yale University Press, 1962. 620 pp.

A new perspective on Tsarist war aims during the Great War is often gained in this collection of essays.

1772. Louis, Wm. Roger. *Great Britain and Germany's Lost Colonies, 1914-1919*. New York: Oxford University Press, 1967. 165 pp.

This is an important and succinct study of one aspect of British war objectives that is solidly grounded on archival sources. Many British statesmen believed that the future security of the British Empire depended upon the destruction of the German position in Africa.

1773. Renzi, William A. "Great Britain, Russia, and the Straits, 1914-1915." *Jour. Mod. Hist.* 42 (March 1970): 1-20.

Renzi takes a fresh look at the motives of the French and especially of the British in signing the Straits Agreement, one of the most important of the "secret treaties" which Wilson first learned of in 1917.

1774. ———. "Italy's Neutrality and Entrance into the Great War: A Re-Examination." *AHR* 73 (June 1968): 1414-32.

Renzi takes the position that Italian diplomacy, 1914-1915, was "no more deceitful or 'Machiavellian'" than the diplomacy of the other great powers.

1775. ———. "Who Composed 'Sazanov's Thirteen Points'? A Re-Examination of Russia's War Aims of 1914." *AHR* 88 (April 1983): 347-54.

Renzi casts doubt on the importance to the Tsarist government and even the authorship of Sazanov's "Thirteen Points," which hitherto has been accepted as one of the two attempts by an Allied leader to propose a specific list of war objectives. Wilson's Fourteen Points was the other attempt.

1776. Rothwell, V.H. *British War Aims and Peace Diplomacy 1914-
       1918*. Oxford: Clarendon Press, 1971. 315 pp.

       This impressively researched volume makes an original contri-
       bution to the understanding of the development of British war
       aims, considerations of a compromise peace with Germany, and
       efforts to detach members of the Central Powers. Rothwell
       concentrates on the period after the formation of Lloyd
       George's ministry in December 1916. He argues that the growing
       commitment of the United States to the war strengthened the
       British resolve in 1918 to reject a negotiated peace and seek
       total victory over the enemy.

1777. Smith, C. Jay, Jr. "Great Britain and the 1914-1915 Straits
       Agreement with Russia: The British Promise of November 1914."
       AHR 70 (July 1965): 1015-34.

       Smith contends that a central motive of Sir Edward Grey in
       concluding the Straits Agreement with Russia was to divert
       Russian war aims from Eastern Europe to the Near East. The
       Asquith papers are extensively utilized.

1778. ———. *The Russian Struggle for Power, 1914-1917: A Study
       of Russian Foreign Policy During the First World War*. New
       York: Philosophical Library, 1956. 553 pp.

       This is the first English-language examination of Tsarist
       war objectives, based on thorough research in Russian sources.
       Smith argues that Tsarist diplomacy, 1914-1917, is similar in
       many respects to Stalin's diplomacy, 1941-1948. A more recent
       examination of Tsarist diplomacy can be found in Lederer in
       this section.

1779. Stein, Leonard. *The Balfour Declaration*. New York: Simon &
       Schuster, 1961. 681 pp.

       This is a comprehensive examination of the origins of the
       Balfour Declaration of November 2, 1917. The author is an
       English lawyer.

1780. Stevenson, David. *French War Aims Against Germany 1914-1919*.
       New York: Oxford University Press, 1982. 320 pp.

       This well-researched monograph is the first systematic treat-
       ment of French war objectives against Britain during and im-
       mediately after World War I. The development of French war
       aims toward Germany, the consideration of a negotiated settle-
       ment, and the French approach to containing Germany at the
       Paris Peace Conference are examined.

1781. Swartz, Marvin. *The Union of Democratic Control in British
       Politics During the First World War*. New York: Oxford Uni-
       versity Press, 1971. 267 pp.

       The UDC was formed by nonpacifist critics of Britain's entry
       into the war. Opposed to annexationist war objectives, the
       UDC championed parliamentary control of diplomacy. This well-
       documented monograph examines the UDC's impact on both British

war aims and the unity of the liberal party. There is information on the British liberals' view of President Wilson's
peace diplomacy and war objectives. See also the author's
1969 Yale University dissertation.

1782. *The War of Democracy: The Allies' Statement.* Garden City, N.Y.:
      Doubleday, Page & Co., 1917. 441 pp.

      This volume does not really contain the official war aims
      statements of the Allied governments. Rather the views of
      fifteen statesmen and publicists such as Balfour, Lord Bryce,
      and G.M. Trevelyan are published in the form of interviews,
      speeches, and essays.

*   Woodward, David R. "Britain's 'Brass Hats' and the Question
      of a Compromise Peace, 1916-1918." Cited above as item 356.

1783. ———. "David Lloyd George, A Negotiated Peace with Germany,
      and the Kühlmann Peace Kite of September, 1917." *Can. Jour.
      of Hist.* 6 (March 1971): 75-93.

      Lloyd George's consideration of a negotiated peace with
      Germany at Russia's expense is considered in this article.

1784. ———. "Great Britain and President Wilson's Efforts to End
      World War I in 1916." *Maryland Historian.* 1 (Spring 1970):
      45-58.

      This article, which is based on research in British archives,
      focuses on the House-Grey Memorandum. It should be read in
      conjunction with the Cooper article in this section.

1785. ———. "The Origins and Intent of David Lloyd George's
      January 5 War Aims Speech." *Historian* 34 (November 1971):
      22-39.

      In this article based on the papers of Britain's war leaders
      and the Cabinet Papers, the author asserts that one of Lloyd
      George's primary motives in making this liberal interpretation
      of British war objectives was to make possible a compromise
      peace.

4. Central Powers

1786. Epstein, Klaus. "The Development of German-Austrian War Aims
      in the Spring of 1917." *Jour. of Central Eur. Affairs* 17
      (April 1957): 24-47.

      General Ludendorff's dominant diplomatic influence over the
      civilians is emphasized by Epstein.

1787. Farrar, L.L., Jr. *Divide and Conquer: German Efforts to Con-
      clude a Separate Peace, 1914-1918.* Boulder, Colo.: East
      European Quarterly, distributed by Columbia University Press,
      1978. 180 pp.

      Farrar makes a questionable attack on the Fischer school,
      arguing that German efforts to divide the Entente offer a better

explanation of German wartime policy than do German expansionist goals.

1788. ────. "Opening to the West: German Efforts to Conclude a Separate Peace with England, July 1917-March 1918." *Can. Jour. of Hist.* 10 (April 1975): 73-90.

This well-researched article gives the German side of the peace discussion in Berlin and London in late 1917 and early 1918. For the British side, see Woodward (item 1783) and Rothwell (item 1776). Farrar's article is also revealing on civil-military relations in Germany.

1789. Fedyshyn, Oleh S. *Germany's Drive to the East and the Ukrainian Revolution, 1917-1918*. New Brunswick, N.J.: Rutgers University Press, 1971. 401 pp.

The first third of this volume is a careful examination of the development of German policy toward the Ukraine. In opposition to Fritz Fischer, Fedyshyn concludes that German objectives in southern Russia were a product of the war rather than a result of long-range plans of expansionism. Russian, German, and Ukrainian sources are utilized.

1790. Feldman, Gerald D. *German Imperialism, 1914-1918: The Development of a Historical Debate*. New York: John Wiley & Sons, 1972. 221 pp.

This book, one of the volumes in the "Major Issues in History" series, presents raw source materials and then interprets these primary sources. Part one deals with pre-1945 documents and interpretations and part two concerns post-1945 documents and interpretations of German imperialism during the Great War.

*   Fischer, Fritz. *Germany's Aims in the First World War*. Cited above as item 108.

1791. ────. *World Power or Decline: The Controversy over Germany's Aims in the First World War*. New York: W.W. Norton & Co., 1974. 131 pp.

Critics of Fischer's *Germany's Aims in the First World War* and *War of Illusions* are answered on substantive and methodological levels by the author himself. Fischer's counterattack is especially directed against Zechlin and Ritter, two German historians in considerable disagreement with Fischer's views on German responsibility for the war and the nature of German war objectives.

1792. Gatzke, Hans W. *Germany's Drive to the West (Drang Nach Westen): A Study of Germany's Western War Aims During the First World War*. Baltimore, Md.: Johns Hopkins Press, 1950. 316 pp.

German western expansionism during World War I receives detailed treatment in this scholarly monograph. Gatzke relates domestic politics to war objectives, arguing that *drang nach westen* was more popular in Germany than *drang nach osten*. The

more recent works of Fischer and others, which are based on
archival sources denied the author, have gone beyond Gatzke's
findings. See also his 1947 Harvard doctoral dissertation.

1793. Herwig, Holger H. "Admirals Versus Generals: The War Aims of
the Imperial German Navy, 1914-1918." *Central Eur. Hist.* 5
(September 1972): 208-33.

The conflicting war aims of the army and navy are revealed
in this well-documented article.

1794. Koehl, Robert Lewis. "A Prelude to Hitler's Greater Germany."
AHR 59 (October 1953): 43-65.

The German false start in creating a greater Germany during
World War I is critically examined in this article.

1795. Pribran, Alfred Francis. *Austrian Foreign Policy, 1908-1918.*
London: Allen & Unwin, 1923. 128 pp.

Despite its age, this volume remains a standard source.
G.P. Gooch has written the foreword.

*   Ritter, Gerhard. *The Sword and the Scepter: The Problem of
Militarism in Germany.* Cited above as item 354.

1796. Silberstein, Gerard E. "The Serbian Campaign of 1915: Its
Diplomatic Background." *AHR* 73 (October 1967): 51-69.

This article probes the connection between the Serbian campaign and Berlin's desire to win Bulgaria as an ally.

1797. Trumpener, Ulrich. *Germany and the Ottoman Empire, 1914-1918.*
Princeton: Princeton University Press, 1968. 433 pp.

This is a solid analysis of the German-Ottoman alliance,
describing the political and diplomatic aspects of this at
times uneasy alliance. Unfortunately the author was denied
access to the Turkish state archives.

1798. Weber, Frank G. *Eagles on the Crescent: Germany, Austria,
and the Diplomacy of the Turkish Alliance, 1914-1918.*
Ithaca, N.Y.: Cornell University Press, 1970. 284 pp.

The author conducted extensive research in Austrian and
German archives.

1799. Wheeler-Bennett, John W. *Brest-Litovsk: The Forgotten Peace,
March 1918.* London: Macmillan & Co., 1938. 478 pp.

This remains the standard work on the first peace treaty of
World War I. It is superbly written and is based on official
documents, the memoirs and diaries of the participants, and
the contemporary press. Wheeler-Bennett's purpose is to examine Soviet-German relations in the context of the Brest-
Litovsk negotiations, to explain the motives of both sides,
and to "establish the very prominent place which the Forgotten
Peace holds in world history."

G. COALITION DIPLOMACY

1. U.S. Relations with Allies
(*See also* VII:F, War Objectives
and Peace Diplomacy, 1914-1918)

1800. Bridges, Sir Tom. *Alarms & Excursions: Reminiscences of a Soldier*. London: Longmans, Green & Co., 1938. 361 pp.

Bridges includes information on the Balfour mission to Washington in 1917 and British efforts to brigade American soldiers with British divisions.

1801. Burk, Kathleen. "Great Britain in the United States, 1917-1918: The Turning Point." *International Hist. Rev.* 1 (April 1979): 228-45.

The growing dependence of Great Britain on the United States is the theme of this first-rate article. This thoroughly researched and enlightening study analyzes the work of the British war missions concerning supply and finance. See also Burk's 1976 Oxford University D. Phil. thesis, "British War Missions to the United States 1914-1918."

1802. Davenport, E.H., and Cooke, Sidney Russell. *The Oil Trusts and Anglo-American Relations*. New York: Macmillan Co., 1924. 272 pp.

The authors attempt to trace and analyze the influence of oil on Anglo-American relations. They carry their examination into the postwar period.

* Fowler, Wilton B. *British-American Relations, 1917-1918: The Role of Sir William Wiseman*. Cited above as item 1628.

1803. Fry, M.G. "The Imperial War Cabinet, the United States, and the Freedom of the Seas." *JRUSI* 110 (November 1965): 353-62.

The issue of freedom of the seas, which served to divide Washington and London over maritime policy, is examined in this balanced and well-researched article.

1804. Halsey, Francis W., ed. *Balfour, Viviani and Joffre: Their Speeches and Other Public Utterances in America*. New York: Funk & Wagnalls Co., 1917. 369 pp.

Using contemporary accounts, the compiler describes the activities and records the speeches of the Allied leaders who journeyed to the United States to encourage rapid American mobilization. He also describes the arrival of the first American forces in Europe. The period from April 21 to July 4, 1917, is covered.

1805. Kaufman, B.I. *Efficiency and Expansion: Foreign Trade Organization in the Wilson Administration, 1913-1921*. Westport, Conn.: Greenwood Press, 1974. 300 pp.

This is an important source on financial and commercial conflict between the United States and Great Britain during the
period of the Great War.

1806. Klachko, Mary. "Anglo-American Naval Competition, 1918-1922."
       Doctoral dissertation, Columbia University, 1962. 406 pp.

       Among other topics, Klachko examines how Wilson used the
       potential of the U.S. Navy to gain support for his peace pro-
       gram. Anglo-American economic rivalry also receives some at-
       tention.

1807. Lyddon, W.G. *British War Missions to the United States 1914-*
       1918. New York: Oxford University Press, 1938. 233 pp.

       The great number and variety of British war missions to the
       United States are reflected in this matter-of-fact unofficial
       history. The British war missions ranged from timber to pur-
       chasing to tanks. For a more critical evaluation of the same
       subject, see Burk.

1808. MacVeagh, Ewen Cameron, and Brown, Lee D. *The Yankees in the*
       British Zone. New York: G.P. Putnam's Sons, 1920. 418 pp.

       Two former U.S. officers record the history of the few U.S.
       divisions which fought alongside the BEF in the British sector
       on the western front.

1809. Parrini, Carl P. *Heir to Empire: United States Economic Dip-*
       lomacy, 1916-1923. Pittsburgh: University of Pittsburgh
       Press, 1969. 303 pp.

       Well researched and competently written, this volume attempts
       to examine the economic motives in American foreign policy.
       Prior to and during World War I, the British considered the
       United States to be a competitor in world trade, but after the
       war, they proposed an economic alliance in world trade. See
       also Parrini's 1963 University of Wisconsin doctoral disserta-
       tion directed by William A. Williams.

1810. Parsons, Edward B. "Why the British Reduced the Flow of
       American Troops to Europe in August-October 1918." *Can.*
       Jour. of Hist. 12 (December 1977): 173-91.

       Utilizing British sources such as the Lloyd George papers
       and the Cabinet papers, Parsons advances the questionable
       thesis that the British refused to furnish shipping for American
       forces in the summer of 1918 in order to limit America's in-
       fluence on the peace settlement and to check her economic ex-
       pansion. The full record in the British archives, however,
       reveals a contrary interpretation.

1811. ————. *Wilsonian Diplomacy: Allied-American Rivalries in*
       War and Peace. St. Louis, Mo.: Forum Press, 1978. 213 pp.

       This controversial book does not bring into question Wilson's
       high ideals. But it places emphasis on his anti-British senti-
       ment and "Machiavellian strategic thinking," with the author

arguing that Wilson often viewed the Allies as economic and
maritime rivals. American and British archives were researched.
See also Parsons's 1971 S.U.N.Y., Buffalo, doctoral dissertation, "Admiral Sims' Mission in Europe in 1917-1919 and Some
Aspects of United States Naval and Foreign Wartime Policy."

1812. Réquin, E.J. *America's Race to Victory.* New York: Frederick
A. Stokes Co., 1919. 211 pp.

This account by a French officer who accompanied Joffre to
America in 1917 offers some insight into the activities of the
French mission.

1813. Salter, James A. *Allied Shipping Control: An Experiment in
International Administration.* Oxford: Clarendon Press, 1921.
372 pp.

This valuable work focuses on the activities of the Allied
Maritime Transport Council and its permanent organization, the
Allied Maritime Transport Executive. Salter covers the peace
conference as well as the war years.

1814. Smith, Gaddis George. "Nation and Empire: Canadian Diplomacy
During the First World War." Doctoral dissertation, Yale
University, 1960. 389 pp.

This is a detailed examination of Canadian relations with
Great Britain and the United States during the war. Smith
shows in this superior dissertation that a major Canadian
foreign objective was to improve communications with the
United States.

1815. Stafford, Jeffrey J. "Anglo-American Maritime Relations
During the Two World Wars: A Comparative Analysis." *American
Neptune* 41 (October 1981): 262-79.

Anglo-American maritime relations are shown to have been far
stormier during World War I than during World War II.

1816. ————. "Experiment in Containment: The U.S. Steel Embargo
and Japan, 1917-18." *Pac. Hist. Rev.* 39 (November 1970):
439-51.

This article concerns the Wilson administration's attempt to
thwart Japanese imperial growth and to support Chinese integrity through economic means. This American policy failed.
Japan became convinced that it needed iron and steel from
other sources, a decision that could only result in further
territorial expansion.

1817. Stevenson, David. "French War Aims and the American Challenge,
1914-1918." *Hist. Jour.* (December 1979): 877-94.

This article by a British scholar examines the growing tension between Washington and Paris over the European settlement
as the French to their unease became more and more dependent
upon American economic and military assistance.

1818.   Trask, David F. *Captains & Cabinets: Anglo-American Naval Re-
        lations, 1917-1918*. Columbia: University of Missouri Press,
        1972. 396 pp.

        Trask's examination of Anglo-American naval-political rela-
        tions is solidly based on recently opened archival material.
        There was often conflict between British and American policy
        and tactics, but in the end cooperation more often than not
        prevailed. Admiral William S. Sims emerges as a central figure
        in these pages.

1819.   U.S. Navy Department. Office of Naval Records and Library,
        Historical Section. *The American Planning Section, London*.
        Washington, D.C.: Government Printing Office, 1923. 537 pp.

        In November 1917 a planning section was created in London to
        enable U.S. naval officers to have more effective communica-
        tions with the British Admiralty. This volume provides a de-
        tailed history of the important activities and plans of this
        body.

1820.   White, Dorothy Shipley. "Franco-American Relations in 1917-
        1918: War Aims and Peace Prospects." Doctoral dissertation,
        University of Pennsylvania, 1954. 557 pp.

        The emerging conflict between French war objectives and
        President Wilson's peace program prior to the Paris Peace
        Conference is given detailed treatment.

1821.   Willert, Arthur. *The Road to Safety: A Study in Anglo-American
        Relations*. New York: Frederick A. Praeger, 1953. 184 pp.

        Willert was the London *Times* correspondent in Washington
        during World War I and he has some interesting comments to
        make about President Wilson, Lord Northcliffe, Wiseman,
        Spring-Rice, and Lord Reading. This work is an essential
        source for any study of Anglo-American relations during and
        immediately after the war.

                        2. The Supreme War Council, the
                    Generalissimo, and the Creation of an
                      Independent American Army in Europe

1822.   Beadon, Lieut.-Col. R.H. "The Supreme War Council of the
        Allied Associated Nations: Its Origins, Organization, and
        Work." *JRUSI* 65 (February 1920): 105-15.

        Beadon vigorously defends the creation and work of the SWC
        and provides a convenient summary of its organization. "If
        the Supreme War Council never fulfilled any other purpose
        than that of a mere stepping stone to unified command--subse-
        quently so brilliantly justified by results--it would have
        more than rewarded those who were responsible for its creation,"
        he writes.

*   Bliss, Tasker H. "The Evolution of the Unified Command."
        Cited above as item 218.

*   ———. "Report of General T.H. Bliss on the Supreme War
         Council." Cited above as item 219.

1823.   *The Genesis of the American First Army.* Washington, D.C.:
         Government Printing Office, 1928. 81 pp.

         This slim monograph was prepared in the historical section
         of the Army War College. Based on records in the archives of
         the War Department, it traces the evolution of an independent
         American army in Europe. The principal author, according to
         the preface, was Major Julian F. Barnes.

1824.   Grant, Colonel C.J.C. "Marshal Foch: 26th of March to the 11th
         of November, 1918." *Army Quar.* 1 (January 1921): 263-89.

         This is a rather perceptive article on the personality and
         practices of Foch as the Allied generalissimo.

*   Harbord, James G. *The American Army in France, 1917-1919.*
         Cited above as item 241.

1825.   Lonergan, Thomas C. *It Might Have Been Lost! A Chronicle
         from Alien Sources of the Struggle to Preserve the National
         Identity of the A.E.F.* New York: G.P. Putnam's Sons, 1929.
         327 pp.

         This is a very valuable documentary record of the conflict
         over the creation of the AEF by a member of its general staff.
         Lonergan was able to gain access to many sensitive documents,
         especially from the British.

1826.   Maurice, Sir Frederick. *Lessons of Allied Co-Operation: Naval,
         Military and Air, 1914-1918.* New York: Oxford University
         Press, 1942. 195 pp.

         Maurice was the director of military operations on the Im-
         perial General Staff and the alter ego of Sir William Robertson,
         who was hostile to the concept of the Supreme War Council.
         This is not a balanced or comprehensive account of the contro-
         versial and ultimately successful struggle to achieve a unified
         command, but Maurice is right in faulting the machinery of the
         SWC when it was first created. Naval and air cooperation are
         also discussed.

1827.   ———. "The Versailles Supreme War Council." *Army Quar.* 1
         (January 1921): 232-40.

         Maurice is not always fair in this account of the creation
         of the Supreme War Council and the generalissimo. He does,
         however, correctly emphasize the often overlooked achieve-
         ments of the SWC after Foch became generalissimo.

1828.   Ohl, John Kennedy. "The Keystone Division in the Great War."
         Prologue 10 (Summer 1978): 82-99.

         French misuse of the Keystone or 28th Division in three opera-
         tions during the summer of 1918, Ohl contends, demonstrates the
         fallacy of the Anglo-French argument that American forces would

be better served by amalgamation than by the creation of an
independent American army.

*   Palmer, Frederick. *America in France: The Story of the Making
        of an Army*. Cited above as item 185.

1829.   Shumate, Thomas D., Jr. "The Allied Supreme War Council, 1917-
        1918." Doctoral dissertation, University of Virginia, 1952.
        247 pp.

        This pioneering study of the attempt to wage coalition war-
        fare more effectively has been superseded by Trask's account.

1830.   Trask, David F. "Political-Military Consultation Among Allies."
        Mil. Rev. 39 (September 1959): 20-28.

        In this comparison of the united commands of the two world
        wars, Trask argues that the Supreme War Council in 1917-1918
        accomplished more than is usually thought and would have been
        even more important if some of its basic weaknesses had been
        removed.

1831.   ————. *The United States in the Supreme War Council: American
        War Aims and Inter-Allied Strategy, 1917-1918*. Middletown,
        Conn.: Wesleyan University Press, 1961. 244 pp.

        This well-researched study is the best examination of the
        relationship between Wilsonian diplomacy and American military
        strategy. The focus is on the SWC, which was created in late
        1917. Allied intervention in Russia was a major topic of de-
        liberation by this body.

1832.   Wright, Captain Peter E. *At the Supreme War Council*. New York:
        G.P. Putnam's Sons, 1921. 201 pp.

        Anyone wanting to discover the inside story of the Supreme
        War Council will have to look elsewhere. Wright includes some
        interesting anecdotes, but he has nothing to say of great sig-
        nificance about either the leading personalities or the de-
        cisions of the SWC. Wright served as an interpreter for this
        Allied body at Versailles.

                              H. ARMISTICE

1833.   Barclay, C.N. *Armistice 1918*. London: J.M. Dent & Sons, 1968.
        155 pp.

        Barclay, a veteran of both world wars and a prolific writer
        on military subjects, makes clear that this study, which has
        no bibliography or footnotes, was written with the general
        reader rather than the scholar in mind. The result is a book
        which makes no contribution to our understanding of the course
        of the armistice negotiations. Much of this volume, in fact,
        concentrates on military operations leading up to the armis-
        tice negotiations. President Wilson's role in the armistice
        negotiations is almost ignored.

1834. Halperin, S. William. Anatomy of an Armistice." *Jour. Mod. Hist.* 43 (March 1971): 107-12.

This is a review essay of Pierre Renouvin's important *L'Armistice de Rethondes: 11 November 1918* (Paris, 1968). Renouvin exploits previously unresearched material in the French archives and questions basic assumptions made about the armistice. Renouvin argues that the specter of Bolshevism influenced equally the supporters of a soft or a harsh armistice.

1835. Lowry, Bullitt. "Pershing and the Armistice." *JAH* 55 (September 1968): 281-96.

Lowry sheds new light on Pershing's famous letter to the Allied Supreme War Council expressing opposition to an armistice. Lowry shows that Pershing was not really opposed to an armistice, only to one of moderation. See also his 1963 Duke doctoral dissertation, "The Generals, the Armistice, and the Treaty of Versailles, 1919."

1836. Maurice, Sir Frederick. *The Armistices of 1918.* New York: Oxford University Press, 1943. 104 pp.

Issued under the auspices of the Royal Institute of International Affairs, this slim volume when published brought together the most recent material on the Allied side of the armistice negotiations. Maurice's conclusions are worthy of careful consideration.

1837. Nelson, Keith L. "What Colonel House Overlooked in the Armistice." *Mid-Amer.* 51 (April 1968): 75-91.

Nelson maintains that Colonel House unwittingly undermined Wilson's peace plan by accepting certain military clauses in the armistice which supported the war objectives of the Allies.

1838. Noring, Nina J. "American Coalition Diplomacy and the Armistice, 1918-1919." Doctoral dissertation, University of Iowa, 1972. 374 pp.

This dissertation focuses on the American role in the signing of the armistice and the tension between the United States and her wartime partners which resulted from the execution of the armistice. American willingness to cooperate with the Entente powers over the armistice declined along with the military potential of Germany.

1839. Ritter, Gerhard. *The Sword and the Scepter: The Problem of Militarism in Germany*, vol. 4: *The Reign of German Militarism and the Disaster of 1918.* Coral Gables, Fla.: University of Miami Press, 1973. 496 pp.

The German side of the armistice negotiations is thoroughly examined in this exhaustively researched study. President Wilson's policies in October are characterized as "not only wavering but downright contradictory."

1840. Rudin, Harry Rudolph. *Armistice 1918.* New Haven: Yale University Press, 1944. 442 pp.

This exhaustive monograph serves as a corrective to the
"stab in the back" legend promoted by the German military.
The author demonstrates in his comprehensive and well-documented study that the initiative for peace came from the generals,
especially Ludendorff, rather than the civil authorities.
Lengthy excerpts from unpublished sources are included.

1841. Snell, John L. "Wilson on Germany and the Fourteen Points."
       Jour. Mod. Hist. 26 (December 1954): 364-69.

       Snell comments on and quotes in full a Wilson-Wiseman inter-
       view which sheds light on Wilson's views on constitutional
       reforms in Germany and his interpretation of his Fourteen
       Points in October when Germany began its search for peace.

                       I. RUSSO-AMERICAN RELATIONS
                   (INCLUDING U.S. AND ALLIED MILITARY ROLE
                          IN RUSSIAN CIVIL WAR)

              1. Background and Allied Intervention in Russia

1842. Bailey, Thomas A. *America Faces Russia: Russian-American Re-
       lations from Early Times to Our Day.* Ithaca, N.Y.: Cornell
       University Press, 1950. 375 pp.

       Approximately two-thirds of this survey of American-Russian
       relations is concerned with the Tsarist period. Bailey demon-
       strates that there were many differences between Russia and
       America prior to the creation of the Soviet regime in 1917.

1843. Bradley, John. *Allied Intervention in Russia.* New York:
       Basic Books, 1968. 251 pp.

       Bradley counters the one-dimensional view found in Soviet
       and some western literature that fear of Communism was the
       motive force of Allied intervention. He argues that there
       was little that the Allies could agree upon. This volume is
       based on extensive research in British, French, German, and
       Austrian archives. White Russian materials at Columbia Uni-
       versity and the Hoover Institution are also utilized.

1844. Brinkley, George. *The Volunteer Army and Allied Intervention
       in South Russia 1917-1921: A Study in the Politics and Dip-
       lomacy of the Russian Civil War.* Notre Dame, Ind.: Univer-
       sity of Notre Dame Press, 1966. 446 pp.

       This scholarly study, based on extensive research in the
       United States and Soviet Union, gives a comprehensive poli-
       tical history of the Volunteer Army, the first White army to
       take the field against Bolshevism.

1845. Carley, Michael Jabara. "The Origins of the French Interven-
       tion in the Russian Civil War, January-May 1918: A Re-
       appraisal." *Jour. Mod. Hist.* 48 (September 1976): 413-39.

Carley examines the frequently conflicting motives of French soldiers and politicians, concluding that ultimately the most important motive for intervention was the desire to save France's "preponderant interests" in Russia which were going to be destroyed if the Soviet regime survived.

1846. ————. *Revolution and Intervention: The French Government and the Russian Civil War, 1917-1919*. Montreal: McGill-Queens University Press, distributed by University of Toronto Press, 1983. 280 pp.

British intervention in Russia has been extensively treated by scholars, but the same cannot be said about French intervention. This scholarly study fills that void, answering many questions about French motivation and anti-Bolshevik strategy.

1847. Cummings, C.K., and Pettit, Walter W., comps. and eds. *Russian-American Relations March, 1917-March, 1920*. New York: Harcourt, Brace & Howe, 1920. 375 pp.

This volume contains published documents in English, translations of Russian official and unofficial newspapers, and previously unpublished documents. One of the compilers, Pettit, was with Bullitt on his famous mission to Petrograd in March 1919.

1848. Davis, Donald E., and Trani, Eugene P. "An American in Russia: Russell M. Storey and the Bolshevik Revolution, 1917-1919." *Historian* 36 (August 1974): 704-21.

Utilizing the Storey papers in the Hoover Institution Archives and Russian materials in the YMCA Historical Library in New York, the authors discuss Storey's understanding of Russian events while he was the YMCA representative in Russia.

1849. Debo, Richard K. *Revolution and Survival: The Foreign Policy of Soviet Russia, 1917-1918*. Toronto: University of Toronto Press, 1979. 462 pp.

This important study is based on multi-archival research. Unfortunately, as long as the Soviet archives remain closed to western scholars, a definitive study of Soviet diplomacy of this period remains to be written. This volume sheds new light on such topics as Allied intervention and the Brest-Litovsk negotiations.

1850. Degras, Jane, ed. *Soviet Documents on Foreign Policy*, vol. 1: *1917-1924*. New York: Oxford University Press, 1951. 501 pp.

Treaties, speeches, newspaper interviews, and other items are arranged in chronological order. There is no commentary on the documents. The year 1918 receives the most attention.

*   *Dollars and Diplomacy: Ambassador David Rowland Francis and the Fall of Tsarism, 1916-1917*. Cited above as item 1560.

1851. Fike, Claude E. "The Influence of the Creel Committee and the

American Red Cross on Russian-American Relations, 1917-1919."
Jour. Mod. Hist. 31 (June 1959): 93-109.

This article examines the activities of the Creel Committee
and the American Red Cross in Russia. The author concludes
that the activities of this "ad hoc diplomatic corps of un-
diplomatic Americans" was generally detrimental to Russian-
American relations.

*   ————. "The United States and Russian Territorial Problems,
1917-1920." Cited above as item 1748.

1852. Filene, Peter G. *Americans and the Soviet Experiment, 1917-
1933.* Cambridge: Harvard University Press, 1967. 389 pp.

Filene attempts to examine American attitudes toward the
Soviet Union rather than Communism in general. Only the first
two chapters in this well-documented volume deal with the
period of World War I. Many diverse sources, including official papers, newspapers, and journals, are utilized.

1853. Fischer, Louis. *The Soviets in World Affairs: A History of
Relations Between the Soviet Union and the Rest of the
World, 1917-1929.* New York: Cape & Smith, 1930. 2 vols.

This work covers the period of the revolution, civil war,
and the New Economic Policy and is based on considerable research and an intimate knowledge of Russian affairs. Fischer,
a journalist, conducted numerous interviews with Soviet leaders
such as Chicherin and Litvinov. The result is an account generally sympathetic to the Soviets. The first six chapters are
pertinent to Russo-American relations during the war.

1854. Footman, David. *Civil War in Russia.* New York: Frederick A.
Praeger, 1962. 328 pp.

This work does not provide a comprehensive treatment of
either Allied intervention or the Russian Civil War. Rather
it focuses in depth on selected aspects of this complex episode. Footnotes are not provided but sources used, some of
them Russian, are listed at the end of chapters.

*   Fowler, Wilton B. *British-American Relations, 1917-1918: The
Role of Sir William Wiseman.* Cited above as item 1628.

*   Francis, David R. *Russia from the American Embassy, April
1916-November 1918.* Cited above as item 1559.

1855. Gankin, Olga Hess, and Fisher, H.H., eds. *The Bolsheviks and
the World War: The Origin of the Third International.* Stanford, Calif.: Stanford University Press, 1940. 856 pp.

This is a collection of documents on the Bolsheviks and
World War I and on the origin of the Third International.
This study concludes with the meeting of European leftists at
the Stockholm Conference in the summer of 1917. The editors
provide a very judicious commentary on the documents.

1856. Gardner, Lloyd C. *Wilson and Revolutions: 1913-1921*. Phila-
       delphia: J.B. Lippincott Co., 1976. 149 pp.

       This recent study emphasizes anti-Bolshevism as the primary
       reason for Wilson's decision to send an American force to
       Siberia.

1857. Gaworek, Norbert Horst. "Allied Economic Warfare Against
       Soviet Russia from November 1917 to March 1921." Doctoral
       dissertation, University of Wisconsin, 1970. 439 pp.

       This dissertation examines an often overlooked aspect of
       western policy toward the Soviet regime: the economic war to
       undermine and destroy Bolshevism. As in the case with armed
       intervention, this anti-Soviet program was handicapped by the
       failure of the Allies to coordinate their efforts.

1858. Goldhurst, Richard. *The Midnight War: The American Interven-
       tion in Russia, 1918-1920*. New York: McGraw-Hill Book Co.,
       1978. 288 pp.

       This popular history is long on anecdotes and superficial
       characterization and short on scholarship.

1859. Grayson, Benson Lee. *Russian-American Relations in World
       War I*. New York: Frederick Ungar, 1979. 151 pp.

       This slim monograph accurately portrays the differences
       (mistreatment of Jews, Tsarist political oppression, and
       rivalry in the Far East) which separated Washington from
       Petrograd. The title is misleading because the period covered
       is from the beginning of the war to the recognition of the
       Provisional Government in early 1917. Many recent secondary
       and primary sources are neglected and there is little utiliza-
       tion of Russian sources.

1860. Ingram, Alton Earl. "The Root Mission to Russia, 1917." Doc-
       toral dissertation, Louisiana State University, 1970. 332
       pp.

       The origins and activities of the nine-man Root mission to
       Russia in 1917 are examined. Sources include State Department
       material in the National Archives and the private papers and
       diaries of many of the participants.

1861. Jackson, Robert. *At War with the Bolsheviks: The Allied Inter-
       vention into Russia, 1917-1920*. London: Tom Stacey, 1972.
       251 pp.

       Largely based on printed works, this volume is a survey of
       military operations rather than a political history. There
       are numerous illustrations. The author is a free-lance writer
       who specializes in military history.

1862. Kennan, George F. *Russia and the West Under Lenin and Stalin*.
       Boston: Atlantic-Little, Brown, 1961. 411 pp.

       The first half of this work provides a thought-provoking in-
       terpretation of western relations with Russia during the Russian

Revolution and Civil War and the Paris Peace Conference. Kennan argues that it was a great tragedy for western civilization that a negotiated settlement of the war was not possible
in 1917. He is also critical of Allied pressure on the Russian
Provisional Government to continue the war. The result of this
pressure, he argues, was the triumph of Bolshevism. This study
is especially noteworthy for its clarity and boldness of interpretation.

1863.   ————. *Soviet-American Relations, 1917-1920*. Princeton:
         Princeton University Press, 1956-1958. 2 vols.

         This is a judicious study of the origins of Allied interven-
         tion in Russia and of how the United States came to be drawn
         into that controversial episode. The first volume, *Russia
         Leaves the War*, won the Bancroft Prize and the Pulitzer Prize.
         Certain aspects of Kennan's brilliant study are now somewhat
         dated by the availability of many new archival sources, es-
         pecially in France and Great Britain.

1864.   ————. "Soviet Historiography and America's Role in the
         Intervention." *AHR* 65 (January 1960): 302-22.

         This former American ambassador to the USSR and distinguished
         historian shows the blatant distortions and unsupported state-
         ments of the Soviet historian S.F. Naida's treatment of Ameri-
         can intervention in Russia. In a chapter of thirty-five pages,
         Naida, for example, uses the phrase "American imperialists"
         some eighty times.

1865.   Kernez, Peter. *Civil War in South Russia, 1919-1920*. Ber-
         keley: University of California Press, 1977. 378 pp.

         Kernez succeeds in his attempt to fill a large gap in the
         literature on the Russian Civil War. Much has been written
         on the triumph of the Reds; almost nothing has been published
         on their rivals, the Whites. One should look elsewhere for
         an account of Allied intervention, but this scholarly and
         clearly-written monograph helps explain why Allied intervention
         failed.

1866.   Kettle, Michael. *The Allies and the Russian Collapse*. Minnea-
         polis: University of Minnesota Press, 1981. 287 pp.

         Not surprisingly, Great Britain, the country most centrally
         involved in intervention in Russia, receives the most attention
         in this superbly researched study. This volume, the first of
         a projected five-volume set, ends with the Treaty of Brest-
         Litovsk. It provides broader treatment than Ullman's study of
         British intervention and makes use of material not available
         when Ullman's *Intervention and the War* was published in 1961.

1867.   Killen, Linda. *The Russian Bureau: A Case Study in Wilsonian
         Diplomacy*. Lexington: University Press of Kentucky, 1983.
         216 pp.

         This scholarly work focuses on the Russian Bureau of the
         War Trade Board, October 1918 to June 1919, which sought trade

with Russia. American misconceptions about Russia are emphasized and corrected.

1868. Lasch, Christopher. *The American Liberals and the Russian Revolution*. New York: McGraw-Hill Book Co., 1972. 290 pp.

Lasch, a specialist in American social history, examines the influence of the Russian Revolution on American liberals in this well-documented volume. Attention is given to the divisions in American liberalism caused by events in Russia.

1869. Laserson, Max M. *The American Impact on Russia--Diplomatic and Ideological--1784-1917*. New York: Macmillan Co., 1950. 441 pp.

This volume attempts to trace America's impact on Russian thought, domestic politics, and foreign policy from the 1780s to the Elihu Root Mission in 1917.

* Marye, George T. *Nearing the End in Imperial Russia*. Cited above as item 1585.

1870. Radosh, Ronald. "John Spargo and Wilson's Russian Policy." *JAH* 52 (December 1965): 548-65.

This is a well-documented analysis of the support that John Spargo, an American prowar socialist, gave to Wilson's anti-Bolshevik policies in Russia.

1871. Rothstein, Andrew. *The Soldiers' Strikes of 1919*. Atlantic Highlands, N.J.: Humanities Press, 1980. 114 pp.

This pithy study of the little-known protests of British soldiers in early 1919 is pertinent to the larger topic of Allied intervention in Russia. Fearing that their demobilization might be delayed by involvement in the Russian Civil War, some soldiers struck. It is no wonder that Winston Churchill, the British Secretary of State for War, looked to the United States for the necessary manpower to crush Bolshevism.

1872. Savage, Harry Howard. "Official Policies and Relations of the United States with the Provisional Government of Russia, March-November 1917." Doctoral dissertation, University of Minnesota, 1971. 399 pp.

Savage contends that historians who examine U.S. relations with the Provisional Government as little more than a prelude to the Bolshevik Revolution have distorted American policy. He also makes the sensible assertion that under the circumstances no American policy could have altered events in Russia.

1873. Schuman, Frederick Lewis. *American Policy Toward Russia Since 1917*. New York: International Publishers, 1928. 399 pp.

This work, based primarily on American sources, is a description and analysis of Russo-American relations since the Russian Revolution. The first half of this volume covers the period of the Revolution, civil war, and Allied intervention. Schuman,

very critical of American participation in that intervention,
asserts that "a more complete and tragic debacle would be difficult to imagine." Valuable in its time, this work is now
dated.

1874. Silverlight, John. *The Victor's Dilemma: Allied Intervention
       in the Russian Civil War*. New York: Weybright & Talley,
       1970. 392 pp.

       The British Cabinet papers constitute the author's most im-
       portant unpublished source. His research does not compare with
       the much more thorough multi-archival research of John Bradley.

1875. Sisson, Edgar Grant. *One Hundred Red Days: A Personal Chronicle
       of the Bolshevik Revolution*. New Haven: Yale University
       Press, 1931. 502 pp.

       Sisson, who was sent to Russia by Wilson as his special rep-
       resentative to Kerensky's Provisional Government, arrived after
       the Bolsheviks had seized power. His personal and detailed
       account constitutes an important source on the American em-
       bassy in Petrograd during this confused period. The appendix
       includes a copy of the discredited Sisson report, which at-
       tempted to prove a German-Bolshevik conspiracy.

1876. Strakhovsky, Leonid I. *American Opinion About Russia, 1917-
       1920*. Toronto: University of Toronto Press, 1961. 135 pp.

       The editorials of the *New York Times* and the *Washington Eve-
       ning Star* are emphasized in this well-researched and well-
       documented monograph. Strakhovsky contends that policymakers
       in Washington had very little reliable information about
       Russia upon which to base their decisions. The press had many
       misconceptions, and American representatives were amateurs.

1877. Tompkins, Pauline. *American-Russian Relations in the Far East*.
       New York: Macmillan Co., 1949. 426 pp.

       Japanese-American relations, the Russian Revolution, and U.S.
       intervention in Siberia are some of the topics discussed by the
       author in this balanced and well-researched work.

1878. Trani, Eugene P. "Woodrow Wilson and the Decision to Intervene
       in Russia: A Reconsideration." *Jour. Mod. Hist.* 48 (Septem-
       ber 1976): 440-61.

       This article, based on archival research in both Great Britain
       and the United States, contends that Wilson accepted interven-
       tion in Russia largely because of pressure applied by the
       British and French.

1879. Ullman, Richard H. *Anglo-Soviet Relations, 1917-1921*. Prince-
       ton: Princeton University Press, 1961-1972. 3 vols.

       Vol. 1 of this standard study includes information on Lon-
       don's efforts to involve the United States in intervention in
       Russia. This volume is based on thorough research in available
       primary and secondary sources, but was published before the

opening of British state papers and many important private manuscript collections. Vol. 2 makes excellent use of this new material and includes a detailed account of the Prinkipo proposal, the Bullitt mission, and the steps leading to the recognition of Kolchak.

1880. United States Department of State. *Papers Relating to the Foreign Relations of the United States, 1918, Russia.* Washington, D.C.: Government Printing Office, 1931-1932. 3 vols.

These volumes, the single most important collection of documents concerning America's role in intervention in Russia, cover political questions and diplomatic relations (Vol. 1); the Allies and the White movement (Vol. 2); and economic questions such as loans to the Provisional Government and the Soviet repudiation of the Tsarist debt (Vol. 3).

1881. ————. *Papers Relating to the Foreign Relations of the United States, 1919, Russia.* Washington, D.C.: Government Printing Office, 1937. 807 pp.

This volume covers the last year of America's involvement in the Russian civil war.

* ————. *Papers Relating to the Foreign Relations of the United States: The Lansing Papers, 1914-1920.* Cited above as item 1577.

1882. Unterberger, Betty Miller, ed. *American Intervention in the Russian Civil War.* Lexington, Mass.: D.C. Heath & Co., 1969. 113 pp.

This volume in the Problems in American Civilization series includes a collection of official documents. There is an excellent source for the conflicting interpretations of American intervention.

1883. Upton, Anthony F. *The Finnish Revolution, 1917-1918.* Minneapolis: University of Minnesota Press, 1981. 608 pp.

This is a comprehensive and detailed study of Finland's struggle for independence from Russia and the Finnish Civil War by a University of St. Andrew's professor.

1884. Wade, Rex A. *The Russian Search for Peace: February-October 1917.* Stanford, Calif.: Stanford University Press, 1969. 196 pp.

This book focuses on the moderate, as opposed to Bolshevik, socialists in the Petrograd Soviet. The failure of the moderates to liberalize the war aims of the belligerents and open general peace negotiations was catastrophic to their political fortunes. This well-documented study sheds light on Allied attempts to keep Russia in the war. See also Wade's 1963 University of Nebraska-Lincoln doctoral dissertation.

1885. Warth, Robert D. *The Allies and the Russian Revolution: From the Fall of the Monarchy to the Peace of Brest-Litovsk.* Durham, N.C.: Duke University Press, 1954. 294 pp.

Based on many manuscript sources and printed works in the
relevant languages, this volume examines the efforts of the
Allies and the "associated" United States to keep Russia in
the war. Particular attention is given to the anti-German
coalition's reaction to Russian efforts to liberalize war objectives.

1886. Weeks, Charles J., Jr., and Baylen, Joseph O. "Admiral Kol-
       chak's Mission to the United States, 10 September-9 November
       1917." *Mil. Affairs* 40 (April 1976): 63-67.

       This examination of Kolchak's three-month visit to the United
       States makes clear that his visit had little impact on American-
       Russian relations.

1887. Williams, William Appleman. "American Intervention in Russia:
       1917-1920." In *Containment and Revolution*, edited by David
       Horowitz, pp. 26-75. Boston: Beacon Press, 1967.

       Williams argues that "American intervention in Russia was a
       long-debated and long-delayed tactical move in support of the
       basic anti-Bolshevik strategy that had been established in
       December 1917."

1888. ————. *American Russian Relations, 1781-1947*. New York:
       Rinehart & Co., 1952. 367 pp.

       The author contends that the roots of the Soviet-American
       conflict can be found during the 1917-1920 period. Williams
       is critical of President Wilson's approach to the new Soviet
       regime which he characterizes as misguided and vacillating.
       Approximately one-half of the text is devoted to World War I
       and the Russian Revolution.

1889. Woodward, David R. "British Intervention in Russia During the
       First World War." *Mil. Affairs* 41 (December 1977): 171-75.

       The role of the British military authorities in armed inter-
       vention in Russia is explored in this article which is based
       on unpublished sources.

                    2. U.S. Intervention in North Russia

1890. "Chronicler." *Archangel, The American War with Russia*. Chicago:
       A.C. McClurg & Co., 1924. 216 pp.

       The author, who wished to remain anonymous, attacks his
       government for sending U.S. soldiers to fight in Russia. This
       is not good scholarship, but it is an accurate reflection of
       the views of many of the U.S. soldiers who served in North
       Russia.

*   Gordon, Dennis, ed. *Quartered in Hell: The Story of American
       North Russian Expeditionary Force, 1918-1919*. Cited above
       as item 411.

1891. Halliday, E.M. *The Ignorant Armies*. New York: Harper & Brothers, 1958. 232 pp.

This is a dramatic narrative of Allied intervention in North Russia with emphasis on the role of the American North Russian Expeditionary Force. Brief and inadequate notes concerning sources are included. The author's interviews with participants are especially valuable. The foreword is by S.L.A. Marshall.

* Moore, J.R., and others, eds. *History of the American Expedition Fighting the Bolsheviki: Campaigning in North Russia, 1918-1919*. Cited above as item 429.

1892. Shapiro, Sumner. "Intervention in Russia (1918-1919)." *U.S. Naval Inst., Proc.* 99 (April 1973): 52-61.

This article agrees in the main with the critical assessment of American intervention in North Russia found in Tolley's 1969 article in this journal. As was the case with Tolley, the author served as an assistant U.S. naval attaché in Moscow.

1893. Strakhovsky, Leonid J. *Intervention at Archangel: The Story of Allied Intervention and Russian Counter-Revolution in North Russia, 1918-1920*. Princeton: Princeton University Press, 1944. 336 pp.

A sequel to Strakhovsky's 1937 study on the origins of American involvement, this well-documented and detailed study offers insight into Allied diplomacy and the interworkings of the White government in North Russia. Strakhovsky served with the Whites in the Russian Civil War and his work is perhaps not without bias.

1894. ————. *The Origins of American Intervention in North Russia, 1918*. Princeton: Princeton University Press, 1937. 140 pp.

This is a pioneering study with documentation by a Russian emigré historian.

1895. Tolley, Kemp. "Our Russian War of 1918-1919." *U.S. Naval Inst., Proc.* 95 (February 1969): 58-72.

Tolley, a retired rear admiral who at one time served as an assistant naval attaché in Moscow, is critical of American involvement in Allied intervention in North Russia. Rear Admiral Newton McCully, however, is singled out for special praise for his understanding of Russian conditions.

3. U.S. Intervention in Siberia

1896. Dupuy, R. Ernest. *Perish by the Sword: The Czechoslovakian Anabasis and Our Supporting Campaigns in North Russia and Siberia*. Harrisburg, Pa.: Military Service Publishing Co., 1939. 302 pp.

The Czechoslovakian Legion played an important role in Wilson's decision to send American troops to Siberia in 1918. The

author, an American officer with experience as a war correspondent, examines the political and military aspects of the Czech
and Slovak prisoners of war in Russia. Footnotes and a short
bibliography are included, but errors of fact and interpretation
abound. The eighty-nine photographs which illustrate the work
are very good.

1897. Feist, Joe Michael. "Theirs Not to Reason Why: The Case of
the Russian Railway Service Corps." *Mil. Affairs* 42 (February 1978): 1-6.

Feist presents the history of the RRSC, including the court
fight by some of its members to gain recognition that they
were serving in the AEF in Siberia.

*   Graves, William S. *America's Siberian Adventure*. Cited above
as item 238.

1898. Guins, George C. "The Siberian Intervention, 1918-1919."
Russian Rev. 28 (October 1969): 428-40.

This article provides a general account of intervention in
Asiatic Russia by a strongly anti-Soviet Russian emigré who
was deputy minister of foreign affairs in Kolchak's White
government.

1899. Hosoya, Chihiro. "Japanese Documents on the Siberian Intervention, 1917-1922. Part 1, November, 1917-January, 1919."
Hitotsubashi Journal of Law and Politics 1 (April 1960):
30-53.

This valuable collection of unpublished documents helps make
sense of Japanese policy in Siberia.

1900. ———. "Origin of the Siberian Intervention, 1917-1918."
Annals of the Hitotsubashi Academy 9 (October 1958): 91-108.

Materials in the Japanese Foreign Office archives are utilized
in this article which the author originally prepared for a
seminar at the Russian Institute at Columbia University in 1956.

1901. Kindall, Sylvian G. *American Soldiers in Siberia*. New York:
R.R. Smith, 1945. 251 pp.

This is a personal account by a member of the AEF in Siberia
rather than a history of that intervention. The hostility of
American soldiers toward the Japanese is a thread running
through this account.

1902. Lasch, Christopher. "American Intervention in Siberia: A Reinterpretation." *Pol. Sci. Quar.* 77 (June 1962): 205-23.

This critical examination of American intervention in Siberia
argues that the primary justification was based on an illusion:
that the Bolsheviks were agents of Berlin rather than true
revolutionaries. Lasch also rejects the interpretation that
President Wilson sent troops to Siberia to restrain the Japanese.

*   McClellan, Edwin N. "American Marines in Siberia During the
         World War." Cited above as item 831.

1903.   Maddox, Robert J. "Doughboys in Siberia." *Amer. Hist. Ill.*
         12 (August 1977): 10-21.

         Maddox in this well-illustrated article argues that American
         intervention in Asiatic Russia succeeded only in "prolonging
         the civil war in Russia."

1904.   ————. *The Unknown War with Russia: Wilson's Siberian Inter-
         vention.* San Rafael, Calif.: Presidio Press, 1977. 156 pp.

         This is an interpretative study of Wilson's motives in inter-
         vening in Siberia which presents new evidence from the War
         Trade Board. Maddox argues that Wilson's opposition to Bol-
         shevism and his desire to strengthen liberal or democratic
         forces in Russia were central to his decision to intervene.
         The open door and concern for the plight of the Czechoslovak
         Legion were minor issues.

1905.   ————. "Woodrow Wilson, the Russian Embassy, and Siberian
         Intervention." *Pac. Hist. Rev.* 36 (November 1967): 435-48.

         Maddox argues that Wilson, instead of following a policy of
         nonintervention in Russian domestic affairs, sought to destroy
         the Bolshevik regime. A transcript of an oral recording (Col-
         umbia University Library) of Boris Bakhmetev, the Provisional
         Government's ambassador to the United States, is utilized.

1906.   Manning, Clarence A. *The Siberian Fiasco.* New York: Library
         Publishers, 1952. 210 pp.

         This volume is helpful in understanding the objectives of
         the multinational people of Siberia, but Allied intervention
         is better treated in the works of White and Unterberger.

1907.   Morley, James William. *The Japanese Thrust into Siberia, 1918.*
         London: Oxford University Press, 1957. 395 pp.

         This book by a leading authority on Japanese-American rela-
         tions is the best examination of Japanese motives in inter-
         vention in Asiatic Russia. Morley illuminates the structure
         of Japanese decision making. Japanese, Chinese, Russian and
         American sources are utilized.

1908.   St. John, Jacqueline D. "John F. Stevens: American Assistance
         to Russian and Siberian Railroads, 1917-1922." Doctoral dis-
         sertation, University of Oklahoma, 1969. 348 pp.

         The breakdown of Russian railways undermined the Russian war
         effort. Encouraged by the British, President Wilson sent
         Stevens to Russia in the spring of 1917 to see what could be
         done to repair Russian railways. The Bolshevik Revolution
         made an already difficult task impossible.

1909.   Smith, Canfield F. *Vladivostock Under Red and White Rule:
         Revolution and Counterrevolution in the Russian Far East,*

1920-1922. Seattle: University of Washington Press, 1976.
304 pp.

This volume provides valuable background material for the
conflict between the Soviets, Japanese, and Americans in the
Maritime Province during the immediate post-Kolchak period.

1910. Smith, Gaddis. "Canada and the Siberian Intervention, 1918-
1919." *AHR* 64 (July 1959): 866-77.

This article reveals that Canada, following an independent
policy in Siberian intervention, acted as a "buffer" between
Great Britain and the United States. The Borden papers were
extensively used.

1911. Unterberger, Betty Miller. *America's Siberian Expedition, 1918-
1919: A Study of National Policy.* Durham, N.C.: Duke University Press, 1956. 271 pp.

This thorough, extensively researched study stresses that
Wilson's primary and hitherto misunderstood motive in agreeing
to intervention in Siberia was to restrain Japanese imperial-
ist designs and to protect the open door in Siberia and North
Manchuria. Unterberger's work offers a fuller picture of
American policy than White's *The Siberian Intervention* (1950).

1912. ————. "President Wilson and the Decision to Send American
Troops to Siberia." *Pac. Hist. Rev.* 24 (February 1955):
63-74.

Wilson's concern over Japanese expansion in the Far East is
emphasized as one of Wilson's motives for intervention.

1913. ————. "The Russian Revolution and Wilson's Far Eastern
Policy." *Russian Rev.* 16 (April 1957): 35-46.

The origins of American intervention in Siberia are critically examined in this article.

1914. White, John Albert. *The Siberian Intervention.* Princeton:
Princeton University Press, 1950. 471 pp.

This volume covers Allied intervention in Siberia, including
the period after U.S. forces were withdrawn. It is a superior
work based on American, Japanese, and Russian sources.

1915. Woodward, David R. "The British Government and Japanese Intervention in Russia During World War I." *Jour. Mod. Hist.* 46
(December 1974): 663-85.

Based on new sources, this article demonstrates that British
statesmen were often as skeptical as Wilson about Japanese
motives.

4. Russia and the Paris Peace Conference

*   Bullitt, William C. *The Bullitt Mission to Russia: Testimony Before the Committee on Foreign Relations, United States Senate.*
Cited above as item 1555.

*   Farnsworth, Beatrice. *William C. Bullitt and the Soviet Union*.
         Cited above as item 1556.

1916. Mayer, Arno J. *Politics and Diplomacy of Peacemaking: Con-
         tainment and Counterrevolution at Versailles, 1918-1919*.
         New York: Alfred A. Knopf, 1967. 893 pp.

         This is a sequel to his *Political Origins of the New Diplo-
         macy, 1917-1918*. It includes much material on the west's at-
         tempts to contain Bolshevik Russia. The relationship between
         domestic and international politics is thoroughly delineated
         in this unconventional history, with Mayer asserting the primacy
         of the former. His view of the influence of Bolshevism on the
         peacemaking of the victor powers is challenged by John Thompson.

1917. Thompson, John M. *Russia, Bolshevism and the Versailles Peace*.
         Princeton: Princeton University Press, 1966. 429 pp.

         The manner in which the Russian Revolution and the threat of
         Bolshevism influenced the peace settlement is judiciously ex-
         amined. This volume is well documented through Russian as
         well as English-language sources. The author argues that although
         U.S. and Allied policy toward Russia was often misguided and a
         failure, it probably exercised little influence on the creation
         of a totalitarian socialist regime hostile to the west. Thompson
         makes a case that Arno J. Mayer is wrong in his contention that
         the Bolshevik threat dominated the proceedings of the peace
         conference.

VIII. THE PEACE SETTLEMENT
(*SEE ALSO* VII:F, WAR OBJECTIVES AND PEACE DIPLOMACY, 1914-1918)

A. GENERAL ACCOUNTS AND CRITICAL EVALUATIONS OF THE PEACEMAKING

1918. Birdsall, Paul. *Versailles Twenty Years After*. New York: Reynal & Hitchcock, 1941. 350 pp.

This is an outstanding history of the making of peace which is sympathetic to President Wilson, who the author asserts fought heroically for his principles, succeeding far more often in living up to his Fourteen Points than his critics have conceded. This volume serves as a corrective to the critical accounts of Keynes and others.

1919. Churchill, Winston S. *The Aftermath, 1918-1928*. New York: Charles Scribner's Sons, 1929. 502 pp.

The first half of this volume focuses on the peace settlement and the Russian question. Churchill discusses the opportunities missed at the peace conference and during Allied intervention in Russia during which he attempted to lead an anti-Communist crusade. Neither notes nor a bibliography are included.

1920. Czernin, Ferdinand. *Versailles, 1919: The Forces, Events and Personalities That Shaped the Treaty*. New York: Capricorn Books, 1965. 437 pp.

This documentary account focuses on the evolution of the five main clauses of the Treaty of Versailles, allowing the peacemakers to speak for themselves. Except for his conclusion, the author expresses no opinions.

1921. Dillon, E.J. *The Inside Story of the Peace Conference*. New York: Harper & Brothers, 1919. 513 pp.

Dillon promises more than he can deliver, because he was often on the outside of the peace negotiations looking in. Dillon was a graduate of two Russian universities, a university professor, the editor of two Russian newspapers, and a contributor to *Contemporary Review*.

1922. Haskins, Charles Homer, and Lord, Robert Howard. *Some Problems of the Peace Conference*. Cambridge: Harvard University Press, 1920. 307 pp.

The "problems" referred to by the authors concern the territorial settlement in Europe. This is the publication of a
series of lectures at the Lowell Institute in 1920. This
work is of special interest because both Lord and Haskins
were members of the American peace commission.

*   Hoover, Herbert C. *America's First Crusade*. Cited above as
         item 886.

1923.   House, Edward M., and Seymour, Charles, eds. *What Really
         Happened at Paris*. New York: Charles Scribner's Sons, 1921.
         528 pp.

         Based on a series of lectures by American delegates to Ver-
         sailles, this book provides a firsthand discussion of the
         problems and debates of the peace conference.

1924.   Israel, Fred L., ed. *Major Peace Treaties of Modern History,
         1648-1967*. New York: Chelsea House Publishers in association
         with McGraw-Hill Book Co., 1967. 4 vols.

         Some 1,000 pages are devoted to the treaties of 1919.
         Emanuel Chill provides commentaries. Colored maps are in-
         cluded.

1925.   Mee, Charles L., Jr. *The End of Order: Versailles, 1919*.
         New York: E.P. Dutton, 1980. 301 pp.

         This is an impressionistic account of the peacemaking
         written in a dramatic fashion by a free-lance writer. The
         leading personalities come alive on these pages. But the
         author's anecdotal approach often entertains more than it en-
         lightens. This work is based primarily on published sources.

1926.   Miller, David H. *My Diary at the Conference of Paris, with
         Documents*. New York: Appeal Printing, 1924. 21 vols.

         Miller was a legal expert who served on the Inquiry. His
         diary and collection of documents constitute one of the most
         important sources for studying peacemaking in 1919, especially
         the discussions concerning reparations and the League of
         Nations. Vol. 1 consists of Miller's valuable diary.

1927.   Nicolson, Harold. *Peacemaking, 1919*. Boston: Houghton Mifflin
         Co., 1933. 378 pp.

         This volume is divided into two parts: part one concerns
         Nicolson's analysis of the peace negotiations and part two is
         composed of excerpts from the diary he kept during the peace
         conference. A central thesis of this veteran British diplomat
         is that the hysteria provoked by the long war made a balanced
         and moderate peace settlement impossible. He is also critical
         of those who would portray Wilson as the leader of the "Powers
         of Light" against Clemenceau and the "Powers of Darkness."

1928.   Nowak, Karl Friederich. *Versailles*. New York: Payson & Clarke,
         1929. 287 pp.

         This English translation gives the German view of the peace
         settlement and Wilsonian diplomacy. Wilson, according to Nowak,

was "a child in all European problems" who "advanced into territory as strange to him as the mountains of the moon."

1929. Schmitt, Bernadotte E. "The Peace Conference of 1919." *Jour. Mod. Hist.* 16 (March 1944): 49-59.

Schmitt both assesses the importance of and previews the publication of the U.S. diplomatic record of the peace conference found in *Papers Relating to the Foreign Relations of the United States.*

1930. Scott, Arthur Pearson. *An Introduction to the Peace Treaties.* Chicago: University of Chicago Press, 1920. 292 pp.

Scott gives an evenhanded appraisal of the peace treaties, with emphasis on the Treaty of Versailles. His sources, however, are primarily newspapers and magazines.

1931. Shotwell, James T. *At the Paris Peace Conference.* New York: Macmillan Co., 1937. 444 pp.

This is a valuable and revealing description and analysis of peacemaking by a historian and former member of the Inquiry. This volume is divided into two parts: Shotwell's attempt to explain what went awry in the negotiations and his diary while at the peace conference.

1932. Tardieu, André. *The Truth About the Treaty.* Indianapolis: Bobbs-Merrill Co., 1921. 473 pp.

This volume is especially valuable in providing the French view of American statesmanship at the Paris Peace Conference. Tardieu was a conservative and nationalist French politician who was involved in the creation of the League of Nations.

1933. Temperley, H.W.V., ed. *A History of the Peace Conference.* London: Henry Frowde, and Hodder & Stoughton, 1920-1924. 6 vols.

This massive and monumental work remains a basic source for the peace conference. Published under the auspices of the Institute of International Affairs, it is a mine of information and documentary material. Temperley did not compile these volumes with a particular point of view; rather he presents the material both topically and chronologically in such a way that the reader can reach his own conclusions.

1934. Thompson, Charles Thaddeus. *Peace Conference Day by Day: A Presidential Pilgrimage Leading to the Discovery of Europe.* New York: Brentano's, 1920. 423 pp.

Thompson, an American reporter who covered the peace negotiations, has written an entertaining and at times enlightening account of the negotiations and leading personalities.

1935. Tillman, Seth P. *Anglo-American Relations at the Paris Peace Conference of 1919.* Princeton: Princeton University Press, 1961. 442 pp.

This is a balanced and thoroughly researched study of the
mutual interests and differences between Anglo-American peacemakers at the Paris Peace Conference. The two world powers
were more often than not in agreement on important issues;
the relationship would have been even closer, Tillman concludes,
if the chemistry between Lloyd George and Wilson had been
better.

1936. United States Department of State. *Papers Relating to the
       Foreign Relations of the United States, 1919, The Paris Peace
       Conference.* Washington, D.C.: Government Printing Office,
       1942-1947. 13 vols.

       These volumes, published by the Department of State, are
       essential to any study of the peace settlement. They contain
       material from the private papers of such participants as Wil-
       son, House, and Lansing, the official minutes of the Council
       of Ten and Council of Four, and documents from the files of
       the Department of State and the American commission to nego-
       tiate peace.

1937. Walworth, Arthur. *America's Moment: 1918, American Diplomacy
       at the End of World War I.* New York: W.W. Norton & Co.,
       1977. 309 pp.

       Walworth, a Pulitzer Prize-winning historian for his biog-
       raphy of Wilson, describes the often neglected period between
       the Armistice and the beginning of the peace conference. This
       is an original contribution and the research is impressive.
       Walworth conducted his research in the United States, Britain,
       France, and Canada. He also makes use of the recollections,
       either oral or in writing, of the peacemakers.

1938. Woodward, E.L., and Butler, Rohan, eds. *Documents on British
       Foreign Policy, 1919-1939.* First Series. London: H.M. Sta-
       tionery Office, 1947-1966. Vols. 1-14.

       The official British record of the peace settlement can be
       found in these volumes, which should be used to supplement
       Papers Relating to the Foreign Relations of the United States.
       Vols. 1 through 14 are most relevant to the 1919-1920 period.

          B. THE BIG FOUR AND OTHER LEADING PEACEMAKERS

1939. Bailey, Thomas A. *Woodrow Wilson and the Lost Peace.* New
       York: Macmillan Co., 1944. 325 pp.

       This is a major work on Wilson at Versailles. It is balanced
       and points out Wilson's mistakes as well as his triumphs.
       Bailey thoroughly approves of Wilson's war aims, but is con-
       cerned by his losing of the peace. He concludes that Wilson's
       mistakes are overstated by his opponents.

1940. Baker, Ray Stannard. *Woodrow Wilson and the World Settlement.*
       Garden City, N.Y.: Doubleday, Page & Co., 1922. 3 vols.

These volumes, written from Wilson's unpublished and personal material, provide a narrative of Wilson's work at Versailles. Topically organized, these volumes contain many important Wilson documents.

1941. Bonsal, Stephen. *Unfinished Business*. Garden City, N.Y.:
Doubleday, Doran & Co., 1944. 313 pp.

This is the diary of the multilingual Bonsal, who often
served as an interpreter for House and Wilson in their meetings
with statesmen at the Paris Peace Conference. It gives an
insider's view of the often complex negotiations and brings to
life the leading participants.

1942. Curry, George. "Woodrow Wilson, Jan Smuts, and the Versailles
Settlement." *AHR* 66 (July 1961): 968-86.

This article, based primarily on printed sources, delineates
Smuts's influence, both positive and negative, on Wilson
during the Paris Peace Conference. The papers of Lansing and
Wilson are utilized.

1943. Elcock, Howard. *Portrait of a Decision: The Council of Four
and the Treaty of Versailles*. London: Eyre Methuen, 1972.
386 pp.

The passage of time and availability of new papers and documents are given as justification for this new study of the
making of the Treaty of Versailles. This is good narrative
history supported by research in published English-language
sources and the British archives.

1944. Ferrell, R.H. "Woodrow Wilson and Open Diplomacy." In *Issues
and Conflicts*, edited by G.L. Anderson, pp. 193-209. Lawrence: University of Kansas Press, 1959.

Ferrell argues that although Wilson believed in closed negotiations, he wanted the results published.

* Floto, Inga. *Colonel House in Paris: A Study of American Policy
at the Paris Peace Conference, 1919*. Cited above as item
1570.

1945. Hankey, Lord. *The Supreme Control at the Paris Peace Conference 1919: A Commentary*. London: Allen & Unwin, 1963.
206 pp.

This work is valuable for its treatment of the procedure of
the Paris Peace Conference. It is a sequel to Hankey's more
important work on the war years, *The Supreme Command, 1914-
1918*.

1946. Harris, H. Wilson. *The Peace in the Making*. New York: E.P.
Dutton & Co., 1920. 235 pp.

The author, a correspondent for the London *Daily News* at the
peace conference, is especially good in his treatment of the
key peacemakers.

1947. Headlam-Morley, Sir James. *A Memoir of the Paris Peace Con-
       ference 1919.* London: Methuen & Co., 1972. 230 pp.

       Extracts from Headlam-Morley's diary, notes, letters, and
       memoranda have been brought together by Agnes Headlam-Morley,
       Russell Bryant, and Anna Cienciala. This volume concerns many
       aspects of the peacemaking, including Anglo-American relations.

1948. Holt, W. Stull. "What Wilson Sent and What House Received:
       Or Scholars Need to Check Carefully." *AHR* 65 (April 1960):
       569-71.

       Holt points out that there were at times substantial differ-
       ences between the wording of the cables sent by Wilson and the
       decoded versions at House's end in Paris.

1949. King, Jere Clemens. *Foch Versus Clemenceau: France and German
       Dismemberment, 1918-1919.* Cambridge: Harvard University
       Press, 1960. 137 pp.

       King extends his early study of French civil-military rela-
       tions during the war with this slim volume focusing on the
       different approaches of Foch and Clemenceau toward the German
       question at the peace conference. Both men sought a peace that
       would guarantee French security, but Clemenceau, unlike Foch,
       was sensitive to the possibility that France might drive a
       wedge between herself and her wartime allies if the demand for
       an independent Rhineland was pressed too hard.

1950. Lansing, Robert. *The Big Four and Others of the Peace Con-
       ference.* Boston: Houghton Mifflin Co., 1921. 213 pp.

       Lansing's pen-portraits of the character and personality,
       foibles included, of the leading figures at the peace conferences
       make for fascinating reading. The reader, however, may not
       always agree with the pictures painted by Lansing. See also
       Lansing's general account of the peace negotiations (1575).

1951. Lloyd George, David. *Memoirs of the Peace Conference.* New
       Haven: Yale University Press, 1939. 2 vols.

       This is the U.S. edition of *The Truth About the Treaties.*
       The British title more accurately reflects the intent of the
       author. These volumes constitute a valuable source for peace-
       making and the treaties, but Lloyd George often magnified his
       own role at the expense of Wilson and others. The work con-
       tains numerous inconsistencies and distortions of the historical
       record.

1952. *Lord Riddell's Intimate Diary of the Peace Conference and
       After, 1918-1923.* New York: Reynal & Hitchcock, 1934. 435
       pp.

       Riddell, an intimate of Lloyd George, provides some inside
       information. Only about one-fourth of this volume concerns
       the Paris Peace Conference.

1953. Mantoux, Paul. *Paris Peace Conference, 1919: Proceedings of
       the Council of Four, March 24-April 18.* Geneva: Publications

de l'Institut Universitaire de Hautes Études Internationales, 1964. 227 pp.

This is the English translation of Mantoux's work, which was originally published in two volumes in 1955. It is an important source for the decisions of the Council of Four during the period when no official minutes were taken. Mantoux, the official interpreter for the Council of Four, kept daily personal notes.

1954. Nevins, Allan. *Henry White: Thirty Years of American Diplomacy.* New York: Harper & Brothers, 1930. 518 pp.

The part played by and the perspective of this important U.S. diplomat at the peace conference are revealed through his letters and diaries. This is a superior biography by a distinguished historian.

1955. [Seymour, Charles.] *Letters from the Paris Peace Conference.* Edited by Harold B. Whiteman, Jr. New Haven: Yale University Press, 1965. 289 pp.

These letters by Charles Seymour are an important source on Wilson's diplomacy and the activities of the peace conference. Seymour, a specialist on Austro-Hungarian questions, sheds light on the House-Wilson relationship.

1956. Startt, James Dill. "American Editorial Opinion of Woodrow Wilson and the Main Problems of Peacemaking in 1919." Doctoral dissertation, University of Maryland, 1965. 360 pp.

One hundred and seventy-four newspapers and thirty-four magazines are examined in this analysis of the treatment accorded President Wilson's peacemaking by the American press.

1957. ————. "The Uneasy Partnership: Wilson and the Press at Paris." *Mid-Amer.* 52 (January 1970): 55-69.

Startt discusses the reasons for Wilson's less-than-happy relationship with the press at the Paris Peace Conference.

1958. ————. "Wilson's Mission to Paris: The Making of a Decision." *Historian* 30 (August 1968): 599-616.

The author contends that Wilson's compassion for war-torn Europe and his moralistic ideas were essential to his decision to lead the American delegation to the Paris Peace Conference.

1959. Wells, Wells. *Wilson the Unknown: An Explanation of an Enigma of History.* New York: Charles Scribner's Sons, 1931. 358 pp.

As portrayed by Wells, Wilson emerges as a brilliant, calculating man who failed at Versailles because of illness.

C. SPECIFIC COUNTRIES, AREAS, AND ISSUES

1960. Albrecht-Carrié, René. "Italy and Her Allies, June, 1919."
       AHR 46 (July 1941): 837-43.

       The original text of a British-French-American communication,
       June 28, 1919, which exerted pressure on the Italians, is pub-
       lished in full in French.

1961. ———. *Italy at the Paris Peace Conference*. New York: Colum-
       bia University Press, 1938. 575 pp.

       This remains an important work on Italy's negotiations with
       the other powers at the Paris Peace Conference in spite of its
       paucity of Italian sources. Twelve maps and over 200 pages
       of documents are included.

1962. Almond, Nina, and Lutz, Ralph Haswell, comps. *The Treaty of
       St. Germain: A Documentary History of Its Territorial and
       Political Clauses with a Survey of the Documents of the
       Supreme Council of the Paris Peace Conference*. Stanford,
       Calif.: Stanford University Press, 1935. 712 pp.

       This is a valuable collection of documents concerning the
       making of peace with Austria. The organization is topical
       rather than chronological.

1963. Ambrosius, Lloyd Eugene. "The United States and the Weimar
       Republic 1918-1923: From the Armistice to the Ruhr Occupa-
       tion." Doctoral dissertation, University of Illinois,
       1967. 426 pp.

       Focusing attention on relations between the United States
       and Germany in the postwar period, this study underlines
       problems stemming from debates over postwar policy toward
       Germany.

1964. ———. "Wilson, the Republicans, and French Security After
       World War I." *JAH* 59 (September 1972): 341-52.

       This article deals with Wilson's conflict with the Republican
       "Irreconcilables" and the French security question. He argues
       that the Republicans offered a reasonable plan for French
       security apart from the League of Nations. However, President
       Wilson refused to compromise in his belief that the League of
       Nations would guarantee French security.

1965. Bane, Suda Lorena, and Lutz, Ralph Haswell, eds. *The Blockade
       of Germany After the Armistice, 1918-1919: Selected Documents
       of the Supreme Economic Council, Superior Blockade Council,
       American Relief Administration, and Other Wartime Organiza-
       tions*. Stanford, Calif.: Stanford University Press, 1942.
       874 pp.

       This is a comprehensive documentary history of the food
       blockade, published by the Hoover Library on War, Revolution
       and Peace. The arrangement is chronological and no attempt
       has been made to interpret the documents.

1966. Beer, George Louis. *African Questions at the Paris Peace Conference*. New York: Macmillan Co., 1923. 628 pp.

This is an especially valuable source because Beer headed the colonial division of the American delegation at Paris and served on the commission on mandates. Many of the author's papers are included.

1967. Bethlen, Count Steven. *The Treaty of Trianon and European Peace*. New York: Arno Press and the New York Times, 1971. 187 pp.

This is a collection of the lectures of the former prime minister of Hungary which were delivered in London in 1933. This is a reprint of the 1934 edition.

1968. Bonsal, Stephen. *Suitors and Suppliants: The Little Nations at Versailles*. New York: Prentice-Hall, 1946. 301 pp.

Bonsal, Colonel House's assistant, was involved in many interviews with the representatives of small nations at Versailles. His diary entries make interesting reading, but provide little significant information on the diplomacy of the small countries.

1969. Cobban, Alfred. *National Self-Determination*. London: Oxford University Press, 1945. 186 pp.

This balanced historical analysis of the development of the concept of national self-determination sheds light on the European peace settlement in 1919. It was issued under the auspices of the Royal Institute of International Affairs.

1970. Coston, Glen Howard. "The American Reaction to the Post-First World War Search of France for Security 1919-1930: A Periodical and Period Piece Study." Doctoral dissertation, University of Georgia, 1971. 317 pp.

This dissertation attempts to discern and discuss the attitudes, opinions, and ideas of American correspondents, editors, and historians who wrote about the French security thesis in the 1920s.

1971. Crosby, Gerda Richards. *Disarmament and Peace in British Politics, 1914-1919*. Cambridge: Harvard University Press, 1957. 192 pp.

Two of the six chapters focus on disarmament and peace in British politics. The remainder of the book examines efforts at arms limitations following the armistice and has much to say about American and French policy.

1972. Deák, Francis. *Hungary at the Paris Peace Conference: The Diplomatic History of the Treaty of Trianon*. New York: Columbia University Press, 1942. 594 pp.

The numerous new materials unearthed by Professor Deák in Hungarian archives make this work especially valuable. The Hungarian delegation to the peace conference is pictured in a most favorable light by the author.

1973. Dockrill, Michael, and Goold, Douglas J. *Peace Without*
       Promise: Britain and the Peace Conference, 1919-1923.
       Hamden, Conn.: Shoe String Press, 1981. 287 pp.

       This useful volume examines all of the treaties signed by
       Great Britain between 1919 and 1923. Each treaty is evaluated
       by the authors in a separate section. The first half of the
       book covers the Paris Peace Conference.

1974. Fifield, Russell H. *Woodrow Wilson and the Far East: The*
       Diplomacy of the Shantung Question. New York: Thomas Y.
       Crowell Co., 1952. 383 pp.

       This is a balanced study of the Shantung question based on
       unpublished sources which concentrates on negotiations at the
       Paris Peace Conference. This issue helped bring Wilson into
       conflict with the Japanese, who had seized German-controlled
       Shantung during the war. To gain Japan's support for the
       League of Nations, Wilson ultimately gave way.

*   Gerson, Louis L. *Woodrow Wilson and the Rebirth of Poland,*
       1914-1920: A Study in the Influence on American Policy of
       Minority Groups of Foreign Origin. Cited above as item 1720.

1975. Glazebrook, G.P. deT. *Canada at the Paris Peace Conference.*
       London: Oxford University Press, 1942. 156 pp.

       This slim volume fills a gap in the historical literature
       of the peace conference.

1976. Helmreich, Paul C. *From Paris to Sèvres: The Partition of the*
       Ottoman Empire at the Paris Peace Conference of 1919-1920.
       Columbus: Ohio State University Press, 1974. 376 pp.

       This expanded version of the author's doctoral dissertation
       is a first-rate description and analysis of both the drafting
       of the peace treaty with the Ottoman Empire and its partition.
       Although the United States was obviously not as involved in
       these negotiations as Britain and France, the question of an
       American mandate in Armenia is scrutinized.

1977. Huston, James A. "The Allied Blockade of Germany, 1918-1919."
       Jour. of Central Eur. Affairs 10 (July 1950): 145-66.

       Huston examines the reasons behind the continuation of the
       blockade of Germany for eight months after the Armistice.

*   Komarnicki, Titus. *Rebirth of the Polish Republic: A Study in*
       the Diplomatic History of Europe, 1914-1920. Cited above as
       item 1518.

1978. Lederer, Ivo J. *Yugoslavia at the Paris Peace Conference: A*
       Study in Frontiermaking. New Haven: Yale University Press,
       1963. 351 pp.

       This is an important, scholarly, and detailed examination
       of the Yugoslavian delegation's efforts at the Paris Peace
       Conference to achieve a nation state for the South Slavs.

Among many other primary sources, the papers of the Yugoslav foreign minister and the minutes of the Yugoslav delegation have been utilized.

1979. Louis, Wm. Roger. "Great Britain and the African Peace Settlement of 1919." *AHR* (April 1966): 875-92.

This article examines the British decision to accept a system of mandates rather than outright annexation of territory in Africa. Extensive use was made of the Milner papers.

* **Lowe, Cedric James, and Marzari, F.** *Italian Foreign Policy, 1870-1940.* Cited above as item 1526.

* ————, and Marzari, F. *Italian Foreign Policy, 1870-1940.* Cited above as item 1526.

1980. Luckau, Alma. *The German Delegation at the Paris Peace Conference.* New York: Columbia University Press, 1941. 522 pp.

This is a collection of documents that pertain to a subject broader than the title would indicate. The documents begin with Wilson's Fourteen Points in January 1918 and conclude with German acceptance of the Versailles Treaty in June 1919. Luckau provides a balanced introduction to the documents.

1981. ————. "Unconditional Acceptance of the Treaty of Versailles by the German Government, June 22-28, 1919." *Jour. Mod. Hist.* 17 (September 1945): 215-20.

Luckau publishes an important memorandum which was not included in *The German Delegation at the Paris Peace Conference.*

1982. McDougall, Walter A. *France's Rhineland Diplomacy, 1914-1924: The Last Bid for a Balance of Power in Europe.* Princeton: Princeton University Press, 1978. 410 pp.

This scholarly reassessment of French motives includes some provocative comparisons of French and American policy at the Paris Peace Conference.

1983. Maier, Charles S. "The Truth About the Treaties?" *Jour. Mod. Hist.* 51 (March 1979): 56-67.

Maier discusses some of the more recent studies of the Treaty of Versailles by such revisionists as McDougall and Trachtenberg.

1984. Marks, Sally. *Innocent Abroad: Belgium at the Paris Peace Conference of 1919.* Chapel Hill: University of North Carolina Press, 1981. 461 pp.

This well-researched and thoughtful study of a neglected topic is a model for the writing of traditional diplomatic history. It received the 1981 George Louis Beer Prize.

1985. Miller, David Hunter. "The Adriatic Negotiations at Paris." *Atlantic Monthly* 128 (August 1921): 267-77.

All in all, this is a sympathetic discussion of Wilson's role in the thorny Adriatic negotiations at the peace conference.

1986. Morrow, I.F.D. *The Peace Settlement in the German-Polish Borderlands*. London: Oxford University Press, 1936. 558 pp.

This is a scholarly and balanced treatment of the controversial peace settlement in the German-Polish borderlands. It is published under the auspices of the Royal Institute of International Affairs. Morrow was assisted by L.M. Sieveking.

1987. Nelson, Harold I. *Land and Power: British and Allied Policy on Germany's Frontiers, 1916-1919*. Toronto: University of Toronto Press, 1963. 402 pp.

The focus of this monograph is on the British position, but the French and American role in determining Germany's frontiers also receives considerable attention. Some surprising conclusions about Wilson's peacemaking emerge in this well-documented study.

1988. Nelson, Keith L. *Victors Divided: America and the Allies in Germany, 1918-1923*. Berkeley: University of California Press, 1975. 441 pp.

The author uses the American presence on the Rhine, 1918-1923, as a case study to reveal how American policymakers, especially during the Harding administration, dealt with the questions not resolved by the Paris Peace Conference. Will Rogers once said that American forces remained in Europe until 1923 "because two of them weren't married yet." Nelson, of course, improves upon this facetious interpretation, noting that many factors were involved. His multi-archival research is impressive. See also his 1965 University of California, Berkeley, dissertation.

1989. Noble, George Bernard. *Policies and Opinions at Paris, 1919: Wilsonian Diplomacy, the Versailles Peace, and French Public Opinion*. New York: Macmillan Co., 1935. 465 pp.

This is a solid account of certain aspects of the diplomacy of peacemaking as well as French public opinion. Professor Noble's role during the peace conference was to furnish the American delegation with a daily summary of the reaction of the French press to the decisions of the peacemakers.

1990. Page, Stanley W. *The Formation of the Baltic States: A Study of the Effects of Great Power Politics upon the Emergence of Lithuania, Latvia, and Estonia*. Cambridge: Harvard University Press, 1959. 193 pp.

This scholarly monograph criticizes the diplomacy of the Paris peacemakers for its lack of candor and inconsistency toward the Baltic states.

1991. Passivirta, Juhani. *The Victors in World War I and Finland: Finland's Relations with the British, French and United*

States Governments in 1918-1919. Helsinki: Finnish Historical Society, 1965. 198 pp.

This work was originally published in Finnish. It is based on extensive research in unpublished sources and gives a balanced treatment of Finland's quest for recognition and her relationship to Allied intervention in Russia.

1992. Spector, Sherman D. *Rumania at the Paris Peace Conference: A Study of the Diplomacy of Ioan I.C. Bratianu*. New York: Bookman Associates, 1962. 368 pp.

Romanian-American relations at the peace conference receive considerable attention in this scholarly monograph.

1993. Strickland, Roscoe Lee, Jr. "Czechoslovakia at the Paris Peace Conference, 1919." Doctoral dissertation, University of North Carolina, 1958. 378 pp.

Attention is given to the drawing of the borders for the new state of Czechoslovakia.

1994. Tarulis, Albert N. *American-Baltic Relations 1918-1922: The Struggle Over Recognition*. Washington, D.C.: Catholic University of America Press, 1965. 386 pp.

Wilson's approach to the Baltic peoples, who were struggling for their independence from Russia, is strongly criticized by this Lithuanian scholar. Many foreign archives were explored in researching this work.

1995. Yates, Louis A.R. *United States and French Security, 1917-1921: A Study in American Diplomatic History*. New York: Twayne Publishers, 1957. 252 pp.

The abortive Guarantee Treaties and their role in determining the peace settlement are examined in this scholarly monograph. Unlike some historians, Yates argues that Wilson negotiated the treaties in good faith.

D. REPARATIONS

1996. Baruch, Bernard M. *The Making of the Reparation and Economic Sections of the Treaty*. New York: Harper & Brothers, 1920. 353 pp.

Baruch was an economic advisor to the American peace commission and a member of the economic drafting committee, the reparation commission, and the economic commission. He gives his views of the reparation and economic sections of the peace treaty, which have been reprinted verbatim in the back of this volume.

1997. Bergmann, Karl. *History of Reparations*. Boston: Houghton Mifflin Co., 1927. 333 pp.

Bergmann was the German representative on the Reparations
Commission; he gives an insider's and surprisingly objective
point of view. His organization is chronological.

1998. Bunselmeyer, Robert E. *The Cost of the War, 1914-1919: British
Economic War Aims and the Origins of Reparation*. Hamden,
Conn.: Archon Books, 1975. 249 pp.

The evolution of British economic war aims which culminated
in Article 231 in the Treaty of Versailles is traced in this
scholarly monograph which is solidly grounded in archival research. The escalating tension between Washington and London
during the war over economic questions also receives some
attention. See also his 1968 Yale University dissertation.

1999. Burnett, Philip Mason. *Reparation at the Paris Peace Conference from the Standpoint of the American Delegation*.
New York: Columbia University Press, 1940. 2 vols.

This is an exhaustive examination, with many important documents, of the American side of the reparations issue at the
peace conference. American sources were researched.

2000. Feis, Herbert. "Keynes in Retrospect." *For. Affairs* 29 (July
1951): 564-77.

This is a thoughtful analysis of the impact of Keynes's
polemic against the Treaty of Versailles and the peacemaking
of Woodrow Wilson.

2001. Fish, Carl Russell. "The German Indemnity and the South."
AHR 26 (April 1921): 489-90.

This brief note by Fish compares the South's condition after
the Civil War with that of Germany after World War I. He concludes that the South was treated harshly.

2002. Keynes, John Maynard. *The Economic Consequences of the Peace*.
London: Macmillan & Co., 1919. 279 pp.

Keynes, a famous English monetary authority, makes a blister-
ing attack on the reparations settlement, arguing that it
created an impossible economic situation for Germany. His
one-sided views, in fact, helped defeat the Treaty of Versailles
in the American Senate. This volume should be supplemented by
Mantoux's critical evaluation of Keynes's conclusions.

2003. Mantoux, Étienne. *The Carthaginian Peace, or the Economic
Consequences of Mr. Keynes*. New York: Charles Scribner's
Sons, 1952. 210 pp.

Mantoux raises serious questions about Keynes's critical interpretation of the reparation settlement by demonstrating that
the English economist used faulty statistical methods. Mantoux
argues that the Germans could actually have paid the reparations
demanded of them.

2004. Marks, Sally. "The Myths of Reparations." *Central Eur. Hist.*
11 (September 1978): 231-55.

Marks takes a fresh look at an old controversy and offers some provocative conclusions. She faults many historians for concentrating on Germany's "capacity to pay" rather than on her "will" to pay.

2005. Rhodes, Benjamin Dagwell. "The United States and the War Debt Question, 1917-1934." Doctoral dissertation, University of Colorado, 1965. 410 pp.

The roots of the war debt problem are linked to American loan policy during World War I.

2006. Trachtenberg, Marc. *Reparation in World Politics: France and European Diplomacy, 1916-1923*. New York: Columbia University Press, 1980. 423 pp.

Based on extensive research in British and French archives, this volume challenges the traditional interpretations of the French approach to reparations. The French, Trachtenberg argues, were much more reasonable about collecting reparations from Germany than their public position often indicated.

E. LEAGUE OF NATIONS AND ITS REJECTION BY UNITED STATES

2007. Bagby, Wesley M. *The Road to Normalcy: The Presidential Campaign and Election of 1920*. Baltimore, Md.: Johns Hopkins Press, 1962. 206 pp.

The election of 1920, which resulted in the rejection of membership in the League of Nations, receives scholarly attention from this history professor at West Virginia University.

2008. ———. "Woodrow Wilson, a Third Term, and the Solemn Referendum." *AHR* 60 (April 1955): 567-75.

This article deals with the speculation as to whether or not Wilson would be a candidate for a third term. Until his breakdown in 1919, the possibility existed that he might be a viable candidate. He had hoped to make the election a solemn referendum on the League.

2009. Bailey, Thomas A. *Woodrow Wilson and the Great Betrayal*. Chicago: Quadrangle Books, 1963. 429 pp.

Bailey gives an outstanding account of the supreme tragedy of U.S. rejection of the Versailles Treaty. This work is written from the American point of view. Bailey concludes that Senator Lodge by himself did not keep the United States out of the League of Nations, and that some kind of an agreement on the Republican reservations should have been worked out. See also the survey by D.F. Fleming.

2010. Bartlett, Ruhl J. *The League to Enforce the Peace*. Chapel Hill: University of North Carolina Press, 1944. 214 pp.

Early in World War I a group was formed in the United States
to develop policies to prevent another war of such magnitude.
This bipartisan movement gained much public support during the
war. Yet most of the Republicans who supported a "league"
turned their backs on it during the election of 1918. Bartlett speculates that if the organization had been active when
Wilson collapsed, the United States would have ratified the
treaty.

2011. Boothe, Leon. "A Fettered Envoy: Lord Grey's Special Mission
       to the United States, 1919-1920." *Rev. Pol.* 33 (January
       1971): 78-94.

       Boothe examines Grey's often neglected mission to the United
       States on behalf of the League of Nations, assigning "heroic"
       status to the British statesman for his efforts.

2012. ————. "Woodrow Wilson's Cold War, the President, the Pub-
       lic, and the League Fight, 1919-1920." Doctoral disserta-
       tion, University of Illinois at Urbana-Champaign, 1966.
       333 pp.

       Boothe takes a broad view of this conflict, examining or-
       ganizations and foreign governments, as well as the leading
       political figures, that were involved. President Wilson re-
       ceives much of the blame for the defeat of the peace treaty.

2013. Brand, Carl F. "The Attitude of British Labor Toward Presi-
       dent Wilson During the Peace Conference." *AHR* 42 (January
       1937): 244-55.

       Newspapers such as the *Daily Herald* and *Labour Leader* consti-
       tute the chief source for this article. Labor's support for
       Wilson's peace program was an important element in his popular
       support.

2014. Cranston, Alan M. *The Killing of the Peace.* New York: Viking
       Press, 1945. 304 pp.

       Written in diary form, this narrative is interesting and at
       times enlightening. It covers the period from 1916 to 1923.

*   Creel, George. *The War, the World and Wilson.* Cited above as
       item 874.

2015. Duff, John B. "The Versailles Treaty and the Irish-Americans."
       JAH 55 (December 1968): 582-98.

       This article examines the attempts by Irish-Americans to
       gain Irish freedom through the Paris peace negotiations.
       President Wilson felt that the peace conference was not the
       place to air the Irish situation. Duff criticizes Wilson for
       alienating Irish-Americans from his administration.

2016. Egerton, George W. "Britain and the 'Great Betrayal': Anglo-
       American Relations and the Struggle for United States Ratifi-
       cation of the Treaty of Versailles." *Hist. Jour.* 21 (Decem-
       ber 1978): 885-911.

The failure of Sir Edward Grey's mission to the United States to encourage the ratification of the Versailles Treaty is viewed by Egerton as a great failure for "British strategy and foreign policy."

2017. ————. *Great Britain and the Creation of the League of Nations: Strategy, Politics, and International Organization, 1914-1919.* Chapel Hill: University of North Carolina Press, 1979. 273 pp.

This well-researched and balanced account sheds some new light on the British approach to the Covenant. Lloyd George's position is particularly well treated.

2018. ————. "The Lloyd George Government and the Creation of the League of Nations." *AHR* 79 (April 1974): 419-44.

The generally neglected British side of the creation of the League of Nations is well described in this article based on extensive research in unpublished British materials.

*   Fischer, Robert James. "Henry Cabot Lodge's Concept of Foreign Policy and the League of Nations." Cited above as item 904.

2019. Fleming, Denna F. *The United States and the League of Nations 1918-1920.* New York: G.P. Putnam's Sons, 1932. 559 pp.

This scholarly and balanced treatment has retained its value over the years. There is extensive documentation but only a one-page select bibliography.

*   Francesconi, Robert A. "A Burkeian Analysis of Selected Speeches of Woodrow Wilson and Henry Cabot Lodge on the League of Nations." Cited above as item 905.

2020. Garvin, J.L. *The Economic Foundations of Peace: Or World-Partnership as the True Basis of the League of Nations.* London: Macmillan & Co., 1919. 574 pp.

This volume places emphasis on economic factors in causing war and peace. The author sees the war as one of food and raw materials, and as an effort by Germany to become master of her oceanic fate. The war forced the Allies to cooperate with one another. Garvin hopes that this cooperation will continue into the period of peace. He urges the formation of a council to examine questions that might cause disputes.

2021. Grubbs, Frank L. "Organized Labor and the League to Enforce Peace." *Labor Hist.* 14 (Spring 1973): 247-58.

American labor's cooperation with the L.T.E.P. is examined, including its struggle to get the Treaty of Versailles ratified by the Senate.

2022. Helbich, Wolfgang J. "American Liberals in the League of Nations Controversy." *Public Opinion Quar.* 31 (Winter 1967-1968): 568-96.

By focusing on the views and activities of a liberal committee (known by different names), which was initiated by Paul
Kellogg, the editor of *Survey*, the author concludes that "the
lack of liberal ardor for the Versailles Treaty should not
have come as a surprise to anyone."

2023. Herman, Sondra R. *Eleven Against War: Studies in American
Internationalist Thought, 1898-1921.* Stanford, Calif.:
Hoover Institution Press, 1969. 264 pp.

The author sees American internationalism as more hope than
action as she examines eleven leading internationalists, including Woodrow Wilson and Elihu Root. Her internationalists
were chosen because their philosophy had some relationship to
their philosophy of life. Herman concludes that failure of
the League was due to nationalism being stronger than internationalism.

2024. Holt, W. Stull. *Treaties Defeated by the Senate: A Study of
the Struggle Between President and Senate over the Conduct
of Foreign Relations.* Gloucester, Mass.: Peter Smith,
1964. 328 pp.

Holt's competent study of rejected treaties ends with the
Versailles Treaty. He concludes that the most persistent
factors in the treaty's rejection were the Senate's determination to assert its power and the general American desire to
return to isolationism.

2025. Howard-Ellis, Charles. *The Origins, Structure and Working of
the League of Nations.* Boston: Houghton Mifflin Co., 1928.
528 pp.

This journalistic account by an Englishman was well received
by reviewers when published, and rightly so. It remains a
valuable and very readable survey.

2026. Knock, Thomas J. "Woodrow Wilson and the Origins of the League
of Nations." Doctoral dissertation, Princeton University,
1982. 362 pp.

The intellectual, political, and diplomatic roots of Wilson's
advocacy of the League of Nations are examined.

2027. Kuehl, Warren F. *Seeking World Order: The United States and
International Organization to 1920.* Nashville: Vanderbilt
University Press, 1969. 385 pp.

This well-researched monograph traces the growth in the United
States from 1890 to 1920 of internationalist sentiment and the
desire for a world league or association. The internationalists, although they agreed on the merits of an international
organization, could not reach agreement on the machinery or
nature of the new body.

2028. Lancaster, James L. "The Protestant Churches and the Fight for
Ratification of the Versailles Treaty." *Public Opinion Quar.*
31 (Winter 1967-1968): 597-619.

The role of the Protestant churches in the League fight is carefully analyzed in this scholarly article.

2029. Marburg, Theodore. *Development of the League of Nations Idea: Documents and Correspondence.* Edited by John H. Latane. New York: Macmillan Co., 1932. 2 vols.

The extensive papers of the chairman of the foreign organization committee of the League to Enforce Peace provide background for the origins of the League of Nations. John H. Latané has done a competent job of editing.

2030. Maxwell, Kenneth R. "Irish-Americans and the Fight for Treaty Ratification." *Public Opinion Quar.* 31 (Winter 1967-1968): 620-41.

How Irish-Americans "organized and manipulated public opinion in opposition to the president's program" is the subject of this article.

2031. Miller, David Hunter. *The Drafting of the Covenant.* New York: G.P. Putnam's Sons, 1928. 2 vols.

Miller, a member of the Inquiry and one of the legal advisors to the American delegation at the peace conference, has written a solid interpretative history of the drafting of the Covenant. His insider background makes his comments on the motives of the supporters of the Covenant especially valuable. The second volume contains a valuable collection of documents. A subject index and an index of the articles of the Covenant are included.

2032. Schwabe, Klaus. "Woodrow Wilson and Germany's Membership in the League of Nations, 1918-1919." *Central Eur. Hist.* 8 (March 1975): 3-22.

President Wilson's views on including Germany in the League are examined from their origins.

2033. Stone, Ralph. "The Irreconcilables' Alternatives to the League of Nations." *Mid-Amer.* 49 (July 1967): 163-73.

This interesting article argues that the irreconcilables offered an alternative to the League. However, they were unclear as to what that should be. They did agree that the League must be defeated.

2034. ————. *The Irreconcilables: The Fight Against the League of Nations.* Lexington: University Press of Kentucky, 1970. 208 pp.

This monograph, based upon a thorough use of primary and secondary sources, focuses attention on the sixteen senators who fought for the total rejection of the Versailles Treaty. Stone concludes that the senators were wise to question the League as a cure-all for the diplomatic ills of the world.

2035. ————. "Two Illinois Senators Among the Irreconcilables." *MVHR* 50 (December 1963): 443-63.

This article focuses attention on Medill McCormick and Lawrence

Yarnell Sherman of Illinois--the only state with two irrecon-
cilable senators. It concludes that both played an important
role in the Treaty's defeat.

2036.   ————, ed. *Wilson and the League of Nations: Why America's
        Rejection?* New York: Holt, Rinehart & Winston, 1967. 122 pp.

        This is a useful collection of readings on such topics as
        "The Role of Woodrow Wilson," "The Constitutional Interpretation,"
        and "Wilson and the Lessons of History." There is an annotated
        bibliography.

2037.   Vinson, J. Chalmers. *Referendum for Isolation: Defeat of Ar-
        ticle Ten of the League of Nations Covenant.* Athens: Uni-
        versity of Georgia Press, 1961. 148 pp.

        Vinson succeeds in reviewing the logical rather than the emo-
        tional reasons for the rejection of the League in the United
        States in this scholarly monograph. He focuses on the "honest
        difference of opinion" concerning Article Ten.

2038.   Walters, Francis Paul. *A History of the League of Nations.*
        London: Oxford University Press, 1960. 833 pp.

        The birth of the League of Nations at the Paris Peace Con-
        ference receives some attention in this standard history. It
        was originally published in two volumes in 1952.

*   Widenor, William C. *Henry Cabot Lodge and the Search for an
        American Foreign Policy.* Cited above as item 907.

2039.   Wimer, Kurt. "Senator Hitchcock and the League of Nations."
        Neb. Hist. 44 (September 1963): 189-204.

        This article examines the role of Senator Gilbert M. Hitchcock
        of Nebraska as he attempted to influence the Senate and Woodrow
        Wilson to compromise.

2040.   ————. "Woodrow Wilson Tries Conciliation: An Effort That
        Failed." *Historian* 25 (August 1963): 419-38.

        The author argues that Wilson was more flexible with the
        Senate than most scholars have thought. He made a serious
        effort at conciliation, and he did try to compromise with
        moderate Republicans. It was the moderates, according to Wimer,
        who failed to bring about a compromise.

2041.   Zimmern, Alfred. *The League of Nations and the Rule of Law,
        1918-1935.* London: Macmillan & Co., 1939. 542 pp.

        Zimmern sheds light on American influence on the character
        of the Covenant.

CHRONOLOGY OF EVENTS

1914

August

1   Outbreak of World War I; German declaration of war on Russia

4   Wilson's proclamation of U.S. neutrality

14   Battle of the Frontiers begins

26   Opening of Battle of Tannenberg

September

5   Opening of the First Battle of the Marne

14   Opening of the First Battle of the Aisne; start of trench warfare

December

8   Battle of the Falkland Islands

21   First German air raid on Britain

1915

January

18   Japan's Twenty-One Demands on China

February

4   Germany announces "war zone" in British waters

19   British begin naval action against the Dardanelles

March

1   American citizen dies in sinking of first passenger ship, the
     British liner *Falaba*

11   British announce blockade of German ports

April

22   Second Battle of Ypres begins

25   British landing on Gallipoli Peninsula

26   France, Russia, Italy, and Britain conclude secret Treaty of
     London

May

2   Opening of great Austro-German offensive in Galicia (Gorlice-
     Tarnow)

7   *Lusitania* sunk by German U-boat off Irish coast

9   Opening of the Second Battle of Artois on western front

23   Italy declares war on Austria-Hungary

25   Asquith reorganizes his liberal ministry as a coalition

June

8   Bryan balks at second *Lusitania* note and resigns as American
     Secretary of State; succeeded by Lansing

29   First of twelve battles of the Isonzo begins on the Italian
     front

August

10   Civilian military training camp started at Plattsburg

19   Two Americans die in sinking of *Arabic* off Ireland

September

1   *Arabic* pledge by German Ambassador von Bernstorff

22   Opening of Second Battle of Champagne on western front

October

3-5 Anglo-French force lands at Salonika, Greece

December

4   Henry Ford's peace ship *Oskar II* begins its voyage to Europe

15   Haig becomes commander in chief of BEF

                                  1916

February

21   Beginning of ten-month Battle of Verdun

22   House-Grey Memorandum drawn up in London

23   Ministry of Blockade created in Britain

29   First British "blacklist" compiled

March

3-7 Gore-McLemore resolutions tabled in Congress

7   Newton D. Baker appointed Secretary of War

9   Pancho Villa's raid on Columbus, New Mexico

15   Pershing starts his pursuit of Villa into Mexico

24   French passenger ship *Sussex* torpedoed

April

24   Rebellion begins in Ireland on Easter Monday

May

19   Britain and France conclude the Sykes-Picot Agreement

31   Opening of Battle of Jutland

June

3   National Defense Act authorizes five-year expansion of U.S. Army

4   Beginning of the Brusilov offensive against Austria-Hungary

July

1   Battle of the Somme opens; British suffer some 60,000 casualties
    on first day

29   U.S. Marines land in Haiti

30   Black Tom Island munitions plant destroyed; German sabotage sus-
    pected

August

29   Council of National Defense established under Army Appropriations
    Act
    Hindenburg succeeds von Falkenhayn as chief of staff of German
    field armies; beginning of military dictatorship in Germany

31   Germany suspends submarine assaults

September

15   Tanks introduced on the Somme battlefield by the British

October

15   Germany resumes U-boat attacks under search and destroy rules

November

7-9   Wilson wins reelection, which was in doubt until California
     votes were counted

28   First German airplane raid on London

29   U.S. occupation of Santo Domingo proclaimed

December

5   Asquith resigns as prime minister; replaced by Lloyd George

12   Germans issue peace note suggesting compromise peace

18   Wilson requests statements of war objectives from warring nations
    in peace note

1917

January

9   German leaders decide to launch unrestricted U-boat warfare

10   Allies state war objectives in response to Wilson's peace note
     of December 18

February

1   Germany resumes unrestricted U-boat warfare

3   United States breaks off relations with Germany

26   Wilson requests authority from Congress to arm U.S. merchant
     ships

March

1   Zimmermann Note released to press by State Department

11   British capture Baghdad

15   Culmination of "February Revolution"; Nicholas II abdicates

28   Admiral Sims ordered to Great Britain as liaison to Admiralty

31   General Munitions Board to coordinate war industry established
     by Council of National Defense

April

6   U.S. declaration of war

14   Committee on Public Information established by executive order

16   Lenin arrives in Russia
     Neville's offensive begins (Second Battle of the Aisne)

24   Wilson signs Liberty Loan Act
     U.S. destroyers despatched overseas

May

11   Wilson appoints American commission to Russia with Elihu Root as
     chairman

18   Selective Service Act signed by President Wilson

24   Voyage of first Atlantic convoy to Great Britain begins

26   General Pershing chosen to command American Expeditionary Force

29   Rear Admiral Gleaves chosen as commander of convoy operations
     in Atlantic

June

15   Espionage Act

26   First U.S. troops (1st Division) arrive in France

July

16   Start of July demonstrations in Petrograd against Provisional
     Government

19   Peace Resolution in favor of peace without annexations or in-
      demnities passed by German Reichstag

28   War Industries Board established by Council of National Defense;
      supersedes General Munitions Board

31   Passchendaele offensive (Third Battle of Ypres) opens in Flanders

August

1   Papal peace proposal

10   Lever Food and Fuel Control Act
      Hoover appointed Food Administrator

29   Wilson rejects Pope's call for negotiations with Germany

September

1   Pershing establishes his general headquarters at Chaumont

October

3   War Revenue Act; graduated income tax authorized

6   Trading with the Enemy Act; government controls all foreign trade

24   Austro-German breakthrough at Caporetto on Italian front

November

2   Lansing-Ishii Agreement

7   Bolsheviks seize power in Russia
      Allied Supreme War Council created at Rapallo, Italy

20   British launch surprise tank attack at Cambrai

December

7   United States and Austria-Hungary at war

9   Jerusalem captured by British

22   Central Powers and Soviets open peace negotiations at Brest-
      Litovsk

1918

January

5   Lloyd George's war aims address to Trades Union Congress

8   Wilson's Fourteen Points speech to joint session of Congress

February

11   Wilson's Four Principles speech to joint session of Congress

March

3   Soviet Russia and Central Powers make peace with Treaty of Brest-
      Litovsk

4   Bernard M. Baruch appointed head of War Industries Board

5   British landing at Murmansk in North Russia

21   Germans launch first of their great 1918 assaults against British
      (Battle of Picardy)

26   Doullens Agreement gives General Foch "co-ordinating authority"
      over the western front

April

5   War Finance Corporation established to finance war industries
      Japanese landing at Vladivostok

8   National War Labor Board appointed to mediate labor conflicts

9   Germans launch second assault of their 1918 offensive (Battle of
      the Lys) in British sector of Armentières

14   Foch appointed commander in chief of Allied forces on western
      front

May

16   Sedition Act; amendment to Espionage Act of 1917

25   German U-boats make their first appearance in U.S. waters

27   Third phase of 1918 German offensive (Third Battle of the Aisne)
      begins in French sector along Chemin des Dames

28   28th Regiment of U.S. 1st Division goes into action at town
      of Cantigny

June

6   2nd Division captures Bouresches and southern part of Belleau
      Wood

9   Opening of fourth phase of 1918 German offensive (Battle of the
      Matz) in French section between Noyon and Montdidier

July

2   Allied Supreme War Council supports intervention in Siberia

6   Wilson agrees to American intervention in Siberia

15   Opening of last phase of German offensive (Second Battle of
      the Marne)

18   Allied counterattack seizes strategical initiative from Germans;
      nine U.S. divisions participate

August

3   Large-scale Allied intervention begins at Vladivostok

8   Battle of Amiens opens; Ludendorff's "Black Day" for German
      army

10   1st U.S. Army organized under Pershing

September

4   American troops land at Archangel in North Russia

12   United States launches St. Mihiel offensive

19   Opening of British offensive in Palestine (Battle of Megiddo)

26   Meuse-Argonne offensive opens; greatest offensive of war for
     U.S. forces

27   Wilson's Five Particulars speech in New York City

29   Bulgaria signs armistice

October

3-4 Germans and Austrians send notes to Wilson requesting an armis-
     tice

12   Pershing forms 2nd Army under the command of General Bullard

21   Germany ceases unrestricted U-boat warfare

November

3   Mutiny of the German fleet at Kiel

5   Congressional elections result in Republican control of Congress

11   Armistice goes into effect at 11 A.M.

18   Wilson announces that he will attend peace conference

December

13   Wilson aboard the liner *George Washington* arrives at Brest,
     France

14   Khaki Election in Britain

1919

January

5   Spartacist (Communist) revolt begins in Berlin

18   Peace negotiations start at Paris

25   Peace conference accepts principle of League of Nations

February

6   German National Assembly meets at Weimar

14   Draft Covenant of League of Nations completed

24   Wilson arrives at Boston aboard the *George Washington*

28   Lodge starts his campaign against League of Nations

March

4   Founding of Comintern (Third International) at Moscow
     Lodge introduces Republican Round Robin

13   Admiral Kolchak begins his offensive against Bolsheviks in
     Russian Civil War

14   Wilson returns to Paris after a month's absence

April

3   Wilson becomes sick with influenza

7   Allies evacuate Odessa

23   Wilson appeals directly to Italians in an effort to gain their
     support for his views on peace settlement

24   Italian Premier Orlando walks out of peace conference over Fiume
     issue

May

6   Peace conference disposes of Germany's colonies

7   Treaty of Versailles submitted to German delegation

June

21   German High Seas Fleet scuttled at Scapa Flow

28   Treaty of Versailles signed in Hall of Mirrors at Versailles

ABBREVIATIONS

Aerospace Hist.	*Aerospace Historian*
AHR	*American Historical Review*
Air Power Hist.	*Air Power History*
Amer. Heritage	*American Heritage*
Amer. Hist. Ill.	*American History Illustrated*
Amer. Jour. of Pub. Health	*American Journal of Public Health*
Amer. Mercury	*American Mercury*
Amer. Mil. Institute	*American Military Institute*
Amer. Quarterly	*American Quarterly*
Amer. Slavic and East Eur. Rev.	*American Slavic and East European Review*
Amer. Speech	*American Speech*
Ann. Am. Ac. of Pol. Sci. and Soc. Sci.	*Annals of the American Academy of Political Science and Social Science*
Army Quar.	*Army Quarterly*
Brit. Hist. Ill.	*British History Illustrated*
Bull. Hist. of Med.	*Bulletin of the History of Medicine*
Bus. Hist. Rev.	*Business History Review*
Can. Jour. Econ. Pol. Sci.	*Canadian Journal of Economics and Political Science*
Can. Jour. of Hist.	*Canadian Journal of History*
Can. Rev. Amer. Stud.	*Canadian Review of American Studies*
Central Eur. Hist.	*Central European History*
Field Artillery Jour.	*Field Artillery Journal*
For. Affairs	*Foreign Affairs*
Hist. Jour.	*Historical Journal*
Illus. World	*Illustrated World*
Infantry Jour.	*Infantry Journal*
International Hist. Rev.	*International History Review*
JAH	*Journal of American History*
Jour. Contemp. Hist.	*Journal of Contemporary History*
Jour. Home Econ.	*Journal of Home Economics*
Jour. Mod. Hist.	*Journal of Modern History*
Jour. Negro Educ.	*Journal of Negro Education*
Jour. Negro Hist.	*Journal of Negro History*
Jour. of Central Eur. Affairs	*Journal of Central European Affairs*
Jour. Pol. Econ.	*Journal of Political Economy*
Jour. Presby. Hist.	*Journal of Presbyterian History*
JRUSI	*Journal of the Royal United Services Institute*
JSH	*Journal of Southern History*
Labor Hist.	*Labor History*
Mid-Amer.	*Mid-America*
Mil. Affairs	*Military Affairs*
Mil. Engin.	*Military Engineer*

Mil. Rev.	*Military Review*
MVHR	*Mississippi Valley Historical Review*
Nat. Mun. Rev.	*National Municipal Review*
Nav. War Col. Rev.	*Naval War College Review*
Neb. Hist.	*Nebraska History*
New Mexico Hist. Rev.	*New Mexico Historical Review*
Ohio Archaeol. and Hist. Quar.	*Ohio Archaeological and Historical Quarterly*
Pac. Hist. Rev.	*Pacific Historical Review*
Pol. Sci. Quar.	*Political Science Quarterly*
Princeton Lib. Chron.	*Princeton Library Chronicle*
Proc. Acad. Pol. Sci.	*Proceedings of the Academy of Political Science*
Pub. Admin. Rev.	*Public Administration Review*
Public Opinion Quar.	*Public Opinion Quarterly*
Quar. Jour. Econ.	*Quarterly Journal of Economics*
Rev. Pol.	*Review of Politics*
Russian Rev.	*Russian Review*
S.A.E. Bull.	*S.A.E. Bulletin*
Slav. Rev.	*Slavic Review*
So. Atl. Quar.	*South Atlantic Quarterly*
So. Cal. Quar.	*Southern California Quarterly*
So. Dak. Hist. Coll.	*South Dakota History Collections*
U.S. Naval Inst., Proc.	*United States Naval Institute, Proceedings*
Yale Rev.	*Yale Review*

AUTHOR INDEX

SUBJECT INDEX